Edited by STUART SANDLER and JACKIE BROGAN
Published by Newsquest (Herald and Times) Ltd,
200 Renfield Street, Glasgow, G2 3QB.
ISBN: 978-0-903216-21-0

BIG GAME DATES
FRIENDLY

Scotland v Belgium...September 7, 2018
Scotland v Portugal...October 14, 2018

UEFA NATIONS LEAGUE

Scotland v Albania.. September 10, 2018
Israel v Scotland... October 11, 2018
Albania v Scotland... November 17, 2018
Scotland v Israel...November 20, 2018

PREMIERSHIP PLAY-OFFS

QUARTER-FINALS................................... Wednesday/Saturday, May 8/11, 2019
SEMI-FINALS...Wednesday/Saturday, May 15/18, 2019
FINAL .... Thursday/Sunday, May 23/26, 2019

CHAMPIONSHIP PLAY-OFFS

SEMI-FINALS... Wednesday/Saturday, May 8/11, 2019
FINAL .... Wednesday/Sunday, May 15/19, 2019

LEAGUE ONE PLAY-OFFS

SEMI-FINALS... Wednesday/Saturday, May 8/11, 2019
FINAL .... Wednesday/Saturday, May 15/18, 2019

LEAGUE TWO PLAY-OFFS

FINAL..Saturday, May 11/18, 2019

SCOTTISH CUP

FIRST ROUND ....Saturday, September 22, 2018
SECOND ROUND.. Saturday, October 20, 2018
THIRD ROUND.. Saturday, November 24, 2018
FOURTH ROUND..Saturday, January 29, 2019
FIFTH ROUND ....Saturday, February 9, 2019
QUARTER-FINALS... Saturday, March 2, 2019
SEMI-FINALS...Saturday/Sunday, April 13/14, 2019
FINAL .... Saturday, May 25, 2019

BETFRED CUP

GROUP STAGE MATCHDAY 1 .... Saturday, July 14, 2018
GROUP STAGE MATCHDAY 2 ....Tuesday/Wednesday, July 17/18, 2018
GROUP STAGE MATCHDAY 3 .... Saturday, July 21, 2018
GROUP STAGE MATCHDAY 4 ....Tuesday/Wednesday, July 24/25, 2018
GROUP STAGE MATCHDAY 5 .... Saturday, July 28, 2018
SECOND ROUND ....Saturday, August 18, 2018
QUARTER-FINALS....................Tuesday-Thursday, September 25-27, 2018
SEMI-FINALS.. Saturday/Sunday, October 27/28, 2018
FINAL .... Sunday, December 2, 2018

IRN-BRU CUP (Challenge Cup)

FIRST ROUND ....Tuesday/Wednesday, August 14/15, 2018
SECOND ROUND.......................Saturday/Sunday, September 8/9, 2018
THIRD ROUND............................Saturday/Sunday, October 13/14, 2018
QUARTER-FINALS.................... Saturday/Sunday, November 17/18, 2018
SEMI-FINALS............................ Saturday/Sunday, February 16/17, 2019
FINAL .... Saturday/Sunday, March 23/24, 2019

UEFA CHAMPIONS LEAGUE

FIRST QUALIFYING ROUND ....July 10/11 and July 17/18, 2018
SECOND QUALIFYING ROUND..........July 24/25 and July 31/August 1, 2018
THIRD QUALIFYING ROUND ....August 7/8 and August 14, 2018

PLAY-OFF ROUND ....August 21/22 and August 28/29, 2018
GROUP STAGE................. September 18/19, October 2/3, October 23/24, 2018
..............................November 6/7, November 27/28 and December 11/12, 2018
ROUND OF 16.. February 12/13/19/20, 2019
....March 5/6/12/13, 2019
QUARTER-FINALS... April 9/10 and April 16/17, 2019
SEMI-FINALS..May 1 and May 7/8, 2019
FINAL...June 1, 2019 (Estadio Metropolitano, Madrid)

EUROPA LEAGUE

FIRST QUALIFYING ROUND ....July 12 and July 19, 2018
SECOND QUALIFYING ROUND.............................July 26 and August 2, 2018
THIRD QUALIFYING ROUND ....August 9 and August 16, 2018
PLAY-OFF ROUND .... August 23 and August 30, 2018
GROUP STAGE.....................September 20, October 4, October 25, 2018
....November 8, November 29, December 13 2018
ROUND OF 32................................... February 14 and February 21, 2019
ROUND OF 16... March 7 and March 14, 2019
QUARTER-FINALS... April 11 and April 18, 2019
SEMI-FINALS...May 2 and May 9, 2019
FINAL... May 29, 2019 (Olympic Stadium, Baku)

FINAL LEAGUE TABLES 2017-2018

PREMIERSHIP

	P	W	D	L	F	A	Pt
Celtic	38	24	10	4	73	25	82
Aberdeen	38	22	7	9	56	37	73
Rangers	38	21	7	10	76	50	70
Hibernian	38	18	13	7	62	46	67
Kilmarnock	38	16	11	11	49	47	59
Hearts	38	12	13	13	39	39	49
Motherwell	38	13	9	16	43	49	48
St J'stone	38	12	10	16	42	53	46
Dundee	38	11	6	21	36	57	39
Hamilton	38	9	6	23	47	68	33
Partick Th	38	8	9	21	31	61	33
Ross County	38	6	11	21	40	62	29

CHAMPIONSHIP

	P	W	D	L	F	A	Pt
St Mirren	36	23	5	8	63	36	74
Livingston	36	17	11	8	56	37	62
Dundee Utd	36	18	7	11	52	42	61
Dunfermline	36	16	11	9	60	35	59
ICT	36	16	9	11	53	37	57
QoS	36	14	10	12	59	53	52
Morton	36	13	11	12	47	40	50
Falkirk	36	12	11	13	45	49	47
Dumbarton	36	7	9	20	27	63	30
Brechin	36	0	4	32	20	90	4

LEAGUE ONE

	P	W	D	L	F	A	Pt
Ayr United	36	24	4	8	92	42	76
R Rovers	36	22	9	5	68	32	75
Alloa Athletic	36	17	9	10	56	43	60
Arbroath	36	17	8	11	70	51	59
Stranraer	36	16	5	15	58	66	53
East Fife	36	13	3	20	49	67	42
Airdrieonians	36	10	11	15	46	60	41
Forfar	36	11	5	20	40	65	38
Queen's P	36	7	10	19	42	72	31
Albion R	36	8	6	22	57	80	30

LEAGUE TWO

	P	W	D	L	F	A	Pt
Montrose	36	23	8	5	60	35	77
Peterhead	36	24	4	8	79	39	76
S Albion	36	16	7	13	61	52	55
Stenh'muir	36	15	19	12	56	47	54
Clyde	36	14	9	13	52	50	51
Elgin City	36	14	7	15	54	61	49
Annan Ath	36	12	11	13	49	41	47
B Rangers	36	9	10	17	31	59	37
E'burgh C	36	7	9	20	37	62	30
C'beath	36	4	10	22	23	56	22

WESTERN REGION SJFA LEAGUES
2017-2018

McBOOKIE.COM SUPER LEAGUE
PREMIER DIVISION

	P	W	D	L	F	A	Pts
Beith Juniors F.C.	22	14	3	5	61	21	45
Auchinleck Talbot	22	14	2	6	56	25	44
Pollok F.C.	22	11	7	4	46	27	40
Kilwinning R.	22	12	4	5	42	27	40
Kilbirnie L	22	9	7	6	35	37	34
Kirkintilloch RR	22	9	4	9	45	53	31
Glenafton	22	8	6	8	30	30	30
Hurlford Utd	22	8	5	9	37	36	29
Cumnock	22	7	6	9	36	40	27
Clydebank	22	7	3	12	32	44	24
Girvan	22	2	6	14	24	59	12
Arthurlie	22	2	5	15	20	64	11

McBOOKIE.COM SUPER LEAGUE
FIRST DIVISION

	P	W	D	L	F	A	Pts
Petershill	26	19	4	3	65	30	61
Cambuslang R	26	16	2	8	62	39	50
Largs Thistle	26	15	5	6	42	27	50
Renfrew	26	15	4	7	48	36	49
Irvine Meadow	26	15	4	7	45	33	49
Troon	26	14	5	7	62	42	47
Rutherglen G	26	13	4	9	56	46	43
Cumbernauld	26	13	2	11	51	45	41
Darvel Juniors	26	9	4	13	48	55	31
Kilsyth Rangers	26	8	4	14	42	53	28
Larkhall Thistle	26	7	4	15	45	62	25
Kello Rovers	26	6	5	15	38	55	23
Maryhill	26	2	6	18	24	62	12
Shettleston	26	2	3	21	19	62	9

McBOOKIE.COM CENTRAL
DISTRICT LEAGUE FIRST DIVISION

	P	W	D	L	F	A	Pts
Rossvale J	28	20	4	4	65	33	64
St. Roch's	28	19	5	4	73	40	62
Benburb	28	18	4	6	81	38	58
Neilston	28	16	4	8	75	45	52
Blantyre Vic	28	14	4	10	61	47	46
Wishaw	28	13	2	13	68	48	41
Gla'gow P'shire	28	11	6	11	52	47	39
Port Glasgow	28	12	3	13	38	50	39
Shotts	28	12	1	15	58	52	37
Yoker Athletic	28	10	6	12	53	58	36
East Kilbride	28	11	3	14	47	61	36
Greenock	28	10	4	14	38	52	34
Forth W'rers	28	9	3	16	53	77	30
Thorniewood	28	5	3	20	44	89	18
Lesmahagow	28	3	2	23	35	103	11

McBOOKIE.COM LEAGUE CENTRAL
DISTRICT SECOND DIVISION

	P	W	D	L	F	A	Pts
Royal Albert	22	16	4	2	65	25	52
Gartcairn	22	16	3	3	75	27	51
Bellshill Athletic	22	14	2	6	49	29	44
St. Anthony's	22	12	1	9	43	32	37
Ashfield	22	11	2	9	42	31	35
Lanark United	22	8	7	7	52	40	31
Vale of Clyde	22	9	2	11	53	45	29
Vale of Leven	22	9	2	11	49	41	29
Johnstone Burgh	22	8	4	10	41	55	28
Carluke Rovers	22	7	5	10	39	41	26
Dunipace	22	5	2	15	27	51	17
Newmains United	22	0	0	22	15	133	0

**PETERSHILL celebrate
winning the McBookie Super
League First Division**

McBOOKIE.COM AYRSHIRE
DISTRICT LEAGUE

	P	W	D	L	F	A	Pts
Dalry Thistle	20	16	3	1	80	63	51
Irvine Victoria	20	15	1	4	60	30	46
Craigmark	20	14	1	5	50	27	43
Whitletts Victoria	20	12	4	4	44	33	40
Lugar Boswell Th	20	10	1	9	55	47	31
Ardrossan Winton	20	8	3	9	45	41	27
Maybole	20	8	2	10	55	36	26
Muirkirk	20	6	3	11	33	59	21
Saltcoats Victoria	20	4	1	15	22	73	13
Ardeer Thistle	20	4	0	16	23	51	12
Annbank United	20	3	1	16	31	84	10

SCOTTISH PROFESSIONAL FOOTBALL LEAGUE PREMIERSHIP 2018-2019

*FIXTURES SUBJECT TO CHANGE FOR LIVE TV COVERAGE,
AND CORRECT AT TIME OF GOING TO PRESS*

Saturday, August 4, 2018
Celtic v Livingston
Hamilton Accies v Hearts
Hibernian v Motherwell
Kilmarnock v St Johnstone
St Mirren v Dundee

Sunday, August 5, 2018
Aberdeen v Rangers

Saturday, August 11, 2018
Dundee v Aberdeen
Hearts v Celtic
Livingston v Kilmarnock
Motherwell v Hamilton Accies
Rangers v St Mirren
St Johnstone v Hibernian

Saturday, August 25, 2018
Celtic v Hamilton Accies
Hibernian v Aberdeen
Kilmarnock v Hearts
Motherwell v Rangers
St Johnstone v Dundee
St Mirren v Livingston

Saturday, September 1, 2018
Aberdeen v Kilmarnock
Celtic v Rangers
Dundee v Motherwell
Hamilton Accies v St Johnstone
Hearts v St Mirren
Livingston v Hibernian

Saturday, September 15, 2018
Hibernian v Kilmarnock
Livingston v Hamilton Accies
Motherwell v Hearts
Rangers v Dundee
St Johnstone v Aberdeen
St Mirren v Celtic

Saturday, September 22, 2018
Aberdeen v Motherwell
Dundee v Hibernian
Hamilton Accies v St Mirren
Hearts v Livingston
Kilmarnock v Celtic
Rangers v St Johnstone

Saturday, September 29, 2018
Celtic v Aberdeen
Hamilton Accies v Dundee
Hearts v St Johnstone
Kilmarnock v Motherwell
Livingston v Rangers
St Mirren v Hibernian

Saturday, October 6, 2018
Aberdeen v St Mirren
Dundee v Kilmarnock
Hibernian v Hamilton Accies
Motherwell v Livingston
Rangers v Hearts
St Johnstone v Celtic

Saturday, October 20, 2018
Celtic v Hibernian
Hamilton Accies v Rangers
Hearts v Aberdeen
Livingston v Dundee
Motherwell v St Johnstone
St Mirren v Kilmarnock

Saturday, October 27, 2018
Aberdeen v Livingston
Celtic v Motherwell
Dundee v Hearts
Hibernian v Rangers
Kilmarnock v Hamilton Accies
St Johnstone v St Mirren

Wednesday, October 31, 2018
Aberdeen v Hamilton Accies
Dundee v Celtic
Hearts v Hibernian
Livingston v St Johnstone
Rangers v Kilmarnock
St Mirren v Motherwell

Saturday, November 3, 2018
Celtic v Hearts
Hamilton Accies v Livingston
Hibernian v St Johnstone
Kilmarnock v Aberdeen
Motherwell v Dundee
St Mirren v Rangers

Saturday, November 10, 2018
Aberdeen v Hibernian
Dundee v St Mirren
Hearts v Kilmarnock
Livingston v Celtic
Rangers v Motherwell
St Johnstone v Hamilton Accies

Saturday, November 24, 2018
Hamilton Accies v Celtic
Hibernian v Dundee
Motherwell v Aberdeen
Rangers v Livingston
St Johnstone v Kilmarnock
St Mirren v Hearts

Saturday, December 1, 2018
Aberdeen v Dundee
Celtic v St Johnstone
Hearts v Rangers
Kilmarnock v Hibernian
Livingston v Motherwell
St Mirren v Hamilton Accies

Wednesday, December 5, 2018
Dundee v Hamilton Accies
Hibernian v St Mirren
Kilmarnock v Livingston
Motherwell v Celtic
Rangers v Aberdeen
St Johnstone v Hearts

Saturday, December 8, 2018
Aberdeen v St Johnstone
Celtic v Kilmarnock
Dundee v Rangers
Hamilton Accies v Hibernian
Hearts v Motherwell
Livingston v St Mirren

Saturday, December 15, 2018
Hibernian v Celtic
Kilmarnock v Dundee
Livingston v Hearts
Rangers v Hamilton Accies
St Johnstone v Motherwell
St Mirren v Aberdeen

Saturday, December 22, 2018
Aberdeen v Hearts
Celtic v Dundee
Hamilton Accies v Kilmarnock
Hibernian v Livingston
Motherwell v St Mirren
St Johnstone v Rangers

Wednesday, December 26, 2018
Aberdeen v Celtic
Dundee v Livingston
Hearts v Hamilton Accies
Motherwell v Kilmarnock
Rangers v Hibernian
St Mirren v St Johnstone

Saturday, December 29, 2018
Dundee v St Johnstone
Hamilton Accies v Motherwell
Hibernian v Hearts
Kilmarnock v St Mirren
Livingston v Aberdeen
Rangers v Celtic

Wednesday, January 23, 2019
Celtic v St Mirren
Hamilton Accies v Aberdeen
Hearts v Dundee
Kilmarnock v Rangers
Motherwell v Hibernian
St Johnstone v Livingston

Saturday, January 26, 2019
Aberdeen v Kilmarnock
Celtic v Hamilton Accies
Dundee v Motherwell
Hearts v St Johnstone
Livingston v Rangers
St Mirren v Hibernian

Saturday, February 2, 2019
Hamilton Accies v Dundee
Hibernian v Aberdeen
Kilmarnock v Hearts
Motherwell v Livingston
Rangers v St Mirren
St Johnstone v Celtic

Wednesday, February 6, 2019
Aberdeen v Rangers
Celtic v Hibernian
Dundee v Kilmarnock
Hamilton Accies v St Johnstone
Hearts v Livingston
St Mirren v Motherwell

Saturday, February 16, 2019
Aberdeen v St Mirren
Hibernian v Hamilton Accies
Kilmarnock v Celtic
Livingston v Dundee
Motherwell v Hearts
Rangers v St Johnstone

Saturday, February 23, 2019
Celtic v Motherwell
Dundee v Hibernian
Hamilton Accies v Rangers
Hearts v St Mirren
Livingston v Kilmarnock
St Johnstone v Aberdeen

Wednesday, February 27, 2019
Aberdeen v Hamilton Accies
Hearts v Celtic
Kilmarnock v Motherwell

Rangers v Dundee
St Johnstone v Hibernian
St Mirren v Livingston

Saturday, March 9, 2019
Celtic v Aberdeen
Dundee v Hearts
Hibernian v Rangers
Livingston v St Johnstone
Motherwell v Hamilton Accies
St Mirren v Kilmarnock

Saturday, March 16, 2019
Aberdeen v Livingston
Dundee v Celtic
Hamilton Accies v Hearts
Hibernian v Motherwell
Rangers v Kilmarnock
St Johnstone v St Mirren

Saturday, March 30, 2019
Celtic v Rangers
Hearts v Aberdeen
Kilmarnock v Hamilton Accies
Livingston v Hibernian
Motherwell v St Johnstone
St Mirren v Dundee

Wednesday, April 3, 2019
Aberdeen v Motherwell
Hibernian v Kilmarnock
Livingston v Hamilton Accies
Rangers v Hearts
St Johnstone v Dundee
St Mirren v Celtic

Saturday, April 6, 2019
Celtic v Livingston
Dundee v Aberdeen
Hamilton Accies v St Mirren
Hearts v Hibernian
Kilmarnock v St Johnstone
Motherwell v Rangers

LEAGUE WILL NOW SPLIT IN TWO FOR FINAL FIVE GAMES. DATES TO BE ARRANGED.

SPFL CHAMPIONSHIP 2018-2019

Saturday, August 4, 2018
Ayr United v Partick Thistle
Dundee United v Dunfermline
Falkirk v Inverness CT
Morton v Queen of South
Ross County v Alloa Athletic

Saturday, August 11, 2018
Alloa Athletic v Morton
Dunfermline v Ross County
Inverness CT v Ayr United
Partick Thistle v Falkirk
Queen of South v Dundee United

Saturday, August 25, 2018
Ayr United v Dunfermline
Dundee United v Partick Thistle
Falkirk v Queen of South
Inverness CT v Alloa Athletic
Morton v Ross County

Saturday, September 1, 2018
Alloa Athletic v Dundee United
Dunfermline v Inverness CT
Partick Thistle v Morton
Queen of South v Ayr United
Ross County v Falkirk

Saturday, September 15, 2018
Ayr United v Falkirk
Dundee United v Morton
Dunfermline v Alloa Athletic
Inverness CT v Partick Thistle
Queen of South v Ross County

Saturday, September 22, 2018
Alloa Athletic v Ayr United
Falkirk v Dundee United
Morton v Dunfermline
Partick Thistle v Queen of South
Ross County v Inverness CT

Saturday, September 29, 2018
Alloa Athletic v Falkirk
Dundee United v Ross County
Dunfermline v Partick Thistle
Inverness CT v Queen of South
Morton v Ayr United

Saturday, October 6, 2018
Ayr United v Dundee United
Falkirk v Dunfermline
Inverness CT v Morton
Partick Thistle v Ross County
Queen of South v Alloa Athletic

Saturday, October 20, 2018
Alloa Athletic v Partick Thistle
Dundee United v Inverness CT
Dunfermline v Queen of South
Morton v Falkirk
Ross County v Ayr United

Saturday, October 27, 2018
Alloa Athletic v Inverness CT
Dunfermline v Dundee United
Partick Thistle v Ayr United
Queen of South v Falkirk
Ross County v Morton

Tuesday, October 30, 2018
Ayr United v Alloa Athletic
Falkirk v Ross County
Inverness CT v Dunfermline
Partick Thistle v Dundee United
Queen of South v Morton

Saturday, November 3, 2018
Alloa Athletic v Dunfermline
Dundee United v Queen of South
Falkirk v Ayr United
Inverness CT v Ross County
Morton v Partick Thistle

Saturday, November 10, 2018
Ayr United v Queen of South
Dunfermline v Falkirk
Morton v Alloa Athletic
Partick Thistle v Inverness CT
Ross County v Dundee United

Saturday, November 17, 2018
Ayr United v Morton
Dundee United v Alloa Athletic
Falkirk v Partick Thistle
Queen of South v Inverness CT
Ross County v Dunfermline

Saturday, December 1, 2018
Alloa Athletic v Ross County
Dundee United v Ayr United
Dunfermline v Morton
Inverness CT v Falkirk
Queen of South v Partick Thistle

Saturday, December 8, 2018
Ayr United v Inverness CT
Falkirk v Alloa Athletic
Morton v Dundee United
Partick Thistle v Dunfermline
Ross County v Queen of South

Saturday, December 15, 2018
Ayr United v Ross County
Falkirk v Morton
Inverness CT v Dundee United
Partick Thistle v Alloa Athletic
Queen of South v Dunfermline

Saturday, December 22, 2018
Alloa Athletic v Queen of South
Dundee United v Falkirk
Dunfermline v Ayr United
Morton v Inverness CT
Ross County v Partick Thistle

Saturday, December 29, 2018
Alloa Athletic v Dundee United
Falkirk v Dunfermline
Partick Thistle v Morton
Queen of South v Ayr United
Ross County v Inverness CT

Saturday, January 5, 2019
Ayr United v Falkirk
Dundee United v Partick Thistle
Dunfermline v Alloa Athletic
Inverness CT v Queen of South
Morton v Ross County

Saturday, January 12, 2019
Alloa Athletic v Morton
Dundee United v Dunfermline
Inverness CT v Ayr United
Partick Thistle v Falkirk
Queen of South v Ross County

Saturday, January 26, 2019
Ayr United v Dundee United
Falkirk v Inverness CT
Morton v Dunfermline
Partick Thistle v Queen of South
Ross County v Alloa Athletic

Saturday, February 2, 2019
Alloa Athletic v Ayr United
Dundee United v Morton
Dunfermline v Ross County
Falkirk v Queen of South
Inverness CT v Partick Thistle

Saturday, February 16, 2019
Alloa Athletic v Partick Thistle
Dunfermline v Inverness CT
Morton v Ayr United
Queen of South v Dundee United
Ross County v Falkirk

Saturday, February 23, 2019
Ayr United v Dunfermline
Falkirk v Dundee United
Inverness CT v Morton
Partick Thistle v Ross County
Queen of South v Alloa Athletic

Tuesday, February 26, 2019
Alloa Athletic v Falkirk
Dundee United v Inverness CT
Dunfermline v Partick Thistle
Morton v Queen of South
Ross County v Ayr United

Saturday, March 2, 2019
Ayr United v Partick Thistle
Dundee United v Ross County
Dunfermline v Queen of South
Inverness CT v Alloa Athletic
Morton v Falkirk

Saturday, March 9, 2019
Alloa Athletic v Dunfermline
Falkirk v Ayr United
Partick Thistle v Dundee United
Queen of South v Inverness CT
Ross County v Morton

Saturday, March 16, 2019
Ayr United v Queen of South
Dunfermline v Dundee United
Falkirk v Partick Thistle
Inverness CT v Ross County
Morton v Alloa Athletic

Saturday, March 23, 2019
Ayr United v Morton
Dundee United v Alloa Athletic
Partick Thistle v Inverness CT
Queen of South v Falkirk
Ross County v Dunfermline

Saturday, March 30, 2019
Alloa Athletic v Ross County
Dundee United v Queen of South
Dunfermline v Ayr United
Inverness CT v Falkirk
Morton v Partick Thistle

Saturday, April 6, 2019
Ayr United v Inverness CT
Falkirk v Alloa Athletic
Partick Thistle v Dunfermline
Queen of South v Morton
Ross County v Dundee United

Saturday, April 13, 2019
Alloa Athletic v Queen of South
Dundee United v Ayr United
Dunfermline v Falkirk
Morton v Inverness CT
Ross County v Partick Thistle

Saturday, April 20, 2019
Ayr United v Ross County
Falkirk v Morton
Inverness CT v Dundee United
Partick Thistle v Alloa Athletic
Queen of South v Dunfermline

Saturday, April 27, 2019
Alloa Athletic v Inverness CT
Dundee United v Falkirk
Dunfermline v Morton
Partick Thistle v Ayr United
Ross County v Queen of South

Saturday, May 4, 2019
Ayr United v Alloa Athletic
Falkirk v Ross County
Inverness CT v Dunfermline
Morton v Dundee United
Queen of South v Partick Thistle

SPFL LEAGUE 1 2018-2019

Saturday, August 4, 2018
East Fife v Dumbarton
Forfar Athletic v Airdrieonians
Stenhousemuir v Brechin City
Stranraer v Raith Rovers

Saturday, August 11, 2018
Airdrieonians v Montrose
Arbroath v Stranraer
Brechin City v East Fife
Dumbarton v Forfar Athletic
Raith Rovers v Stenhousemuir

Saturday, August 18, 2018
Dumbarton v Arbroath
Forfar Athletic v Stranraer
Montrose v Brechin City
Raith Rovers v East Fife
Stenhousemuir v Airdrieonians

Saturday, August 25, 2018
Airdrieonians v Raith Rovers
Brechin City v Dumbarton
East Fife v Arbroath
Forfar Athletic v Stenhousemuir
Stranraer v Montrose

Saturday, September 1, 2018
Airdrieonians v Stranraer
Arbroath v Brechin City
Montrose v East Fife
Raith Rovers v Forfar Athletic
Stenhousemuir v Dumbarton

Saturday, September 15, 2018
Arbroath v Forfar Athletic
Brechin City v Raith Rovers
Dumbarton v Montrose
East Fife v Airdrieonians
Stranraer v Stenhousemuir

Saturday, September 22, 2018
Airdrieonians v Dumbarton
Forfar Athletic v Brechin City
Raith Rovers v Montrose
Stenhousemuir v Arbroath
Stranraer v East Fife

Saturday, September 29, 2018
Arbroath v Airdrieonians
Brechin City v Stranraer
Dumbarton v Raith Rovers
East Fife v Stenhousemuir
Montrose v Forfar Athletic

Saturday, October 6, 2018
Airdrieonians v Brechin City
Forfar Athletic v East Fife
Raith Rovers v Arbroath
Stenhousemuir v Montrose
Stranraer v Dumbarton

Saturday, October 20, 2018
Arbroath v Dumbarton
East Fife v Brechin City
Montrose v Airdrieonians
Raith Rovers v Stranraer
Stenhousemuir v Forfar Athletic

Saturday, October 27, 2018
Airdrieonians v Stenhousemuir
Brechin City v Montrose
Dumbarton v East Fife
Forfar Athletic v Raith Rovers
Stranraer v Arbroath

Saturday, November 3, 2018
Airdrieonians v Forfar Athletic
Arbroath v East Fife
Montrose v Dumbarton
Raith Rovers v Brechin City
Stenhousemuir v Stranraer

Saturday, November 10, 2018
Arbroath v Montrose
Brechin City v Forfar Athletic
Dumbarton v Stenhousemuir
East Fife v Raith Rovers
Stranraer v Airdrieonians

Saturday, November 17, 2018
Airdrieonians v East Fife
Brechin City v Arbroath
Forfar Athletic v Dumbarton
Montrose v Stranraer
Stenhousemuir v Raith Rovers

Saturday, December 1, 2018
Arbroath v Stenhousemuir
Dumbarton v Brechin City
East Fife v Montrose
Raith Rovers v Airdrieonians
Stranraer v Forfar Athletic

Saturday, December 8, 2018
Brechin City v Stenhousemuir
Dumbarton v Airdrieonians
East Fife v Stranraer
Forfar Athletic v Arbroath
Montrose v Raith Rovers

Saturday, December 15, 2018
Airdrieonians v Arbroath
Forfar Athletic v Montrose
Raith Rovers v Dumbarton
Stenhousemuir v East Fife
Stranraer v Brechin City

Saturday, December 22, 2018
Arbroath v Raith Rovers
Brechin City v Airdrieonians
Dumbarton v Stranraer
East Fife v Forfar Athletic
Montrose v Stenhousemuir

Saturday, December 29, 2018
Airdrieonians v Stranraer
Forfar Athletic v Brechin City
Montrose v Arbroath
Raith Rovers v East Fife
Stenhousemuir v Dumbarton

Saturday, January 5, 2019
Arbroath v Brechin City
Dumbarton v Forfar Athletic
East Fife v Airdrieonians
Raith Rovers v Stenhousemuir
Stranraer v Montrose

Saturday, January 12, 2019
Airdrieonians v Raith Rovers
Brechin City v Dumbarton
Forfar Athletic v Stranraer
Montrose v East Fife
Stenhousemuir v Arbroath

Saturday, January 26, 2019
Arbroath v Forfar Athletic
Brechin City v Raith Rovers
Dumbarton v Montrose
Stenhousemuir v Airdrieonians
Stranraer v East Fife

Saturday, February 2, 2019
Airdrieonians v Dumbarton
East Fife v Arbroath
Montrose v Brechin City
Raith Rovers v Forfar Athletic
Stranraer v Stenhousemuir

Saturday, February 9, 2019
Arbroath v Stranraer
Brechin City v East Fife
Dumbarton v Raith Rovers
Forfar Athletic v Airdrieonians
Stenhousemuir v Montrose

Saturday, February 16, 2019
Airdrieonians v Brechin City
East Fife v Stenhousemuir
Montrose v Forfar Athletic
Raith Rovers v Arbroath
Stranraer v Dumbarton

Saturday, February 23, 2019
Arbroath v Airdrieonians
Brechin City v Stranraer
East Fife v Dumbarton
Forfar Athletic v Stenhousemuir
Raith Rovers v Montrose

Saturday, March 2, 2019
Airdrieonians v Montrose
Dumbarton v Arbroath
Forfar Athletic v East Fife
Stenhousemuir v Brechin City
Stranraer v Raith Rovers

Saturday, March 9, 2019
Arbroath v Stenhousemuir
Brechin City v Forfar Athletic
East Fife v Stranraer
Montrose v Dumbarton
Raith Rovers v Airdrieonians

Saturday, March 16, 2019
Arbroath v East Fife
Brechin City v Montrose
Dumbarton v Airdrieonians
Forfar Athletic v Raith Rovers
Stenhousemuir v Stranraer

Saturday, March 23, 2019
Airdrieonians v Forfar Athletic
East Fife v Brechin City
Montrose v Stenhousemuir
Raith Rovers v Dumbarton
Stranraer v Arbroath

Saturday, March 30, 2019
Brechin City v Airdrieonians
Dumbarton v Stenhousemuir
East Fife v Raith Rovers
Forfar Athletic v Arbroath
Montrose v Stranraer

Saturday, April 6, 2019
Airdrieonians v East Fife
Arbroath v Montrose
Dumbarton v Brechin City
Stenhousemuir v Raith Rovers
Stranraer v Forfar Athletic

Saturday, April 13, 2019
Airdrieonians v Stenhousemuir
Brechin City v Arbroath
East Fife v Montrose
Forfar Athletic v Dumbarton
Raith Rovers v Stranraer

Saturday, April 20, 2019
Arbroath v Raith Rovers
Dumbarton v East Fife
Montrose v Airdrieonians
Stenhousemuir v Forfar Athletic
Stranraer v Brechin City

Saturday, April 27, 2019
Airdrieonians v Arbroath
Dumbarton v Stranraer
Forfar Athletic v Montrose
Raith Rovers v Brechin City
Stenhousemuir v East Fife

Saturday, May 4, 2019
Arbroath v Dumbarton
Brechin City v Stenhousemuir
East Fife v Forfar Athletic
Montrose v Raith Rovers
Stranraer v Airdrieonians

DON'T MISS OUR

BIG
TWO
IN SPORT!

John Hartson

Lee McCulloch

ONLY IN YOUR
EveningTimes

SPFL LEAGUE 2 2018-2019

Saturday, August 4, 2018
Annan Athletic v Elgin City
Berwick Rangers v Stirling Albion
Clyde v Cowdenbeath
Edinburgh City v Albion Rovers
Peterhead v Queen's Park

Saturday, August 11, 2018
Albion Rovers v Peterhead
Cowdenbeath v Annan Athletic
Elgin City v Edinburgh City
Queen's Park v Berwick Rangers
Stirling Albion v Clyde

Saturday, August 18, 2018
Albion Rovers v Elgin City
Annan Athletic v Queen's Park
Cowdenbeath v Berwick Rangers
Edinburgh City v Stirling Albion
Peterhead v Clyde

Saturday, August 25, 2018
Berwick Rangers v Annan Athletic
Clyde v Edinburgh City
Elgin City v Cowdenbeath
Queen's Park v Albion Rovers
Stirling Albion v Peterhead

Saturday, September 1, 2018
Albion Rovers v Berwick Rangers
Annan Athletic v Clyde
Elgin City v Stirling Albion
Peterhead v Edinburgh City
Queen's Park v Cowdenbeath

Saturday, September 15, 2018
Berwick Rangers v Elgin City
Clyde v Albion Rovers
Cowdenbeath v Peterhead
Edinburgh City v Annan Athletic
Stirling Albion v Queen's Park

Saturday, September 22, 2018
Clyde v Elgin City
Cowdenbeath v Albion Rovers
Peterhead v Berwick Rangers
Queen's Park v Edinburgh City
Stirling Albion v Annan Athletic

Saturday, September 29, 2018
Albion Rovers v Stirling Albion
Annan Athletic v Peterhead
Berwick Rangers v Clyde
Edinburgh City v Cowdenbeath
Elgin City v Queen's Park

Saturday, October 6, 2018
Annan Athletic v Albion Rovers
Cowdenbeath v Stirling Albion
Edinburgh City v Berwick Rangers
Peterhead v Elgin City
Queen's Park v Clyde

Saturday, October 27, 2018
Albion Rovers v Queen's Park
Berwick Rangers v Cowdenbeath
Clyde v Peterhead
Elgin City v Annan Athletic
Stirling Albion v Edinburgh City

Saturday, November 3, 2018
Cowdenbeath v Elgin City
Edinburgh City v Clyde
Peterhead v Albion Rovers
Queen's Park v Annan Athletic
Stirling Albion v Berwick Rangers

Saturday, November 10, 2018
Albion Rovers v Edinburgh City
Annan Athletic v Cowdenbeath
Clyde v Stirling Albion
Elgin City v Berwick Rangers
Queen's Park v Peterhead

QUEENS Park, winners of the inaugural Scottish Cup, (back row, l-r) Angus McKinnon, John Dickson, Thomas Lawrie, Charles Campbell, Robert Neill; (front row, l-r) Robert Leckie, Joseph Taylor, Harry McNeil, JJ Thomson, James Weir, William McKinnon on April 1, 1874

Saturday, November 17, 2018
Annan Athletic v Stirling Albion
Berwick Rangers v Albion Rovers
Cowdenbeath v Queen's Park
Edinburgh City v Peterhead
Elgin City v Clyde

Saturday, December 1, 2018
Albion Rovers v Cowdenbeath
Clyde v Berwick Rangers
Edinburgh City v Queen's Park
Peterhead v Annan Athletic
Stirling Albion v Elgin City

Saturday, December 8, 2018
Annan Athletic v Edinburgh City
Berwick Rangers v Peterhead
Cowdenbeath v Clyde
Elgin City v Albion Rovers
Queen's Park v Stirling Albion

Saturday, December 15, 2018
Berwick Rangers v Queen's Park
Clyde v Annan Athletic
Edinburgh City v Elgin City
Peterhead v Cowdenbeath
Stirling Albion v Albion Rovers

Saturday, December 22, 2018
Albion Rovers v Clyde
Annan Athletic v Berwick Rangers
Cowdenbeath v Edinburgh City
Peterhead v Stirling Albion
Queen's Park v Elgin City

Saturday, December 29, 2018
Albion Rovers v Annan Athletic
Berwick Rangers v Edinburgh City
Clyde v Queen's Park
Elgin City v Peterhead
Stirling Albion v Cowdenbeath

Saturday, January 5, 2019
Annan Athletic v Elgin City
Cowdenbeath v Berwick Rangers
Edinburgh City v Stirling Albion
Peterhead v Clyde
Queen's Park v Albion Rovers

Saturday, January 12, 2019
Albion Rovers v Peterhead
Berwick Rangers v Clyde
Elgin City v Cowdenbeath
Queen's Park v Edinburgh City
Stirling Albion v Annan Athletic

Saturday, January 19, 2019
Clyde v Elgin City
Cowdenbeath v Albion Rovers
Edinburgh City v Annan Athletic
Peterhead v Berwick Rangers
Stirling Albion v Queen's Park

Saturday, January 26, 2019
Albion Rovers v Stirling Albion
Annan Athletic v Peterhead
Clyde v Cowdenbeath
Elgin City v Edinburgh City
Queen's Park v Berwick Rangers

Saturday, February 2, 2019
Berwick Rangers v Annan Athletic
Cowdenbeath v Peterhead
Edinburgh City v Albion Rovers
Elgin City v Queen's Park
Stirling Albion v Clyde

Saturday, February 9, 2019
Albion Rovers v Elgin City
Annan Athletic v Clyde
Berwick Rangers v Stirling Albion
Peterhead v Edinburgh City
Queen's Park v Cowdenbeath

Saturday, February 16, 2019
Clyde v Albion Rovers
Cowdenbeath v Annan Athletic
Edinburgh City v Berwick Rangers
Elgin City v Stirling Albion
Peterhead v Queen's Park

Saturday, February 23, 2019
Annan Athletic v Albion Rovers
Berwick Rangers v Elgin City
Edinburgh City v Cowdenbeath
Queen's Park v Clyde
Stirling Albion v Peterhead

Saturday, March 2, 2019
Albion Rovers v Berwick Rangers
Annan Athletic v Queen's Park
Clyde v Edinburgh City
Cowdenbeath v Stirling Albion
Peterhead v Elgin City

Saturday, March 9, 2019
Berwick Rangers v Cowdenbeath
Edinburgh City v Queen's Park
Elgin City v Clyde
Peterhead v Annan Athletic
Stirling Albion v Albion Rovers

Saturday, March 16, 2019
Albion Rovers v Cowdenbeath
Annan Athletic v Edinburgh City
Berwick Rangers v Peterhead
Clyde v Stirling Albion
Queen's Park v Elgin City

Saturday, March 23, 2019
Clyde v Annan Athletic
Cowdenbeath v Queen's Park
Edinburgh City v Peterhead
Elgin City v Albion Rovers
Stirling Albion v Berwick Rangers

Saturday, March 30, 2019
Albion Rovers v Clyde
Berwick Rangers v Edinburgh City
Elgin City v Annan Athletic
Peterhead v Cowdenbeath
Queen's Park v Stirling Albion

Saturday, April 6, 2019
Albion Rovers v Queen's Park
Annan Athletic v Berwick Rangers
Clyde v Peterhead
Cowdenbeath v Edinburgh City
Stirling Albion v Elgin City

Saturday, April 13, 2019
Annan Athletic v Stirling Albion
Berwick Rangers v Queen's Park
Cowdenbeath v Elgin City
Edinburgh City v Clyde
Peterhead v Albion Rovers

Saturday, April 20, 2019
Albion Rovers v Edinburgh City
Clyde v Berwick Rangers
Elgin City v Peterhead
Queen's Park v Annan Athletic
Stirling Albion v Cowdenbeath

Saturday, April 27, 2019
Annan Athletic v Cowdenbeath
Berwick Rangers v Albion Rovers
Clyde v Queen's Park
Edinburgh City v Elgin City
Peterhead v Stirling Albion

Saturday, May 4, 2019
Albion Rovers v Annan Athletic
Cowdenbeath v Clyde
Elgin City v Berwick Rangers
Queen's Park v Peterhead
Stirling Albion v Edinburgh City

LEADING EXECUTIVES/SECRETARIES

SCOTTISH FA – Ian Maxwell, Chief Executive, Hampden Park, Glasgow, G42 9AY. Tel: 0141 616 6000. Website: scottishfa.co.uk

SCOTTISH PROFESSIONAL FOOTBALL LEAGUE– N. Doncaster, Chief Executive, Hampden Park, Glasgow, G42 9DE. 0141 620 4140. Website: spfl.co.uk

ENGLISH FA – M. Glenn, Chief Executive, Wembley Stadium, PO Box 1966, London, SW1P 9EQ. Tel: 0800 169 1862. Website: thefa.com

ENGLISH PREMIER LEAGUE – R. Scudamore, Chief Executive, 30 Gloucester Place, London, W14 8PL. Tel: 0207 864 9000. Website: premierleague.com

ENGLISH FOOTBALL LEAGUE – S. Harvey, Chairman, EFL House, 10-12 West Cliff, Preston, PR1 8HU. Tel: 01722 325800. Website: football-league.co.uk

FA OF WALES – J. Ford, Chief Executive, 11 / 12 Neptune Court, Vanguard Way, Cardiff, CF24 5PJ. Tel: 02920 435 830. Website: faw.org.uk

NORTHERN IRELAND FA – P. Nelson, Chief Executive, Donegall Avenue, Belfast, BT12 6LU. Tel: 02890 669458. Website: irishfa.com

FA OF IRELAND – J. Delaney, Chief Executive, National Sports Campus, Abbotstown, Dublin 15. Website: fai.ie

UEFA – Aleksander Ceferin, President, Route de Geneve 46, CH-1260 Nyon 2, Switzerland. Tel: 00 41 848 00 2727. Website: uefa.com

FIFA – G. Infantino, President, FIFA-Strasse 20, P.O. Box 8044 Zurich, Switzerland. Tel : 00 43 222 7777, Fax : 00 43 222 7878. Website: fifa.com

PFA SCOTLAND F. Wishart, Chief Executive, Woodside House, 2 Woodside Place, Glasgow, G3 7QF. 0141 353 0199. Website: www.pfascotland.co.uk

SCOTTISH JUNIOR FA – T. Johnston, Secretary, Hampden Park, Glasgow, G42 9DD. Tel: 0141 620 4560. Website: www.scottishfa.co.uk/sjfa

WEST OF SCOTLAND REGION – J. Scott Robertson. Secretary. 01698 266 725. Website: www.scottishfa.co.uk/sjfa

SCOTTISH WOMEN'S FOOTBALL – V. MacLaren, Chair, Hampden Park, Glasgow G42. Tel: 0141 620 4580. Website: scotwomensfootball.com

KILMARNOCK manager Steve Clarke with assistant manager Alex Dyer (left) and goalkeeping coach Billy Thomson with the Ladbrokes Premiership Manager of the Month Award for February

2017-2018 SPFL MONTHLY AWARDS

AUGUST

Ladbrokes Premiership Manager of Month: Tommy Wright (St Johnstone)

Ladbrokes Championship Manager of Month: Allan Johnston (Dunfermline)

Ladbrokes League 1 Manager of Month: Barry Smith (Raith Rovers)

Ladbrokes League 2 Manager of Month: Dave Mackay (Stirling Albion)

Ladbrokes Premiership Player of Month: Michael O'Halloran (St Johnstone)

Ladbrokes Championship Player of Month: Joe Cardle (Dunfermline)

Ladbrokes League 1 Player of Month: Lewis Vaughan (Raith Rovers)

Ladbrokes League 2 Player of Month: Darren Smith (Stirling Albion)

BRENDAN Rodgers with his manager of the month award
Pics: SNS

SEPTEMBER

Ladbrokes Premiership Manager of Month: Brendan Rodgers (Celtic)

Ladbrokes Championship Manager of Month: David Hopkin (Livingston)

Ladbrokes League 1 Manager of Month: Brian Kerr (Albion Rovers)

Ladbrokes League 2 Manager of Month: Brown Ferguson (Stenhousemuir)

Ladbrokes Premiership Player of Month: Louis Moult (Motherwell)

Ladbrokes Championship Player of Month: Lewis Morgan (St Mirren)

Ladbrokes League 1 Player of Month: Ryan McCord (Arbroath)

Ladbrokes League 2 Player of Month: Mark McGuigan (Stenhousemuir)

2017-2018 SPFL MONTHLY AWARDS

OCTOBER

Ladbrokes Premiership Manager of Month: Neil Lennon (Hibernian)

Ladbrokes Championship Manager of Month: John Robertson (Inverness CT)

Ladbrokes League 1 Manager of Month: Ian McCall (Ayr United)

Ladbrokes League 2 Manager of Month: Gavin Price (Elgin City)

Ladbrokes Premiership Player of Month: Kieran Tierney (Celtic)

Ladbrokes Championship Player of Month: Carl Tremarco (Inverness CT)

Ladbrokes League 1 Player of Month: Michael Moffat (Ayr United)

Ladbrokes League 2 Player of Month: Craig Johnston (Montrose)

NOVEMBER

Ladbrokes Premiership Manager of Month: Martin Canning (Hamilton Accies)

Ladbrokes Championship Manager of Month: Stephen Aitken (Dumbarton)

Ladbrokes League 1 Manager of Month: Ian McCall (Ayr United)

Ladbrokes League 2 Manager of Month: Stewart Petrie (Montrose)

Ladbrokes Premiership Player of Month: David Templeton (Hamilton Accies)

Ladbrokes Championship Player of Month: Scott Fraser (Dundee United)

Ladbrokes League 1 Player of Month: Lawrence Shankland (Ayr United)

Ladbrokes League 2 Player of Month: Cammy Ballantyne (Montrose)

DECEMBER

Ladbrokes Premiership Manager of Month: Steve Clarke (Kilmarnock)

Ladbrokes Championship Manager of Month: Jack Ross (St Mirren)

Ladbrokes League 1 Manager of Month: Barry Smith (Raith Rovers)

Ladbrokes League 2 Manager of Month: Jim McInally (Peterhead)

2017-2018 SPFL MONTHLY AWARDS

Ladbrokes Premiership Player of Month: Kris Boyd (Kilmarnock)

Ladbrokes Championship Player of Month: Stephen Dobbie (Queen of the South)

Ladbrokes League 1 Player of Month: Alan Trouten (Albion Rovers)

Ladbrokes League 2 Player of Month: Rory McAllister (Peterhead)

JANUARY

Ladbrokes Premiership Manager of Month: No award due to winter break

Ladbrokes Championship Manager of Month: Jack Ross (St Mirren)

Ladbrokes League 1 Manager of Month: Dick Campbell (Arbroath)

Ladbrokes League 2 Manager of Month: Jim McInally (Peterhead)

Ladbrokes Premiership Player of Month: No award due to winter break

Ladbrokes Championship Player of Month: Stephen McGinn (St Mirren)

Ladbrokes League 1 Player of Month: Angus Beith (Stranraer)

Ladbrokes League 2 Player of Month: Darren Smith (Stirling Albion)

FEBRUARY

Ladbrokes Premiership Manager of Month: Steve Clarke (Kilmarnock)

Ladbrokes Championship Manager of Month: David Hopkin (Livingston)

Ladbrokes League 1 Manager of Month: Dick Campbell (Arbroath)

Ladbrokes League 2 Manager of Month: Dave Mackay (Stirling Albion)

Ladbrokes Premiership Player of Month: Josh Windass (Rangers)

Ladbrokes Championship Player of Month: Ryan Hardie (Livingston)

Ladbrokes League 1 Player of Month: Willis Furtado (Raith Rovers)

Ladbrokes League 2 Player of Month: Peter MacDonald (Stirling Albion)

2017-2018 SPFL AWARDS

MARCH

Ladbrokes Premiership Manager of Month: Steve Clarke (Kilmarnock)

Ladbrokes Championship Manager of Month: Jack Ross (St Mirren)

Ladbrokes League 1 Manager of Month: Ian McCall (Ayr United)

Ladbrokes League 2 Manager of Month: Danny Lennon (Clyde)

Ladbrokes Premiership Player of Month: Stephen O'Donnell (Kilmarnock)

Ladbrokes Championship Player of Month: Nicky Clark (Dunfermline)

Ladbrokes League 1 Player of Month: Lawrence Shankland (Ayr United)

Ladbrokes League 2 Player of Month: Chris McStay (Clyde)

Pic: SNS

FORMER St Mirren boss Jack Ross won the Ladbrokes Championship Manager of the Year Award

SEASON 2017/18 OVERALL AWARDS

Ladbrokes Premiership Manager of Year: Brendan Rodgers (Celtic)

Ladbrokes Championship Manager of Year: Jack Ross (St Mirren)

Ladbrokes League 1 Manager of Year: Ian McCall (Ayr United)

Ladbrokes League 2 Manager of Year: Stewart Petrie (Montrose)

Ladbrokes Premiership Player of Year: Scott Brown (Celtic)

Ladbrokes Championship Player of Year: Lewis Morgan (St Mirren)

Ladbrokes League 1 Player of Year: Lawrence Shankland (Ayr United)

Ladbrokes League 2 Player of Year: Sean Dillon (Montrose)

PFA SCOTLAND TEAMS OF THE SEASON

PREMIERSHIP:

Jon McLaughlin (Hearts), **James Tavernier** (Rangers), **Christophe Berra** (Hearts), **Scott McKenna** (Aberdeen), **Kieran Tierney** (Celtic), **Dylan McGeough** (Hibernian), **Scott Brown** (Celtic), **John McGinn** (Hibernian), **James Forrest** (Celtic), **Kris Boyd** (Kilmarnock), **Alfredo Morelos** (Rangers)

CHAMPIONSHIP:

Neil Alexander (Livingston), **Ryan Williamson** (Dunfermline), **Thomas O'Ware** (Morton), **Craig Halkett** (Livingston), **Liam Smith** (St Mirren), **Cammy Smith** (St Mirren). **Stephen McGinn** (St Mirren), **Iain Vigurs** (Inverness Caledonian Thistle), **Gavin Reilly** (St Mirren), **Stephen Dobbie** (Queen of the South), **Lewis Morgan** (St Mirren)

LEAGUE ONE:

Neil Parry (Alloa Athletic), **Scott Taggart** (Alloa Athletic), **Iain Davidson** (Raith Rovers), **Thomas O'Brien** (Arbroath), **Jason Thomson** (Raith Rovers), **Declan McDaid** (Ayr United), **Lewis Vaughan** (Raith Rovers), **Iain Flannigan** (Alloa Athletic), **Michael Moffat** (Ayr United) **Lawrence Shankland** (Ayr United), **Alan Trouten** (Albion Rovers)

LEAGUE TWO:

Greg Fleming (Peterhead), **Jason Brown** (Peterhead) **David McCracken** (Peterhead), **Sean Dillon** (Montrose), **Andrew Steeves** (Montrose), **Harry Paton** (Stenhousemuir), **Thomas Reilly** (Elgin City), **Willie Gibson** (Peterhead), **Mark McGuigan** (Stenhousemuir), **Rory McAllister** (Peterhead), **Darren Smith** (Stirling Albion)

2017-2018 SFA YOUTH CUP

FIRST ROUND: Inverurie Loco Works 2-2 Nairn County (Inverurie win 4-1 on pens); Inverness Caledonian Thistle 6-1 Banks O'Dee; Deveronvale 2-1 Formartine United; Lossiemouth 0-2 Keith; Ross County 10-0 Elgin City; Albion Rovers 1-1 Clyde (Albion win 6-5 on pens); Cowdenbeath 2-3 Whitehill Welfare; Dundee 1-2 Raith Rovers; East Kilbride 4-1 Airdrieonians; Stranraer 4-3 Mid-Annandale; Bonnyton Thistle 0-1 Selkirk

SECOND ROUND: Turriff United 8-0 Lossiemouth; Deveronvale FC 0-12 Ross County; Inverurie Loco Works 3-0 Montrose FC; Forfar Athletic 1-3 Inverness Caledonian Thistle (AET) Fraserburgh FC 3-0 Clachnacuddin; Albion Rovers 0-1Alloa Athletic; Lothian Thistle Hutchison Vale 0-4 Stirling Albion; Whitehill Welfare 0-4 East Kilbride; Edusport Academy 1-0 BSC Glasgow; Burntisland Shipyard 3-2 Livingston FC; Hamilton Academical 4-2 Queen's Park (AET); Tynecastle FC 1-4 Cumbernauld Colts; Berwick Rangers 1-2 University of Stirling; St Mirren 4-0 Heriot Watt University; Edinburgh City 0-1 Raith Rovers; Stranraer FC 2-0 Selkirk FC

THIRD ROUND: Rangers 5-2 Partick Thistle; Alloa Athletic 0-8 Celtic; Morton 3-0 Turriff Utd; Queen of the South 0-1 Stranraer; Motherwell 9-0 Burntisland Shipyard; Edusport Academy 0-6 Aberdeen; Hamilton Academicals 4-2 Falkirk; St Johnstone 2-1 Dundee Utd; Inverness Caledonian Thistle 2-0 University of Stirling FC; Inverurie Loco Works 1-2 Raith Rovers; Ross County 2-0 Fraserburgh; Heart of Midlothian 5-1 Ayr Utd; Spartans 0-3 Kilmarnock; Hibernian 2-1 East Kilbride; Stirling Albion 4-2 Cumbernauld Colts.

FOURTH ROUND: Stranraer FC 0-11; Stirling Albion 3-4 Ross County; St Johnstone 2-1 Rangers; Inverness Caledonian Thistle 1-2 Hibernian; Kilmarnock 3-1 Heart of Midlothian; Hamilton Academical 2-4 Aberdeen; Morton 3-1 St Mirren; Celtic 5-0 Raith Rovers

QUARTER-FINALS: Motherwell 2-3 Kilmarnock; Aberdeen 2-1 Ross County; Celtic 3-0 St Johnstone; Hibernian 3-1 Morton

SEMI-FINALS: Hibernian 0-0 Celtic (Hibernian won 4-2 on penalties); Kilmarnock 0-3 Aberdeen

FINAL
Aberdeen 1-3 Hibernian

GLASGOW CUP 2017-2018

FIRST ROUND

Celtic....................................4 Partick Thistle....................3
Rangers...............................8 Queen's Park.....................0

SECOND ROUND

Partick Thistle........................1 Queen's Park.....................3
Celtic....................................5 Rangers.............................2

THIRD ROUND

Queen's Park.........................2 Celtic.................................2
Rangers...............................1 Partick Thistle....................2

FOURTH ROUND

Partick Thistle........................1 Celtic.................................5
Queen's Park.........................1 Rangers.............................1

FIFTH ROUND

Queen's Park.........................3 Partick Thistle....................0
Rangers...............................4 Celtic.................................2

SEMI FINAL

Celtic....................................4 Queen's Park.....................0
Partick Thistle........................1 Rangers.............................3

FINAL

Rangers...............................3 Celtic.................................0

**THE Rangers youngsters celebrate winning the
Glasgow Cup, beating Celtic 3-0   Pic: SNS**

Pic: SNS

**KILMARNOCK'S Kris Boyd was the Premiership's
top goalscorer with 18 goals**

TOP SCORERS – 2017/18

SCOTLAND

Premiership.................. Kris Boyd (Kilmarnock).....................18

Championship.............. Stephen Dobbie (QoS) 18

League One...................Lawrence Shankland (Ayr United). 26

League Two ....David Goodwillie (Clyde) 25

ENGLAND

Premier League........... Mohamed Salah (Liverpool) 32

Championship.............. Matej Vydra (Derby) 21

League One.................. Jack Marriott (Peterborough).......... 27

League Two ....Billy Kee (Accrington) 25

.................................Marc McNulty (Coventry) 25

SPAIN

Primera Liga .... Lionel Messi (Barcelona)................. 34

ITALY

Serie A ....Ciro Immobile (Lazio)...................... 29

.................................Mauro Icardi (Inter Milan)................ 29

FRANCE

Ligue One .... Edinson Cavani (Paris St Germain)28

GERMANY

Bundesliga................... Robert Lewandowski (B Munich)... 29

HOLLAND

Eredivisie .... Alireza Jahanbakhsh (AZ Alkmaar)21

PORTUGAL

Primera Liga .... Jonas (Benfica)................................ 34

CHAMPIONS LEAGUE

Cristiano Ronaldo (Real Madrid) 15

EUROPA LEAGUE

Aduriz (A Bilbao)..8

Ciro Immobile (Lazio) 8

SCOTLAND MANAGERS

NAME	DATES	P	W	D	L	F	A
Andy Beattie	2/54-6/54	6	2	1	3	6	14
Sir Matt Busby	9/58-12/58	2	1	1	0	5	2
Andy Beattie	3/59-10/60	12	3	3	6	19	23
Ian McColl	11/60-5/65	28	17	3	8	77	52
Jock Stein	5/65-12/65	7	3	1	3	11	11
John Prentice	3/66-9/66	4	0	1	3	4	9
Malcolm McDonald	10/66-11/66	2	1	1	0	3	2
Bobby Brown	2/67-7/71	28	9	8	11	37	35
Tommy Docherty	9/71-12/72	12	7	2	3	17	8
Willie Ormond	1/73-5/77	38	18	8	12	55	38
Ally McLeod	5/77-9/78	17	7	5	5	26	21
Jock Stein	10/78-9/85	61	26	12	23	80	70
Alex Ferguson	10/85-6/86	10	3	4	3	8	5
Andy Roxburgh	7/86-9/93	61	23	19	19	67	60
Craig Brown	11/93-10/01	70	32	18	20	85	60
Berti Vogts	3/02-11/04	31	8	7	16	23	50
Walter Smith	12/04-1/07	16	7	4	5	16	8
Alex McLeish	1/07- 11/07	10	7	0	3	14	9
George Burley	1/08-11/09	14	3	3	8	8	21
Craig Levein	12/09-11/12	24	10	5	9	30	31
Gordon Strachan	01/13-10/17	40	19	9	12	59	45
Alex McLeish	02/18-present	4	1	0	2	1	4

RESULTS FOR SEASON 2017/18

(Scotland scores first)

Opponents	Venue	Res	Scorers	Competition
Lithuania	A	3-0	Armstrong, Robertson, McArthur	World Cup Qualifier
Malta	H	2-0	Berra, Griffiths	World Cup Qualifier
Slovakia	H	1-0	Skrtel OG,	World Cup Qualifier
Slovenia	A	2-2	Griffiths, Snodgrass	World Cup Qualifier
Holland	H	0-1		Friendly
Costa Rica	H	0-1		Friendly
Hungary	A	1-0	Phillips	Friendly
Peru	A	0-2		Friendly
Mexico	A	0-1		Friendly

SCOTT MCTOMINAY made his Scotland debut in the
1-0 defeat to Costa Rica in March 2018

ABERDEEN

NICKNAME:	The Dons
COLOURS:	Red and white
GROUND:	Pittodrie
TELEPHONE:	01224 650400
EMAIL:	feedback@afc.co.uk
WEBSITE:	afc.co.uk
CAPACITY:	20,961
RECORD ATT:	45,061 (v Hearts, 1954)
RECORD VICTORY:	13-0 (v Peterhead, 1923)
RECORD DEFEAT:	0-9 (v Celtic, 2010)
MANAGER:	Derek McInnes
CHAIRMAN:	Stewart Milne
MOST LEAGUE	
GOALS (1 SEASON):	38, Benny Yorston, 1929-30
GOALS (OVERALL):	206, Joe Harper

HONOURS

LEAGUE-CHAMPIONSHIP-(4):-Division A -1954-55. Premier
Division – 1979-80, 1983-84, 1984-85. SCOTTISH CUP (7):
1947, 1970, 1982, 1983, 1984,
1986, 1990. LEAGUE CUP (6): 1955-56, 1976-77,
1985-86, 1989-90, 1995-96, 2013-14. EUROPEAN CUP-
WINNERS' CUP: 1983. EUROPEAN SUPER CUP: 1983-84.

LEAGUE RESULTS 2017-2018

Aberdeen 2-0 Hamilton	Aberdeen 1-0 Partick Thistle
Ross County 1-2 Aberdeen	Aberdeen 0-0 Hearts
Aberdeen 2-1 Dundee	Aberdeen 4-1 St. Mirren
Partick Thistle 3-4 Aberdeen	Rangers 2-0 Aberdeen
Hearts 0-0 Aberdeen	Aberdeen 3-1 Kilmarnock
Aberdeen 1-1 Kilmarnock	Ross County 2-4 Aberdeen
Motherwell 0-1 Aberdeen	Aberdeen 3-0 Hamilton
Aberdeen 3-0 St Johnstone	Hibernian 2-0 Aberdeen
Hibernian 1-0 Aberdeen	Aberdeen 0-2 Celtic
Aberdeen 0-3 Celtic	Partick Thistle 0-0 Aberdeen
Aberdeen 2-1 Ross County	Aberdeen 1-0 Dundee
Hamilton 2-2 Aberdeen	Aberdeen 4-1 St. Johnstone
Aberdeen 0-2 Motherwell	Motherwell 0-2 Aberdeen
Rangers 3-0 Aberdeen	Hearts 0-2 Aberdeen
Aberdeen 1-2 Rangers	Kilmarnock 0-2 Aberdeen
Dundee 0-1 Aberdeen	Aberdeen 2-0 Hearts
St. Johnstone 0-3 Aberdeen	Aberdeen 0-0 Hibernian
Aberdeen 4-1 Hibernian	Aberdeen 1-1 Rangers
Celtic 3-0 Aberdeen	Celtic 0-1 Aberdeen

AIRDRIEONIANS

NICKNAME:	The Diamonds
COLOURS:	White and red
GROUND:	Penny Cars Stadium
TELEPHONE No:	01236 622000
EMAIL:	enquiries@airdriefc.com
WEBSITE:	airdriefc.com
CAPACITY:	10,170
RECORD ATT:	9843 (v Rangers, 2013)
RECORD VICTORY:	11-0 (v Gala Fairydean, 2011)
RECORD DEFEAT:	0-7 (v Partick Thistle, 2012)
HEAD COACH:	Stephen Findlay
CHAIRMAN:	Jim Ballantyne
MOST LEAGUE	
GOALS (1 SEASON):	21, Ryan Donnelly, 2011-12

HONOURS
LEAGUE CHAMPIONSHIP: Second Division – 2003-04.
CHALLENGE CUP: 2008-2009.

LEAGUE RESULTS 2017-2018

Forfar 2-1 Airdrieonians
Airdrieonians 1-1 Arbroath
Albion Rovers 1-2 Airdrieonians
Airdrieonians 2-0 Alloa
Stranraer 3-1 Airdrieonians
Airdrieonians 0-1 East Fife
Raith Rovers 2-0 Airdrieonians
Airdrieonians 4-2 Queens Park
Ayr United 2-2 Airdrieonians
Arbroath 7-1 Airdrieonians
Airdrieonians 2-2 Albion Rovers
Alloa 1-0 Airdrieonians
Airdrieonians 2-0 Stranraer
East Fife 6-1 Airdrieonians
Airdrieonians 2-1 Forfar Athletic
Airdrieonians 2-2 Raith Rovers
Queen's Park 1-1 Airdrieonians
Airdrieonians 2-0 Ayr United

Albion Rovers 2-2 Airdrieonians
Airdrieonians 0-0 East Fife
Stranraer 3-2 Airdrieonians
Airdrieonians 0-0 Arbroath
Forfar Athletic 0-1 Airdrieonians
Raith Rovers 2-1 Airdrieonians
Airdrieonians 2-1 Queen's Park
Ayr United 3-0 Airdrieonians
East Fife 2-1 Airdrieonians
Airdrieonians 2-1 Stranraer
Alloa Athletic 2-2 Airdrieonians
Airdrieonians 2-2 Alloa Athletic
Airdrieonians 1-2 Raith Rovers
Queen's Park 0-0 Airdrieonians
Airdrieonians 1-2 Ayr United
Airdrieonians 2-0 Albion Rovers
Arbroath 2-0 Airdrieonians
Airdrieonians 1-2 Forfar Athletic

ALBION ROVERS

NICKNAME:	Wee Rovers
COLOURS:	Yellow and red
GROUND:	The Exsel Group Stadium
TELEPHONE No:	01236 606334
EMAIL:	paul.reilly@ albionroversfc.com
CAPACITY:	1238
RECORD ATT:	27,381 (v Rangers, 1936)
RECORD VICTORY:	12-0 (v Airdriehill, 1887)
RECORD DEFEAT:	1-11 (v Partick Thistle, 1993)
MANAGER:	John Brogan
CHAIRMAN:	Ronnie Boyd
MOST LEAGUE GOALS (1 SEASON):	41, Jim Renwick, 1932-33

HONOURS

LEAGUE CHAMPIONSHIP: Division II – 1933-34. Second Division – 1988-89. League Two 2014-2015.

LEAGUE RESULTS 2017-2018

Albion Rovers 1-5 Ayr United	Alloa Athletic 3-1 Albion Rovers
Queen's Park 2-5 Albion Rovers	Forfar Athletic 4-2 Albion Rovers
Albion Rovers 1-2 Airdrieonians	Albion Rovers 1-3 Stranraer
Forfar Athletic 0-2 Albion Rovers	Arbroath 1-0 Albion Rovers
Arbroath 1-4 Albion Rovers	Raith Rovers 3-1 Albion Rovers
Albion Rovers 0-4 Stranraer	Albion Rovers 2-2 Raith Rovers
Alloa 2-5 Albion Rovers	East Fife 2-0 Albion Rovers
Albion Rovers 2-1 Raith Rovers	Stranraer 2-3 Albion Rovers
East Fife 5-4 Albion Rovers	Albion Rovers 1-1 Queen's Park
Albion Rovers 0-1 Queen's Park	Albion Rovers 1-2 Arbroath
Airdrie 2-2 Albion Rovers	Albion Rovers 2-3 Ayr United
Albion Rovers 3 - 4 Forfar Athletic	Albion Rovers 1-3 Alloa Athletic
Albion Rovers 0-2 Alloa Athletic	Albion Rovers 1-2 Arbroath
Ayr United 3-2 Albion Rover	Raith Rovers 2-0 Albion Rovers
Stranraer 2-2 Albion Rovers	Albion Rovers 0-1 Forfar Athletic
Albion Rovers 3-2 East Fife	Airdrieonians 2-0 Albion Rovers
Queen's Park 2-2 Albion Rovers	Albion Rovers 1-0 East Fife
Albion Rovers 2-2 Airdrieonians	Ayr United 2-0 Albion Rovers

BRIAN KERR with the League One Manager of the Month Award for September. The former midfielder left his role with Albion Rovers in May 2018

ALLOA

NICKNAME:	The Wasps
COLOURS:	Gold and black
GROUND:	Indodrill Stadium
TELEPHONE No:	01259 722695
WEBSITE:	alloaathletic.co.uk
EMAIL:	fcadmin@alloaathletic.co.uk
CAPACITY:	3100
RECORD ATT:	13,000
	(v Dunfermline, 1939)
RECORD VICTORY:	9-0 (v Selkirk, 2005)
RECORD DEFEAT:	0-10 (v Dundee, 1937),
	0-10 (v Third Lanark, 1953)
MANAGER:	Jim Goodwin
CHAIRMAN:	Mike Mulraney
MOST LEAGUE	
GOALS (1 SEASON):	49, William Crilley, 1921-22

HONOURS

LEAGUE CHAMPIONS: Division II – 1921-22. Third Division – 1997-98, 2011-12. CHALLENGE CUP: 1999-00.

LEAGUE RESULTS 2017-2018

Alloa 1-1 Raith Rovers	Alloa 3-1 Albion Rovers
East Fife 1-0 Alloa	East Fife 2-1 Alloa
Alloa 1-0 Queen's Park	Alloa 0-0 Raith Rovers
Airdrie 2-0 Alloa	Ayr United 1-2 Alloa
Alloa 2-1 Forfar	Alloa 1-0 Forfar Athletic
Ayr Utd 3-3 Alloa	Arbroath 0-0 Alloa
Alloa 2-5 Albion Rovers	Stranraer 1-0 Alloa
Arbroath 1-1 Alloa	Alloa 5-3 Arbroath
Stranraer 2-0 Alloa	Queen's Park 1-2 Alloa
Alloa 4-1 East Fife	Alloa 1-2 East Fife
Queen's Park 0-4 Alloa	Alloa 2-2 Airdrieonians
Alloa 1-0 Airdrie	Airdrieonians 2-2 Alloa
Albion Rovers 0-2 Alloa	Albion Rovers 1-3 Alloa
Alloa 1-2 Ayr	Alloa 3-2 Arbroath
Raith Rovers 2-1 Alloa	Alloa 0-1 Stranraer
Forfar 0-2 Alloa	Forfar Athletic 0-1 Alloa
Alloa 1-0 Stranraer	Alloa 2-1 Ayr United
Alloa 1-0 Stranraer	Raith Rovers 0-0 Alloa
Alloa 2-2 Queen's Park	

ANNAN

NICKNAME:	Galabankies
COLOURS:	Black and gold
GROUND:	Galabank
TELEPHONE No:	01461 204108
EMAIL:	annanathletic.
	enquiries@btconnect.com
CAPACITY:	2517
RECORD ATT:	2517 (v Rangers, 2012)
RECORD VICTORY:	18-0 (v Newton Stewart, 2004)
RECORD DEFEAT:	2-5 (v Brechin, 2011)
PLAYER MANAGER:	Peter Murphy
CHAIRMAN:	Phillip Jones
MOST LEAGUE	
GOALS (1 SEASON):	22, Peter Weatherson, 2014-15

LEAGUE RESULTS 2017-2018

Annan 1-2 Peterhead
Clyde 2-1 Annan
Berwick Rangers1-5 Annan
Annan 0-1 Montrose
Elgin City 0-1 Annan
Annan 1-1 Stenhousemuir
Stirling Albion 3-2 Annan
Annan 1-0 Cowdenbeath
Edinburgh City 0-1 Annan
Peterhead 1-0 Annan
Annan 0-0 Berwick
Montrose 1-1 Annan
Cowdb'th 1-1 Annan
Annan 0-0 Clyde
Annan 2-0 Elgin
Stenh'muir 1-3 Annan
Annan 1-1 Stirling Albion
Annan 2-1 Edinburgh City

Clyde 0-0 Annan
Annan 0-1 Montrose
Berwick Rangers 0-2 Annan
Edinburgh City 3-2 Annan
Annan 1-1 Cowdenbeath
Elgin City 2-1 Annan
Stirling Albion 3-0 Annan
Annan 3-3 Peterhead
Annan 2-0 Stenhousemuir
Annan 2-3 Edinburgh City
Montrose 2-1 Annan
Annan 1-1 Clyde
Peterhead 1-0 Annan
Annan 0-0 Berwick Rangers
Annan 4-1 Elgin City
Stenhousemuir 3-2 Annan
Annan 3-1 Stirling Albion
Cowdenbeath 0-2 Annan

ARBROATH

NICKNAME:	The Red Lichties
COLOURS:	Maroon and white
GROUND:	Gayfield Park
TELEPHONE No:	01241 872157
EMAIL:	contact@arbroathfc.co.uk
WEBSITE:	arbroathfc.co.uk
CAPACITY:	6600
RECORD ATT:	13,510
	(v Rangers, 1952)
RECORD VICTORY:	36-0 (v Bon Accord, 1885)
RECORD DEFEAT:	1-9 (v Celtic, 1993)
MANAGER:	Dick Campbell
CHAIRMAN:	Mike Caird
MOST LEAGUE	
GOALS (1 SEASON):	45, Dave Easson, 1958-59

HONOURS

LEAGUE CHAMPIONS: Third Division – 2010-11, League Two – 2016-2017

LEAGUE RESULTS 2017-2018

Arbroath 2-0 Queen's Park
Airdrie 1-1 Arbroath
Arbroath 2-3 East Fife
Ayr United 1-2 Arbroath
Arbroath 1-4 Albion Rovers
Forfar 0-5 Arbroath
Stranraer 2-6 Arbroath
Arbroath 1-1 Alloa
Raith Rovers 2-0 Arbroath
Arbroath 7-1 Airdrie
East Fife 3-1 Arbroath
Arbroath 1-4 Ayr United
Queen's Park 0-2 Arbroath
Arbroath 2-1 Forfar Athletic
Arbroath 1-2 Stranraer
Arbroath 1-2 Raith Rovers
Arbroath 1-1 East Fife
Forfar Athletic 0-1 Arbroath

Ayr United 1-2 Arbroath
Arbroath 2-1 Queen's Park
Airdrieonians 0-0 Arbroath
Arbroath 1-0 Albion Rovers
Arbroath 0-0 Alloa Athletic
Stranraer 1-4 Arbroath
Raith Rovers 2-2 Arbroath
Alloa Athletic 5-3 Arbroath
Arbroath 2-0 Forfar Athletic
Arbroath 1-1 Ayr United
Albion Rovers 1-2 Arbroath
Arbroath 2-3 Stranraer
Albion Rovers 1-2 Arbroath
Alloa Athletic 3-2 Arbroath
Arbroath 1-1 Raith Rovers
East Fife 0-5 Arbroath
Arbroath 2-0 Airdrieonians
Queen's Park 3-0 Arbroath

AYR UNITED

NICKNAME:	The Honest Men
COLOURS:	White and black
GROUND:	Somerset Park
TELEPHONE No:	01292 263435
EMAIL:	info@ayrunitedfc.co.uk
WEBSITE:	ayrunitedfc.co.uk
CAPACITY:	10,184
RECORD ATT:	25,225 (v Rangers, 1969)
RECORD VICTORY:	11-1 (v Dumbarton, 1952)
RECORD DEFEAT:	0-9 (v Rangers, 1929; v Hearts, 1931; v Third Lanark, 1954)
MANAGER:	Ian McCall
CHAIRMAN:	Lachlan Cameron
MOST LEAGUE GOALS (1 SEASON):	66, Jimmy Smith, 1927-28
GOALS (OVERALL):	213, Peter Price, 1955-61

HONOURS

LEAGUE CHAMPIONS: Division II (6) – 1911-12, 1912-13, 1927-28, 1936-37, 1958-59, 1965-66. Second Division (2) – 1987-88, 1996-97. League One 2017-18.

LEAGUE RESULTS 2017-2018

Albion Rovers 1-5 Ayr United	Stranraer 1-5 Ayr United
Ayr United 3-0 Forfar	Ayr United 1-2 Arbroath
Stranraer 3-4 Ayr United	Raith Rovers 1-1 Ayr United
Ayr United 1-2 Arbroath	Queen's Park 1-4 Ayr United
Raith Rovers 2-1 Ayr United	Ayr United 1-2 Alloa Athletic
Ayr United 3-3 Alloa	Ayr United 3-0 East Fife
Queen's Park 0-2 Ayr United	Ayr United 3-0 Airdrieonians
Ayr United 3-0 East Fife	Ayr United 3-0 Raith Rovers
Ayr United 2-2 Airdrie	Arbroath 1-1 Ayr United
Forfar Athletic 0-5 Ayr United	Forfar Athletic 0-2 Ayr United
Ayr United 2-0 Stranraer	Albion Rovers 2-3 Ayr United
Arbroath 1-4 Ayr United	Ayr United 4-0 Queen's Park
Ayr United 3-0 Raith Rov	East Fife 2-3 Ayr United
Alloa Athletic 1-2 Ayr United	Airdrieonians 1-2 Ayr United
Ayr United 3-2 Albion Rovers	Ayr United 1-2 Stranraer
Ayr United 3-2 Queen's Park	Alloa Athletic 2-1 Ayr United
East Fife 1-4 Ayr United	Ayr United 2-0 Albion Rovers
Airdrie 2-0 Ayr United	
Ayr United 2-3 Forfar Athletic	

BERWICK RANGERS

NICKNAME:	The Borderers
COLOURS:	Black and gold
GROUND:	Shielfield Park
TELEPHONE No:	01289 307424
EMAIL:	club@berwickrangers.com
WEBSITE:	berwickrangers.com
CAPACITY:	4500
RECORD ATT:	13,365 (v Rangers, 1967)
RECORD VICTORY:	8-1 (v Forfar Athletic, 1965; Vale of Leithen, 1966)
RECORD DEFEAT:	1-9 (v Hamilton, 1980)
MANAGER:	Robbie Horn
CHAIRMAN:	Len Eyre
MOST LEAGUE GOALS (1 SEASON):	33, Ken Bowron, 1963-64

HONOURS

LEAGUE CHAMPIONSHIP: Second Division – 1978-79. Third Division – 2006-07.

LEAGUE RESULTS 2017-2018

Berwick Rangers 3-1 Clyde
Stirling 4-0 Berwick Rangers
Berwick Rangers 1-5 Annan
Cowd'bth 0-1 Berwick Rangers
Edin'gh Cty 1-0 Berwick Rangers
Berwick Rangers 3-2 Elgin City
Stenh'muir 3-0 Berwick Rangers
Peterhead 0-2 Berwick Rangers
Berwick Rangers 0-1 Montrose
Berwick Rangers 1-0 Cowdenbeath
Annan 0-0 Berwick Rangers
Berwick Rangers 1-1 Edinb'gh City
Elgin City 5-1 Berwick Rangers
Berwick Rangers 1-0 Stirling Albion
Montrose 3-0 Berwick Rangers
Clyde 0-0 Berwick Rangers
Edinburgh City 3-0 Berwick Rangers
Stirling Albion 2-0 Berwick Rangers

Berwick Rangers 0-2 Annan
Cowdenbeath 1-3 Berwick Rangers
Berwick Rangers 2-3 Peterhead
Stenhousemuir 4-0 Berwick Rangers
Berwick Rangers 0-1 Clyde
Peterhead 1-1 Berwick Rangers
Berwick Rangers 2-2 Montrose
Elgin City 3-0 Berwick Rangers
Berwick Rangers 0-1 Stirling Albion
Berwick Rangers 1-1 Edinburgh City
Berwick Rangers 2-2 Elgin City
Annan Athletic 0-0 Berwick Rangers
Berwick Rangers 1-3 Peterhead
Montrose 1-0 Berwick Rangers
Berwick Rangers 0-0 Stenhousemuir
Berwick Rangers 1-0 Cowdenbeath
Berwick Rangers 2-2 Stenhousemuir
Clyde 1-2 Berwick Rangers

BRECHIN CITY

NICKNAME:	The City
COLOURS:	Red and white
GROUND:	Glebe Park
TELEPHONE No:	01356 622856
EMAIL:	secretary@ brechincityfc.com
WEBSITE:	brechincity.com
CAPACITY:	3960
RECORD ATT:	8122 (v Aberdeen, 1973)
RECORD VICTORY:	12-1 (v Thornhill, 1926)
RECORD DEFEAT:	0-10 (v Airdrie, Albion, Cowdenbeath, all 1937-38)
MANAGER:	Darren Dods
CHAIRMAN:	Ken Ferguson
MOST LEAGUE GOALS (1 SEASON):	26, W McIntosh, 1959-60

HONOURS

LEAGUE CHAMPIONS: Second Division (3) – 1982-83, 1989-90, 2004-05. Third Division – 2001-02. C Division – 1953-54.

LEAGUE RESULTS 2017-2018

Queen of S'th 4-1 Brechin City	Dundee United 4-1 Brechin City
Brechin City 2-2 Livingston	Brechin City 1-1 Morton
Dundee Utd 1-0 Brechin City	Brechin City 0-2 Livingston
Brechin City 0-4 Inverness CT	Queen of S'th 3-1 Brechin City
Brechin City 1-1 Falkirk	Falkirk 3-1 Brechin City
Dumbarton 2-1 Brechin City	Brechin City 0-1 Falkirk
Brechin City 0-3 Dunfermline	St. Mirren 1-0 Brechin City
St Mirren 2-1 Brechin City	Dumbarton 1-0 Brechin City
Brechin City 0-1 Morton	Brechin City 1-3 Dumbarton
Brechin City 0-1 Queen of the S'th	Brechin City 0-3 Dunfermline
Livingston 3-2 Brechin City	Morton 2-0 Brechin City
Brechin City 0-1 Dumbarton	Falkirk 3-0 Brechin City
Brechin City 1-1 Dundee United	Inverness CT 4-0 Brechin City
Inverness CT 4-0 Brechin City	Brechin City 0-1 St. Mirren
Morton 4-1 Brechin City	Dunfermline 4-0 Brechin City
Brechin City 1-2 St. Mirren	Brechin City 0-5 Dundee Utd
Dunfermline 2-1 Brechin City	Livingston 3-0 Brechin City
Brechin City 2-3 Inverness CT	Brechin City 1-5 Queen of S'th

CELTIC

NICKNAME:	The Bhoys
COLOURS:	Green and white
GROUND:	Celtic Park
TELEPHONE No:	0871 226 1888
EMAIL:	webhelp@celticfc.com
WEBSITE:	celticfc.net
CAPACITY:	60,506
RECORD ATT:	92,000
	(v Rangers, 1938)
RECORD VICTORY:	11-0 (v Dundee, 1895)
RECORD DEFEAT:	0-8 (v Motherwell, 1937)
MANAGER:	Brendan Rodgers
CHIEF EXECUTIVE:	Peter Lawwell
MOST LEAGUE	
GOALS (1 SEASON):	50, Jimmy McGrory, 1935-36
GOALS (OVERALL):	472, Jimmy McGrory, 1922-37

HONOURS

LEAGUE CHAMPIONS (49): 1892-93, 1893-94, 1895-96, 1897-98, 1904-05, 1905-06, 1906-07, 1907-08, 1908-09, 1909-10, 1913-14, 1914-15, 1915-16, 1916-17, 1918-19, 1921-22, 1925-26, 1935-36, 1937-38, 1953-54, 1965-66, 1966-67, 1967-68, 1968-69, 1969-70, 1970-71, 1971-72, 1972-73, 1973-74, 1976-77, 1978-79, 1980-81, 1981-82, 1985-86, 1987-88, 1997-98, 2000-01, 2001-02, 2003-2004, 2005-2006, 2006-07, 2007-08, 2011-12, 2012-13, 2013-14, 2014-2015, 2015-2016, 2016-2017, 2017-2018.

SCOTTISH CUP (38): 1892, 1899, 1900, 1904, 1907, 1908, 1911, 1912, 1914, 1923, 1925, 1927, 1931, 1933, 1937, 1951, 1954, 1965, 1967, 1969, 1971, 1972, 1974, 1975, 1977, 1980, 1985, 1988, 1989, 1995, 2001, 2004, 2005, 2007, 2011, 2013, 2017, 2018.

LEAGUE CUP (17): 1956-57, 1957-58, 1965-66, 1966-67, 1967-68, 1968-69, 1969-70, 1974-75, 1982-83, 1997-98, 1999-00, 2000-01, 2005-06, 2008-09, 2014-2015, 2016-2017, 2017-2018.

EUROPEAN CUP: 1966-67.

Pics: SNS

SCOTT BROWN　　　**ODSONNE EDOUARD**

LEAGUE RESULTS 2017-2018

Celtic 4-1 Hearts	Celtic 3-0 Aberdeen
Partick Thistle 0-1 Celtic	Dundee 0-2 Celtic
Kilmarnock 0-2 Celtic	Celtic 0-0 Rangers
Celtic 1-1 St. Johnstone	Partick Thistle 1-2 Celtic
Hamilton 1-4 Celtic	Celtic 1-0 Hibernian
Celtic 4-0 Ross County	Celtic 3-1 Hearts
Rangers 0-2 Celtic	Kilmarnock 1-0 Celtic
Celtic 2-2 Hibernian	Celtic 0-0 St. Johnstone
Celtic 1-0 Dundee	Aberdeen 0-2 Celtic
Aberdeen 0-3 Celtic	Rangers 2-3 Celtic
Celtic 1-1 Kilmarnock	Motherwell 0-0 Celtic
St. Johnstone 0-4 Celtic	Celtic 3-0 Ross County
Ross County 0-1 Celtic	Celtic 0-0 Dundee
Motherwell 1-1 Celtic	Hamilton 1-2 Celtic
Celtic 5-1 Motherwell	Hibernian 2-1 Celtic
Hibernian 2-2 Celtic	Celtic 5-0 Rangers
Celtic 3-1 Hamilton	Hearts 1-3 Celtic
Hearts 4-0 Celtic	Celtic 0-0 Kilmarnock
Celtic 2-0 Partick Thistle	Celtic 0-1 Aberdeen

AYR United celebrate winning the League One title

AYR United's Lawrence Shankland won the Ladbrokes League 1 Player of the Year Award   **Pics: SNS**

CLYDE

NICKNAME:	The Bully Wee
COLOURS:	White and red
GROUND:	Broadwood Stadium
TELEPHONE No:	01236 451511
EMAIL:	info@clydefc.co.uk
WEBSITE:	clydefc.co.uk
CAPACITY:	8029
RECORD ATT:	52,000 (v Rangers, 1908, at Shawfield)
RECORD VICTORY:	11-1 (v Cowdenbeath, 1951)
RECORD DEFEAT:	0-11 (v Dumbarton 1879, Rangers, 1880)
FOUNDED:	1877
MANAGER:	Danny Lennon
CHAIRMAN:	Norrie Innes
MOST LEAGUE GOALS (1 SEASON):	32, Bill Boyd, 1932-33

HONOURS

LEAGUE CHAMPIONS: Division II (5) – 1904-05, 1951-52, 1956-57, 1961-62, 1972-73. **Second Division (4)** – 1977-78, 1981-82, 1992-93, 1999-00. **SCOTTISH CUP (3):** 1939, 1955, 1958.

LEAGUE RESULTS 2017-2018

Berwick Rangers 3-1 Clyde	Montrose 1-3 Clyde
Clyde 2-1 Annan	Clyde 1-0 Peterhead
Elgin City 3-2 Clyde	Clyde 3-2 Edinburgh City
Clyde 1-1 Stenhousemuir	Berwick Rangers 0-1 Clyde
Stirling Albion 2-3 Clyde	Clyde 2-0 Cowdenbeath
Clyde 2-3 Edinburgh City	Stirling Albion 2-1 Clyde
Clyde 1-1 Cowdenbeath	Peterhead 2-1 Clyde
Montrose 3-2 Clyde	Stenhousemuir 2-3 Clyde
Clyde 1-4 Peterhead	Clyde 1-0 Elgin City
Clyde 2-4 Elgin City	Annan Athletic 1-1 Clyde
Stenhousemuir 1-1 Clyde	Edinburgh City 0-3 Clyde
Clyde 1-1 Stirling Albion	Clyde 3-0 Montrose
Annan Athletic 0-0 Clyde	Cowdenbeath 0-3 Clyde
Clyde 0-0 Montrose	Peterhead 3-0 Clyde
Clyde 0-0 Berwick Rangers	Cowdenbeath 1-0 Clyde
Clyde 0-0 Annan Athletic	Clyde 2-1 Stirling Albion
Elgin City 2-1 Clyde	Edinburgh City 1-3 Clyde
Clyde 0-3 Stenhousemuir	Clyde 1-2 Berwick Rangers

COWDENBEATH

NICKNAME:	**The Blue Brazil**
COLOURS:	**Royal blue and white**
GROUND:	**Central Park**
TELEPHONE No:	**01383 610166**
EMAIL:	**office@cowdenbeathfc.com**
WEBSITE:	**cowdenbeathfc.com**
CAPACITY:	**4370**
RECORD ATT:	25,586 (v Rangers, 1949)
RECORD VICTORY:	12-0 (v Johnstone, 1928)
RECORD DEFEAT:	1-11 (v Clyde, 1951)
FOUNDED:	**1881**
HEAD COACH:	**Gary Bollan**
CHAIRMAN:	**Donald Findlay QC**
MOST LEAGUE GOALS (1 SEASON):	54, Rab Walls 1938-39
GOALS (OVERALL):	127, Willie Devlin, 1922-26/1929-1930

HONOURS
LEAGUE CHAMPIONSHIP: Division II (3) – 1913-14, 1914-15, 1938-39.
Second Division – 2011-12. Third Division – 2005-06.

LEAGUE RESULTS 2017-2018

Elgin City 1-1 Cowdenbeath
Cowdenbeath 1-0 Edinburgh City
Montrose 1-0 Cowdenbeath
Cowdenbeath 0-1 Berwick
Stenh'muir 1-0 Cowdenbeath
Cowdenbeath 0-4 Peterhead
Clyde 1-1 Cowdenbeath
Annan 1-0 Cowdenbeath
Cowdenbeath 0-3 Stirling Albion
Berwick Rangers 1-0 Cowdenbeath
Cowdenbeath 1-3 Montrose
Cowdenbeath 1-3 Elgin City
Cowdenbeath 1-1 Annan Athletic
Edinburgh City 0-0 Cowdenbeath
Cowdenbeath 1-1 Stenhousemuir
Peterhead 3-2 Cowdenbeath
Montrose 1-1 Cowdenbeath
Cowdenbeath 0-2 Edinburgh City

Elgin City 1-0 Cowdenbeath
Cowdenbeath 1-3 Berwick Rangers
Stirling Albion 1-0 Cowdenbeath
Annan Athletic 1-1 Cowdenbeath
Cowdenbeath 1-2 Stirling Albion
Clyde 2-0 Cowdenbeath
Cowdenbeath 0-2 Peterhead
Edinburgh City 1-1 Cowdenbeath
Cowdenbeath 3-1 Elgin City
Stenhousemuir 1-2 Cowdenbeath
Stirling Albion 2-2 Cowdenbeath
Cowdenbeath 0-3 Clyde
Cowdenbeath 1-1 Stenhousemuir
Cowdenbeath 1-0 Clyde
Cowdenbeath 0-3 Montrose
Peterhead 1-0 Cowdenbeath
Berwick Rangers 1-0 Cowdenbeath
Cowdenbeath 0-2 Annan Athletic

DUMBARTON

NICKNAME:	The Sons
COLOURS:	White, gold, and black
GROUND:	C&G Systems Stadium
TELEPHONE No:	01389 762569
EMAIL:	enquiries@dumbartonfc.com
WEBSITE:	dumbartonfootballclub.com
CAPACITY:	2020
RECORD ATT:	18,000 (v Raith, 1957)
RECORD VICTORY:	13-1 (v Kirkintilloch, 1888)
RECORD DEFEAT:	1-11 (v Albion, 1926; v Ayr United, 1952)
FOUNDED:	1872
MANAGER:	Stephen Aitken
CHAIRMAN:	John Steele
GOALS (1 SEASON):	38, Kenny Wilson, 1971-72

HONOURS
LEAGUE CHAMPIONS: Division I (2) – 1890-91 (shared with Rangers), 1891-92. Division II (2) – 1910-11, 1971-72. Second Division – 1991-92. Division 3 – 2008-09. **SCOTTISH CUP:** 1883.

LEAGUE RESULTS 2017-2018

Dumbarton 0-0 Morton	Dumbarton 0-1 Dunfermline
Falkirk 1-1 Dumbarton	Dumbarton 0-2 St. Mirren
Queen of S'th 1-0 Dumbarton	Livingston 2-0 Dumbarton
Dumbarton 0-4 Dunfermline	Dumbarton 0-1 Morton
Dundee Utd 1-1 Dumbarton	Falkirk 0-0 Dumbarton
Dumbarton 2-1 Brechin City	Dumbarton 0-1 Queen of S'th
Dumbarton 2-1 Inverness CT	Dumbarton 1-0 Brechin City
Livingston 2-1 Dumbarton	Brechin City 1-3 Dumbarton
Dumbarton 0-2 St. Mirren	St. Mirren 5-0 Dumbarton
Morton 1-1 Dumbarton	Dumbarton 0-3 Livingston
Dumbarton 0-2 Dundee United	Dundee Utd 2-0 Dumbarton
Brechin City 0-1 Dumbarton	Dumbarton 3-2 Dundee Utd
Dunfermline 2-2 Dumbarton	Morton 3-2 Dumbarton
Dumbarton 2-2 Queen of S'th	Inverness CT 5-1 Dumbarton
St. Mirren 0-1 Dumbarton	Dumbarton 0-1 Inverness CT
Inverness CT 1-0 Dumbarton	Dumbarton 2-5 Falkirk
Dumbarton 0-0 Falkirk	Dunfermline 4-0 Dumbarton
Dumbarton 1-4 Livingston	
Queen of S'th 0-0 Dumbarton	

DUNDEE

NICKNAME:	The Dark Blues
COLOURS:	Dark blue, red and white
GROUND:	Kilmac Stadium at Dens Park
TELEPHONE No:	01382 889966
EMAIL:	reception@dundeefc.co.uk
WEBSITE:	dundeefc.co.uk
CAPACITY:	11,200
RECORD ATT:	43,024 (v Rangers, 1953)
RECORD VICTORY:	10-0 (v Alloa, 1957; v Dunfermline, 1957)
RECORD DEFEAT:	0-11 (v Celtic, 1895)
MANAGER:	Neil McCann
MANAGING DIRECTOR:	Tim Keys
MOST LEAGUE GOALS (1 SEASON):	38, Dave Halliday, 1923-24
GOALS (OVERALL):	113, Alan Gilzean

HONOURS

LEAGUE CHAMPIONS: 1961-62. First Division (3) – 1978-79, 1991-92, 1997-98. Championship – 2013-14. Division II – 1946-47. SCOTTISH CUP: 1910. LEAGUE CUP WINNERS (3): 1951-52, 1952-53, 1973-74. CHALLENGE CUP (2): 1990-91, 2009-10.

LEAGUE RESULTS 2017-2018

Dundee 1-2 Ross County	Motherwell 1-1 Dundee
Hamilton 3-0 Dundee	Dundee 0-2 Celtic
Aberdeen 2-1 Dundee	St. Johnstone 0-2 Dundee
Dundee 1-1 Hibernian	Dundee 0-1 Hibernian
Rangers 4-1 Dundee	Hamilton 1-2 Dundee
Dundee 3-2 St Johnstone	Dundee 1-4 Ross County
Kilmarnock 1-1 Dundee	Kilmarnock 3-2 Dundee
Dundee 2-1 Hearts	Partick Thistle 1-2 Dundee
Celtic 1-0 Dundee	Dundee 0-1 Motherwell
Partick Thistle 2-1 Dundee	Dundee 0-4 St. Johnstone
Dundee 0-1 Motherwell	Aberdeen 1-0 Dundee
Dundee 1-3 Hamilton	Dundee 1-1 Hearts
Hibernian 2-1 Dundee	Celtic 0-0 Dundee
Dundee 0-0 Kilmarnock	Rangers 4-0 Dundee
Dundee 2-1 Rangers	Dundee 2-1 St. Johnstone
Ross County 2-0 Dundee	Motherwell 2-1 Dundee
Dundee 0-1 Aberdeen	Dundee 1-0 Hamilton
Hearts 2-0 Dundee	Ross County 0-1 Dundee
Dundee 3-0 Partick Thistle	Dundee 0-1 Partick Thistle

DUNDEE UNITED

NICKNAME:	**The Terrors**
COLOURS:	**Tangerine**
	and black
GROUND:	**Tannadice Park**
TELEPHONE No:	**01382 833166**
EMAIL:	**admin@dundeeunitedfc.co.ul**
WEBSITE:	**dundeeunitedfc.co.uk**
CAPACITY:	**14,209**
RECORD ATT:	**28,000 (v Barcelona, 1966)**
RECORD VICTORY:	**14-0 (v Nithsdale, 1931)**
RECORD DEFEAT:	**1-12 (v Motherwell, 1954)**
MANAGER:	**Csaba László**
CHAIRMAN:	**Mike Martin**
MOST LEAGUE	
GOALS (1 SEASON):	**41, John Coyle, 1955-56**
GOALS (OVERALL):	**158, Peter Mackay**

HONOURS

LEAGUE CHAMPIONS: 1982-83. Division 2 (2) – 1924-25, 1928-29. **SCOTTISH CUP** (2): 1994, 2010. **LEAGUE CUP** (2): 1979-80, 1980-81. **CHALLENGE CUP:** 2016-17.

LEAGUE RESULTS 2017-2018

Inverness CT 0-1 Dundee Utd	Dundee Utd 4-1 Brechin City
Dundee Utd 2-1 Queen of S'th	Falkirk 6-1 Dundee Utd
Dundee Utd 1-0 Brechin City	Dunfermline 0-0 Dundee Utd
St. Mirren 3-0 Dundee Utd	Dundee Utd 0-3 Morton
Dundee Utd 1-1 Dumbarton	Livingston 2-1 Dundee Utd
Falkirk 0-0 Dundee Utd	Queen of S'th 1-3 Dundee Utd
Dundee Utd 2-1 Morton	Dundee Utd 1-1 Inverness CT
Dunfermline 1-3 Dundee Utd	Dundee Utd 2-3 Queen of S'th
Livingston 2-0 Dundee Utd	Dundee Utd 1-1 Dunfermline
Dundee Utd 0-2 Inverness CT	Inverness CT 1-0 Dundee Utd
Dumbarton 0-2 Dundee Utd	Morton 1-1 Dundee Utd
Dundee Utd 2-1 St. Mirren	Dundee Utd 2-0 Dumbarton
Dundee Utd 3-0 Falkirk	Dumbarton 3-2 Dundee Utd
Brechin City 1-1 Dundee Utd	Dundee Utd 1-0 St. Mirren
Dundee Utd 2-1 Dunfermline	Dundee Utd 1-0 Falkirk
Morton 0-2 Dundee Utd	Brechin City 0-5 Dundee Utd
Dundee Utd 3-0 Livingston	Queen of the S'th 3-0 Dundee Utd
St. Mirren 2-0 Dundee Utd	Dundee Utd 2-0 Livingston

DUNFERMLINE

NICKNAME:	The Pars
COLOURS:	Black and white
GROUND:	East End Park
TELEPHONE No:	01383 724295
EMAIL:	enquiries@dafc.co.uk
WEBSITE:	dafc.co.uk
CAPACITY:	11,508
RECORD ATT:	27,816 (v Celtic, 1968)
RECORD VICTORY:	11-2 (v Stenhousemuir, 1930)
RECORD DEFEAT:	0-10 (v Dundee, 1947)
MANAGER:	Allan Johnston
CHAIRMAN:	Ross McArthur
MOST LEAGUE	
GOALS (1 SEASON):	53, Bobby Skinner, 1925-26

HONOURS

LEAGUE CHAMPIONS: Division II – 1925-26. Second Division – 1985-86. First Division (3) – 1988-89, 1995-96, 2010-11. League One – 2015-16. SCOTTISH CUP (2): 1961, 1968.

LEAGUE RESULTS 2017-2018

Livingston 1-1 Dunfermline	Dunfermline 2-0 Falkirk
Dunfermline 5-1 Inverness CT	Dumbarton 0-1 Dunfermline
Dunfermline 3-1 Falkirk	Dunfermline 0-0 Dundee United
Dumbarton 0-4 Dunfermline	Dunfermline 1-2 St. Mirren
Morton 3-2 Dumbarton	Morton 2-1 Dunfermline
Dunfermline 3-0 St Mirren	Livingston 0-0 Dunfermline
Brechin City 0-3 Dunfermline	Queen of S'th 0-0 Dunfermline
Dunfermline 1-3 Dundee Utd	St. Mirren 2-0 Dunfermline
Queen of S'th 0-0 Dunfermline	Dunfermline 1-0 Inverness CT
Dunfermline 3-1 Livingston	Dunfermline 0-0 Morton
Inverness CT 1-0 Dunfermline	Brechin City 0-3 Dunfermline
Falkirk 1-1 Dunfermline	Dundee United 1-1 Dunfermline
Dunfermline 1-1 Morton	Dunfermline 3-1 Queen of S'th
Dunfermline 2-2 Dumbarton	Dunfermline 1-0 Livingston
Dundee Utd 2-1 Dunfermline	Falkirk 1-2 Dunfermline
Dunfermline 2-5 Queen of S'th	Dunfermline 4-0 Brechin City
St. Mirren 1-0 Dunfermline	Inverness CT 2-2 Dunfermline
Dunfermline 2-1 Brechin City	Dunfermline 4-0 Dumbarton

EAST FIFE

NICKNAME:	The Fifers/The Fife
COLOURS:	Black and gold
GROUND:	Locality Hub
	Bayview Stadium
TELEPHONE No:	01333 426323
EMAIL:	office@eastfifefc.info
WEBSITE:	eastfifefc.info
CAPACITY:	1992
RECORD ATT:	22,515 (v Raith,1950)
RECORD VICTORY:	13-2 (v Edinburgh City, 1937)
RECORD DEFEAT:	0-9 (v Hearts, 1957)
MANAGER:	Darren Young
CHAIRMAN:	Jim Stevenson
MOST LEAGUE	
GOALS (1 SEASON):	42, Jock Wood, 1926-27

HONOURS

LEAGUE CHAMPIONSHIP: Division II – 1947-48.
Third Division – 2007-08. League Two – 2015-16. SCOTTISH
CUP: 1938. LEAGUE CUP (3): 1947-48, 1949-50, 1953-54.

LEAGUE RESULTS 2017-2018

Stranraer 1-0 East Fife	Arbroath 1-1 East Fife
East Fife 1-0 Alloa	East Fife 2-3 Raith Rovers
Arbroath 2-3 East Fife	Airdrieonians 0-0 East Fife
East Fife 0-5 Raith Rovers	East Fife 2-1 Alloa Athletic
East Fife 0-1 Queen's Park	East Fife 1-2 Forfar Athletic
Airdrie 0-1 East Fife	Stranraer 0-2 East Fife
East Fife 3-0 Forfar	East Fife 0-2 Queen's Park
Ayr Utd 3-0 East Fife	Ayr United 3-0 East Fife
East Fife 5-4 Albion Rovers	East Fife 2-0 Albion Rovers
Alloa Athletic 4-1 East Fife	East Fife 2-1 Airdrieonians
East Fife 3-1 Arbroath	Alloa Athletic 1-2 East Fife
Raith Rovers 1-0 East Fife	Forfar Athletic 2-0 East Fife
Forfar Athletic 2-0 East Fife	Raith Rovers 2-0 East Fife
East Fife 6-1 Airdrieonians	East Fife 2-3 Ayr United
Queen's Park 2-1 East Fife	Queen's Park 2-3 East Fife
East Fife 1-1 Stranraer	East Fife 0-5 Arbroath
East Fife 1-4 Ayr United	Albion Rovers 1-0 East Fife
Albion Rovers 3-2 East Fife	East Fife 2-3 Stranraer

EDINBURGH CITY

NICKNAME:	The Citizens
COLOURS:	Black and white
GROUND:	Ainslie Park Stadium
TELEPHONE No:	0845 463 1932
EMAIL:	admin@edinburghcityfc.com
WEBSITE:	edinburghcityfc.com
CAPACITY:	7,500
RECORD ATT:	5,740 (v Cowdenbeath 1936)
RECORD VICTORY:	10-0 (v Heriot-Watt, 1996)
RECORD DEFEAT:	2-13 (v East Fife 1937)
HEAD COACH:	James McDonaugh
CHAIRMAN:	Jim Brown
MOST LEAGUE GOALS (1 SEASON):	Ross Allum, 22, 2015/16, Willie Bauld, 22, 1947/48

HONOURS

LEAGUE CHAMPIONS: Lowland Football League Winners (2): 2014–15, 2015–16, East of Scotland Football League Winners (1): 2005–06, East of Scotland Football League First Division Winners (1): 1995–96

LEAGUE RESULTS 2017-2018

Edinburgh City 1-3 Montrose	Cowdenbeath 0-2 Edinburgh City
Cowdb'th 1-0 Edinburgh City	Edinburgh City 0-2 Montrose
Stirling Albion 2-0 Edinburgh City	Edinburgh City 3-2 Annan
Edinburgh City 0-3 Elgin City	Clyde 3-2 Edinburgh City
Edinburgh City 1-0 Berwick	Edinburgh City 0-0 Peterhead
Clyde 2-3 Edinburgh City	Stenhousemuir 1-0 Edinburgh City
Edinburgh City 0-3 Peterhead	Edinburgh City 4-0 Elgin City
Stenh'muir 3-0 Edinburgh City	Annan 2-3 Edinburgh City
Edinburgh City 0-1 Annan	Edinburgh City 1-1 Cowdenbeath
Montrose 1-0 Edinburgh City	Edinburgh City 2-2 Stirling Albion
Edinburgh City 1-2 Stirling Albion	Edinburgh City 0-3 Clyde
Berwick 1-1 Edinburgh City	Berwick Rangers 1-1 Edinburgh City
Edinburgh City 0-0 Cowdenb'th	Stirling Albion 2-2 Edinburgh City
Peterhead 3-0 Edinburgh City	Montrose 3-0 Edinburgh City
Elgin City 1-1 Edinburgh City	Edinburgh City 1-4 Stenhousemuir
Edinburgh City 1-2 Stenhousemuir	Elgin City 1-1 Edinburgh City
Annan 2-1 Edinburgh City	Edinburgh City 1-3 Clyde
Edinburgh City 3-0 Berwick Rangers	Peterhead 2-1 Edinburgh City

ELGIN CITY

NICKNAME:	The City
	or Black & Whites
COLOURS:	Black and white
GROUND:	Borough Briggs
TELEPHONE No:	01343 551114
EMAIL:	office@elgincity.com
WEBSITE:	elgincity.com
CAPACITY:	3716
RECORD ATT:	12,608
	(v Arbroath,1968)
RECORD VICTORY:	18-1 (v Brora Rangers, 1960)
RECORD DEFEAT:	1-14 (v Hearts, 1939)
MANAGER:	Gavin Price
CHAIRMAN:	Graham Tatters
MOST LEAGUE	
GOALS (1 SEASON):	66, Willie Grant, 1960-61

LEAGUE RESULTS 2017-2018

Elgin City 1-1 Cowdb'th

Peterhead 3-0 Elgin City

Elgin City 3-2 Clyde

Edinburgh City 0-3 Elgin City

Elgin City 0-1 Annan

Berwick 3-2 Elgin City

Elgin City 3-0 Montrose

Stirling Albion 2-2 Elgin City

Elgin City 2-0 Stenhousemuir

Clyde 2-4 Elgin City

Elgin City 0-2 Peterhead

Cowdenbeath 1-3 Elgin City

Elgin City 5-2 Berwick

Annan Athletic 2-0 Elgin City

Elgin City 1-1 Edinburgh City

Montrose 3-0 Elgin City

Stenhou'muir 4-1 Elgin City

Peterhead 7-0 Elgin City

Elgin City 2-1 Clyde

Elgin City 1-0 Cowdenbeath

Elgin City 2-0 Stenhousemuir

Stirling Albion 3-1 Elgin City

Elgin City 2-1 Annan Athletic

Elgin City 2-2 Montrose

Edinburgh City 4-0 Elgin City

Elgin City 3-0 Berwick Rangers

Clyde 1-0 Elgin City

Cowdenbeath 3-1 Elgin City

Elgin City 0-2 Stirling Albion

Stenhousemuir 0-2 Elgin City

Berwick Rangers 2-2 Elgin City

Elgin City 3-0 Stirling Albion

Annan Athletic 4-1 Elgin City

Elgin City 1-1 Edinburgh City

Elgin City 0-1 Peterhead

Montrose 1-1 Elgin City

FALKIRK

NICKNAME:	The Bairns
COLOURS:	Navy blue and white
GROUND:	The Falkirk Stadium
TELEPHONE No:	01324 624121
EMAIL:	marketing@falkirkfc.co.uk
WEBSITE:	falkirkfc.co.uk
CAPACITY:	8750
RECORD ATT:	23,100 (v Celtic, 1953)
RECORD VICTORY:	12-1 (v Laurieston, 1893)
RECORD DEFEAT:	1-11 (v Airdrie, 1951)
MANAGER:	Paul Hartley
CHAIRMAN:	Margaret Laing
MOST LEAGUE GOALS (1 SEASON):	43, Evelyn Morrison, 1928-29
GOALS (OVERALL):	243, Kenny Dawson, 1934-51

FALKIRK

HONOURS

LEAGUE CHAMPIONS: Division II (3) – 1935-36, 1969-70, 1974-75. First Division (4) – 1990-91, 1993-94, 2002-03, 2004-05. Second Division – 1979-80. **SCOTTISH CUP (2):** 1913, 1957. **CHALLENGE CUP (4):** 1993-94, 1997-98, 2004-05, 2011-12.

LEAGUE RESULTS 2017-2018

St. Mirren 3-1 Falkirk
Falkirk 1-1 Dumbarton
Dunfermline 3-1 Falkirk
Falkirk 1-4 Queen of the S'th
Brechin City 1-1 Falkirk
Falkirk 0-0 Dundee Utd
Falkirk 0-2 Livingston
Morton 0-1 Falkirk
Falkirk 0-0 Inverness CT
Falkirk 0-0 St. Mirren
Queen of S'th 4-2 Falkirk
Falkirk 1-1 Dunfermline
Dundee Utd 3-0 Falkirk
Falkirk 0-3 Morton
Livingston 0-0 Falkirk
Dumbarton 0-0 Falkirk
Dumbarton 0-0 Falkirk
Falkirk 3-2 Queen of the S'th

Dunfermline 2-0 Falkirk
Falkirk 6-1 Dundee United
Inverness CT 4-1 Falkirk
Morton 0-1 Falkirk
Falkirk 3-1 Inverness CT
Falkirk 1-3 Livingston
Falkirk 3-1 Brechin City
Brechin City 0-1 Falkirk
Falkirk 0-0 Dumbarton
Falkirk 3-1 Greenock Morton
Livingston 0-0 Falkirk
Falkirk 3-0 Brechin City
Queen of S'th 2-2 Falkirk
Falkirk 1-2 Dunfermline At...
Inverness CT 1-0 Falkirk
Dundee United 1-0 Falkirk
St. Mirren 1-2 Falkirk
Dumbarton 2-5 Falkirk
Falkirk 1-0 St. Mirren

FORFAR ATHLETIC

NICKNAME:	The Loons
COLOURS:	Sky/navy
GROUND:	Station Park
TELEPHONE:	01307 463576
EMAIL:	info@forfarathletic.co.uk
WEBSITE:	forfarathletic.co.uk
CAPACITY:	6777
RECORD ATT:	10,780
	(v Rangers, 1970)
RECORD VICTORY:	14-1 (v Lindertis, 1888)
RECORD DEFEAT:	2-12 (v King's Park, 1930)
MANAGER:	Jim Weir
CHAIRMAN:	Ross Graham
MOST LEAGUE	
GOALS (1 SEASON):	45, Dave Kilgour, 1929-30

HONOURS

**LEAGUE CHAMPIONSHIP: Second Division – 1983-84.
Third Division – 1994-95.**

LEAGUE RESULTS 2017-2018

Forfar Athletic 2-1 Airdrie	Ayr United 2-3 Forfar Athletic
Ayr United 3-0 Forfar Athletic	Forfar Athletic 0-1 Arbroath
Raith Rovers 3-1 Forfar Athletic	Raith Rovers 2-1 Forfar Athletic
Forfar Athletic 0-2 Albion Rovers	Forfar Athletic 4-2 Albion Rovers
Alloa 2-1 Forfar Athletic	East Fife 1-2 Forfar Athletic
Forfar Athletic 0-5 Arbroath	Forfar Athletic 0-1 Airdrieonians
East Fife 3-0 Forfar Athletic	Alloa Athletic 1-0 Forfar Athletic
Forfar Athletic 1-1 Stranraer	Forfar Athletic 5-1 Stranraer
Queen's Park 1-1 Forfar Athletic	Queen's Park 2-2 Forfar Athletic
Forfar Athletic 0-5 Ayr United	Arbroath 2-0 Forfar Athletic
Forfar Athletic 1-1 Raith Rovers	Forfar Athletic 2-1 Raith Rovers
Albion Rovers 3-4 Forfar Athletic	Forfar Athletic 0-2 Ayr United
Forfar Athletic 2-0 East Fife	Forfar Athletic 2-0 East Fife
Arbroath 2-1 Forfar Athletic	Stranraer 2-0 Forfar Athletic
Airdrieonians 2-1 Forfar Athletic	Albion Rovers 0-1 Forfar Athletic
Forfar Athletic 0-2 Alloa Athletic	Forfar Athletic 0-1 Alloa Athletic
Stranraer 3-0 Forfar Athletic	Forfar Athletic 1-1 Queen's Park
Forfar Athletic 0-3 Queen's Park	Airdrieonians 1-2 Forfar Athletic

HAMILTON ACCIES

NICKNAME:	The Accies
COLOURS:	Red and white
GROUND:	SuperSeal Stadium
TELEPHONE No:	01698 368652
EMAIL:	office@acciesfc.co.uk
WEBSITE:	hamiltonacciesfc.co.uk
CAPACITY:	6014
RECORD ATT:	28,690 (v Hearts, 1937)
RECORD VICTORY:	11-1 (v Chryston, 1885)
RECORD DEFEAT:	1-11 (v Hibs, 1965)
MANAGER:	Martin Canning
CHAIRMAN:	Ronnie MacDonald
MOST LEAGUE	
GOALS (1 SEASON):	35, David Wilson, 1936-37

HONOURS

LEAGUE CHAMPIONS (3): First Division: 1985-86, 1987-88, 2007-08. Second Division: 1903-04. Third Division: 2000-01. CHALLENGE CUP (2); 1991-92, 1992-93.

LEAGUE RESULTS 2017-2018

Aberdeen 2-0 Hamilton	Partick Thistle 1-0 Hamilton
Hamilton 3-0 Dundee	Motherwell 1-3 Hamilton
Hibernian 1-3 Hamilton	Hamilton 0-3 Hearts
Kilmarnock 2-2 Hamilton	Hamilton 1-2 Dundee
Hamilton 1-4 Celtic	Aberdeen 3-0 Hamilton
Hamilton 1-2 Hearts	Hamilton 3-5 Rangers
St Johnstone 2-1 Hamilton	Hamilton 2-1 Partick Thistle
Hamilton 1-4 Rangers	Hamilton 2-0 Motherwell
Hamilton 1-2 Motherwell	Ross County 2-2 Hamilton
Ross County 2-1 Hamilton	St. Johnstone 1-0 Hamilton
Hamilton 0-0 Partick Thistle	Kilmarnock 2-0 Hamilton
Dundee 1-3 Hamilton	Hibernian 3-1 Hamilton
Hamilton 2-2 Aberdeen	Hamilton 1-2 Celtic
Rangers 0-2 Hamilton	Hamilton 1-2 Kilmarnock
Hamilton 1-1 Hibernian	Partick Thistle 2-1 Hamilton
Hearts 1-1 Hamilton	Hamilton 2-0 Ross County
Hamilton 0-1 St. Johnstone	Dundee 1-0 Hamilton
Celtic 3-1 Hamilton	Hamilton 1-2 St. Johnstone
Hamilton 3-2 Ross County	Motherwell 3-0 Hamilton

HEART OF MIDLOTHIAN

NICKNAME:	The Jambos
COLOURS:	Maroon and white
GROUND:	Tynecastle Park
TELEPHONE No:	0333 043 1874
EMAIL:	supporterservices@homplc.co.uk
WEBSITE:	heartsfc.co.uk
CAPACITY:	20,099
RECORD ATT:	53,396 (v Rangers, 1932)
RECORD VICTORY:	21-0 (v Anchor, 1880)
RECORD DEFEAT:	1-8 (v Vale of Leven, 1882)
HEAD COACH:	Craig Levein
CHAIRWOMAN:	Ann Budge
MOST LEAGUE GOALS (1 SEASON):	44, Barney Battles
GOALS (OVERALL):	214, John Robertson

HONOURS

LEAGUE CHAMPIONS: Division I (4) – 1894-95, 1896-97, 1957-58, 1959-60. First Division – 1979-80. Championship: 2014-15. SCOTTISH CUP (8): 1891, 1896, 1901, 1906, 1956, 1998, 2006, 2012. LEAGUE CUP (4): 1954-55, 1958-59, 1959-60, 1962-63.

LEAGUE RESULTS 2017-2018

Celtic 4-1 Hearts	St. Johnstone 0-0 Hearts
Kilmarnock 0-1 Kilmarnock	Hearts 0-0 Hibernian
Rangers 0-0 Hearts	Aberdeen 0-0 Hearts
Motherwell 2-1 Hearts	Hamilton 0-3 Hearts
Hearts 0-0 Aberdeen	Hearts 1-1 Motherwell
Hamilton 1-2 Hearts	Celtic 3-1 Hearts
Partick Thistle 1-1 Hearts	Hearts 1-0 St. Johnstone
Dundee 2-1 Hearts	Ross County 1-1 Hearts
Ross County 1-2 Hearts	Rangers 2-0 Hearts
Hearts 1-0 St. Johnstone	Hearts 1-1 Kilmarnock
Hibernian 1-0 Hearts	Hibernian 2-0 Hearts
Hearts 1-3 Rangers	Hearts 3-0 Partick Thistle
Hearts 1-2 Kilmarnock	Dundee 1-1 Hearts
Hearts 1-1 Partick Thistle-	Hearts 2-0 Aberdeen
Hearts 0-0 Ross County	Rangers 2-1 Hearts
Hearts 1-1 Hamilton	Aberdeen 2-0 Hearts
Hearts 1-0 Motherwell	Hearts 1-3 Celtic
Hearts 2-0 Dundee	Hearts 2-1 Hibernian
Hearts 4-0 Celtic	Kilmarnock 1-0 Hearts

HIBERNIAN

NICKNAME:	The Hibees
COLOURS:	Green and white
GROUND:	Easter Road
TELEPHONE No:	0131 661 2159
EMAIL:	reception@ hibernianfc.co.uk
WEBSITE:	hibernianfc.co.uk
CAPACITY:	20,400
RECORD ATT:	65,860 (v Hearts, 1950)
RECORD VICTORY:	22-1 (v 42nd Highlanders, 1881)
RECORD DEFEAT:	0-10 (v Rangers, 1898)
MANAGER:	Neil Lennon
CHAIRMAN:	Rod Petrie
MOST LEAGUE GOALS (1 SEASON):	42, Joe Baker, 1959-60
GOALS (OVERALL):	364, Gordon Smith

HONOURS
LEAGUE CHAMPIONS: Division I (4) – 1902-03, 1947-48, 1950-51,1951-52. Division II (3) – 1893-94, 1894-94, 1932-33. First Division (2) – 1980-81, 1998-99. Championship (1) – 2016-17. SCOTTISH CUP (3): 1887, 1902, 2016. LEAGUE CUP (3): 1972-73, 1991-92, 2006-07.

LEAGUE RESULTS 2017-2018

Hibernian 3-1 Partick Thistle	Hibernian 2-1 Ross County
Rangers 2-3 Hibernian	Hearts 0-0 Hibernian
Hibernian 1-3 Hamilton	Hibernian 1-1 Kilmarnock
Dundee 1-1 Hibernian	Dundee 0-1 Hibernian
St Johnstone 1-1 Hibernian	Celtic 1-0 Hibernian
Hibernian 2-2 Motherwell	Hibernian 2-1 Motherwell
Ross County 0-1 Hibernian	Rangers 1-2 Hibernian
Celtic 2-2 Hibernian	Hibernian 2-0 Aberdeen
Hibernian 0-1 Aberdeen	Kilmarnock 2-2 Hibernian
Hibernian 1-0 Hearts	Hibernian 2-0 Hearts
Motherwell 0-1 Hibernian	St. Johnstone 1-1 Hibernian
Kilmarnock 0 -3 Hibernian	Hibernian 2-0 Partick Thistle
Hibernian 2-1 Dundee	Hibernian 3-1 Hamilton
Hibernian1-2 St. Johnstone	Ross County 1-1 Hibernian
Hamilton 1-1 Hibernian	Hibernian 2-1 Celtic
Partick Thistle 0-1 Hibernian	Hibernian 5-3 Kilmarnock
Hibernian 2-2 Celtic	Aberdeen 0-0 Hibernian
Hibernian 1-2 Rangers	Hearts 2-1 Hibernian
Aberdeen 4-1 Hibernian	Hibernian 5-5 Rangers

INVERNESS CT

NICKNAME:	Caley Thistle
COLOURS:	Blue and red
GROUND:	Tulloch
	Caledonian Stadium
TELEPHONE No:	01463 222880
EMAIL:	info@ictfc.co.uk
WEBSITE:	ictfc.co.uk
CAPACITY:	7812
RECORD ATT:	7753
	(v Rangers, 2008)
RECORD VICTORY:	8-1
	(v Annan, 1998)
RECORD DEFEAT:	0-6 (v Airdrie 2001/Celtic 2014)
MANAGER:	John Robertson
CHAIRMAN:	Graham Rae
MOST LEAGUE	
GOALS (1 SEASON):	29, Iain Stewart, 1996-97

HONOURS

LEAGUE CHAMPIONS: Third Division – 1996-97. First Division (2)
– 2003-04, 2009-10. **CHALLENGE CUP** – 2003-04, 2017-18
SCOTTISH CUP-2015.

LEAGUE RESULTS 2017-2018

Inverness CT 0-1 Dundee Utd	St. Mirren 1-0 Inverness CT
Dunfermline 5-1 Inverness CT	Inverness CT 4-1 Falkirk
Inverness CT 1-1 Morton	Inverness CT 3-1 Queen of S'th
Brechin City 0-4 Inverness CT	Falkirk 3-1 Inverness CT
St Mirren 4-2 Inverness CT	Inverness CT 0-2 Morton
Inverness CT 1-3 Livingston	Dunfermline 1-0 Inverness CT
Dumbarton 2-1 Inverness CT	Dundee Utd 1-1 Inverness CT
Inverness CT 0-0 Queen of S'th	Inverness CT 1-0 Dundee United
Falkirk 0-0 Inverness CT	Inverness CT 2-2 St. Mirren
Dundee Utd 0-2 Inverness CT	Inverness CT 4-0 Brechin City
Inverness CT 1-0 Dunfermline	Queen of S'th 0-2 Inverness CT
Livingston 0-0 Inverness CT	Inverness CT 1-0 Falkirk
Inverness CT 0-2 St. Mirren	Inverness CT 5-1 Dumbarton
Inverness CT 4-0 Brechin City	Dumbarton 0-1 Inverness CT
Queen of S'th 0-0 Inverness CT	Inverness CT 2-2 Dunfermline
Inverness CT 1-0 Dumbarton	Livingston 0-1 Inverness CT
Morton 1-0 Inverness CT	Morton 0-3 Inverness CT
Brechin City 2-3 Inverness CT	
Inverness CT 1-1 Livingston	

KILMARNOCK

NICKNAME:	Killie
COLOURS:	Blue and white
GROUND:	Rugby Park
TELEPHONE No:	01563 545300
EMAIL:	info@kilmarnockfc.co.uk
WEBSITE:	kilmarnockfc.co.uk
CAPACITY:	18,128
RECORD ATT:	35,995 (v Rangers, 1962)
RECORD VICTORY:	11-1 (v Paisley Academical, 1930)
RECORD DEFEAT:	1-9 (v Celtic, 1938)
MANAGER:	Steve Clarke
MOST LEAGUE GOALS (1 SEASON):	34, Harry Cunningham, 1927-28/ Andy Kerr, 1960-61
GOALS (OVERALL):	148, W Culley, 1912-23

HONOURS

LEAGUE CHAMPIONS: Division I – 1964-65. Division II (2) – 1897-98, 1898-99. SCOTTISH CUP (3): 1920, 1929, 1997. LEAGUE CUP: 2011-12.

LEAGUE RESULTS 2017-2018

Kilmarnock 1-2 St. Johnstone	Kilmarnock 2-1 Rangers
Kilmarnock 0-1 Hearts	Hibernian 1-1 Kilmarnock
Kilmarnock 0-2 Celtic	Aberdeen 3-1 Kilmarnock
Kilmarnock 2-2 Hamilton	Kilmarnock 1-0 Celtic
Motherwell 2-0 Kilmarnock	Kilmarnock 3-2 Dundee
Aberdeen 1-1 Kilmarnock	Motherwell 0-1 Kilmarnock
Kilmarnock 1-1 Dundee	Kilmarnock 2-2 Hibernian
Kilmarnock 0-2 Ross County	Hearts 1-1 Kilmarnock
Partick Thistle 0-2 Kilmarnock	Kilmarnock 2-0 St. Johnstone
Rangers 1-1 Kilmarnock	Kilmarnock 3-2 Ross County
Celtic 1-1 Kilmarnock	Rangers 0-1 Kilmarnock
Kilmarnock 0-3 Hibernian	Kilmarnock 2-0 Hamilton
Hearts 1-2 Kilmarnock	Partick Thistle 0-1 Kilmarnock
Dundee 0-0 Kilmarnock	Hamilton 1-2 Kilmarnock
Kilmarnock 1-3 Aberdeen	Kilmarnock 0-2 Aberdeen
St. Johnstone 1-2 Kilmarnock	Hibernian 5-3 Kilmarnock
Kilmarnock 5-1 Partick Thistle	Rangers 1-0 Kilmarnock
Ross County 2-2 Kilmarnock	Celtic 0-0 Kilmarnock
Kilmarnock 1-0 Motherwell	Kilmarnock 1-0 Hearts

LIVINGSTON

NICKNAME:	Livi Lions
COLOURS:	Amber and Black
GROUND:	Tony Macaroni Arena
TELEPHONE No:	01506 417000
EMAIL:	lfcreception@ livingstonfc.co.uk
WEBSITE:	livingstonfc.co.uk
CAPACITY:	10,122
RECORD ATT:	10,112 (v Rangers, 2001)
RECORD VICTORY:	8-0 (v Stranraer, 2012)
RECORD DEFEAT:	0-8 (v Hamilton Accies, 1974)
MANAGER:	VACANT (at the time of press)
CHAIRMAN:	Robert Wilson
MOST LEAGUE GOALS (1 SEASON):	22, Iain Russell 2010-2011 Liam Buchanan, 2016-17

HONOURS
LEAGUE CHAMPIONS: Third Division (2) – 1995-96, 2009-10.
Second Division (3) – 1986-87, 1998-99, 2010-11.
First Division (1) – 2000-01. League One (1) 2016-2017.
LEAGUE CUP: 2003-04. CHALLENGE CUP: 2014-2015

LEAGUE RESULTS 2017-2018

Livingston 1-1 Dunfermline	Livingston 0-1 Queen of S'th
Brechin City 2-2 Livingston	Brechin City 0-2 Livingston
Livingston 1-3 St. Mirren	Livingston 2-0 Dumbarton
Morton 0-1 Livingston	Falkirk 1-3 Livingston
Livingston 2-2 Queen of Sth	Livingston 0-0 Dunfermline
Inverness CT 1-3 Livingston	Livingston 4-1 St. Mirren
Falkirk 0-2 Livingston	Livingston 2-1 Dundee Utd
Livingston 2-1 Dumbarton	Morton 0-1 Livingston
Livingston 2-0 Dundee United	Livingston 1-1 Morton
Dunfermline 3-1 Livingston	Livingston 0-0 Falkirk
Livingston 3-2 Brechin City	Queen of S'th 3-3 Livingston
Livingston 0-0 Inverness CT	Dumbarton 0-3 Livingston
Queen of S'th 0-3 Livingston	Dunfermline 1-0 Livingston
St. Mirren 3-1 Livingston	Livingston 3-2 Morton
Livingston 0-0 Falkirk	St. Mirren 0-0 Livingston
Dundee Utd 3-0 Livingston	Livingston 3-0 Brechin City
Dumbarton 1-4 Livingston	Livingston 0-1 Inverness CT
Inverness CT 1-1 Livingston	Dundee Utd 2-0 Livingston

LIVINGSTON celebrate their 3-1 aggregate win over Partick Thistle to win promotion

MONTROSE

NICKNAME:	The Gable Endies
COLOURS:	Blue and white
GROUND:	Links Park Stadium
TELEPHONE No:	01674 673200
EMAIL:	office@montrosefc.co.uk
WEBSITE:	montrosefc.co.uk
CAPACITY:	4936
RECORD ATT:	8983
	(v Dundee, 1973)
RECORD VICTORY:	12-0 (v Vale of
	Leithen, 1975)
RECORD DEFEAT:	0-13 (v Aberdeen, 1951)
MANAGER:	Stewart Petrie
CHAIRMAN:	John Crawford
MOST LEAGUE	
GOALS (1 SEASON):	28, Brian Third, 1972-73

HONOURS

LEAGUE CHAMPIONSHIP: Second Division – 1984-85. League Two 2017-18.

LEAGUE RESULTS 2017-2018

Edinburgh City 1-3 Montrose	Montrose 1-1 Cowdenbeath
Montrose 1-1 Stenhousemuir	Annan Athletic 0-1 Montrose
Montrose 1-0 Cowdenbeath	Edinburgh City 0-2 Montrose
Annan Athletic 0-1 Montrose	Montrose 1-3 Clyde
Peterhead 1-1 Montrose	Montrose 2-1 Stirling Albion
Montrose 1-3 Stirling Albion	Peterhead 0-1 Montrose
Elgin City 3-0 Montrose	Montrose 1-0 Stenhousemuir
Montrose 3-2 Clyde	Elgin City 2-2 Montrose
Berwick Rangers 0-1 Montrose	Berwick Rangers 2-2 Montrose
Montrose 1-0 Edinburgh City	Montrose 2-1 Annan Athletic
Cowdenbeath 1 - 3 Montrose	Montrose 3-2 Peterhead
Montrose 1 - 1 Annan Athletic	Clyde 3-0 Montrose
Stenhousemuir 0-1 Montrose	Montrose 3-0 Edinburgh City
Clyde 0-0 Montrose	Stirling Albion 0-5 Montrose
Montrose 3-0 Berwick Rangers	Cowdenbeath 0-3 Montrose
Montrose 3-0 Elgin City	Montrose 1-0 Berwick Rangers
Stirling Albion 0-1 Montrose	Stenhousemuir 0-2 Montrose
Montrose 2-6 Peterhead	Montrose 1-1 Elgin City

MONTROSE celebrate winning the Ladbrokes League Two title   Pic: SNS

THE new Rangers boss Steven Gerrard, unveiled in May 2018

MORTON

NICKNAME:	The Ton
COLOURS:	Blue and white
GROUND:	Cappielow Park
TELEPHONE No:	01475 723571
EMAIL:	admin@gmfc.net
WEBSITE:	gmfc.net
CAPACITY:	11,841
RECORD ATT:	23,500 (v Celtic, 1922)
RECORD VICTORY:	11-0 (v Carfin Shamrock, 1886)
RECORD DEFEAT:	1-10 (v Port Glasgow Athletic, 1894; v St Bernard's, 1933)
MANAGER:	Ray McKinnon
CHAIRMAN:	Crawford Rae
MOST LEAGUE GOALS (1 SEASON):	58, Allan McGraw, 1963-64

HONOURS

LEAGUE CHAMPIONS: First Division (3) – 1977-78, 1983-84, 1986-87. Division II (3) – 1949-50, 1963-64, 1966-67. Second Division (2)– 1994-95, 2006-07. Third Division – 2002-03. League One (1) 2014-2015. SCOTTISH CUP: 1922.

LEAGUE RESULTS 2017-2018

Dumbarton 0-0 Morton	Brechin City 1-1 Morton
Morton 4-1 St. Mirren	Morton 0-1 Falkirk
Inverness CT 1-1 Morton	Dundee United 0-3 Morton
Morton 0-1 Livingston	Morton 2-1 Dunfermline
Morton 3-2 Dunfermline	Queen of S'th 1-1 Morton
Queen of S'th 1-2 Morton	Dumbarton 0-1 Morton
Dundee Utd 2-1 Morton	Inverness CT 0-2 Morton
Morton 0-1 Falkirk	Morton 0-1 Livingston
Brechin City 0-1 Morton	Falkirk 3-1 Morton
Morton 1-1 Dumbarton	Livingston 1-1 Morton
St. Mirren 2-2 Morton	Dunfermline 0-0 Morton
Morton 1-2 Queen of S'th	Morton 2-0 Brechin City
Dunfermline 1-1 Morton	Morton 1-1 Dundee United
Falkirk 0-3 Morton	Livingston 3-2 Morton
Morton 4-1 Brechin City	Morton 3-2 Dumbarton
Morton 0-2 Dundee United	Morton 0-1 Queen of S'th
Morton 1-0 Inverness CT	St. Mirren 2-1 Morton
Morton 1-1 St. Mirren	Morton 0-3 Inverness CT

MOTHERWELL

NICKNAME:	The Steelmen
COLOURS:	Claret and amber
GROUND:	Fir Park
TELEPHONE No:	01698 333333
EMAIL:	enquiries@ motherwellfc.co.uk
WEBSITE:	motherwellfc.co.uk
CAPACITY:	13,742
RECORD ATT:	35,632 (v Rangers, 1952)
RECORD VICTORY:	12-1 (v Dundee United, 1954)
RECORD DEFEAT:	0-8 (v Aberdeen, 1979)
MANAGER:	Stephen Robinson
CHAIRMAN:	Jim McMahon
MOST LEAGUE GOALS (1 SEASON):	52, William McFadyen, 1931-32
GOALS (OVERALL):	283, Hugh Ferguson, 1916-25

HONOURS

LEAGUE CHAMPIONSHIP: Division I – 1931-32. Division II (2) – 1953-54, 1968-69. First Division (2) – 1981-82, 1984-85. SCOTTISH CUP: (2) 1952, 1991. LEAGUE CUP: 1950-51.

LEAGUE RESULTS 2017-2018

Motherwell 1-2 Rangers	Rangers 2-0 Motherwell
St. Johnstone 4-1 Motherwell	Motherwell 1-3 Hamilton
Motherwell 2-0 Ross County	Motherwell 2-0 Ross County
Motherwell 2-1 Hearts	Hearts 1-1 Motherwell
Motherwell 2-0 Kilmarnock	Hibernian 2-1 Motherwell
Hibernian 2-2 Motherwell	Motherwell 1-1 Partick Thistle
Motherwell 0-1 Aberdeen	Motherwell 2-0 St. Johnstone
Motherwell 3-0 Partick Thistle	Motherwell 0-1 Kilmarnock
Hamilton 1-2 Motherwell	Dundee 0-1 Motherwell
Dundee 0-1 Motherwell	Hamilton 2-0 Motherwell
Motherwell 0-1 Hibernian	Motherwell 0-0 Celtic
Ross County 3-2 Motherwell	Motherwell 2-2 Rangers
Aberdeen 0-2 Motherwell	Motherwell 0-2 Aberdeen
Motherwell 1-1 Celtic	St. Johnstone 0-0 Motherwell
Celtic 5-1 Motherwell	Ross County 0-0 Motherwell
Hearts 1-0 Motherwell	Motherwell 2-1 Dundee
Partick Thistle 3-2 Motherwell	Motherwell 1-5 St. Johnstone
Kilmarnock 1-0 Motherwell	Partick Thistle 0-1 Motherwell
Motherwell 1-1 Dundee	Motherwell 3-0 Hamilton

PARTICK THISTLE

NICKNAME:	The Jags
COLOURS:	Red and yellow
GROUND:	The Energy Check Stadium at Firhill
TELEPHONE No:	0141 579 1971
EMAIL:	mail@ptfc.co.uk
WEBSITE:	ptfc.co.uk
CAPACITY:	10,102
RECORD ATT:	49,838 (v Rangers, 1922) *RECORD*
VICTORY:	16-0 (v Royal Albert, 1931)
RECORD DEFEAT:	0-10 (v Queen's Park, 1881)
MANAGER:	Alan Archibald
CHAIRMAN:	David Beattie
MOST LEAGUE GOALS (1 SEASON):	41, Alex Hair, 1926-27

HONOURS

LEAGUE CHAMPIONS: Division II (3) – 1896-97, 1899-1900, 1970-71. First Division (3) – 1975-76, 2001-2002, 2012-13. Second Division – 2000-01. SCOTTISH CUP: 1921. LEAGUE CUP: 1971-72.

LEAGUE RESULTS 2017-2018

Hibernian 3-1 Partick Thistle
Partick Thistle 0-1 Celtic
St. Johnstone 1-0 Partick Thistle
Partick Thistle 3-4 Aberdeen
Ross County 1-1 Partick Thistle
Partick Thistle 2-2 Rangers
Partick Thistle 1-1 Hearts
Motherwell 3-0 Partick Thistle
Partick Thistle 0-2 Kilmarnock
Partick Thistle 2-1 Dundee
Hamilton 0-0 Partick Thistle
Partick Thistle 1-0 St. Johnstone
Rangers 3-0 Partick Thistle
Hearts 1-1 Partick Thistle
Partick Thistle 0-1 Hibernian
Kilmarnock 5-1 Partick Thistle
Partick Thistle 3-2 Motherwell
Dundee 3-0 Partick Thistle
Celtic 2-0 Partick Thistle

Partick Thistle 1-0 Hamilton
Aberdeen 1-0 Partick Thistle
Partick Thistle 2-0 Ross County
Partick Thistle 1-2 Celtic
St. Johnstone 1-3 Partick Thistle
Motherwell 1-1 Partick Thistle
Partick Thistle 0-2 Rangers
Partick Thistle 1-2 Dundee
Hamilton 2-1 Partick Thistle
Partick Thistle 0-0 Aberdeen
Hearts 3-0 Partick Thistle
Hibernian 2-0 Partick Thistle
Ross County 4-0 Partick Thistle
Partick Thistle 0-1 Kilmarnock
Partick Thistle 2-1 Hamilton
St. Johnstone 1-1 Partick Thistle
Partick Thistle 1-1 Ross County
Partick Thistle 0-1 Motherwell
Dundee 0-1 Partick Thistle

PETERHEAD

NICKNAME:	The Blue Toon
COLOURS:	Blue and white
GROUND:	Balmoor Stadium
TELEPHONE:	01779 478256
EMAIL:	office@peterhead fc.co.uk
WEBSITE:	peterheadfc.co.uk
CAPACITY:	3150
RECORD ATT:	8643 (v Raith Rovers, 1987)
RECORD VICTORY:	17-0 (v Fort William, 1998)
RECORD DEFEAT:	0-13 (v Aberdeen, 1923-24)
MANAGER:	Jim McInally
CHAIRMAN:	Rodger Morrison
MOST LEAGUE GOALS (1 SEASON):	32, Rory McAllister, 2013-14

HONOURS
LEAGUE CHAMPIONS: League Two – 2013-14

LEAGUE RESULTS 2017-2018

Annan 1-2 Peterhead
Peterhead 3-0 Elgin City
Stenh'muir 3-1 Peterhead
Peterhead 2-4 Stirling Albion
Peterhead 1-1 Montrose
Cowdenbeath 0-4 Peterhead
Edinburgh City 0-3 Peterhead
Peterhead 0-2 Berwick Rangers
Clyde 1-4 Peterhead
Peterhead 1-0 Annan Athletic
Elgin City 0-2 Peterhead
Peterhead 2-3 Stenhousemuir
Peterhead 3-0 Edinburgh City
Stirling Albion 0-1 Peterhead
Peterhead 3-2 Cowdenbeath
Montrose 2-6 Peterhead
Peterhead 7-0 Elgin City
Stenhousemuir 1-4 Peterhead

Peterhead 4-3 Stirling Albion
Clyde 1-0 Peterhead
Berwick Rangers 2-3 Peterhead
Peterhead 0-1 Montrose
Edinburgh City 0-0 Peterhead
Peterhead 1-1 Berwick Rangers
Annan Athletic 3-3 Peterhead
Cowdenbeath 0-2 Peterhead
Peterhead 2-1 Clyde
Stirling Albion 0-1 Peterhead
Peterhead 1-2 Stenhousemuir
Montrose 3-2 Peterhead
Peterhead 1-0 Annan Athletic
Peterhead 3-0 Clyde
Berwick Rangers 1-3 Peterhead
Peterhead 1-0 Cowdenbeath
Elgin City 0-1 Peterhead
Peterhead 2-1 Edinburgh City

QUEEN OF THE SOUTH

NICKNAME:	The Doonhamers
COLOURS:	Royal blue
GROUND:	Palmerston Park
TELEPHONE No:	01387 254853
EMAIL:	admin@qosfc.com
WEBSITE:	qosfc.com
CAPACITY:	8690
RECORD ATT:	26,552
	(v Hearts, 1952)
RECORD VICTORY:	11-1 (v Stranraer, 1932)
RECORD DEFEAT:	2-10 (v Dundee, 1962)
MANAGER:	Gary Naysmith
CHAIRMAN:	Billy Hewitson
MOST LEAGUE	
GOALS (1 SEASON):	41, Jimmy Rutherford, 1931-32

HONOURS

LEAGUE CHAMPIONS: Division II – 1950-51. Second Division (2) – 2001-02, 2012-13. CHALLENGE CUP (2): 2002-03, 2012-13.

LEAGUE RESULTS 2017-2018

Queen of S'th 4-1 Brechin City	Queen of S'th 0-0 Dumbarton
Dundee Utd 2-1 Queen of S'th	Livingston 0-1 Queen of S'th
Queen of S'th 1-0 Dumbarton	Inverness CT 3-1 Queen of S'th
Falkirk 1-4 Queen of the S'th	Queen of S'th 3-1 Brechin City
Livingston 2-2 Queen of S'th	St. Mirren 2-0 Queen of S'th
Queen of S'th 1-2 Morton	Queen of S'th 1-1 Morton
St Mirren 3-1 Queen of S'th	Queen of S'th 0-0 Dunfermline
Inverness 0-0 Queen of S'th	Dumbarton 0-1 Queen of S'th
Queen of S'th 0-0 Dunfermline	Queen of S'th 1-3 Dundee Utd
Brechin City 0-1 Queen of S'th	Queen of S'th 1-3 St. Mirren
Queen of S'th 4-2 Falkirk	Dundee Utd 2-3 Queen of S'th
Morton 1-2 Queen of S'th	Queen of S'th 3-3 Livingston
Queen of S'th 0-3 Livingston	Dunfermline 3-1 Queen of S'th
Dumbarton 2-2 Queen of South	Queen of S'th 2-2 Falkirk
Queen of S'th 0-0 Inverness CT	Queen of S'th 0-2 Inverness CT
Dunfermline 2-5 Queen of S'th	Morton 0-1 Queen of S'th
Queen of S'th 2-3 St. Mirren	Queen of S'th 3-0 Dundee Utd
Falkirk 3-2 Queen of S'th	Brechin City 1-5 Queen of S'th

QUEEN'S PARK

NICKNAME:	**The Spiders**
COLOURS:	**White and black**
GROUND:	**Hampden Park**
TELEPHONE No:	**0141 632 1275**
EMAIL:	**secretary@**
	queensparkfc.co.uk
WEBSITE:	**queensparkfc.co.uk**
CAPACITY:	**51,866**
RECORD ATT:	**95,772**
	(v Rangers, 1930).
	149,547 (for ground
	Scotland v England, 1937)
RECORD VICTORY:	**16-0 (v St Peter's, 1885)**
RECORD DEFEAT:	**0-9 (v Motherwell, 1930)**
MANAGER:	**Gus MacPherson**
PRESIDENT:	**Gerry Crawley**
MOST LEAGUE	
GOALS (1 SEASON):	**30, William Martin, 1937-38**

HONOURS

LEAGUE CHAMPIONSHIP: Division II – 1922-23. B Division – 1955-56. Second Division – 1980-81. Third Division – 1999-00. SCOTTISH CUP (10): 1874, 1875, 1876, 1880, 1881, 1882, 1884, 1886, 1890, 1893.

LEAGUE RESULTS 2017-2018

Arbroath 2-0 Queen's Park	Queen's Park 2-2 Albion Rovers
Queen's Park 2-5 Albion Rovers	Alloa Athletic 2-2 Queen's Park
Alloa 1-0 Queen's Park	Queen's Park 2-2 Stranraer
Queen's Park 2-2 Stranraer	Arbroath 2-1 Queen's Park
East Fife 0-1 Queen's Park	Queen's Park 1-4 Ayr United
Queen's Park 0-5 Raith Rovers	Queen's Park 1-3 Raith Rovers
Queen's Park 0-2 Ayr Utd	East Fife 0-2 Queen's Park
Airdrie 4-2 Queen's Park	Airdrieonians 2-1 Queen's Park
Queen's Park 1-1 Forfar Athletic	Queen's Park 2-2 Forfar Athletic
Albion Rovers 0-1 Queen's Park	Queen's Park 1-2 Alloa Athletic
Queen's Park 0-4 Alloa Athletic	Albion Rovers 1-1 Queen's Park
Stranraer 3-0 Queen's Park	Stranraer 2-3 Queen's Park
Queen's Park 0-2 Arbroath	Ayr United 4-0 Queen's Park
Raith Rovers 2-0 Queen's Park	Queen's Park 0-0 Airdrieonians
Queen's Park 2-1 East Fife	Queen's Park 2-3 East Fife
Ayr United 3 - 2 Queen's Park	Raith Rovers 2-0 Queen's Park
Queen's Park 1-1 Airdrieonians	Forfar Athletic 1-1 Queen's Park
Forfar Athletic 0-3 Queen's Park	Queen's Park 3-0 Arbroath

RAITH ROVERS

NICKNAME:	The Rovers
COLOURS:	White and navy blue
GROUND:	Stark's Park
TELEPHONE No:	01592 263514
EMAIL:	info@raithrovers.net
WEBSITE:	raithrovers.net
CAPACITY:	8475
RECORD ATT:	31,306 (v Hearts, 1953)
RECORD VICTORY:	10-1 (v Coldstream, 1954)
RECORD DEFEAT:	2-11 (v Morton, 1936)
MANAGER:	Barry Smith
CHAIRMAN:	Bill Clark
MOST LEAGUE	
GOALS (1 SEASON):	42, Norman Haywood, 1937-38

HONOURS

LEAGUE CHAMPIONS: First Division (2) – 1992-93, 1994-95. Second Division – 2002-03, 2008-09. Division II (4) – 1907-08, 1909-10 (shared), 1937-38, 1948-49. **LEAGUE CUP** – 1994-95. **CHALLENGE CUP** – 2013-14.

LEAGUE RESULTS 2017-2018

Alloa 1-1 Raith Rovers	Raith Rovers 2-1 Forfar Athletic
Raith Rovers 3-0 Stranraer	Raith Rovers 1-1 Ayr United
Raith Rovers 3-1 Forfar	Stranraer 1-0 Raith Rovers
East Fife 0-5 Raith Rovers	Alloa Athletic 0-0 Raith Rovers
Raith Rovers 2-1 Ayr Utd	Queen's Park 1-3 Raith Rovers
Queen's Park 0-5 Raith Rovers	Raith Rovers 3-1 Albion Rovers
Raith Rovers 2-0 Airdire	Raith Rovers 2-1 Airdrieonians
Albion Rovers 2-1 Raith Rovers	Albion Rovers 2-2 Raith Rovers
Raith Rovers 2-0 Arbroath	Raith Rovers 2-2 Arbroath
Forfar Athletic 1-1 Raith Rovers	Ayr United 3-0 Raith Rovers
Raith Rovers 1-0 East Fife	Forfar Athletic 2-1 Raith Rovers
Ayr United 3-0 Raith Rovers	Airdrieonians 1-2 Raith Rovers
Raith Rovers 2-0 Queen's Park	Raith Rovers 2-0 East Fife
Raith Rovers 2-1 Alloa Athletic	Raith Rovers 2-0 Albion Rovers
Airdrieonians 2-2 Raith Rovers	Arbroath 1-1 Raith Rovers
Arbroath 1-2 Raith Rovers	Raith Rovers 2-0 Queen's Park
Raith Rovers 3-0 Stranraer	Stranraer 0-3 Raith Rovers
East Fife 2-3 Raith Rovers	Raith Rovers 0-0 Alloa Athletic

RANGERS

NICKNAME:	**The Gers**
COLOURS:	**Blue, red and white**
GROUND:	**Ibrox Stadium**
TELEPHONE No:	**0871 702 1972**
EMAIL:	**webmail@rangers.co.uk**
WEBSITE:	**rangers.co.uk**
CAPACITY:	**51,082**
RECORD ATT:	**118,567 (v Celtic, 1939)**
RECORD VICTORY:	**14-2 (v Blairgowrie, 1934)**
RECORD DEFEAT:	**2-10 (v Airdrie, 1886)**
MANAGER:	**Steven Gerrard**
CHAIRMAN:	**Dave King**
MOST LEAGUE GOALS (1 SEASON):	**44, Sam English, 1931-32**
GOALS (OVERALL):	**355, Ally McCoist**

HONOURS

LEAGUE CHAMPIONSHIP (54): 1890-91 (shared), 1898-99, 1899-1900, 1900-01, 1901-02, 1910-11, 1911-12, 1912-13, 1917-18, 1919-20, 1920-21, 1922-23, 1923-24, 1924-25, 1926-27, 1927-28, 1928-29, 1929-30, 1930-31, 1932-33, 1933-34, 1934-35, 1936-37, 1938-39, 1946-47, 1948-49, 1949-50, 1952-53, 1955-56, 1956-57, 1958-59, 1960-61, 1962-63, 1963-64, 1974-75, 1975-76, 1977-78, 1986-87, 1988-89, 1989-90, 1990-91, 1991-92, 1992-93, 1993-94, 1994-95, 1995-96, 1996-97, 1998-99, 1999-00, 2002-03, 2004-05, 2008-09, 2009-10, 2010-11.
THIRD DIVISION: 2012-2013.
LEAGUE ONE: 2013-2014.
CHAMPIONSHIP: 2015-16

SCOTTISH CUP (33): 1894, 1897, 1898, 1903, 1928, 1930, 1932, 1934, 1935, 1936, 1948, 1949, 1950, 1953, 1960, 1962, 1963, 1964, 1966, 1973, 1976, 1978, 1979, 1981, 1992, 1993, 1996, 1999, 2000, 2002, 2003, 2008, 2009.
LEAGUE CUP (27): 1946-47, 1948-49, 1960-61, 1961-62, 1963-64, 1964-65, 1970-71, 1975-76, 1977-78, 1978-79, 1981-82, 1983-84, 1984-85, 1986-87, 1987-88, 1988-89, 1990-91, 1992-93, 1993-94, 1996-97, 1998-99, 2001-02, 2002-03, 2004-05, 2007-08, 2009-10, 2010-11.

CHALLENGE CUP: 2015-2016

EUROPEAN CUP-WINNERS' CUP: 1971-72.

DANIEL CANDEIAS

JAMES TAVERNIER

LEAGUE RESULTS 2017-2018

Motherwell 1-2 Rangers
Rangers 2-3 Hibernian
Rangers 0-0 Hearts
Ross County 1-3 Rangers
Rangers 4-1 Dundee
Patrick Thistle 2-2 Rangers
Rangers 0-2 Celtic
Hamilton 1-4 Rangers
St. Johnstone 0-3 Rangers
Rangers 1-1 Kilmarnock
Hearts 1-3 Rangers
Rangers 3-0 Partick Thistle
Rangers 0-2 Hamilton
Dundee 2-1 Rangers
Rangers 3-0 Aberdeen
Aberdeen 1-2 Rangers
Rangers 2-1 Ross County
Hibernian 1-2 Rangers
Rangers 1-3 St. Johnstone

Kilmarnock 2-1 Rangers
Rangers 2-0 Motherwell
Celtic 0-0 Rangers
Rangers 2-0 Aberdeen
Ross County 1-2 Rangers
Rangers 1-2 Hibernian
Partick Thistle 0-2 Rangers
Hamilton 3-5 Rangers
Rangers 2-0 Hearts
St. Johnstone 1-4 Rangers
Rangers 2-3 Celtic
Rangers 0-1 Kilmarnock
Motherwell 2-2 Rangers
Rangers 4-0 Dundee
Rangers 2-1 Hearts
Celtic 5-0 Rangers
Rangers 1-0 Kilmarnock
Aberdeen 1-1 Rangers
Hibernian 5-5 Rangers

ROSS COUNTY

NICKNAME:	The Staggies
COLOURS:	Navy blue, white and red
GROUND:	The Global Energy Stadium
TELEPHONE No:	01349 860860
EMAIL:	info@rosscountyfootballclub.co.uk
WEBSITE:	rosscountyfootballclub.co.uk
CAPACITY:	6540
RECORD ATT:	8000 (v Rangers, 1966)
RECORD VICTORY:	11-0 (v St Cuthbert's Wanderers, 1993)
RECORD DEFEAT:	1-10 (v Inverness Thistle)
MANAGERS:	Stuart Kettlewell/Steven Ferguson
CHAIRMAN:	Roy MacGregor
MOST LEAGUE GOALS (1 SEASON):	24, Andy Barrowman, 2007-08

HONOURS

LEAGUE CHAMPIONSHIP: First Division – 2011-12. Second Division – 2007-08. Third Division – 1998-99. CHALLENGE CUP (2): 2006-07, 2010-11. LEAGUE CUP – 2015-16

LEAGUE RESULTS 2017-2018

Dundee 1-2 Ross County	Hibernian 2-1 Ross County
Ross County 1-2 Aberdeen	Ross County 1-1 St. Johnstone
Motherwell 2-0 Ross County	Partick Thistle 2-0 Ross County
Ross County 1-3 Rangers	Motherwell 2-0 Ross County
Ross County 1-1 Patrick Thistle	Ross County 1-2 Rangers
Celtic 4-0 Ross County	Ross County 2-4 Aberdeen
Ross County 0-1 Hibernian	Dundee 1-4 Ross County
Kilmarnock 0-2 Ross County	Ross County 1-1 Hearts
Ross County 1-2 Hearts	St. Johnstone 2-0 Ross County
Ross County 2-1 Hamilton	Kilmarnock 3-2 Ross County
St. Johnstone 0-0 Ross County	Ross County 2-2 Hamilton
Aberdeen 2-1 Ross County	Celtic 3-0 Ross County
Ross County 3-2 Motherwell	Ross County 4-0 Partick Thistle
Ross County 0-1 Celtic	Ross County 1-1 Hibernian
Hearts 0-0 Ross County	Ross County 0-0 Motherwell
Ross County 0-2 Dundee	Hamilton 2-0 Ross County
Rangers 2-1 Ross County	Partick Thistle 1-1 Ross County
Ross County 2-2 Kilmarnock	Ross County 0-1 Dundee
Hamilton 3-2 Ross County	St. Johnstone 1-1 Ross County

ST JOHNSTONE

NICKNAME:	The Saints
COLOURS:	Blue and white
GROUND:	McDiarmid Park
TELEPHONE No:	01738 459090
EMAIL:	enquiries@ perthsaints.co.uk
WEBSITE:	perthstjohnstone fc.co.uk
CAPACITY:	10,673
RECORD ATT:	10,545 (v Dundee, 1999)
RECORD VICTORY:	9-0 (v Albion Rovers, 1946)
RECORD DEFEAT:	1-10 (v Third Lanark, 1903)
MANAGER:	Tommy Wright
CHAIRMAN:	Steve Brown
MOST LEAGUE GOALS (1 SEASON):	36, Jimmy Benson, 1931-32
GOALS (OVERALL):	140, John Brogan, 1977-83

HONOURS

LEAGUE CHAMPIONSHIP: First Division (4) – 1982-83, 1989-90, 1996-97, 2008-09. Division II (3) – 1923-24, 1959-60, 1962-63.
SCOTTISH CUP: 2013-14. CHALLENGE CUP: 2007-08.

LEAGUE RESULTS 2017-2018

Kilmarnock 1-2 St. Johnstone	Ross County 1-1 St. Johnstone
St. Johnstone 4-1 Motherwell	St. Johnstone 0-2 Dundee
St. Johnstone 1-0 Partick Thistle	St. Johnstone 1-3 Partick Thistle
Celtic 1-1 St. Johnstone	Hearts 1-0 St. Johnstone
St Johnstone 1-1 Hibernian	Motherwell 2-0 St. Johnstone
Dundee 3-2 St Johnstone	Celtic 0-0 St. Johnstone
St Johnstone 2-1 Hamilton	St. Johnstone 2-0 Ross County
Aberdeen 3-0 St Johnstone	St. Johnstone 1-4 Rangers
St. Johnstone 0-3 Rangers	Kilmarnock 2-0 St. Johnstone
Hearts 1-0 St. Johnstone	Dundee 0-4 St. Johnstone
St. Johnstone 0-0 Ross County	St. Johnstone 1-1 Hibernian
Partick Thistle 1-0 St. Johnstone	St. Johnstone 1-0 Hamilton
St. Johnstone 0-4 Celtic	Aberdeen 4-1 St. Johnstone
Hibernian 1-2 St. Johnstone	St. Johnstone 0-0 Motherwell
St. Johnstone 1-2 Kilmarnock	Dundee 2-1 St. Johnstone
Hamilton 0-1 St. Johnstone	St. Johnstone 1-1 Partick Thistle
St. Johnstone 0-3 Aberdeen	Motherwell 1-5 St. Johnstone
Rangers 1-3 St. Johnstone	Hamilton 1-2 St. Johnstone
St. Johnstone 0-0 Hearts	St. Johnstone 1-1 Ross County

ST MIRREN

NICKNAME:	The Buddies
COLOURS:	Black and white
GROUND:	The Simple Digital Arena
TELEPHONE No:	0141 889 2558
EMAIL:	info@stmirren.com
WEBSITE:	saintmirren.com
CAPACITY:	8023
RECORD ATT:	47,438 (v Celtic, 1949)
RECORD VICTORY:	15-0 (v Glasgow University, 1960)
RECORD DEFEAT	0-9 (v Rangers, 1897)
MANAGER:	Alan Stubbs
CHAIRMAN:	Gordon Scott
MOST LEAGUE	
GOALS (1 SEASON):	45, Dunky Walker, 1921-22
GOALS (OVERALL):	251, David McCrae

HONOURS

LEAGUE CHAMPIONS: First Division (3) – 1976-77, 1999-00, 2005-06. Division II – 1967-68. Championship 2017-18. SCOTTISH CUP (3): 1926, 1959, 1987. LEAGUE CUP: 2012-2013. CHALLENGE CUP – 2005-06.

LEAGUE RESULTS 2017-2018

St. Mirren 3-1 Falkirk	St. Mirren 2-0 Dundee United
Morton 4-1 St. Mirren	Morton 1-1 St. Mirren
Livingston 1-3 St. Mirren	St. Mirren 1-0 Inverness CT
St. Mirren 3-0 Dundee Utd	Dumbarton 0-2 St. Mirren
St Mirren 4-2 Inverness CT	Dunfermline 1-2 St. Mirren
Dunfermline 3-0 St Mirren	St. Mirren 2-0 Queen of S'th
St Mirren 3-1 Queen of S'th	Livingston 4-1 St. Mirren
St Mirren 2-1 Brechin City	St. Mirren 1-0 Brechin City
Dumbarton 0 -2 St. Mirren	St. Mirren 2-0 Dunfermline
Falkirk 0-0 St. Mirren	Queen of S'th 1-3 St. Mirren
St. Mirren 2-2 Morton	St. Mirren 5-0 Dumbarton
Dundee United 2-1 St. Mirren	Inverness CT 2-2 St. Mirren
Inverness CT 0-2 St. Mirren	Brechin City 0-1 St. Mirren
St. Mirren 3-1 Livingston	Dundee United 1-0 St. Mirren
St. Mirren 0-1 Dumbarton	St. Mirren 0-0 Livingston
Brechin City 1-2 St. Mirren	St. Mirren 1-2 Falkirk
St. Mirren 1-0 Dunfermline	St. Mirren 2-1 Morton
Queen of S'th 2-3 St. Mirren	Falkirk 1-0 St. Mirren

STENHOUSEMUIR

NICKNAME:	The Warriors
COLOURS:	Maroon and white
GROUND:	Ochilview Park
TELEPHONE No:	01324 562992
E-MAIL:	info@stenhousemuirfc.com
WEBSITE:	stenhousemuirfc.com
CAPACITY:	3645
RECORD ATT:	12,500 (v East Fife, 1950)
RECORD VICTORY:	9-2 (v Dundee United, 1937)
RECORD DEFEAT:	2-11 (v Dunfermline, 1930)
MANAGER:	Brown Ferguson
CHAIRMAN:	Gordon Thompson
MOST LEAGUE GOALS (1 SEASON):	32, Robert Taylor, 1925-26

HONOURS
CHALLENGE CUP: 1995-96.

LEAGUE RESULTS 2017-2018

Stenh'semuir 2-3 Stirling Albion	Stenh'semuir 1-4 Peterhead
Montrose 1-1 Stenh'semuir	Clyde 0-3 Stenh'semuir
Stenh'semuir 3-1 Peterhead	Elgin City 2-0 Stenh'semuir
Clyde 1-1 Stenh'semuir	Stenh'semuir 4-0 Berwick
Stenh'semuir 1-0 Cowdenbeath	Montrose 1-0 Stenh'semuir
Annan 1-1 Stenh'semuir	Stenh'semuir 1-0 Edinburgh City
Stenh'semuir 3-0 Berwick	Annan Athletic 2-0 Stenh'semuir
Stenh'semuir 3-0 Edinburgh City	Stenh'semuir 2-3 Clyde
Elgin City 2-0 Stenh'semuir	Peterhead 1-2 Stenh'semuir
Stirling Albion 1-2 Stenh'semuir	Stenh'semuir 1-2 Cowdenbeath
Stenh'semuir 1-1 Clyde	Stenh'semuir 0-2 Elgin City
Peterhead 2-3 Stenh'semuir	Cowdenbeath 1-1 Stenh'semuir
Stenh'semuir 0-1 Montrose	Edinburgh City 1-4 Stenh'semuir
Stenh'semuir 1-3 Annan Athletic	Stenh'semuir 3-2 Annan Athletic
Edinburgh City 1-2 Stenh'semuir	Berwick 0-0 Stenh'semuir
Cowdenbeath 1-1 Stenh'semuir	Stenh'semuir 0-2 Montrose
Stenh'semuir 4-1 Elgin City	Berwick 2-2 Stenh'semuir
Stenh'semuir 2-1 Stirling Albion	Stirling Albion 1-1 Stenh'semuir

STIRLING ALBION

NICKNAME:	The Binos
COLOURS:	Red and white
GROUND:	Forthbank Stadium
TELEPHONE No:	01786 450399
EMAIL:	office@stirling albionfc.co.uk
WEBSITE:	stirlingalbionfc.co.uk
CAPACITY:	3808
RECORD ATT:	26,400 (v Celtic, 1959, at Annfield)
RECORD VICTORY:	20-0 (v Selkirk, 1984)
RECORD DEFEAT:	0-9 (v Dundee United, 1967; v Ross County, 2010)
MANAGER:	Dave Mackay
CHAIRMAN:	Stuart Brown
MOST LEAGUE GOALS (1 SEASON:)	27, Joe Hughes, 1969-70

HONOURS

LEAGUE CHAMPIONS: Division II (4) – 1952-53, 1957-58, 1960-61, 1964-65. Second Division (4) – 1976-77, 1990-91, 1995-96, 2009-10.

LEAGUE RESULTS 2017-2018

Stenhousemuir 2-3 Stirling Albion	Peterhead 4-3 Stirling Albion
Stirling Albion 4-0 Berwick Rangers	Montrose 2-1 Stirling Albion
Stirling Albion 2-0 Edinburgh City	Stirling Albion 1-0 Cowdenbeath
Peterhead 2-4 Stirling Albion	Stirling Albion 3-1 Elgin City
Stirling Albion 2-3 Clyde	Cowdenbeath 1-2 Stirling Albion
Montrose 1-3 Stirling Albion	Stirling Albion 3-0 Annan Athletic
Stirling Albion 3-2 Annan	Stirling Albion 2-1 Clyde
Stirling Albion 2-2 Elgin City	Stirling Albion 0-1 Peterhead
Cowdenbeath 0-3 Stirling Albion	Berwick Rangers 0-1 Stirling Albion
Stirling Albion1-2 Stenhousemuir	Edinburgh City 2-2 Stirling Albion
Edinburgh City 1-2 Stirling Albion	Elgin City 0-2 Stirling Albion
Clyde 1-1 Stirling Albion	Stirling Albion 2-2 Cowdenbeath
Berwick Rangers 1-0 Stirling Albion	Stirling Albion 2-2 Edinburgh City
Stirling Albion 0-1 Peterhead	Elgin City 3-0 Stirling Albion
Annan Athletic 1-1 Stirling Albion	Stirling Albion 0-5 Montrose
Stirling Albion 0-1 Montrose	Clyde 2-1 Stirling Albion
Stenhousemuir 2-1 Stirling Albion	Annan Athletic 3-1 Stirling Albion
Stirling Albion 2-0 Berwick Rangers	Stirling Albion 1-1 Stenhousemuir

STRANRAER

NICKNAME: The Blues
COLOURS: Blue and white
GROUND: Stair Park
TELEPHONE No: 01776 703271
E-MAIL: secretary@
stranraerfc.org
WEBSITE: stranraerfc.org
CAPACITY: 6100
RECORD ATT: 6500 (v Rangers, 1948)
RECORD VICTORY: 9-0 (v St Cuthbert Wanderers, 2011)
RECORD DEFEAT: 1-11 (v Queen of the South, 1932)
MANAGER: Stevie Farrell
CHAIRMAN: Iain Dougan
**MOST LEAGUE
GOALS (1 SEASON):** 27, Derek Frye, 1976-77

HONOURS
LEAGUE CHAMPIONS: Second Division (2) – 1993-94, 1997-98.
Third Division – 2003-04. CHALLENGE CUP: 1996-97.

LEAGUE RESULTS 2017-2018

Stranraer 1-0 East Fife
Raith Rovers 3-0 Stranraer
Stranraer 3-4 Ayr Utd
Queen's Park 2-2 Stranraer
Stranraer 3-1 Airdrieonians
Albion Rovers 0-4 Stranraer
Stranraer 2-6 Arbroath
Forfar 1-1 Stranraer
Stranraer 2-0 Alloa
Ayr United 2-0 Stranraer
Stranraer 3-0 Queen's Park
Airdrieonians 2-0 Stranraer
Arbroath 1-2 Stranraer
East Fife 1-1 Stranraer
Stranraer 3-0 Forfar
Stranraer 2-2 Albion Rovers
Alloa Athletic 1-0 Stranraer
Raith Rovers 3-0 Stranraer

Stranraer 1-5 Ayr United
Queen's Park 2-2 Stranraer
Stranraer 3-2 Airdrieonians
Stranraer 1-0 Raith Rovers
Albion Rovers 1-3 Stranraer
Stranraer 0-2 East Fife
Forfar 5-1 Stranraer
Stranraer 1-4 Arbroath
Stranraer 1-0 Alloa Athletic
Stranraer 2-3 Albion Rovers
Airdrieonians 2-1 Stranraer
Stranraer 2-3 Queen's Park
Arbroath 2-3 Stranraer
Stranraer 2-0 Forfar
Alloa Athletic 0-1 Stranraer
Ayr United 1-2 Stranraer
Stranraer 0-3 Raith Rovers
East Fife 2-3 Stranraer

LEAGUE CHAMPIONS

YEAR	WINNERS
1890-91	RANGERS/ DUMBARTON
1891-92	DUMBARTON
1892-93	CELTIC
1893-94	CELTIC
1894-95	HEARTS
1895-96	CELTIC
1896-97	HEARTS
1897-98	CELTIC
1898-99	RANGERS
1899-1900	RANGERS
1900-01	RANGERS
1901-02	RANGERS
1902-03	HIBERNIAN
1903-04	THIRD LANARK
1904-05	CELTIC
1905-06	CELTIC
1906-07	CELTIC
1907-08	CELTIC
1908-09	CELTIC
1909-10	CELTIC
1910-11	RANGERS
1911-12	RANGERS
1912-13	RANGERS
1913-14	CELTIC
1914-15	CELTIC
1915-16	CELTIC
1916-17	CELTIC
1917-18	RANGERS
1918-19	CELTIC
1919-20	RANGERS
1920-21	RANGERS
1921-22	CELTIC
1922-23	RANGERS
1923-24	RANGERS
1924-25	RANGERS
1925-26	CELTIC
1926-27	RANGERS
1927-28	RANGERS
1928-29	RANGERS
1929-30	RANGERS

YEAR	WINNERS
1930-31	RANGERS
1931-32	MOTHERWELL
1932-33	RANGERS
1933-34	RANGERS
1934-35	RANGERS
1935-36	CELTIC
1936-37	RANGERS
1937-38	CELTIC
1938-39	RANGERS
NO CHAMPIONSHIP	
1946-47	RANGERS
1947-48	HIBERNIAN
1948-49	RANGERS
1949-50	RANGERS
1950-51	HIBERNIAN
1951-52	HIBERNIAN
1952-53	RANGERS
1953-54	CELTIC
1954-55	ABERDEEN
1955-56	RANGERS
1956-57	RANGERS
1957-58	HEARTS
1958-59	RANGERS
1959-60	HEARTS
1960-61	RANGERS
1961-62	DUNDEE
1962-63	RANGERS
1963-64	RANGERS
1964-65	KILMARNOCK
1965-66	CELTIC
1966-67	CELTIC
1967-68	CELTIC
1968-69	CELTIC
1969-70	CELTIC
1970-71	CELTIC
1971-72	CELTIC
1972-73	CELTIC
1973-74	CELTIC
1974-75	RANGERS
1975-76	RANGERS

PREMIER DIVISION

YEAR	WINNERS
1976-77	CELTIC
1977-78	RANGERS
1978-79	CELTIC
1979-80	ABERDEEN
1980-81	CELTIC
1981-82	CELTIC
1982-83	DUNDEE UNITED
1983-84	ABERDEEN
1984-85	ABERDEEN
1985-86	CELTIC
1986-87	RANGERS
1987-88	CELTIC
1988-89	RANGERS
1989-90	RANGERS
1990-91	RANGERS
1991-92	RANGERS
1992-93	RANGERS
1993-94	RANGERS
1994-95	RANGERS
1995-96	RANGERS
1996-97	RANGERS

YEAR	WINNERS
1997-98	CELTIC
1998-99	RANGERS
1999-00	RANGERS
2000-01	CELTIC
2001-02	CELTIC
2002-03	RANGERS
2003-04	CELTIC
2004-05	RANGERS
2005-06	CELTIC
2006-07	CELTIC
2007-08	CELTIC
2008-09	RANGERS
2009-10	RANGERS
2010-11	RANGERS
2011-12	CELTIC
2012-13	CELTIC
2013-14	CELTIC
2014-15	CELTIC
2015-16	CELTIC
2016-17	CELTIC
2017-18	CELTIC

CELTIC celebrate winning their seventh title in a row Pic: SNS

PROMOTION/RELEGATION

1921-1922	**Promoted**	Alloa
	Relegated	Dumbarton, Queen's Park, Clydebank
1922-23	**Promoted**	Queen's Park, Clydebank
	Relegated	Albion Rovers, Alloa
1923-24	**Promoted**	St Johnstone, Cowdenbeath
	Relegated	Clyde, Clydebank
1924-25	**Promoted**	Dundee Utd, Clydebank
	Relegated	Ayr United, Third Lanark
1925-26	**Promoted**	Dunfermline, Clyde
	Relegated	Raith Rovers, Clydebank
1926-27	**Promoted**	Bo'ness, Raith Rovers
	Relegated	Morton, Dundee United
1927-28	**Promoted**	Ayr United, Third Lanark
	Relegated	Bo'ness, Dunfermline
1928-29	**Promoted**	Dundee United, Morton
	Relegated	Third Lanark, Raith Rovers
1929-30	**Promoted**	Leith Ath, East Fife
	Relegated	Dundee United, St Johnstone
1930-31	**Promoted**	Third Lanark, Dundee United
	Relegated	Hibernian, East Fife
1931-32	**Promoted**	East Stirling, St Johnstone
	Relegated	Dundee United, Leith Ath
1932-33	**Promoted**	Hibernian, Queen of the South
	Relegated	Morton, East Stirling
1933-34	**Promoted**	Albion Rovers, Dunfermline
	Relegated	Third Lanark, Cowdenbeath
1934-35	**Promoted**	Third Lanark, Arbroath
	Relegated	St Mirren, Falkirk
1935-36	**Promoted**	Falkirk, St Mirren
	Relegated	Airdrie, Ayr United
1936-37	**Promoted**	Ayr United, Morton
	Relegated	Dunfermline, Albion Rovers
1937-38	**Promoted**	Raith Rovers, Albion Rovers
	Relegated	Dundee, Morton
1938-39	**Promoted**	Cowdenbeath, Alloa
	Relegated	Queen's Park, Raith Rovers
1946-47	**Promoted**	Dundee, Airdrie
	Relegated	Kilmarnock, Hamilton
1947-48	**Promoted**	East Fife, Albion Rovers
	Relegated	Airdrie, Queen's Park
1948-49	**Promoted**	Raith Rovers, Stirling Albion
	Relegated	Morton, Albion Rovers
1949-50	**Promoted**	Morton, Airdrie
	Relegated	Queen of the South, Stirling Alb
1950-51	**Promoted**	Queen of the South, Stirling Alb
	Relegated	Clyde, Falkirk
1951-52	**Promoted**	Clyde, Falkirk
	Relegated	Morton, Stirling Albion
1952-53	**Promoted**	Stirling Albion, Hamilton Accies
	Relegated	Motherwell, Third Lanark
1953-54	**Promoted**	Motherwell, Kilmarnock
	Relegated	Airdrie, Hamilton Accies
1954-55	**Promoted**	Airdrie, Dunfermline
	Relegated	Motherwell, Stirling Albion
1955-56	**Promoted**	Queen's Park, Ayr United
	Relegated	Clyde, Stirling Albion

1956-57	**Promoted**	Clyde, Third Lanark
	Relegated	Dunfermline, Ayr United
1957-58	**Promoted**	Stirling Albion, Dunfermline
	Relegated	East Fife, Queen's Park
1958-59	**Promoted**	Ayr United, Arbroath
	Relegated	Falkirk, Queen of the South
1959-60	**Promoted**	St Johnstone, Dundee United
	Relegated	Stirling Albion, Arbroath
1960-61	**Promoted**	Stirling Albion, Falkirk
	Relegated	Clyde, Ayr United
1961-62	**Promoted**	Clyde, Queen of the South
	Relegated	St Johnstone, Stirling Albion
1962-63	**Promoted**	St Johnstone, East Stirling
	Relegated	Clyde, Raith Rovers
1963-64	**Promoted**	Morton, Clyde
	Relegated	Queen of the South, East Stirling
1964-65	**Promoted**	Stirling Albion, Hamilton Accies
	Relegated	Airdrie, Third Lanark
1965-66	**Promoted**	Ayr United, Airdrie
	Relegated	Morton, Hamilton Accies
1966-67	**Promoted**	Morton, Raith Rovers
	Relegated	St Mirren, Ayr United
1967-68	**Promoted**	St Mirren, Arbroath
	Relegated	Motherwell, Stirling Albion
1968-69	**Promoted**	Motherwell, Ayr United
	Relegated	Falkirk, Arbroath
1969-70	**Promoted**	Falkirk, Cowdenbeath
	Relegated	Raith Rovers, Partick Thistle
1970-71	**Promoted**	Partick Thistle, East Fife
	Relegated	St Mirren, Cowdenbeath
1971-72	**Promoted**	Dumbarton, Arbroath
	Relegated	Clyde, Dunfermline
1972-73	**Promoted**	Clyde, Dunfermline
	Relegated	Kilmarnock, Airdrie
1973-74	**Promoted**	Airdrie, Kilmarnock
	Relegated	East Fife, Falkirk

1974-75 Leagues reformed into Premier, First and Second Divisions

1975-76	**Promoted to Premier** – Kilmarnock, Partick Th
	Relegated to First – Dundee, St Johnstone
	Promoted to First – Clydebank, Raith Rovers
	Relegated to Second – Clyde, Dunfermline
1976-77	**Promoted to Premier** – St Mirren, Clydebank
	Relegated to First – Hearts, Kilmarnock
	Promoted to First – Alloa, Stirling Albion
	Relegated to Second – Falkirk, Raith Rovers
1977-78	**Promoted to Premier** – Morton, Hearts
	Relegated to First – Ayr United, Clydebank
	Promoted to First – Clyde, Raith Rovers
	Relegated to Second – Alloa Athletic, East Fife
1978-79	**Promoted to Premier** – Dundee, Kilmarnock
	Relegated to First – Hearts, Motherwell
	Promoted to First – Berwick Ran, Dunfermline
	Relegated to Second – Montrose, QOS
1979-80	**Promoted to Premier** – Hearts, Airdrie
	Relegated to First – Dundee, Hibernian
	Promoted to First – East Stirling, Falkirk
	Relegated to Second – Arbroath, Clyde
1980-81	**Promoted to Premier** – Dundee, Hibernian

Relegated to First – Hearts, Kilmarnock
Promoted to First – Queen's Park, QOS

1981-82
Relegated to Second – Berwick R, Stirling Alb
Promoted to Premier – Motherwell, Kilmarnock
Relegated to First – Airdrie, Partick Thistle
Promoted to First – Clyde, Alloa Athletic

1982-83
Relegated to Second – QOS, East Stirling
Promoted to Premier – St Johnstone, Hearts
Relegated to First – Kilmarnock, Morton
Promoted to First – Brechin, Meadowbank

1983-84
Relegated to Second – Queen's Pk, Dunf'line
Promoted to Premier – Dumbarton, Morton
Relegated to First – Motherwell, St Johnstone
Promoted to First – East Fife, Forfar

1984-85
Relegated to Second – Alloa, Raith Rovers
Promoted to Premier – Motherwell, Clydebank
Relegated to First — Dumbarton, Morton
Promoted to First — Montrose, Alloa Athletic

1985-86
Relegated to Second – M'dowbank, St Johnstone
Promoted to Premier – Hamilton Accies, Falkirk
No relegation to First – league reorganisation
Promoted to First – Dunfermline, QOS

1986-87
Relegated to Second – Ayr United, Alloa
Promoted to Premier – Morton, Dunfermline Ath
Relegated to First – Clydebank, Hamilton Accies
Promoted to First – Meadowbank Th, Raith Rovers

1987-88
Relegated to Second – Brechin, Montrose
Promoted to Premier – Hamilton Accies
Relegated to First – Falkirk, Dunfermline, Morton
Promoted to First – Ayr United, St Johnstone

1988-89
Relegated to Second – East Fife, Dumbarton
Promoted to Premier – Dunfermline Ath
Relegated to First – Hamilton Accies
Promoted to First – Albion Rovers, Alloa Ath

1989-90
Relegated to Second – QOS, Kilmarnock
Promoted to Premier – St Johnstone
Relegated to First – Dundee
Promoted to First – Brechin, Kilmarnock

1990-91
Relegated to Second – Alloa Ath, Albion Rovers
Promoted to Premier – Falkirk, Airdrie
No relegation to First
Promoted to First – Stirling Albion, Montrose

1991-92
Relegated to Second – Brechin, Clyde
Promoted to Premier – Dundee, Partick Thistle
Relegated to First – Dunfermline Ath, St Mirren
Promoted to First – Dumbarton, Cowdenbeath

1992-93
Relegated to Second – Montrose, Forfar
Promoted to Premier – Raith Rov, Kilmarnock
Relegated to First – Airdrie, Falkirk
Promoted to First – Clyde, Brechin

1993-94
Relegated to Second – Cowdenbeath, Meadowb'k
Promoted to Premier – Falkirk
Relegated to First – St Johnstone, Raith Rovers,
Dundee
Promoted to First – Stranraer
Relegated to Second – Dumbarton, Stirling Alb,
Clyde, Morton, Brechin
Relegated to Third – Alloa, Forfar

East Stirling, Montrose, Queen's Park, Arbroath
Albion Rovers, Cowdenbeath
Leagues reformed into Premier, First, Second and Third Divisions

1994-95   **Promoted to Premier** – Raith Rovers
Relegated to First – Dundee United
Promoted to First – Morton, Dumbarton
Relegated to Second – Ayr United, Stranraer
Relegated to Third – Meadowbank, Brechin City

1995-96   **Promoted to Premier** – Dunfermline, Dundee Utd
Relegated to First – Falkirk, Partick Thistle
Promoted to First – Stirling Albion, East Fife
Relegated to Second – Dumbarton, Hamilton
Promoted to Second – Livingston, Brechin C
Relegated to Third – Forfar, Montrose

1996-97   **Promoted to Premier** – St Johnstone
Relegated to First – Raith Rovers
Promoted to First – Ayr United, Hamilton Accies
Relegated to Second – Clydebank, East Fife
Promoted to Second – Inverness CT, Forfar
Relegated to Third – Dumbarton, Berwick Rangers

1997-98   **Promoted to Premier** – Dundee
Relegated to First – Hibs
Promoted to First – Stranraer, Clydebank
Relegated to Second – Partick Thistle, Stirling Alb
Promoted to Second – Alloa, Arbroath
Relegated to Third – Stenhousemuir, Brechin

1998-99   **Promoted to Premier** – Hibs
Relegated to First – Dunfermline
Promoted to First – Livingston, Inverness CT
Relegated to Second – Hamilton, Stranraer
Promoted to Second – Ross Co, Stenhousemuir
Relegated to Third – East Fife, Forfar Athletic

1999-00   **Promoted to Premier** – St Mirren, Dunfermline
Relegated to First – No relegation
Promoted to First – Clyde, Alloa, Ross County
Relegated to Second – Clydebank
Promoted to Second – Queen's Pk, Berwick Forfar
Relegated to Third – Hamilton Accies
New league entrants – Elgin City, Peterhead
Relegated to Second – Clydebank
New league entrants – Elgin City, Peterhead

2000-01   **Promoted to Premier** – Livingston
Relegated to First – St Mirren
Promoted to First – Partick Thistle, Arbroath
Relegated to Second – Morton, Alloa
Promoted to Second – Hamilton, Cowdenbeath
Relegated to Third – Queen's Park, Stirling Albion

2001-02   **Promoted to Premier** – Partick Thistle
Relegated to First – St Johnstone
Promoted to First – Queen of the South, Alloa
Relegated to Second – Raith Rovers
Promoted to Second – Brechin, Dumbarton
Relegated to Third – Morton

2002-03   **Promoted to Premier** – No promotion
Relegated to First – No relegation
Promoted to First – Raith Rovers, Brechin City
Relegated to Second – Alloa, Arbroath
Promoted to Second – Morton, East Fife
Relegated to Third – Stranraer, Cowdenbeath

2003-04   **Promoted to Premier** – Inverness Caley Thistle
Relegated to First – Partick Thistle
Promoted to First – Airdrie United, Hamilton Accies

	Relegated to Second – Brechin City, Ayr United
	Promoted to Second – Stranraer, Stirling Albion
	Relegated to Third – Stenhousemuir, East Fife
2004-05	**Promoted to Premier** – Falkirk
	Relegated to First – Dundee
	Promoted to First – Brechin, Stranraer
	Relegated to Second – Partick, Raith Rovers
	Promoted to Second – Gretna, Peterhead
	Relegated to Third – Arbroath, Berwick Rangers
2005-06	**Promoted to Premier** – St Mirren
	Relegated to First – Livingston
	Promoted to First – Gretna, Partick Thistle (play-off)
	Relegated to Second – Stranraer (play-off), Brechin
	Promoted to Second – Cowdenbeath
	Relegated to Third – Dumbarton
2006-07	**Promoted to Premier** – Gretna
	Relegated to First – Dunfermline
	Promoted to First – Morton, Stirling (play-off)
	Relegated to Second – Ross Co, Airdrie (play-off)
	Promoted to Second – Berwick, Q Park (play-off)
	Relegated to Third – Forfar, Stranraer (play-off)
2007-08	**Promoted to Premier** – Hamilton
	Relegated to First – Gretna
	Promoted to First – Ross County
	Relegated to Second – Stirling
	Promoted to Second – East Fife, Arbroath (play-off)
	Relegated to Third – Berwick, Cowdenbeath (play-off)
2008-09	**Promoted to Premier** – St Johnstone
	Relegated to First – Inverness CT
	Promoted to First – Raith Rovers, Ayr Utd (play-off)
	Relegated to Second – Clyde, Airdrie Utd (play-off)
	Promoted to Second – Dumbarton, Stenh'semuir (play-off)
	Relegated to Third – Stranraer, Queen's Pk (play-off)
2009-10	**Promoted to Premier** – Inverness CT
	Relegated to First – Falkirk
	Promoted to First – Stirling, Cowdenbeath (play-off)
	Relegated to Second – Ayr United, Airdrie United (play-off)
	Promoted to Second – Livingston, Forfar Athletic (play-off)
	Relegated to Third – Clyde, Arbroath (play-off)
2010-11	**Promoted to Premier** – Dunfermline Athletic
	Relegated to First – Hamilton Accies
	Promoted to First – Livingston, Ayr (play-off)
	Relegated to Second – Stirling, Cowdenbeath (play-off)
	Promoted to Second – Arbroath, Albion Rovers (play-off)
	Relegated to Third – Peterhead, Alloa (play-off)
2011-12	**Promoted to Premier** – Ross County
	Relegated to First – Dunfermline Athletic
	Promoted to First – Cowdenbeath, Dumbarton (play-off)
	Relegated to Second – Queen of Sth, Ayr United (play-off)
	Promoted to Second – Alloa
	Relegated to Third – Stirling
2012-13	**Promoted to Premier** – Partick Thistle
	Relegated to First – Dundee
	Promoted to First – Queen of South, Alloa
	Relegated to Second – Airdrie United, Dunfermline
	Promoted to Second – Rangers
	Relegated to Third – Albion Rovers
	Leagues reformed into Premiership, Championship, League One and League Two.
2013-14	**Promoted to Premiership** – Dundee, Hamilton (play-off)
	Relegated to Championship – Hearts, Hibernian (play-off)
	Promoted to Championship – Rangers
	Relegated to League One – Morton
	Promoted to League One – Peterhead, Stirling (play-off)
	Relegated to League Two – Arbroath, East Fife (play-off)

2014-15	**Promoted to Premiership** – Hearts
	Relegated to Premiership – St Mirren
	Promoted to Championship – Morton
	Relegated to League One – Cowdenbeath
	Promoted to League One – Albion Rovers
	Relegated to League Two – Stirling Albion
2015-16	**Promoted to Premiership** – Rangers
	Relegated to Premiership – Dundee United
	Promoted to Championship – Dunfermline
	Relegated to League One – Alloa Athletic
	Promoted to League One – East Fife
	Relegated to League Two – Forfar
	Promoted to League Two – Edinburgh City
	Relegated to Lowland League – East Stirlingshire
2016-17	**Promoted to Premiership** – Hibernian
	Relegated to Championship – Inverness CT
	Promoted to Championship – Livingston, Brechin City
	Relegated to League One – Ayr United, Raith Rovers
	Promoted to League One – Arbroath, Forfar
	Relegated to League Two – Stenhousemuir, Peterhead
2017-18	**Promoted to Premiership** – St Mirren, Livingston
	Relegated to Championship – Partick Thistle, Ross County
	Promoted to Championship – Ayr United, Alloa
	Relegated to League One – Brechin City, Dumbarton
	Promoted to League One – Montrose, Stenhousemuir
	Relegated to League Two – Queen's Park, Albion Rovers

SCOTTISH COMMUNITIES LEAGUE CUP 2017-2018

FIRST ROUND: Ayr United 1 - 0 Kilmarnock; Berwick Rangers 0 - 1 Morton; Clyde 2 - 1 Annan Athletic; Cowdenbeath 4 - 2 Buckie Thistle; Dundee United 2 - 0 Raith Rovers; Dunfermline 6 - 0 Elgin City; East Kilbride 1 - 3 Hamilton Accies; Falkirk 4 - 1 Stirling Albion; Hibernian 4 - 0 Montrose; Inverness CT 3 - 0 Brechin City; Livingston 1 - 1 Partick Thistle (Livingston win 3-1 on penalties); Peterhead 1 - 0 East Fife; Queen's Park 1 - 5 Motherwell; Ross County 2 - 0 Alloa Athletic; Stenhousemuir 1 - 3 Queen of South (Stranraer 1 - 4 St Mirren; Airdrieonians 3 - 1 Stranraer Albion Rovers 1 - 1 Stenhousemuir (Stenhousemuir win 3-2 on penalties); Alloa Athletic 1 - 1 Arbroath (Arbroath win 6-5 on penalties); Brechin City 1 - 1 Forfar Athletic (Brechin City win 4-3 on penalties); Dumbarton 1 - 3 Ayr United; East Fife 0 - 0 Dunfermline (Dunfermline win 9-8 on penalties); Edinburgh City 2 - 2 Berwick Rangers (Edinburgh City win 4-2 on penalties); Elgin City 0 - 1 Hearts; Kilmarnock 4 - 2 Clyde; Montrose 0 - 6 Ross County; Morton 2 - 2 Queen's Park (Morton win 4-2 on penalties); Queen of South 0 - 2 East Kilbride (East Kilbride win 4-1 on penalties); Raith Rovers 1 - 2 Dundee; St Mirren 0 - 1 Livingston; Stirling Albion 0 - 0 Inverness CT (Inverness CT win 2-0 on penalties); Buckie Thistle 0 - 3 Dundee United; Ross County 0 - 3 Hibernian (Ross County win 5-3 on penalties); Annan Athletic 0 - 2 Kilmarnock; Arbroath 4 - 0 Montrose; Clyde 2 - 1 Dumbarton; Dundee 2 - 0 Buckie Thistle; Dunfermline 5 - 1 Peterhead; East Kilbride 2 - 5 Albion Rovers; Forfar Athletic 1 - 3 Stirling Albion; Hamilton Accies 1 - 1 Queen of South (Hamilton Accies win 6-5 on penalties); Hearts 3 - 0 East Fife; Inverness CT 0 - 2 Falkirk; Livingston 2 - 0 Airdrieonians; Motherwell 4 - 0 Morton; Partick Thistle 5 - 0 St Mirren; Queen's Park 3 - 0 Edinburgh City; Dundee United 4 - 1 Cowdenbeath; Airdrieonians 1 - 2 Partick Thistle; Albion Rovers 4 - 4 Hamilton Accies (Albion Rovers win 4-2 on penalties); Ayr United 5 - 1 Clyde; Berwick Rangers 2 - 3 Queen's Park; Buckie Thistle 1 - 6 Raith Rovers; Dumbarton 0 - 0 Annan Athletic (Annan Athletic win 4-3 on penalties); East Fife 3 - 2 Elgin City; Edinburgh City 1 - 2 Motherwell; Falkirk 4 - 0 Forfar Athletic; Hibernian 6 - 1 Arbroath; Montrose 2 - 1 Alloa Athletic; Peterhead 2 - 1 Hearts; Stenhousemuir 1 - 2 East Fife; Stirling Albion 2 - 0 Brechin City; Stranraer 2 - 4 Livingston; Cowdenbeath 0 - 3 Dundee; Dundee 1 - 1 Dundee United (Dundee United win 4-3 on penalties); Alloa Athletic 0 - 3 Hibernian; Annan Athletic 1 - 6 Ayr United; Arbroath 0 - 0 Ross County (Ross County win 5-4 on penalties); Brechin City 0 - 3 Falkirk; Elgin City 0 - 3 Peterhead; Forfar Athletic 1 - 2 Inverness CT; Hamilton Accies 3 - 0 Stenhousemuir; Hearts 2 - 2 Dunfermline (Dunfermline win 3-1 on penalties); Kilmarnock 3 - 0 Dumbarton; Morton 5 - 0 Edinburgh City; Motherwell 1 - 0 Berwick Rangers; Partick Thistle 1 - 0 Stranraer; Queen of South 2 - 2 Albion Rovers (Queen of South win 4-3 on penalties); Raith Rovers 0 - 0 St Mirren 5 - 0 Airdrieonians; Dundee 1 - 1 Dundee United (Dundee Utd won 4-3 on penalties)

SECOND ROUND: Celtic 5 - 0 Kilmarnock; Dundee 1 - 2 Livingston; Hibernian 5 - 0 Ayr United; St. Johnstone 0 - 3 Partick Thistle; Dundee 2 - 1 Dundee United; Hamilton 0 - 1 Aberdeen; Rangers 6 - 0 Dunfermline Ross County 2 - 3 Motherwell

QUARTER FINAL: Hibernian 3 - 2 Livingston; Partick Thistle 1 - 3 Rangers; Dundee 0 - 4 Celtic and Motherwell 3 - 0 Aberdeen; **SEMI FINAL** Hibernian 2 - 4 Celtic and Rangers 2 Motherwell

FINAL Motherwell 0 - 2 Celtic

LEAGUE CUP WINNERS

1946-47	RANGERS	4	Aberdeen	0
1947-48	EAST FIFE	4	Falkirk	1

(after 0-0 draw)

1948-49	RANGERS	2	Raith Rovers	0
1949-50	EAST FIFE	3	Dunfermline	0
1950-51	MOTHERWELL	3	Hibernian	0
1951-52	DUNDEE	3	Rangers	2
1952-53	DUNDEE	2	Kilmarnock	0
1953-54	EAST FIFE	3	Partick Thistle	2
1954-55	HEARTS	4	Motherwell	2
1955-56	ABERDEEN	2	St Mirren	1
1956-57	CELTIC	3	Partick Thistle	0
1957-58	CELTIC	7	Rangers	1
1958-59	HEARTS	5	Partick Thistle	1
1959-60	HEARTS	2	Third Lanark	1
1960-61	RANGERS	2	Kilmarnock	0
1961-62	RANGERS	3	Hearts	1

(after 1-1 draw)

1962-63	HEARTS	1	Kilmarnock	0
1963-64	RANGERS	5	Morton	0
1964-65	RANGERS	2	Celtic	1
1965-66	CELTIC	2	Rangers	1
1966-67	CELTIC	1	Rangers	0
1967-68	CELTIC	5	Dundee	3
1968-69	CELTIC	6	Hibs	2
1969-70	CELTIC	1	St Johnstone	0
1970-71	RANGERS	1	Celtic	0
1971-72	PARTICK THISTLE	4	Celtic	1
1972-73	HIBS	2	Celtic	1
1973-74	DUNDEE	1	Celtic	0
1974-75	CELTIC	6	Hibs	3
1975-76	RANGERS	1	Celtic	0
1976-77	ABERDEEN	2	Celtic	1

(after extra time)

1977-78	RANGERS	2	Celtic	1

(after extra time)

1978-79	RANGERS	2	Aberdeen	1
1979-80	DUNDEE UNITED	3	Aberdeen	0

(after 0-0 draw)

1980-81	DUNDEE UNITED	3	Dundee	0
1981-82	RANGERS	2	Dundee United	1
1982-83	CELTIC	2	Rangers	1
1983-84	RANGERS	3	Celtic	2

(after extra time)

1984-85	RANGERS	1	Dundee United	0
1985-86	ABERDEEN	3	Hibernian	0
1986-87	RANGERS	2	Celtic	1
1987-88	RANGERS	3	Aberdeen	3

(after extra time, Rangers won 5-3 on penalties)

1988-89	RANGERS	3	Aberdeen	2
1989-90	ABERDEEN	2	Rangers	1

(after extra time)

1990-91	RANGERS	2	Celtic	1

(after extra time)

1991-92	HIBERNIAN	2	Dunfermline	0
1992-93	RANGERS	2	Aberdeen	1

(after extra time)

1993-94	RANGERS	2	Hibernian	1
1994-95	Celtic	2	RAITH ROVERS	2

(after extra time, Raith Rovers won 6-5 on penalties)

1995-96	ABERDEEN	2	Dundee	0
1996-97	RANGERS	4	Hearts	3
1997-98	CELTIC	3	Dundee United	0
1998-99	RANGERS	2	St Johnstone	1
1999-00	CELTIC	2	Aberdeen	0
2000-01	CELTIC	3	Kilmarnock	0
2001-02	RANGERS	4	Ayr United	0
2002-03	RANGERS	2	Celtic	1
2003-04	LIVINGSTON	2	Hibernian	0
2004-05	RANGERS	5	Motherwell	1
2005-06	CELTIC	3	Dunfermline	0
2006-07	HIBERNIAN	5	Kilmarnock	1
2007-08	RANGERS	2	Dundee United	2

(after extra time, Rangers won 3-2 on penalties)

2008-09	CELTIC	0	Rangers	0

(after extra time, Celtic won 2-0)

2009-10	RANGERS	1	St Mirren	0
2010-11	RANGERS	2	Celtic	1

(after extra time)

2011-12	KILMARNOCK	1	Celtic	0
2012-13	ST MIRREN	3	Hearts	2
2013-14	ABERDEEN	0	Inverness CT	0

(after extra time, Aberdeen won 4-2 on penalties)

2014-15	CELTIC	2	Dundee United	0
2015-16	ROSS COUNTY	2	Hibernian	1
2016-17	CELTIC	3	Aberdeen	0
2017-18	CELTIC	2	Motherwell	0

SPFL PLAY-OFFS

LEAGUE TWO PLAY-OFF FINAL FIRST LEG

Cove Rangers 0-0 Cowdenbeath

LEAGUE TWO PLAY-OFF FINAL SECOND LEG

Cowdenbeath 3-2 Cove Rangers

(Agg 3-2, Cowdenbeath stay in League Two)

LEAGUE ONE PLAY-OFF SEMI-FINAL FIRST LEG

Stenhousemuir 1-1 Queen's Park
Stirling Albion 0-1 Peterhead

LEAGUE ONE PLAY-OFF SEMI-FINAL SECOND LEG

Queen's Park 1-2 Stenhousemuir
Peterhead 3-0 Stirling Albion

LEAGUE ONE PLAY-OFF FINAL

Stenhousemuir 2-0 Peterhead
Peterhead 1-0 Stenhousemuir

(Stenhousemuir win 2-1 on agg and promotion to League One)

CHAMPIONSHIP PLAY-OFF SEMI-FINAL FIRST LEG

Alloa 2-0 Raith Rovers
Arbroath 1-2 Dumbarton

CHAMPIONSHIP PLAY-OFF SEMI-FINAL SECOND LEG

Raith Rovers 1-2 Alloa Athletic

(Alloa win 4-1 on aggregate)

Dumbarton 1-1 Arbroath

(Dumbarton win 3-2 on aggregate)

CHAMPIONSHIP PLAY-OFF FINAL

Alloa 0-1 Dumbarton
Dumbarton 0-2 Alloa

(Alloa win promotion to Championship and Dumbarton are relegated)

PREMIERSHIP PLAY-OFF QUARTER FINAL

Dundee United 2-1 Dunfermline
Dunfermline 0-0 Dundee United

PREMIERSHIP PLAY-OFF SEMI-FINAL

Dundee United 2-3 Livingston
Livingston 1-1 Dundee United

PREMIERSHIP PLAY-OFF FINAL

Livingston 2-1 Partick Thistle
Partick Thistle 0-1 Livingston

(Livingston win 3-1 on agg and promotion to the Premiership and Partick Thistle are relegated)

IRN BRU CUP 2017-2018

FIRST ROUND

Dumbarton 2-1 Rangers U20; Dundee U20 2-4 Alloa Athletic
East Stirlingshire 1-5 Ayr United; Motherwell U20 2-1 Queen's
Park; Aberdeen U20 1-0 St Johnstone U20; Albion Rovers 0-3
Spartans; Annan Athletic 3-1 Celtic U20; Buckie Thistle 2-1
Brechin City; Clyde 2-3 Stranraer; Dundee Utd 2-0 Cowden-
beath; Dunfermline 2-0 Arbroath; East Fife 0-2 Peterhead;
Formartine 2-3 Hearts U20; Hamilton Accies U20 1-0 Edin-
burgh City; Hibernian U20 1-2 Elgin City; Kilmarnock U20 0-2
Berwick Rangers; Morton 0-2 Livingston; Patrick Thistle U20
6-1 Stirling University Queen of the South 4-0 Airdrie Raith
Rovers 3-0 Brora Rangers Ross County U20 2-1 Forfar Ath-
letic St Mirren 2-1 East Kilbride Stenhousemuir 0-2 Cove
Rangers and Stirling Albion 1-3 Montrose

SECOND ROUND

The New Saints 1-1 Livingston (The New Saints win 6-5 on
penalties); Aberdeen U20 2-4 Inverness CT; Berwick
Rangers 0-5 Queen of the South; Buckie Thistle 0-3 Dunfer-
mline; Crusaders FC 3-2 Motherwell U20; Dumbarton 2-1 Con-
nah's Quay; Dundee Utd 3-1 Alloa Athletic; Elgin City 2-0 Bray
Wanderers; Hamilton Accies U20 1-2 Cove Rangers; Peter-
head 2-0 Annan Athletic; Raith Rovers 4-0 Ross County U20;
Sligo Rovers 1-2 Falkirk; Spartans 1-2 Linfield; St Mirren 3-1
Hearts U20; Stranraer 2-0 Patrick Thistle U20 and Ayr Utd 1-1
Montrose (Montrose win 6-5 on penalties)

THIRD ROUND

Cove Rangers 0-3 Crusaders FC; Dundee Utd 1-0 Linfield;
Falkirk 2-0 Dunfermline; Inverness CT 3-0 Peterhead; Montrose
1-2 Queen of the South; St Mirren 1-3 Raith Rovers; The New
Saints 4-0 Elgin City and Dumbarton 2-1 Stranraer

QUARTER FINALS

The New Saints 0-0 Queen of South (The New Saints win 4-3
on penalties): Dumbarton 2-0 Raith Rovers; Dundee United 1-2
Crusaders FC and Inverness CT 1-0 Falkirk

SEMI FINALS

Inverness CT 3-2 Crusaders FC
The New Saints 1-2 Dumbarton

FINAL

Dumbarton 0-1 Inverness CT

WILLIAM HILL SCOTTISH CUP 2017-2018

FIRST ROUND

Banks O'Dee 4-0 Huntly; Brora Rangers 5-0 Girvan; BSC Glasgow 1-0 Dalbeattie Star; Civil Service Strollers 2-1 Strathspey Thistle; Clachnacuddin 8-0 Fort William; Colville Park 2-1 Cumbernauld Colts; Deveronvale 3-1 Hawick Royal Albert; Edinburgh University 2-1 Lossiemouth; Edusport Academy 1-1 Rothes; Formartine United 2-1 Turriff United; Fraserburgh 2-1 Forres Mechanics; Gala Fairydean Rovers 0-2 Keith; Glenafton Athletic 4-0 Threave Rovers; Lothian Thistle Hutchison Vale 3-2 Inverurie Loco Works; Nairn County 1-0 Whitehill Welfare; Selkirk 4-0 Gretna 2008; Spartans 3-0 Vale of Leithen; Wick Academy 2-2 University of Stirling

FIRST ROUND REPLAYS

University of Stirling 1-0 Wick Academy 0; Rothes 1-3 Edusport Academy

SECOND ROUND

Edinburgh City 0-1 Stenhousemuir; Berwick Rangers 1-0 Annan Athletic; Deveronvale 0-2 Glenafton Athletic; Elgin City 3-1 Edusport Academy; Nairn County 1-2 Cove Rangers; Stirling Albion 3-5 Lothian Thistle; Montrose 4-1 University of Stirling; Formartine United 4-0 East Stirlingshire; Cowdenbeath 0-1 East Kilbride; Civil Service Strollers 0-5 Brora Rangers; Banks O'Dee 2-0 Selkirk; Keith FC 0-3 Clyde; Edinburgh University 0-2 Fraserburgh; Buckie Thistle 6-2 BSC Glasgow; Spartans 5-0 Clachnacuddin; Peterhead 9-0 Colville Park

THIRD ROUND

Lothian Thistle 1-7 St Mirren; Montrose 0-0 QoS; Buckie Thistle 2-3 Brechin; Airdrieonians 2-3 Cove Rangers; Formartine United 1-0 Forfar; Clyde 0-2 East Fife; Stenhousemuir 1-2; Alloa Athletic; Stranraer 0-1 Brora Rangers; Banks O'Dee 2-6 Ayr; East Kilbride 3-4 Albion Rovers; Livingston 2-0 Glenafton; Peterhead 3-0 Raith; Spartans 2 Fraserburgh; Queen's Park 1-4 Dunfermline; Dumbarton 1-0 Elgin City; Arbroath 3-0 Berwick Rangers

THIRD ROUND REPLAYS

QoS 2-1 Montrose

FOURTH ROUND

Aberdeen 4-1 St Mirren; East Fife 0-1 Brora Rangers; Kirmarnock 1-0 Ross County; Dundee 2-2 Inverness CT; Alloa Athletic 0-2 Dundee United; QoS 1-2 Partick Thistle; Dunfermline 1-2 Greenock Morton; Motherwell 2-0 Hamilton; Ayr 4-1 Arbroath; Celtic 5-0 Brechin; Hearts 1-0 Hibernian; Livingston 0-1 Falkirk; Peterhead 2-3 Dumbarton; Albion Rovers 4-4 St Johnstone; Formartine United 0-2 Cove Rangers; Fraserburgh 0-3 Rangers

FOURTH ROUND REPLAYS

Inverness CT 0-1 Dundee

FIFTH ROUND

Celtic 3-2 Partick Thistle; Kilmarnock 4-0 Brora Rangers; Greenock Morton 3-0 Dumbarton; Hearts 3-0 St Johnstone; Cove Rangers 1-3 Falkirk; Dundee 0-2 Motherwell; Ayr 1-6 Rangers; Aberdeen 4-2 Dundee United

QUARTER-FINALS

Aberdeen 1-1 Kilmarnock; Celtic 3-0 Greenock Morton; Motherwell 2-1 Hearts; Rangers 4-1 Falkirk;

QUARTER-FINAL REPLAYS

Kilmarnock 1-1 Aberdeen (Aberdeen win 3-2 on penalties)

SEMI-FINALS

Motherwell 3-0 Aberdeen; Celtic 4-0 Rangers

FINAL

Celtic 2-0 Motherwell

PREVIOUS WINNERS

1873-74	QUEEN'S PARK	2	Clydesdale	0
1874-75	QUEEN'S PARK	3	Renton	0
1875-76	QUEEN'S PARK	2	3rd Lanark Rifles	0

(after 1-1 draw)

| 1876-77 | VALE OF LEVEN | 3 | Rangers | 2 |

(After two replays 0-0, 1-1)

| 1877-78 | VALE OF LEVEN | 1 | 3rd Lanark Rifles | 0 |
| 1878-79 | VALE OF LEVEN | 1 | Rangers | 1 |

(Vale of Leven awarded cup, Rangers failed to appear)

| 1879-80 | QUEEN'S PARK | 3 | Thornliebank | 0 |
| 1880-81 | QUEEN'S PARK | 3 | Dumbarton | 1 |

(after Dumbarton protested first game)

| 1881-82 | QUEEN'S PARK | 4 | Dumbarton | 1 |

(after 2-2 draw)

| 1882-83 | DUMBARTON | 2 | Vale of Leven | 1 |

(after 2-2 draw)

| 1883-84 | QUEEN'S PARK | wo | Vale of Leven | |

(Queen's Park awarded cup, Vale of Leven failed to appear.)

| 884-85 | RENTON | 3 | Vale of Leven | 1 |

(after 0-0 draw)

1885-86	QUEEN'S PARK	3	Renton	1
1886-87	HIBERNIAN	2	Dumbarton	1
1887-88	RENTON	6	Cambuslang	1
1888-89	THIRD LANARK	2	Celtic	1

(after replay by order of Scottish FA because of playing
conditions in first match)

| 1889-90 | QUEEN'S PARK | 2 | Vale of Leven | 1 |

(after 1-1 draw)

| 1890-91 | HEARTS | 1 | Dumbarton | 0 |
| 1891-92 | CELTIC | 5 | Queen's Park | 1 |

(after mutually-protested first game)

| 1892-93 | QUEEN'S PARK | 2 | Celtic | 1 |

(after 0-0 draw)

1893-94	RANGERS	3	Celtic	1
1894-95	ST BERNARD'S	2	Renton	1
1895-96	HEARTS	3	Hibernian	1
1896-97	RANGERS	5	Dumbarton	1
1897-98	RANGERS	2	Kilmarnock	0
1898-99	CELTIC	2	Rangers	0
1899-00	CELTIC	4	Queen's Park	3
1900-01	HEARTS	4	Celtic	3
1901-02	HIBS	1	CELTIC	0
1902-03	RANGERS	2	Hearts	0

(after two replays, 1-1, 0-0)

| 1903-04 | CELTIC | 3 | Rangers | 2 |
| 1904-05 | THIRD LANARK | 3 | Rangers | 1 |

(after 0-0 draw)

1905-06	HEARTS	1	Third Lanark	0
1906-07	CELTIC	3	Hearts	0
1907-08	CELTIC	5	St Mirren	1
1908-09	Celtic	–	Rangers	–

(owing to riot, cup was withheld after two drawn games)

| 1909-10 | DUNDEE | 2 | Clyde | 1 |

(after two draws, 2-2, 0-0)

| 1910-11 | CELTIC | 2 | Hamilton Accies | 0 |

(after 0-0 draw)

1911-12	CELTIC	2	Clyde	0
1912-13	FALKIRK	2	Raith Rovers	0
1913-14	CELTIC	4	HIBS	1

(after 0-0 draw)

1919-20	KILMARNOCK	3	Albion Rovers	2
1920-21	PARTICK THISTLE	1	Rangers	0
1921-22	MORTON	1	Rangers	0
1922-23	CELTIC	1	Hibernian	0
1923-24	AIRDRIE	2	Hibernian	0
1924-25	CELTIC	2	Dundee	1
1925-26	ST MIRREN	2	Celtic	0
1926-27	CELTIC	3	East Fife	1
1927-28	RANGERS	4	Celtic	0
1928-29	KILMARNOCK	2	Rangers	0
1929-30	RANGERS	2	Partick Thistle	1

(after 0-0 draw)

| 1930-31 | CELTIC | 4 | Motherwell | 2 |

(after 2-2 draw)

| 1931-32 | RANGERS | 3 | Kilmarnock | 0 |

(after 1-1 draw)

1932-33	CELTIC	1	Motherwell	0
1933-34	RANGERS	5	St Mirren	0
1934-35	RANGERS	2	Hamilton Accies	1
1935-36	RANGERS	1	Third Lanark	0
1936-37	CELTIC	2	Aberdeen	1
1937-38	EAST FIFE	4	Kilmarnock	2

(after 1-1 draw)

1938-39	CLYDE	4	Motherwell	0
1946-47	ABERDEEN	2	Hibernian	1
1947-48	RANGERS	1	Morton	0

(after extra time; after 1-1 draw)

| 1948-49 | RANGERS | 4 | Clyde | 1 |
| 1949-50 | RANGERS | 3 | East Fife | 0 |

1950-51	CELTIC	1	Motherwell	0
1951-52	MOTHERWELL	4	Dundee	0
1952-53	RANGERS	1	Aberdeen	0
	(after 1-1 draw)			
1953-54	CELTIC	2	Aberdeen	1
1954-55	CLYDE	1	Celtic	0
	(after 1-1 draw)			
1955-56	HEARTS	3	Celtic	1
1956-57	FALKIRK	2	Kilmarnock	1
	(after extra time; after 1-1 draw)			
1957-58	CLYDE	1	Hibernian	0
1958-59	ST MIRREN	3	Aberdeen	1
1959-60	RANGERS	2	Kilmarnock	0
1960-61	DUNFERMLINE	2	Celtic	0
	(after 0-0 draw)			
1961-62	RANGERS	2	St Mirren	0
1962-63	RANGERS	3	Celtic	0
	(after 1-1 draw)			
1963-64	RANGERS	3	Dundee	1
1964-65	CELTIC	3	Dunfermline Athletic	2
1965-66	RANGERS	1	Celtic	0
	(after 0-0 draw)			
1966-67	CELTIC	2	Aberdeen	0
1967-68	DUNFERMLINE	3	Hearts	1
1968-69	CELTIC	4	Rangers	0
1969-70	ABERDEEN	3	Celtic	1
1970-71	CELTIC	2	Rangers	1
	(after 1-1 draw)			
1971-72	CELTIC	6	Hibernian	1
1972-73	RANGERS	3	Celtic	2
1973-74	CELTIC	3	Dundee United	0
1974-75	CELTIC	3	Airdrie	1
1975-76	RANGERS	3	Hearts	1
1976-77	CELTIC	1	Rangers	0
1977-78	RANGERS	2	Aberdeen	1
1978-79	RANGERS	3	Hibernian	2
	(after two 0-0 draws, and extra time)			
1979-80	CELTIC	1	Rangers	0
	(after extra time)			
1980-81	RANGERS	4	Dundee United	1
	(after 0-0 draw)			
1981-82	ABERDEEN	4	Rangers	1
	(after extra time)			
1982-83	ABERDEEN	1	Rangers	0
	(after extra time)			

1983-84	ABERDEEN 2	Celtic 1
	(after extra time)	
1984-85	CELTIC 2	Dundee United 1
1985-86	ABERDEEN 3	Hearts 0
1986-87	ST MIRREN.............1	Dundee United 0
	(after extra time)	
1987-88	CELTIC 2	Dundee United 1
1988-89	CELTIC 1	Rangers..........................0
1989-90	ABERDEEN 0	Celtic 0
	(after extra time, Aberdeen won 9-8 on penalties)	
1990-91	MOTHERWELL 4	Dundee United 3
	(after extra time)	
1991-92	RANGERS 2	Airdrie............................1
1992-93	RANGERS 2	Aberdeen 1
1993-94	DUNDEE UTD............1	Rangers..........................0
1994-95	CELTIC 1	Airdrie............................0
1995-96	RANGERS 5	Hearts 1
1996-97	KILMARNOCK 1	Falkirk............................0
1997-98	HEARTS.................2	Rangers..........................1
1998-99	RANGERS 1	Celtic 0
1999-00	RANGERS 4	Aberdeen 0
2000-01	CELTIC 3	Hibernian 0
2001-02	RANGERS 3	Celtic 2
2002-03	RANGERS 1	Dundee............................0
2003-04	CELTIC 3	Dunfermline 1
2004-05	CELTIC 1	Dundee United 0
2005-06	HEARTS.................1	Gretna 1
	(after extra time, Hearts win 4-2 on penalties)	
2006-07	CELTIC 1	Dunfermline....................0
2007-08	RANGERS 3	Queen of the South 2
2008-09	RANGERS 1	Falkirk............................0
2009-10	DUNDEE UNITED 3	Ross County 0
2010-11	CELTIC 3	Motherwell......................0
2011-12	HEARTS.................5	Hibs................................1
2012-13	CELTIC 3	Hibs................................0
2013-14	ST JOHNSTONE.......2	Dundee United 0
2014-15	INVERNESS CT.........2	Falkirk............................1
2015-16	HIBERNIAN 3	Rangers..........................2
2016-17	CELTIC 2	Aberdeen 1
2017-18	CELTIC 2	MOTHERWELL 0

CELTIC celebrate winning the Scottish Cup after a 2-0 win over Motherwell

Pic: SNS

SCOTTISH CUP-WINNING TEAMS

1976-77 – CELTIC: Latchford, McGrain, Lynch, Stanton, McDonald, Aitken, Dalglish, Edvaldsson, Craig, Conn, Wilson.

1977-78 – RANGERS: McCloy, Jardine, Greig, Forsyth, Jackson, MacDonald, McLean, Russell, Johnstone, Smith, Cooper.

1978-79 – RANGERS: McCloy, Jardine, Dawson, Johnstone, Jackson, Watson, McLean, Russell, Parlane, McDonald, Cooper.

1979-80 – CELTIC: Latchford, Sneddon, McGrain, Aitken, Conroy, MacLeod, Provan, Doyle, McCluskey, Burns, McGarvey.

1980-81 – RANGERS: Stewart, Jardine, Dawson, Stevens, Forsyth, Bett, Cooper, Russell, D. Johnstone, Redford, MacDonald.

1981-82 – ABERDEEN: Leighton, Kennedy, Rougvie, McMaster, McLeish, Miller, Strachan, Cooper, McGhee, Simpson, Hewitt.

1982-83 – ABERDEEN: Leighton, Rougvie, McMaster, Cooper, McLeish, Miller, Strachan, Simpson, McGhee, Black, Weir.

1983-84 – ABERDEEN: Leighton, McKimmie, Rougvie, Cooper, McLeish, Miller, Strachan, Simpson, McGhee, Black, Weir.

1984-85 – CELTIC: Bonner, W. McStay, McGrain, Aitken, McAdam, MacLeod, Provan, P. McStay, Johnston, Burns, McGarvey.

1985-86 – ABERDEEN: Leighton, McKimmie, McQueen, McMaster, McLeish, Miller, Hewitt, Cooper, McDougall, Bett, Weir.

1986-87 – ST MIRREN: Money, Wilson, D. Hamilton, Abercromby, Winnie, Cooper, Ferguson, McGarvey, McDowall, B. Hamilton, Lambert.

1987-88 – CELTIC: McKnight, Morris, Rogan, Aitken, McCarthy, Whyte, Miller, McStay, McAvennie, Walker, Burns.

1988-89 – CELTIC: Bonner, Morris, Rogan, Aitken, McCarthy, Whyte, Grant, McStay, Miller, McGhee, Burns.

1989-90 – ABERDEEN: Snelders, McKimmie, Robertson, Grant, McLeish, Irvine, Nicholas, Bett, Mason, Connor, Gillhaus.

1990-91 – MOTHERWELL: Maxwell, Nijholt, Boyd, Griffin, Paterson, McCart, Arnott, Angus, Ferguson (Kirk), O'Donnell, Cooper (O'Neill).

1991-92 – RANGERS: Goram, Stevens, Robertson, Gough, Spackman, Brown, McCall, McCoist, Hateley, Mikhailitchenko, Durrant. Subs: Gordon, Rideout.

1992-93 – RANGERS: Goram, McPherson, Gough, Brown, Robertson, Murray, Ferguson, McCall, Durrant, Hateley, Huistra. Subs: Pressley, McSwegan.

1993-94 – DUNDEE UNITED: Van De Kamp, Cleland, Malpas, McInally, Petric, Welsh, Bowman, Hannah, McLaren, Brewster, Dailly. Subs: Nixon, Bollan.

1994-95 – CELTIC: Bonner, Boyd, McKinlay, Vata, McNally, Grant, McLaughlin, McStay, Van Hooijdonk (Falconer), Donnelly (O'Donnell), Collins.

1995-96 – RANGERS: Goram, Cleland, Robertson, Gough, McLaren, Brown, Durie, Gascoigne, Ferguson (Durrant), McCall, Laudrup.

1996-97 – KILMARNOCK: Lekovic, MacPherson, Kerr, Montgomerie, McGowne, Reilly, Bagan (Mitchell), Holt, Wright (Henry), McIntyre (Brown), Burke.

1997-98 – HEARTS: Rousett, McPherson, Naysmith, Weir, Salvatore, Ritchie, McCann, Fulton, Adam (Hamilton), Cameron, Flogel.

1998-99 – RANGERS: Klos, Porrini (Kanchelskis), Vidmar, Amoruso, Hendry, McCann (I Ferguson), McInnes, Wallace, van Bronckhorst, Amato (Wilson), Albertz.

1999-00 – RANGERS: Klos, Reyna, Moore (Porrini), Vidmar, Numan, Kanchelskis, Ferguson, Albertz, van Bronckhorst (Tugay), Wallace (McCann), Dodds.

2000-01 – CELTIC: Douglas, Mjallby, Vega, Valgaeren, Agathe, Lennon, Lambert (Boyd), Moravcik (McNamara), Thompson (Johnson), Larsson, Sutton.

2001-02 – RANGERS: Klos, Ross, Moore, Amoruso, Numan, Ricksen, de Boer, Ferguson, Lovenkrands, McCann, Caniggia (Arveladze).

2002-03 – RANGERS: Klos, Malcolm, Moore, Amoruso, Numan (Muscat), Ricksen, Ferguson, de Boer, McCann, Arveladze (Thompson), Mols (Ross).

2003-04 – CELTIC: Marshall, Varga, Balde, McNamara, Agathe, Lennon, Petrov, Pearson (Wallace), Thompson, Larsson, Sutton.

2004-05 – CELTIC: Douglas, Agathe, Balde, Varga, McNamara, Petrov, Lennon, Sutton, Thompson (McGeady), Hartson (Valgaeren), Bellamy.

2005-06 – HEARTS: Gordon, Neilson, Pressley, Tall, Fyssas, Cesnauskis (Mikoliunas), Aguiar (Brellier), Hartley, Skacel, Bednar (Pospisil), Jankauskas.

2006-07 – CELTIC: Boruc, Doumbe, McManus, Pressley, Naylor, Nakamura, Lennon (Caldwell), Hartley, McGeady, Miller (Beattie), Vennegoor of Hesselink.

2007-08 – RANGERS: Alexander, Whittaker, Cuellar, Weir, Papac, McCulloch, Ferguson, Thomson, Beasley (Davis), Boyd, Darcheville (Fleck).

2008-09 – RANGERS: Alexander, Whittaker, Bougherra, Weir, Papac, Davis, Ferguson, McCulloch, Lafferty (Dailly), Boyd (Novo), Miller (Naismith).

2009-10 – DUNDEE UNITED: Pernis, Kovacevic (Watson), Webster, Kenneth, Dillon, Swanson (Scott Robertson), Buaben, Gomis, Conway, Daly, Goodwillie (David Robertson).

2010-11 – CELTIC: Forster, Izaguirre, Majstorovic, Wilson, Mulgrew, Loovens, Brown, Ki, Samaras (Stokes), Commons (Forrest), Hooper (McCourt).

2011-12 – HEARTS: MacDonald, McGowan, Webster, Zaliukas, Grainger, Black (Robinson), Barr, Santana (Beattie), Skacel, Driver (Taouil), Elliott.

2012-13 – CELTIC: Forster, Izaguirre, Wilson, Mulgrew, Lustig, Brown (Ambrose), Commons (Samaras), Ledley, Forrest (McCourt), Stokes, Hooper.

2013-14 – ST JOHNSTONE: Mannus, Mackay, Easton, Wotherspoon (McDonald), Wright, Anderson, Millar, Dunne, May, MacLean, O'Halloran (Croft).

2014-15 – INVERNESS CT: Esson, Shinnie, Devine, Meekings, Tremarco, Tansey, Draper, Watkins (Ross), Doran (Williams), Christie (Vincent), Ofere.

2015-16 – HIBERNIAN: Logan, McGregor, Hanlon (Gunnarsson) Fontaine (Henderson), Gray, Fyvie, McGeouch, McGinn, Stevenson, Stokes, Cummings (Keatings).

2016-17 – CELTIC: Gordon, Lustig, Simunovic, Boyata, Tierney (Rogic), McGregor, Brown, Armstrong, Roberts (Sviatchenko), Griffiths, Dembele.

2017-18 – CELTIC: Gordon, Lustig, Boyata, Ajer (Simunovic), Tierney, Ntcham, Brown, Forrest (Sinclair), Rogic (Armstrong), McGregor, Dembele.

PLAYER OF THE YEAR

AWARDED BY THE SCOTTISH FOOTBALL WRITERS' ASSOCIATION.

1965	BILLY McNEILL (Celtic)
1966	JOHN GREIG (Rangers)
1967	RONNIE SIMPSON (Celtic)
1968	GORDON WALLACE (Raith Rovers)
1969	BOBBY MURDOCH (Celtic)
1970	PAT STANTON (Hibernian)
1971	MARTIN BUCHAN (Aberdeen)
1972	DAVE SMITH (Rangers)
1973	GEORGE CONNELLY (Celtic)
1974	WORLD CUP SQUAD
1975	SANDY JARDINE (Rangers)
1976	JOHN GREIG (Rangers)
1977	DANNY McGRAIN (Celtic)
1978	DEREK JOHNSTONE (Rangers)
1979	ANDY RITCHIE (Morton)
1980	GORDON STRACHAN (Aberdeen)
1981	ALAN ROUGH (Partick Thistle)
1982	PAUL STURROCK (Dundee United)
1983	CHARLIE NICHOLAS (Celtic)
1984	WILLIE MILLER (Aberdeen)
1985	HAMISH McALPINE (Dundee United)
1986	SANDY JARDINE (Hearts)
1987	BRIAN McCLAIR (Celtic)
1988	PAUL McSTAY (Celtic)
1989	RICHARD GOUGH (Rangers)
1990	ALEX McLEISH (Aberdeen)
1991	MAURICE MALPAS (Dundee United)
1992	ALLY McCOIST (Rangers)
1993	ANDY GORAM (Rangers)
1994	MARK HATELEY (Rangers)
1995	BRIAN LAUDRUP (Rangers)
1996	PAUL GASCOIGNE (Rangers)
1997	BRIAN LAUDRUP (Rangers)
1998	CRAIG BURLEY (Celtic)
1999	HENRIK LARSSON (Celtic)
2000	BARRY FERGUSON (Rangers)
2001	HENRIK LARSSON (Celtic)
2002	PAUL LAMBERT (Celtic)
2003	BARRY FERGUSON (Rangers)
2004	JACKIE McNAMARA (Celtic)
2005	JOHN HARTSON (Celtic)
2006	CRAIG GORDON (Hearts)
2007	SHUNSUKE NAKAMURA (Celtic)
2008	CARLOS CUELLAR (Rangers)
2009	GARY CALDWELL (Celtic)
2010	DAVID WEIR (Rangers)
2011	EMILIO IZAGUIRRE (Celtic
2012	CHARLIE MULGREW (Celtic)
2013	LEIGH GRIFFITHS (Hibernian)
2014	KRIS COMMONS (Celtic)
2015	CRAIG GORDON (Celtic)
2016	LEIGH GRIFFITHS (Celtic)
2017	SCOTT SINCLAIR (Celtic)
2018	SCOTT BROWN (Celtic)

SPFA PLAYER OF THE YEAR

1977-78
Premier Division .... Derek Johnstone (Rangers)
First Division .... Billy Pirie (Dundee)
Second Division .... Dave Smith (Berwick Rangers)
Young Player .... Graeme Payne (Dundee United)

1978-79
Premier Division .... Paul Hegarty (Dundee United)
First Division .... Brian McLaughlin (Ayr United)
Second Division .... Michael Leonard (Dunfermline Ath)
Young Player .... Raymond Stewart (Dundee United)

1979-80
Premier Division .... Davie Provan (Celtic)
First Division .... Sandy Clark (Airdrie)
Second Division .... Paul Leetion (Falkirk)
Young Player .... John MacDonald (Rangers)

1980-81
Premier Division .... Mark McGhee (Aberdeen)
First Division .... Eric Sinclair (Dundee)
Second Division .... Jimmy Robertson (Queen of the South)
Young Player .... Charlie Nicholas (Celtic)

1981-82
Premier Division .... Sandy Clark (Airdrie)
First Division .... Brian McLaughlin (Motherwell)
Second Division .... Pat Nevin (Clyde)
Young Player .... Frank McAvennie (St Mirren)

1982-83
Premier Division .... Charlie Nicholas (Celtic)
First Division .... Gerry McCabe (Clydebank)
Second Division .... John Colquhoun (Stirling Albion)
Young Player .... Paul McStay (Celtic)

1983-84
Premier Division .... Willie Miller (Aberdeen)
First Division .... Gerry McCabe (Clydebank)
Second Division .... Jim Liddle (Forfar Athletic)
Young Player .... John Robertson (Hearts)

1984-85
Premier Division .... Jim Duffy (Morton)
First Division .... Gerry McCabe (Clydebank)
Second Division .... Bernie Slaven (Albion Rovers)
Young Player .... Craig Levein (Hearts)

1985-86
Premier Division .... Richard Gough (Dundee United)
First Division .... John Brogan (Hamilton)
Second Division .... Mark Smith (Queen's Park)
Young Player .... Craig Levein (Hearts)

1986-87
Premier Division .... Brian McClair (Celtic)
First Division .... Jim Holmes (Morton)
Second Division .... John Sludden (Ayr United)
Young Player .... Robert Fleck (Rangers)

1987-88
Premier Division .... Paul McStay (Celtic)
First Division .... Alex Taylor (Hamilton)
Second Division .... Henry Templeton (Ayr United)
Young Player .... John Collins (Hibernian)

1988-89
Premier Division .... Theo Snelders (Aberdeen)
First Division .... Ross Jack (Dunfermline)
Second Division .... Paul Hunter (East Fife)
Young Player .... Billy McKinlay (Dundee United)

1989-90
Premier Division .... Jim Bett (Aberdeen)
First Division .... Ken Eadie (Clydebank)
Second Division .... Willie Watters (Kilmarnock)
Young Player .... Scott Crabbe (Hearts)

1990-91

Premier Division	Paul Elliott (Celtic)
First Division	Simon Stainrod (Falkirk)
Second Division	Kevin Todd (Berwick Rangers)
Young Player	Eoin Jess (Aberdeen)

1991-92

Premier Division	Ally McCoist (Rangers)
First Division	Gordon Dalziel (Raith Rovers)
Second Division	Andy Thomson (Queen of the South)
Young Player	Phil O'Donnell (Motherwell)

1992-93

Premier Division	Andy Goram (Rangers)
First Division	Gordon Dalziel (Raith Rovers)
Second Division	Sandy Ross (Brechin City)
Young Player	Eoin Jess (Aberdeen)

1993-94

Premier Division	Mark Hateley (Rangers)
First Division	Richard Cadette (Falkirk)
Second Division	Andy Thomson (Queen of the South)
Young Player	Phil O'Donnell (Motherwell)

1994-95

Premier Division	Brian Laudrup (Rangers)
First Division	Stephen Crawford (Raith Rovers)
Second Division	Derek McInnes (Morton)
Third Division	David Bingham (Forfar Ath.)
Young Player	Charlie Miller (Rangers)

1995-96

Premier Division	Paul Gascoigne (Rangers)
First Division	George O'Boyle (St Johnstone)
Second Division	Steven McCormick (Stirling A.)
Third Division	Jason Young (Livingston)
Young Player	Jackie McNamara (Celtic)

1996-97

Premier Division	Paolo di Canio (Celtic)
First Division	Roddy Grant (St Johnstone)
Second Division	Paul Ritchie (Hamilton)
Third Division	Ian Stewart (Inverness CT)
Young Player	Robbie Winters (Dundee United)

1997-98

Premier Division	Jackie McNamara (Celtic)
First Division	James Grady (Dundee)
Second Division	Paul Lovering (Clydebank)
Third Division	Willie Irvine (Alloa)
Young Player	Gary Naysmith (Hearts)

1998-99

Premier Division	Henrik Larsson (Celtic)
First Division	Russell Latapy (Hibs)
Second Division	David Bingham (Livingston)
Third Division	Neil Tarrant (Ross County)
Young Player	Barry Ferguson (Rangers)

1999-2000

Premier Division	Mark Viduka (Celtic)
First Division	Stevie Crawford (Dunfermline)
Second Division	Brian Carrigan (Clyde)
Third Division	Stevie Milne (Forfar)
Young Player	Kenny Miller (Hibs)

2000-2001

Premier Division	Henrik Larsson (Celtic)
First Division	David Bingham (Livingston)
Second Division	Scott McLean (Partick Thistle)
Third Division	Steve Hislop (East Stirling)
Young Player	Stilian Petrov (Celtic)

2001-2002

Premier Division	Lorenzo Amoruso (Rangers)
First Division	Owen Coyle (Airdrie)
Second Division	John O'Neill (Queen of the South)
Third Division	Paul McManus (East Fife)
Young Player	Kevin McNaughton (Aberdeen)

2002-2003

Premier Division ....Barry Ferguson (Rangers)
First Division ....Dennis Wyness (Inverness Caley Thistle)
Second Division ....Chris Templeman (Brechin)
Third Division ....Alex Williams (Morton)
Young Player...............................James McFadden (Motherwell)

2003-2004

Premier Division ....Chris Sutton (Celtic)
First Division ....Ian Harty (Clyde)
Second Division ....Paul Tosh (Forfar)
Third Division ....Michael Moore (Stranraer)
Young Player.............................Stephen Pearson (Celtic)

2004-2005

Premier Division ....John Hartson (Celtic)/Fernando Ricksen (Rangers)
First Division ....Russell Latapy (Falkirk)
Second Division ....Steven Hampshire (Brechin)
Third Division ....David Bingham (Gretna)
Young Player..................................Derek Riordan (Hibs)

2005-2006

Premier Division ....Shaun Maloney (Celtic)
First Division ....John Rankin (Ross County)
Second Division ....James Grady (Gretna)
Third Division ....Markus Paatelainen (Cowdenbeath)
Young Player..................................Shaun Maloney (Celtic)

2006-2007

Premier Division ....Shunsuke Nakamura (Celtic)
First Division ....Colin McMenamin (Gretna)
Second Division ....Iain Russell (Brechin City)
Third Division ....Scott Chaplain (Albion Rovers)
Young Player..........................Steven Naismith (Kilmarnock)

2007-2008

Premier Division ....Aiden McGeady (Celtic)
First Division ....Graham Dorrans (Livingston)
Second Division ....Allan Russell (Airdrie United)
Third Division ....Jonathan Smart (East Fife)
Young Player....................................Aiden McGeady (Celtic)

2008-2009

Premier Division ....Scott Brown (Celtic)
First Division ....Leigh Griffiths (Livingston)
Second Division ....Bryan Prunty (Ayr United)
Third Division ....Bobby Barr (Albion Rovers)
Young Player.............................James McCarthy (Hamilton)

2009-2010

Premier Division ....Steven Davis (Rangers)
First Division ....Adam Rooney (Inverness CT)
Second Division ....Rory McAllister (Brechin City)
Third Division ....Robbie Winters (Livingston)
Young Player..................................Danny Wilson (Rangers)

2010-2011

Premier Division ....Emilio Izaguirre (Celtic)
First Division ....John Baird (Raith Rovers)
Second Division ....Rory McAllister (Brechin City)
Third Division ....Gavin Swankie (Arbroath)
Young Player..........................David Goodwillie (Dundee United)

2011-2012

Premier Division ....Charlie Mulgrew (Celtic)
First Division ....Farid El Alagui (Falkirk)
Second Division ....John Robertson (Cowdenbeath)
Third Division ....Steven May (Alloa)
Young Player..................................James Forrest (Celtic)

2012-2013

Premier Division ....Michael Higdon (Motherwell)
First Division ....Lyle Taylor (Falkirk)
Second Division ....Nicky Clark (Queen of the South)
Third Division ....Lee Wallace (Rangers)
Young Player..............................Leigh Griffiths (Hibernian)

2013-2014

Premiership .... Kris Commons (Celtic)
Championship .... Kane Hemmings (Cowdenbeath)
League One .... Lee Wallace (Rangers)
League Two .... Rory McAllister (Rangers)
Young Player .... Andrew Robertson (Dundee Utd)

2014-2015

Premiership .... Stefan Johansen (Celtic)
Championship .... Scott Allan (Hibernian)
League One .... Declan McManus (Morton)
League Two .... Bobby Linn (Arbroath)
Young Player .... Jason Denayer (Celtic)

2015-2016

Premiership .... Leigh Griffiths (Celtic)
Championship .... Lee Wallace (Rangers)
League One .... Faissal el Bakhtaoui (Dunfermline)
League Two .... Nathan Austin (East Fife)
Young Player .... Kieran Tierney (Celtic)

2016-2017

Premiership .... Scott Sinclair (Celtic)
Championship .... John McGinn(Hibernian)
League One .... Liam Buchanan (Livingston)
League Two .... Shane Sutherland (Elgin)
Young Player .... Kieran Tierney (Celtic)

2017-2018

Premiership .... Scott Brown (Celtic)
Championship .... Lewis Morgan (St Mirren)
League One .... Lawrence Shankland (Ayr Utd)
League Two .... Darren Smith (Stirling Albion)
Young Player .... Kieran Tierney (Celtic)

ENGLISH PLAYER OF THE YEAR

1948 **Stanley Matthews** (Blackpool)	1983 **Kenny Dalglish** Liverpool
1949 **Johnny Carey** (Man U)	1984 **Ian Rush** (Liverpool)
1950 **Joe Mercer** (Arsenal)	1985 **Neville Southall** (Everton)
1951 **Harry Johnston** (Blackpool)	1986 **Gary Lineker** (Everton)
1952 **Billy Wright** (Wolves)	1987 **Clive Allen** (Tottenham H.)
1953 **Nat Lofthouse** (Bolton W.)	1988 **John Barnes** (Liverpool)
1954 **Tom Finney** (Preston NE)	1989 **Steve Nicol** (Liverpool)
1955 **Don Revie** (Man City)	1990 **John Barnes** (Liverpool)
1956 **Bert Trautmann** (Man City)	1991 **Gordon Strachan** (Leeds U)
1957 **Tom Finney** (Preston NE)	1992 **Gary Lineker** (Spurs)
1958 **Danny Blanchflower** (Spurs)	1993 **Chris Waddle** (Sheffield W)
1959 **Syd Owen** (Luton Town)	1994 **Alan Shearer** (Blackburn R)
1960 **Bill Slater** (Wolves)	1995 **Jurgen Klinsmann** (Spurs)
1961 **Danny Blanchflower** (Spurs)	1996 **Eric Cantona** (Man U)
1962 **Jimmy Adamson** (Burnley)	1997 **Gianfranco Zola** (Chelsea)
1963 **Stanley Matthews** (Stoke C)	1998 **Dennis Bergkamp** (Arsenal)
1964 **Bobby Moore** (West Ham)	1999 **David Ginola** (Spurs)
1965 **Bobby Collins** (Leeds U)	2000 **Roy Keane** (Man U)
1966 **Bobby Charlton** (Man U)	2001 **Teddy Sheringham** (Man U)
1967 **Jackie Charlton** (Leeds U)	2002 **Robert Pires** (Arsenal)
1968 **George Best** (Man U)	2003 **Thierry Henry** (Arsenal)
1969 **Dave Mackay** (Derby)	2004 **Thierry Henry** (Arsenal)
Tony Book (Man City)	2005 **Frank Lampard** (Chelsea)
1970 **Billy Bremner** (Leeds U)	2006 **Thierry Henry** (Arsenal)
1971 **Frank McLintock** (Arsenal)	2007 **Cristiano Ronaldo** (Man U)
1972 **Gordon Banks** (Stoke City)	2008 **Cristiano Ronaldo** (Man U)
1973 **Pat Jennings** (Spurs)	2009 **Steven Gerrard** (Liverpool)
1974 **Ian Callaghan** (Liverpool)	2010 **Wayne Rooney** (Man U)
1975 **Alan Mullery** (Fulham)	2011 **Scott Parker** (West Ham)
1976 **Kevin Keegan** (Liverpool)	2012 **Robin van Persie** (Arsenal)
1977 **Emlyn Hughes** (Liverpool)	2013 **Gareth Bale** (Tottenham)
1978 **Kenny Burns** (Notts Forest)	2014 **Luis Suarez** (Liverpool)
1979 **Kenny Dalglish** (Liverpool)	2015 **Eden Hazard** (Chelsea)
1980 **Terry McDermott** (Liverpool)	2016 **Jamie Vardy** (Leicester)
1981 **Frans Thijssen** (Ipswich T)	2017 **N'Golo Kante** (Chelsea)
1982 **Steve Perryman** (Spurs)	2018 **Mohamed Salah** (Liverpool)

The Best FIFA Football Awards.
(formerly Fifa World Player of the Year/Ballon d'Or)

1956	STANLEY MATTHEWS (Blackpool)
1957	ALFREDO DI STEFANO (Real Madrid)
1958	RAYMOND KOPA (Real Madrid)
1959	ALFREDO DI STEFANO (Real Madrid)
1960	LUIS SUAREZ (Barcelona)
1961	OMAR SIVORI (Juventus)
1962	JOSEF MASOPUST (Dukla Prague)
1963	LEV YASHIN (Moscow Dynamo)
1964	DENIS LAW (Manchester United)
1965	EUSEBIO (Benfica)
1966	BOBBY CHARLTON (Manchester United)
1967	FLORIAN ALBERT (Ferencvaros)
1968	GEORGE BEST (Manchester United)
1969	GIANNI RIVERA (AC Milan)
1970	GERD MULLER (Bayern Munich)
1971	JOHAN CRUYFF (Ajax Amsterdam)
1972	FRANZ BECKENBAUER (Bayern Munich)
1973	JOHAN CRUYFF (Barcelona)
1974	JOHAN CRUYFF (Barcelona)
1975	OLEG BLOKHIN (Dynamo Kiev)
1976	FRANZ BECKENBAUER (Bayern Munich)
1977	ALLAN SIMONSEN (Borussia Moenchengladbach)
1978	KEVIN KEEGAN (SV Hamburg)
1979	KEVIN KEEGAN (SV Hamburg)
1980	KARL-HEINZ RUMMENIGGE (Bayern Munich)
1981	KARL-HEINZ RUMMENIGGE (Bayern Munich)
1982	PAOLO ROSSI (Juventus)
1983	MICHEL PLATINI (Juventus)
1984	MICHEL PLATINI (Juventus)
1985	MICHEL PLATINI (Juventus)
1986	IGOR BELANOV (Dynamo Kiev)
1987	RUUD GULLIT (AC Milan)
1988	MARCO VAN BASTEN (AC Milan)
1989	MARCO VAN BASTEN (AC Milan)
1990	LOTHAR MATTHAUS (West Germany)
1991	JEAN-PIERRE PAPIN (Marseilles)
1992	MARCO VAN BASTEN (AC Milan)
1993	ROBERTO BAGGIO (Juventus)
1994	HIRSTO STOICHKOV (Barcelona)
1995	GEORGE WEAH (AC Milan)
1996	MATTHIAS SAMMER (Borussia Dortmund)
1997	RONALDO (Inter Milan)
1998	ZINEDINE ZIDANE (Juventus)
1999	RIVALDO (Barcelona)
2000	LUIS FIGO (Real Madrid)
2001	MICHAEL OWEN (Liverpool)
2002	RONALDO (Real Madrid)
2003	PAVEL NEDVED (Juventus)
2004	ANDRIY SHEVCHENKO (AC Milan)
2005	RONALDINHO (Barcelona)
2006	FABIO CANNAVARO (Italy)
2007	KAKA (AC Milan)
2008	CRISTIANO RONALDO (Manchester United)
2009	LIONEL MESSI (Barcelona)
2010	LIONEL MESSI (Barcelona)
2011	LIONEL MESSI (Barcelona)
2012	LIONEL MESSI (Barcelona)
2013	CRISTIANO RONALDO (Real Madrid)
2014	CRISTIANO RONALDO (Real Madrid)
2015	LIONEL MESSI (Barcelona)
2016	CRISTIANO RONALDO (Real Madrid)
2017	CRISTIANO RONALDO (Real Madrid)

SCOTLAND'S INTERNATIONAL RECORD
v ENGLAND (Scotland scores first)
The year refers to the season, i.e. 1873 is season 1872-73

Year	Score	Venue	Year	Score	Venue
1873	0-0	Partick	1913	0-1	Chelsea
1873	2-4	The Oval	1914	3-1	Hampden
1874	2-1	Partick	1920	4-5	Sheffield
1875	2-2	The Oval	1921	3-0	Hampden
1876	3-0	Partick	1922	1-0	Aston Villa
1877	3-1	The Oval	1923	2-2	Hampden
1878	7-2	Hampden	1924	1-1	Wembley
1879	4-5	The Oval	1925	2-0	Hampden
1880	5-4	Hampden	1926	1-0	Manchester
1881	6-1	The Oval	1927	1-2	Hampden
1882	5-1	Hampden	1928	5-1	Wembley
1883	3-2	Sheffield	1929	1-0	Hampden
1884	1-0	Cathkin	1930	2-5	Wembley
1885	1-1	The Oval	1931	2-0	Hampden
1886	1-1	Hampden	1932	0-3	Wembley
1887	3-2	Blackburn	1933	2-1	Hampden
1888	0-5	Hampden	1934	0-3	Wembley
1889	3-2	The Oval	1935	2-0	Hampden
1890	1-1	Hampden	1936	1-1	Wembley
1891	1-2	Blackburn	1937	3-1	Hampden
1892	1-4	Ibrox	1938	1-0	Wembley
1893	2-5	Richmond	1939	1-2	Hampden
1894	2-2	Celtic Park	1947	1-1	Wembley
1895	0-3	Everton	1948	0-2	Hampden
1896	2-1	Celtic Park	1949	3-1	Wembley
1897	2-1	Crystal Pal	1950	0-1	Hampden
1898	1-3	Celtic Park	1951	3-2	Wembley
1899	1-2	Birmingham	1952	1-2	Hampden
1900	4-1	Celtic Park	1953	2-2	Wembley
1901	2-2	Crystal Pal	1954	2-4	Hampden
1902	2-2	Birmingham	1955	2-7	Wembley
1903	2-1	Sheffield	1956	1-1	Hampden
1904	0-1	Celtic Park	1957	1-2	Wembley
1905	0-1	Crystal Pal	1958	0-4	Hampden
1906	2-1	Hampden	1959	0-1	Wembley
1907	1-1	Newcastle	1960	1-1	Hampden
1908	1-1	Hampden	1961	3-9	Wembley
1909	0-2	Crystal Pal	1962	2-0	Hampden
1910	2-0	Hampden	1963	2-1	Wembley
1911	1-1	Liverpool	1964	1-0	Hampden
1912	1-1	Hampden	1965	2-2	Wembley

1966	3-4	Hampden
1967	3-2	Wembley
1968	1-1	Hampden
1969	1-4	Wembley
1970	0-0	Hampden
1971	1-3	Wembley
1972	0-1	Hampden
1973	0-5	Hampden
1973	0-1	Wembley
1974	2-0	Hampden
1975	1-5	Wembley
1976	2-1	Hampden
1977	2-1	Wembley
1978	0-1	Hampden
1979	1-3	Wembley
1980	0-2	Hampden
1981	1-0	Wembley
1982	0-1	Hampden
1983	0-2	Wembley
1984	1-1	Hampden

SIR STANLEY ROUS CUP

| 1985 | 1-0 | Hampden |
| 1986 | 1-2 | Wembley |

BECAME A THREE-NATION COMPETITION

| 1987 | 0-0 | Hampden |

(Scotland 0 Brazil 2. England 1 Brazil 1; Winners – Brazil)

| 1988 | 0-1 | Wembley |

(Scotland 0 Colombia 0; England 1 Colombia 1. Winners: England)

| 1989 | 0-2 | Hampden |

(Scotland 2 Chile 0; England 0 Chile 0. Winners – England)

1996	0-2	Wembley
1999	0-2	Hampden
1999	1-0	Wembley
2014	2-3	Wembley
2015	1-3	Celtic Park
2017	0-3	Wembley
2017	2-2	Hampden

DENIS LAW heads the ball as Scotland beat England 2-0 at Hampden on April 14, 1962

v NORTHERN IRELAND
(Scotland scores first)

Year	Score	Venue
1884	5-0	Belfast
1885	8-2	Glasgow
1886	7-2	Belfast
1887	4-1	Glasgow
1888	10-2	Belfast
1889	7-0	Glasgow
1890	4-1	Belfast
1891	2-1	Glasgow
1892	3-2	Belfast
1893	6-1	Glasgow
1894	2-1	Belfast
1895	3-1	Glasgow
1896	3-3	Belfast
1897	5-1	Glasgow
1898	3-0	Belfast
1899	9-1	Glasgow
1900	3-0	Belfast
1901	11-0	Glasgow
1902	5-1	Belfast
1903	0-2	Glasgow
1904	1-1	Dublin
1905	4-0	Glasgow
1906	1-0	Dublin
1907	3-0	Glasgow
1908	5-0	Dublin
1909	5-0	Glasgow
1910	0-1	Belfast
1911	2-0	Glasgow
1912	4-1	Belfast
1913	2-1	Dublin
1914	1-1	Belfast
1920	3-0	Glasgow
1921	2-0	Belfast
1922	2-1	Glasgow
1923	1-0	Belfast
1924	2-0	Glasgow
1925	3-0	Belfast
1926	4-0	Glasgow
1927	2-0	Belfast
1928	0-1	Glasgow
1929	7-3	Belfast
1930	3-1	Glasgow
1931	0-0	Belfast
1932	3-1	Glasgow
1933	4-0	Belfast
1934	1-2	Glasgow
1935	1-2	Belfast
1936	2-1	Edinburgh
1937	3-1	Belfast
1938	1-1	Aberdeen
1939	2-0	Belfast
1947	0-0	Glasgow
1948	0-2	Belfast
1949	3-2	Glasgow
1950	8-2	Belfast
1951	6-1	Glasgow
1952	3-0	Belfast
1953	1-1	Glasgow
1954	3-1	Belfast
1955	2-2	Glasgow
1956	1-2	Belfast
1957	1-0	Glasgow
1958	1-1	Belfast
1959	2-2	Glasgow
1960	4-0	Belfast
1961	5-2	Glasgow
1962	6-1	Belfast
1963	5-1	Glasgow
1964	1-2	Belfast
1965	3-2	Glasgow
1966	2-3	Belfast
1967	2-1	Glasgow
1968	0-1	Belfast
1969	1-1	Glasgow
1970	1-0	Belfast
1971	0-1	Glasgow
1972	2-0	Glasgow
1973	1-2	Glasgow
1974	0-1	Glasgow
1975	3-0	Glasgow
1976	3-0	Glasgow
1977	3-0	Glasgow
1978	1-1	Glasgow
1979	1-0	Glasgow
1980	0-1	Belfast
1981	1-1	Glasgow
1981	2-0	Glasgow

1982	0-0	Belfast	1992	1-0	Glasgow
1982	1-1	Belfast	2008	0-0	Glasgow
1983	0-0	Glasgow	2011	3-0	Dublin
1984	0-2	Belfast	2015	1-0	Glasgow

v WALES
(Scotland scores first)

1876	4-0	Glasgow	1914	0-0	Glasgow
1877	2-0	Wrexham	1920	1-1	Cardiff
1878	9-0	Glasgow	1921	2-1	Aberdeen
1879	3-0	Wrexham	1922	1-2	Wrexham
1880	5-1	Glasgow	1923	2-0	Paisley
1881	5-1	Wrexham	1924	2-0	Cardiff
1882	5-0	Glasgow	1925	3-1	Edinburgh
1883	4-1	Wrexham	1926	3-0	Cardiff
1884	4-1	Glasgow	1927	3-0	Glasgow
1885	8-1	Wrexham	1928	2-2	Wrexham
1886	4-1	Glasgow	1929	4-2	Glasgow
1887	2-0	Wrexham	1930	4-2	Cardiff
1888	5-1	Edinburgh	1931	1-1	Glasgow
1889	0-0	Wrexham	1932	3-2	Wrexham
1890	5-0	Paisley	1933	2-5	Edinburgh
1891	4-3	Wrexham	1934	2-3	Cardiff
1892	6-1	Edinburgh	1935	3-2	Aberdeen
1893	8-0	Wrexham	1936	1-1	Cardiff
1894	5-2	Kilmarnock	1937	1-2	Dundee
1895	2-2	Wrexham	1938	1-2	Cardiff
1896	4-0	Dundee	1939	3-2	Edinburgh
1897	2-2	Wrexham	1946	1-3	Wrexham
1898	5-2	Motherwell	1947	1-2	Glasgow
1899	6-0	Wrexham	1948	3-1	Cardiff
1900	5-2	Aberdeen	1949	2-0	Glasgow
1901	1-1	Wrexham	1950	3-1	Cardiff
1902	5-1	Greenock	1951	0-1	Glasgow
1903	1-0	Cardiff	1952	2-1	Cardiff
1904	1-1	Dundee	1953	3-3	Glasgow
1905	1-3	Wrexham	1954	1-0	Cardiff
1906	0-2	Edinburgh	1955	2-0	Glasgow
1907	0-1	Wrexham	1956	2-2	Cardiff
1908	2-1	Dundee	1957	1-1	Glasgow
1909	2-3	Wrexham	1958	3-0	Cardiff
1910	1-0	Kilmarnock	1959	1-1	Glasgow
1911	2-2	Cardiff	1960	0-2	Cardiff
1912	1-0	Edinburgh	1961	2-0	Glasgow
1913	0-0	Wrexham	1962	3-2	Cardiff

1963	2-1	Glasgow
1964	2-3	Cardiff
1965	4-1	Glasgow
1966	1-1	Cardiff
1967	3-2	Glasgow
1969	5-3	Wrexham
1970	0-0	Glasgow
1971	0-0	Cardiff
1972	1-0	Glasgow
1973	2-0	Wrexham
1974	2-0	Glasgow
1975	2-2	Cardiff
1976	3-1	Glasgow
1977	1-0	Glasgow
1977	0-0	Wrexham
1978	2-0	Liverpool

1978	1-1	Glasgow
1979	0-3	Cardiff
1980	1-0	Glasgow
1981	0-2	Swansea
1982	1-0	Glasgow
1983	2-0	Cardiff
1984	2-1	Glasgow
1985	0-1	Glasgow
1986	1-1	Cardiff
1997	0-1	Kilmarnock
2004	0-4	Cardiff
2009	0-3	Cardiff
2011	3-1	Dublin
2013	1-2	Cardiff
2013	1-2	Glasgow

*(Wales' home game in
World Cup qualifier)*

**SCOTLAND v England April 1948, crowds outside Hampden
with no tickets hoping to get lucky**

ARGENTINA
(Scotland scores first)

| 1977 | 1-1 | Buenos Aires | 1990 | 1-0 | Glasgow |
| 1979 | 1-3 | Glasgow | 2008 | 0-1 | Glasgow |

AUSTRALIA
(Scotland scores first)

1986	2-0	Glasgow	2000	0-2	Glasgow
1986	0-0	Melbourne	2013	3-1	Edinburgh
1996	1-0	Glasgow			

AUSTRIA
(Scotland scores first)

1931	0-5	Vienna	1969	2-1	Glasgow
1934	2-2	Glasgow	1970	0-2	Vienna
1937	1-1	Vienna	1979	2-3	Vienna
1951	0-1	Glasgow	1980	1-1	Glasgow
1951	0-4	Vienna	1994	2-1	Vienna
1954	0-1	Zurich	1996	0-0	Vienna
1955	4-1	Vienna	1997	2-0	Glasgow
1956	1-1	Glasgow	2003	0-2	Glasgow
1960	1-4	Vienna	2006	2-2	Graz
1963	4-1	Glasgow	2007	1-0	Vienna

(Referee abandoned match after 79 minutes)

BELARUS
(Scotland scores first)

| 1997 | 1-0 | Minsk | 2005 | 0-0 | Minsk |
| 1998 | 4-1 | Aberdeen | 2006 | 0-1 | Glasgow |

BELGIUM
(Scotland scores first)

1946	2-2	Glasgow	1983	2-3	Brussels
1947	1-2	Brussels	1984	1-1	Glasgow
1948	2-0	Glasgow	1987	1-4	Brussels
1951	5-0	Brussels	1988	2-0	Glasgow
1971	0-3	Liege	2001	2-2	Glasgow
1972	1-0	Aberdeen	2001	0-2	Brussels
1974	1-2	Brussels	2013	0-2	Brussels
1980	0-2	Brussels	2014	0-2	Glasgow
1980	1-3	Glasgow			

BOSNIA
(Scotland scores first)

1999	2-1	Sarajevo	1999	1-0	Glasgow

BRAZIL
(Scotland scores first)

1966	1-1	Glasgow	1982	1-4	Seville
1972	0-1	Rio	1987	0-2	Glasgow
1973	0-1	Glasgow	1990	0-1	Turin
1974	0-0	Frankfurt	1998	1-2	Paris
1977	0-2	Rio	2011	0-2	London

BULGARIA
(Scotland scores first)

1978	2-1	Glasgow	1991	1-1	Sofia
1987	0-0	Glasgow	1991	1-1	Glasgow
1988	1-0	Sofia	2006	5-1	Kobe

CANADA
(Scotland scores first)

1983	2-0	Vancouver	1992	3-1	Toronto
1983	3-0	Edmonton	2003	3-1	Edinburgh
1983	2-0	Toronto	2017	1-1	Edinburgh

CHILE
(Scotland scores first)

1977	4-2	Santiago	1989	2-0	Glasgow

CIS
(Scotland score first)

1992	3-0	Sweden	

COLOMBIA
(Scotland scores first)

1988	0-0	Glasgow	1998	2-2	New Jersey
1996	0-1	Miami			

COSTA RICA
(Scotland score first)

1990	0-1	Genoa	2018	0-1	Glasgow

CROATIA
(Scotland scores first)

2001	1-1	Zagreb	2013	1-0	Zagreb
2002	0-0	Glasgow	2014	2-0	Glasgow
2008	1-1	Glasgow			

CYPRUS
(Scotland scores first)

1969	5-0	Nicosia	1989	2-1	Glasgow
1969	8-0	Glasgow	2011	2-1	Larnaca
1989	3-2	Limassol			

CZECHOSLOVAKIA
(Scotland scores first)

1937	3-1	Prague	1972	0-0	Porto Alegre
1938	5-0	Glasgow	1974	2-1	Glasgow
1961	0-4	Bratislava	1974	0-1	Bratislava
1962	3-2	Glasgow	1977	0-2	Prague
1962	2-4	Brussels	1978	3-1	Glasgow

CZECH REPUBLIC
(Scotland scores first)

1999	1-2	Glasgow	2011	0-1	Prague
1999	2-3	Prague	2012	2-2	Glasgow
2008	1-3	Prague	2016	1-0	Prague
2010	1-0	Glasgow			

DENMARK
(Scotland scores first)

1951	3-1	Glasgow	1976	3-1	Glasgow
1952	2-1	Copenhagen	1986	0-1	Neza
1969	1-0	Copenhagen	1996	0-2	Copenhagen
1971	1-0	Glasgow	1998	0-1	Glasgow
1971	0-1	Copenhagen	2003	0-1	Glasgow
1973	4-1	Copenhagen	2004	0-1	Copenhagen
1973	2-0	Glasgow	2012	2-1	Glasgow
1976	1-0	Copenhagen	2016	1-0	Glasgow

EAST GERMANY
(Scotland scores first)

1975	3-0	Glasgow	1984	1-2	Halle
1978	0-1	East Berlin	1986	0-0	Glasgow
1983	2-0	Glasgow	1990	0-1	Glasgow

ECUADOR
(Scotland score first)

1995 2-1 .... Toyama

EGYPT
(Scotland score first)

1990   1-3 .... Aberdeen

ESTONIA
(Scotland scores first)

1993	3-0 .... Tallinn	1997	0-0 .... Monaco
1993	3-1 .... Aberdeen	1997	2-0 .... Kilmarnock
1997	0-0 .... Tallinn	1998	3-2 .... Tynecastle
(abandoned after 3 seconds,		1999	0-0 .... Tallinn
replay ordered in Monaco)		2004	1-0 .... Tallinn

FAROE ISLANDS
(Scotland scores first)

1995	5-1 .... Glasgow	2004	3-1 .... Glasgow
1995	2-0 .... Torshavn	2007	6-0 .... Glasgow
1998	2-1 .... Aberdeen	2007	2-0 .... Toftir
1999	1-1 .... Toftir	2011	3-0 .... Aberdeen
2003	2-2 .... Toftir		

FINLAND
(Scotland scores first)

1954	2-1 .... Helsinki	1992	1-1 .... Glasgow
1965	3-1 .... Glasgow	1995	2-0 .... Helsinki
1965	2-1 .... Helsinki	1996	1-0 .... Glasgow
1977	6-0 .... Glasgow		

FRANCE
(Scotland scores first)

1930	2-0 .... Paris	1990	0-3 .... Paris
1932	3-1 .... Paris	1998	1-2 .... St Etienne
1948	0-3 .... Paris	2000	0-2 .... Glasgow
1949	2-0 .... Glasgow	2002	0-5 .... Paris
1950	1-0 .... Paris	2007	1-0 .... Glasgow
1951	1-0 .... Glasgow	2008	1-0 .... Paris
1958	1-2 .... Obrero	2016	0-3 .... Metz
1984	0-2 .... Marseilles		
1989	2-0 .... Glasgow		

GEORGIA
(Scotland scores first)

2007	2-1 .... Glasgow	2015	1-0 .... Glasgow
2008	0-2 .... Tbilisi	2016	0-1 .... Tbilisi

TURNING POINT
SCOTLAND

PRESENTS

MUSIC CONNECTS 2018

A NIGHT OF FANTASTIC LIVE MUSIC – TACKLING
HOMELESSNESS THROUGH HOUSING FIRST

FEATURING

Shardlake

PLUS OTHER
ACTS TO BE
CONFIRMED

DOGTOOTH

The Ginhouse Rocks

HOSTED BY
SCOTTISH
STAND UP
ALLAN PARK

SEPTEMBER 19TH 2018

THE FERRY, ANDERSTON QUAY, GLASGOW

Doors open: 6pm

Tickets available: www.ticket-scotland.com
Tickets phone 01698 360085
£10 + £1.50 booking fee

www.turningpointscotland.com
Registered charity SC02882

FIRST Rangers team to play in the Scottish Cup, 1877. Club founder, Moses McNeil (far right)

THE victorious Partick Thistle side who defeated Celtic in the 1971 League Cup final Pic: SNS

CELTIC celebrate winning the treble for a record-breaking two years in a row   Pic: SNS

ST MIRREN celebrate winning the Championship title Pic: SNS

Alex Black
FUNERAL CARE
Caring and Professional Funeral Directors

- 24hr Call Out Service
- Service room available
  with private rest rooms
- Headstones and memorials

Drumchapel:
0141 949 1234

Knightswood:
0141 959 1234

Maryhill:
0141 946 1234

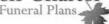
Golden Charter
Funeral Plans

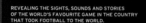

GERMANY
(Scotland scores first)

1929	1-1	Berlin	1999	1-0	Bremen
1937	2-0	Glasgow	2003	1-1	Glasgow
1992	0-2	Sweden	2004	1-2	Dortmund
1993	0-1	Glasgow	2015	1-2	Dortmund
			2016	2-3	Glasgow

GIBRALTAR
(Scotland scores first)

2015	6-1	Glasgow	2016	6-0	Faro

GREECE
(Scotland scores first)

1995	0-1	Athens	1996	1-0	Glasgow

HOLLAND
(Scotland scores first)

1929	2-0	Amsterdam	1994	0-1	Glasgow
1938	3-1	Amsterdam	1994	1-3	Utrecht
1959	2-1	Amsterdam	1996	0-0	Birmingham
1966	0-3	Glasgow	2000	0-0	Arnhem
1968	0-0	Amsterdam	2004	1-0	Glasgow
1972	1-2	Amsterdam	2004	0-6	Amsterdam
1978	3-2	Argentina	2009	0-3	Amsterdam
1982	2-1	Glasgow	2010	0-1	Glasgow
1986	0-0	Eindhoven	2018	0-1	Aberdeen
1992	0-1	Sweden			

HONG KONG
(Scotland score first)

2002	4-0	Hong Kong	

HUNGARY
(Scotland scores first)

1939	3-1	Glasgow	1980	1-3	Budapest
1955	2-4	Glasgow	1988	2-0	Glasgow
1955	1-3	Budapest	2004	0-3	Glasgow
1958	1-1	Glasgow	2018	1-0	Budapest
1960	3-3	Budapest			

ICELAND
(Scotland scores first)

1985	3-0	Glasgow	2003	2-1	Glasgow
1985	1-0	Reykjavik	2008	2-1	Reykjavik
2003	2-0	Reykjavik	2009	2-1	Glasgow

IRAN
(Scotland score first)

1978	1-1	Cordoba	

ISRAEL
(Scotland scores first)

| 1981 | 1-0 | Tel Aviv | 1986 | 1-0 | Tel Aviv |
| 1981 | 3-1 | Glasgow | | | |

ITALY
(Scotland scores first)

1931	0-3	Rome	2005	0-2	Milan
1965	1-0	Glasgow	2006	1-1	Glasgow
1965	0-3	Naples	2007	0-2	Bari
1989	0-2	Perugia	2008	1-2	Glasgow
1993	0-0	Ibrox	2016	0-1	Ta' Qali
1994	1-3	Rome			

JAPAN
(Scotland scores first)

| 1995 | 0-0 | Hiroshima | 2010 | 0-2 | Yokohama |
| 2006 | 0-0 | Saitama | | | |

LATVIA
(Scotland scores first)

| 1997 | 2-0 | Riga | 2000 | 1-0 | Riga |
| 1998 | 2-0 | Celtic Park | 2001 | 2-1 | Glasgow |

LIECHTENSTEIN
(Scotland scores first)

| 2011 | 2-1 | Glasgow | 2012 | 1-0 | Vaduz |

LITHUANIA
(Scotland scores first)

1998	0-0	Vilnius	2008	3-1	Glasgow
1999	3-0	Glasgow	2011	0-0	Kaunas
2003	0-1	Kaunas	2012	1-0	Glasgow
2004	1-0	Glasgow	2017	1-1	Glasgow
2007	2-1	Kaunas	2018	3-0	Vilnius

LUXEMBOURG
(Scotland scores first)

| 1947 | 6-0 | Luxembourg | 1988 | 0-0 | Luxembourg |
| 1987 | 3-0 | Glasgow | 2013 | 2-1 | Luxembourg |

MACEDONIA
(Scotland scores first)

| 2008 | 0-1 | Skopje | 2013 | 1-1 | Glasgow |
| 2010 | 2-0 | Glasgow | 2014 | 2-1 | Skopje |

MALTA
(Scotland scores first)

1988	1-1	Valetta	1997	3-2	Valetta
1990	2-1	Valetta	2017	5-1	Attard
1993	3-0	Glasgow	2018	2-0	Glasgow
1994	2-0	Valetta			

SCOTLAND celebrate a 1-0 win over Italy at Hampden in 1965

MEXICO
(Scotland score first)

2018 0-1................ Mexico City |

MOLDOVA
(Scotland scores first)

2005 1-1.................... Chisinau | 2005 2-0...................... Glasgow

MOROCCO
(Scotland score first)

1998 0-3.................. St Etienne |

NEW ZEALAND
(Scotland scores first)

1982 5-2........................ Malaga | 2003 1-1.................. Edinburgh

NIGERIA
(Scotland score first)

2002 1-2 .... | 2014 2-2...................... London

NORWAY
(Scotland scores first)

1929	7-3	Bergen	1990	1-1	Glasgow
1954	1-0	Glasgow	1992	0-0	Oslo
1954	1-1	Oslo	1998	1-1	Bordeaux
1963	3-4	Bergen	2004	0-0	Oslo
1964	6-1	Glasgow	2005	0-1	Glasgow
1974	2-1	Oslo	2006	2-1	Oslo
1979	3-2	Glasgow	2008	0-0	Glasgow
1979	4-0	Oslo	2010	0-4	Oslo
1989	2-1	Oslo	2014	1-0	Molde

PARAGUAY
(Scotland score first)

1958 2-3.................. Norrkoping |

PERU
(Scotland scores first)

1972 2-0...................... Glasgow | 1980 1-1...................... Glasgow
1978 1-3...................... Cordoba | 2018 0-2.......................... Lima

POLAND
(Scotland scores first)

1958	2-1	Warsaw	1990	1-1	Glasgow
1960	2-3	Glasgow	2001	1-1	Bydgoszcz
1965	1-1	Chorzow	2014	1-0	Warsaw
1966	1-2	Glasgow	2015	2-2	Warsaw
1980	0-1	Poznan	2016	2-2	Glasgow

PORTUGAL
(Scotland scores first)

1950	2-2	Lisbon	1979	1-0	Lisbon
1955	3-0	Glasgow	1980	4-1	Glasgow
1959	0-1	Lisbon	1981	0-0	Glasgow
1966	0-1	Glasgow	1982	1-2	Lisbon
1971	0-2	Lisbon	1993	0-0	Glasgow
1972	2-1	Glasgow	1993	0-5	Lisbon
1975	1-0	Glasgow	2003	0-2	Braga

QATAR

2015	1-0	Edinburgh

REPUBLIC OF IRELAND
(Scotland scores first)

1961	4-1	Glasgow	2000	2-1	Dublin
1961	3-0	Dublin	2003	0-2	Glasgow
1963	0-1	Dublin	2011	0-1	Dublin
1970	1-1	Dublin	2015	1-0	Glasgow
1987	0-0	Dublin	2015	1-1	Dublin
1987	0-1	Glasgow			

ROMANIA
(Scotland scores first)

1975	1-1	Bucharest	1991	2-1	Glasgow
1976	1-1	Glasgow	1992	0-1	Bucharest
1986	3-0	Glasgow	2004	1-2	Glasgow

RUSSIA
(Scotland scores first)

1995	1-1	Glasgow	1995	0-0	Moscow

SAN MARINO
(Scotland scores first)

1991	2-0	Serravalle	1996	5-0	Glasgow
1992	4-0	Glasgow	2000	2-0	Serravalle
1995	2-0	Serravalle	2001	4-0	Glasgow

SAUDI ARABIA
(Scotland score first)

1988	2-2	Riyadh

SERBIA
(Scotland score first)

2013	0-0	Glasgow	2013	0-2	Novi Sad

SLOVAKIA
(Scotland score first)

2017	0-3	Trnava	2018	1-0	Glasgow

SLOVENIA
(Scotland scores first)

2005	0-0	Glasgow	2017	1-0	Glasgow
2006	3-0	Celje	2018	2-2	Ljubljana
2012	1-1	Koper			

SOUTH AFRICA
(Scotland scores first)

2002	0-2	Hong Kong	2008	1-0	Aberdeen

SOUTH KOREA
(Scotland score first)

2002	1-4	Busan	

SOVIET UNION
(Scotland scores first)

1967	0-2	Glasgow	1982	2-2	Malaga
1971	0-1	Moscow	1991	0-1	Glasgow

SPAIN
(Scotland scores first)

1957	4-2	Glasgow	1982	0-3	Valencia
1957	1-4	Madrid	1985	3-1	Glasgow
1963	6-2	Madrid	1985	0-1	Seville
1965	0-0	Glasgow	1988	0-0	Madrid
1975	1-2	Glasgow	2005	1-1	Valencia
1975	1-1	Valencia	2011	2-3	Glasgow
			2012	1-3	Alicante

SWEDEN
(Scotland scores first)

1952	1-3	Stockholm	1990	2-1	Genoa
1953	1-2	Glasgow	1996	0-2	Stockholm
1975	1-1	Gothenburg	1997	1-0	Glasgow
1977	3-1	Glasgow	1997	1-2	Gothenburg
1981	1-0	Stockholm	2005	1-4	Edinburgh
1982	2-0	Glasgow	2011	0-3	Solna

SWITZERLAND
(Scotland scores first)

1931	3-2	Geneva	1983	0-2	Berne
1946	3-1	Glasgow	1983	2-2	Glasgow
1948	1-2	Berne	1991	2-1	Glasgow
1950	3-1	Glasgow	1992	2-2	Berne
1957	2-1	Basel	1993	1-3	Berne
1958	3-2	Glasgow	1994	1-1	Aberdeen
1973	0-1	Berne	1996	1-0	Birmingham
1976	1-0	Glasgow	2006	1-3	Glasgow

TRINIDAD & TOBAGO
(Scotland score first)

2004 4-1.....................Edinburgh |

TURKEY
(Scotland score first)

1960 2-4..........................Ankara |

UKRAINE
(Scotland scores first)

2007 0-2..............................Kiev | 2008 3-1.......................Glasgow

URUGUAY
(Scotland scores first)

| 1954 | 0-7.................Switzerland | 1984 | 2-0.......................Glasgow |
| 1962 | 2-3.....................Glasgow | 1986 | 0-0..............................Neza |

USA
(Scotland scores first)

1952	6-0...................... Glasgow	2006	1-1...................... Glasgow
1992	1-0...................... Denver	2012	1-5........................ Florida
1996	1-2...................... Hartford	2014	0-0...................... Glasgow
1998	0-0..................Washington		

WEST GERMANY
(Scotland scores first)

1957	3-1..................... Stuttgart	1970	2-3..................... Hamburg
1959	3-2..................... Glasgow	1974	1-1..................... Glasgow
1964	2-2.....................Hanover	1974	1-2.....................Frankfurt
1969	1-1..................... Glasgow	1986	1-2..................Queretaro

YUGOSLAVIA
(Scotland scores first)

1955	2-2.....................Belgrade	1974	1-1.....................Frankfurt
1957	2-0..................... Glasgow	1985	6-1..................... Glasgow
1958	1-1.................. Vaasteras	1989	1-1..................... Glasgow
1972	2-2.............. Belo Horizonte	1990	1-3.................. Zagreb

ZAIRE
(Scotland score first)

1974 2-0.....................Dortmund |

SCOTLAND v West Germany at Hampden in May 1959 with captains Bobby Evans and Helmut Rahn. The Scots won 3-2

LIST OF PLAYERS HONOURED

**This is a list of full international appearances by
Scots in matches against the Home Countries and against
foreign nations.**
The code for countries is as follows

A, Austria; Arg, Argentina; Aus, Australia; Bel, Belgium; Blr, Belarus;
Bos, Bosnia; Br, Brazil; Bul, Bulgaria; Ca, Canada; Ch, Chile;
CIS, Commeonwealth of Independent Staes; Co, Colombia;
Cr, Costa Rica; Cro, Croatia; Cy, Cyprus; Cz, Czechoslovakia;
CzR, Czech Republic; D, Denmark; E, England; Ec, Ecuador;
EG, East Germany; Eg, Egypt; Est, Estonia; Fr, France; Fin, Finland; Fi,
Faroes Islands; G, Germany; Geo, Georgia; Gr, Greece; Gib, Gibraltar;
H, Hungary; Holl, Holland; HK, Hong Kong; I, Italy; Ice, Iceland;
Ir, Iran; Is, Israel; J, Japan; L, Luxembourg; La, Latvia;
Li, Liechtenstein; Lth, Lithuania; M, Morocco; Ma, Malta; Mac,
Macedonia; Mx, Mexico; Mo, Moldova; Nig, Nigeria; N, Norway; Ni,
Northern Ireland; Nz, New Zealand; Por, Portugal; Pe, Peru; Pol,
Poland; Q, Qatar; Ei, Republic of Ireland; R, Romania; Ru, Russia;
SAr, Saudi Arabia; Se, Sweden; Sm, San Marino; Ser, Serbia; Slv,
Slovakia; Slo, Slovenia; SA, South Africa; Skor, South Korea; Sp,
Spain; Sw, Switzerland; Trin, Trinidad & Tobago; T, Turkey; U, Uruguay;
Uk, Ukraine; US, United States of America; USSR, Soviet Union; W,
Wales; WG, West Germany; Y, Yugoslavia; Z, Zaire.
**The year refers to the season. For example,
2014 is the 2013-14 season.**

ADAM, C. (Rangers, Blackpool, Liverpool, Stoke) (26): 2007 v A, Fi; 2010 v J, CzR; 2011 v Se, Sp, Fi, Ni, Br, W, Ei; 2012 v D, CzR, Sp, Slo; 2013 v Aus, Mac, W (2), Bel, Est, Ser (2); 2014 v N, Pol; 2015 v Q.

ADAMS, J. (Hearts) (3): 1889 v Ni; 1892 v W; 1893 v Ni.

AGNEW, W. B. (Kilmarnock) (3): 1907 v Ni; 1908 v W, Ni.

AIRD, J. (Burnley) (4): 1954 v N (2); A, U.

AITKEN A. (Newcastle Utd, Middlesbrough, Leicester Fosse) (14): 1901 v E; 1902 v E; 1903 v E, W; 1904 v E; 1905 v E; 1906 v E; 1907 v E, W; 1908 v E; 1910 v E; 1911 v E, Ni.

AITKEN, G. G. (East Fife, Sunderland) (8): 1949 v E, Fr; 1950 v W, Ni, Sw; 1953 v W, Ni; 1954 v E.

AITKEN, R. (Dumbarton) (2): 1886 v E: 1888 v Ni.

AITKEN, R. (Celtic, Newcastle Utd, St Mirren) (57): 1980 v Pe, Bel, W, E, Pol; 1983 v Bel, Ca (2); 1984 v Bel, Ni, W; 1985 v E, Ice; 1986 v W, EG, Aus (2), Is, R, E, D, WG, U; 1987 v Bul, Ei (2), L, Bel, E, Br; 1988 v H, Bel, Bul, L, S.Ar., Ma, Sp, Co, E; 1989 v N, Y, I, Cy, (2), Fr, E, Ch; 1990 v Y, Fr, N, Arg, Pol, Ma, Cr, Se, Br; 1992 v R.

AITKENHEAD, W. A. C. (Blackburn R.) (1): 1912 v Ni.

ALBISTON, A. (Manchester Utd) (14): 1982 v Ni; 1984 v U, Bel, EG, W, E; 1985 v Y, Ice, Sp (2), W; 1986 v EG, Holl, U.

ALEXANDER, D. (East Stirlingshire) (1): 1894 v W, Ni.

ALEXANDER, G. (Preston, Burnley) (40): 2002 v Nig, Skor, SA, HK; 2003 v D, Fi, Can, Por, Ei, Ice, Lth, Nz; 2004 v Lth; 2004 v P; 2005 v Mo, Blr; 2006 v A, I, N, Blr, Slo, US, Sw; 2007 v Lth, Fr, Uk, Geo, I, A, Fi; 2008 v Fr, Geo, Cro; 2009 v Ni, Mac, Ice, Arg, Holl; 2010 v N, Mac.

ALEXANDER, N. (Cardiff) (3): 2006 v Sw, Bul, J.

ALLAN, D. S. (Queen's Park) (3): 1885 v E, W; 1886 v W.

ALLAN, G. (Liverpool) (1): 1897 v E.

ALLAN, H. (Hearts) (1): 1902 v W.

ALLAN, J. (Queen's Park) (2): 1887 v E, W.

ALLAN, T. (Dundee) (2): 1974 v WG, N.

ANCELL, R. F. D. (Newcastle Utd) (2): 1937 v W, Ni.

ANDERSON, A. (Hearts) (23): 1933 v E; 1934 v A, E, W, Ni; 1935 v E, W, Ni; 1936 v E, W, Ni; 1937 v G, E, W, Ni, A; 1938 v E, W, Ni, Cz, Holl; 1939 v W, H.

ANDERSON, F. (Clydesdale) (1): 1874 v E.

ANDERSON, G. (Kilmarnock) (1): 1901 v Ni.

ANDERSON, H. A. (Raith Rovers) (1): 1914 v W.

ANDERSON, J. (Leicester City) (1): 1954 v Fin.

ANDERSON, K. (Queen's Park) (3): 1896 v Ni; 1898 v E, Ni.

ANDERSON, R. (Aberdeen, Sunderland) (11): 2003 v Ice, Can, Por, Ei; 2005 v N, Se; 2006 v A, Bul, J; 2008 v Cro, SA.

ANDERSON, W. (Queen's Park) (6): 1882 v E: 1883 v E, W; 1884 v E; 1885 v E, W.

ANDREWS, P. (Eastern) (1): 1875 v E.

ANYA, I. (Watford, Derby) (29): 2014 v Bel, Mac, Cro, N, Pol, Nig; 2015 v G, Geo, Pol, Ei, E, Ni, Gib, Q, Ei; 2016 v Geo, G, CZR, D, I, Fr; 2017 v Ma, Slv, E, Ca, Slo, E; 2018 v Slv, Slo.

ARCHER, J. (Millwall) (1): 2018 v Pe.

ARCHIBALD, A. (Rangers) (8): 1921 v W; 1922 v W, E; 1923 v Ni; 1924 v E, W; 1931 v E; 1932 v E.

ARCHIBALD, S. (Aberdeen, Tottenham H, Barcelona) (27): 1980 v Por, Ni, Pol, H; 1981 v Se, Is (2), Ni (2), E; 1982 v Ni, Por, Sp, Holl, Nz, Br, USSR; 1983 v EG, Sw, Bel; 1984 v EG, E, Fr; 1985 v Sp, E, Ice; 1986 v WG.

ARMSTRONG, M. W. (Aberdeen) (3): 1936 v W, Ni; 1937 v G.
ARMSTRONG, S. (Celtic) (6): 2017 v Slo, E; 2018 v Lth, Ma, Cr, H.
ARNOTT, W. (Queen's Park) (14): 1883 v W; 1884 v E, Ni; 1885 v E, W; 1886 v E; 1887 v E, W; 1888 v E; 1889 v E; 1890 v E; 1891 v E; 1892 v E; 1893 v E.
AULD, J. R. (Third Lanark) (3): 1887 v E, W; 1889 v W.
AULD, R. (Celtic) (3): 1959 v H, Por; 1960 W.
BAIN, S. (Celtic) (1): 2018 v Mx.
BAIRD, A. (Queen's Park) (2): 1892 v Ni; 1894 v W.
BAIRD, D. (Hearts) (3): 1890 v Ni; 1891 v E; 1892 v W.
BAIRD, H. (Airdrie) (1): 1956 v A.
BAIRD, J. C. (Vale of Leven) (3): 1876 v E; 1878 v W; 1880 v E.
BAIRD, S. (Rangers) (7): 1957 v Y, Sp (2), Sw, WG; 1958 v Fr, Ni.
BAIRD, W. U. (St Bernard's) (1): 1897 v Ni.
BANNAN, B. (Aston Villa, Crystal Palace, Sheffield Wed) (27): 2011 v Fi, Ni, Br, W, Ei; 2012 v D, Lth, Li Sp, Slo, US; 2013 v Cro; 2014 v Mac, Cro, US, N, Pol; 2015 v G, E, Gib; 2016 v CZR; 2017 v Ma, Lth, Slv, Ca; 2018 v Slv, Slo.
BANNON, E. (Dundee Utd) (11): 1980 v Bel; 1983 v Ni, W, E, Ca; 1984 v E, Ei; 1986 v Is, R, E, D, WG.
BARBOUR, A. (Renton) (1): 1885 v Ni.
BARDSLEY, P. (Sunderland) (12): 2011 v Sp, Fi, Ni, W, Ei; 2012 v D, CzR, Lth, Sp, Cy, US; 2014 v Pol.
BARKER, J. B. (Rangers) (2): 1893 v W; 1894 v W.
BARR, D. (Falkirk) (1): 2009 v Ni
BARRETT, F. (Dundee) (2): 1894 v Ni; 1895 v W.
BATTLES, B. (Celtic) (3): 1901 v E, W, Ni.
BATTLES, B. (Hearts) (1): 1931 v W.
BAULD, W. (Hearts) (3): 1950 v E, Sw, Por.
BAXTER, J. C. (Rangers, Sunderland) (34): 1961 v Ni, Ei (2), Cz; 1962 v Ni, W, E, Cz (2), U; 1963 v W, Ni, E, A, N, Ei, Sp; 1964 v W, E, N, WG; 1965 v W, Ni, Fin; 1966 v Por, Br, Ni, W, E, I; 1967 v W, E, USSR; 1968 v W.
BAXTER, R. D. (Middlesbrough) (3): 1939 v E, W, H.
BEATTIE, A. (Preston NE) (7): 1937 v E, A, Cz; 1938 v E; 1939 v W, Ni, H.
BEATTIE, C. (Celtic, West Bromwich Albion) (7): 2006 v I, N; 2007 v Geo, I; 2008 v SA, Lth, Geo.
BEATTIE, R. (Preston NE) (1): 1939 v W.
BEGBIE, I. (Hearts) (4): 1890 v Ni; 1891 v E; 1892 v W; 1894 v E.
BELL, A. (Manchester Utd) (1): 1912 v Ni.
BELL, C. (Kilmarnock) (1): 2011 v Fi.
BELL, J. (Dumbarton, Everton, Celtic) (10): 1890 v Ni; 1892 v W; 1896 v E; 1897 v E; 1898 v E; 1899 v E, W, Ni; 1900 v E, W.
BELL, M. (Hearts) (1): 1901 v W.
BELL, W. J. (Leeds Utd) (1): 1966 v Por, Br.
BENNETT, A. (Celtic, Rangers) (11): 1904 v W; 1907 v Ni; 1908 v W; 1909 v W, Ni, E; 1910 v E, W; 1911 E, W; 1913 v Ni.
BENNIE, R. (Airdrie) (3): 1925 v W, Ni; 1926 v Ni.
BERNARD, P. (Oldham Ath.) (2): 1995 v J, Ec.
BERRA, C. (Hearts, Wolves, Ipswich Town, Hearts) (41): 2008 v CzR; 2009 v Ni, Arg, Holl; 2010 v N, J, CzR; 2011 v Se, Lth, Ni, Br, W, Ei; 2012 v CzR, Lth, Li, Sp, Cy, Slo, US; 2013 v Aus, Mac, W, Bel, Lux, Est, Ser; 2014 v N; 2015 v Ni, Ei; 2016 v Gib, CZR, I; 2017 v E, CA, E; 2018 v Lth, Ma, Slv, Slo, Holl.
BERRY, D. (Queen's Park) (3): 1894 v W; 1899 v W, Ni.
BERRY, W. H. (Queen's Park) (4): 1888 v E; 1889 v E; 1890 v E; 1891 v E.
BETT, J. (Rangers, Lokeren, Aberdeen) (25): 1982 v Holl; 1983 v Bel; 1984 v Bel, W, E, Fr; 1985 v Y, Ice, (2), Sp (2), W, E; 1986 v W, Is, Holl; 1987 v Bel; 1988 v H; 1989 v Y; 1990 v Fr, N, Arg, Eg, Ma, Cr.
BEVERIDGE, W. W. (Glasgow University) (3): 1879 v E, W; 1880 v W.

ALAN BRAZIL played 13 times for Scotland

BLACK, A (Hearts) (3): 1938 v Cz, Holl; 1939 v H.

BLACK, D. (Hurlford) (1): 1889 v Ni.

BLACK, E. (Metz) (2): 1988 v H, L.

BLACK, I. (Rangers) (1): 2013 v Aus.

BLACK, I. H. (Southampton) (1): 1948 v E.

BLACKBURN, J. E. (Royal Engineers) (1): 1873 v E.

BLACKLAW, A. S. (Burnley) (3): 1963 v N, Sp; 1966 v I.

BLACKLEY, J. (Hibernian) (7): 1974 v Cz, E, Bel, Z; 1976 v Sw; 1977 v W, Se.

BLAIR, D. (Clyde, Aston Villa) (8): 1929 v W, Ni; 1931 v E, A, I; 1932 v W, Ni; 1933 v W.

BLAIR, J. (Sheffield W., Cardiff City) (8): 1920 v E, Ni; 1921 v E; 1922 v E; 1923 v E, W, Ni; 1924 v W.

BLAIR, J. (Motherwell) (1): 1934 v W.

BLAIR, J. A. (Blackpool) (1): 1947 v W.

BLAIR, W. (Third Lanark) (1): 1896 v W.

BLESSINGTON, J. (Celtic) (4): 1894 v E, Ni; 1896 v E, Ni.

BLYTH, J. A. (Coventry City) (2): 1978 v Bul, W.

BONE, J. (Norwich City) (2): 1972 v Y; 1973 v D.

BOOTH, S. (Aberdeen, Twente Enschede) (22): 1993 v G, Est (2); 1994 v Sw, Ma; 1995 v Fi, Ru; 1996 v Fin, Sm, Aus, US, Holl, Sw; 1998 v D, Fin, Co, M, US; 2001 v Pol; 2002 v Cro, Bel, La.

BOWIE, J. (Rangers) (2): 1920 v E, Ni.

BOWIE, W. (Linthouse) (1): 1891 v Ni.

BOWMAN, D. (Dundee United) (6): 1992 v Fin, US; 1993 v G, Est; 1994 v Sw, I.

BOWMAN, G. A. (Montrose) (1): 1892 v Ni.

BOYD, J. M. (Newcastle Utd) (1): 1934 v Ni.

BOYD, G. (Hull City) (2): 2013 v Ser; 2014 v Nig.

BOYD, K. (Rangers, Middlesbrough) (18): 2006 v Bul, J; 2007 v Fi (2), Lth, Uk, Geo, I, A; 2008 v SA, Lth, Geo, I, Cro; 2009 v Mac; 2010 v CzR; 2011 v Se, Li.

BOYD, R. (Mossend Swifts) (2): 1889 v Ni; 1891 v W.

BOYD, T. (Motherwell, Chelsea, Celtic) (72): 1991 v R (2), Sw, Bul, USSR; 1992 v Sw, Fin, Ca, N, CIS; 1993 v Sw, Por, I, Ma, G, Est (2); 1994 v I, Ma, Holl, A; 1995 v Fin, Fi, Ru (2), Gr, Sm. 1996 v Gr, Fin, Se, Sm, Aus, D, US, U, Holl, E, Sw; 1997 v A (2), La, Se (2), Est (2), W, Ma, Blr; 1998 v Blr, La, Fr, D, Fin, Co, US, Br, N, M. 1999 v Lth, Est, Fi, CzR (2), G, Fi; 2001 v La, Cro, Aus, Bel, Sm, Pol; 2002 v Bel.

BOYD, W. G. (Clyde) (2): 1931 v I, Sw, Fin.

BRACKENBRIDGE, T. (Hearts) (1): 1888 v Ni.

BRADSHAW, T. (Bury) (1): 1928 v E.

BRAND, R. (Rangers) (8): 1961 v Ni, Cz, Ei. (2); 1962 v Ni, W, Cz, U.

BRANDEN, T. (Blackburn R.) (1): 1896 v E.

BRAZIL, A. (Ipswich Town, Tottenham) (13): 1980 v Pol, H; 1982 v Sp, Holl, Ni, W, E, Nz, USSR; 1983 v EG, Sw, W, La.

BREMNER, D. (Hibernian) (1): 1976 v Sw.

BREMNER, W. J. (Leeds Utd) (54): 1965 v Sp; 1966 v E, Pol, P, Br, I (2); 1967 v W, Ni, E; 1968 v W, E, Ni, D, A, WG, Cy (2); 1970 v Ei, WG, A; 1971 v W, E; 1972 v Por, Bel, Holl, Ni, W, E, Y, Cz (cont...)

Br; 1973 v D (2), E (2), Ni, Sw, Br; 1974 v Cz, WG, Ni, W, E, Bel, N, Z, Br, Y; 1975 v Sp (2); 1976 v D.
BRENNAN, F. (Newcastle Utd) (7): 1947 v W, Ni; 1953 v W, Ni, E; 1954 v Ni, E.
BRESLIN, B. (Hibernian) (1): 1897 v W.
BREWSTER, G. (Everton) (1): 1921 v E.
BRIDCUTT, L. (Brighton, Sunderland) (2): 2013 v Ser; 2016 v D.
BROADFOOT, K. (Rangers) (4): 2009 v Ice, N, Arg; 2011 v Se.
BROGAN, J. (Celtic) (4): 1971 v W, Ni, Por, E.
BROWN, A. (Middlesbrough) (1): 1904 v E.
BROWN, A. (St Mirren) (2): 1890 v W; 1891 v W.
BROWN, A. D. (East Fife, Blackpool) (14): 1950 v Sw, Por, Fr; 1952 v USA, D, Se; 1953 v W; 1954 v W, E, N (2), Fin, A, U.
BROWN, G. C. P. (Rangers) (19): 1931 v W; 1932 v E, W, Ni; 1933 v E; 1935 v A, E, W; 1936 v E, W; 1937 v G, E, W, Ni, Cz; 1938 v E, W, Cz, Holl.
BROWN, H. (Partick Th.) (3): 1947 v W, Bel, L.
BROWN, J. (Cambuslang) (1): 1890 v W.
BROWN, J. B. (Clyde) (1): 1939 v W.
BROWN, J. G. (Sheffield U.) (1): 1975 v R.
BROWN, R. (Dumbarton) (2): 1884 v W, Ni.
BROWN, R. (Rangers) (3): 1947 v Ni; 1949 v Ni; 1952 v E.
BROWN, R. (Dumbarton) (1): 1885 v W.
BROWN, S. (Hibernian, Celtic) (55): 2006 v US; 2007 v Geo, I; 2008 v SA, Lth, Fr, Uk, I, Cro; 2009 v Ni, Mac, Ice (2), N, Arg, Holl; 2010 v N, Mac, Holl, CzR; 2011 v Lth, Li, Br, W, Ei; 2012 v D, CzR, US. 2013 v W, Est; 2014 v E, Bel, Mac, Cro, US, N, Pol, Nig; 2015 v Geo, Pol, Ei, E, Gib, Q, Ei; 2016 v Geo, G, Pol, Gib, D; 2017 v E, Slo, E; 2018 v Lth, Ma.
BROWN, W. D. F. (Dundee, Tottenham H.) (28): 1958 v Fr; 1959 v E, W, Ni; 1960 v W, Ni, Pol, A, H, T; 1962 v W, E, Cz; 1963 v W, Ni, E, A; 1964 v Ni, W, N; 1965 v E, Fin, Pol, Sp; 1966 v Ni, Pol, I.
BROWNING, J. (Celtic) (1): 1914 v W.
BROWNLIE, J. (Hibernian) (7): 1971 v USSR; 1972 v Pe, Ni, E; 1973 v D (2); 1976 v R.
BROWNLIE, J. (Third Lanark) (16): 1909 v E, Ni; 1910 v E, W, Ni; 1911 v W, Ni; 1912 v W, Ni, E; 1913 v W, Ni, E; 1914 v W, Ni, E.
BRUCE, D. (Vale of Leven) (1): 1890 v W.
BRUCE, R. F. (Middlesbrough) (1): 1934 v A.
BRYSON, C. (Kilmarnock, Derby) (3): 2011 v Fi; 2014 v N; 2016 v I.
BUCHAN, M. M. (Aberdeen, Manchester Utd.) (34): 1972 v Por, Bel, W, Y, Cz, Br; 1973 v D (2), E; 1974 v WG, Ni, W, N, Br, Y; 1975 v EG, Sp, Por; 1976 v D, R; 1977 v Fin, Cz, Ch, Arg, Br; 1978 v EG, W, Ni, Pe, Ir, Holl; 1979 v A, N, Por.
BUCHANAN, J. (Cambuslang) (1): 1889 v Ni.
BUCHANAN, J. (Rangers) (2): 1929 v E; 1930 v E.
BUCHANAN, P. S. (Chelsea) (1): 1938 v Cz.
BUCHANAN, R. (Abercorn) (1): 1891 v W.
BUCKLEY, P. (Aberdeen) (3): 1954 v N; 1955 v W, Ni.
BUICK, A. (Hearts) (2): 1902 v W, Ni.
BURCHILL, M. (Celtic) (6): 2000 v Bos, Lth, E (2), Fr, Holl.
BURKE, C. (Rangers, Birmingham) (7): 2006 v Bul, J; 2013 v Est, W, Ser; 2014 v Cro, Pol.
BURKE, O. (Nottingham Forest, RB Leipzig) (5): 2016 v D, I; 2017 v Ma, Lth, Ca.
BURLEY C. (Chelsea, Celtic, Derby) (46): 1995 v J, Ec, Fi. 1996 v Gr, Se, v Blr, La, Fr, Co, US, Br, N, M. 1999 v Fi, CzR. 2000 v Bos (2), (cont...)

Est, Lth, E (2), Holl, Ei; 2001 v Cro, Aus, Bel, Sm; 2002 v Cro, Bel, La; 2003 v A.

BURLEY, G. (Ipswich Town) (11): 1979 v W, Ni, E, Arg, N; 1980 v Por, Ni, E, Pol; 1982 v W, E.

BURNS, F. (Manchester Utd) (1): 1970 v A.

BURNS, K. (Birmingham City, Nottingham F.) (20): 1974 v WG; 1975 v EG, Sp (2); 1977 v Cz, W, (2), Se; 1978 v Ni, W, E, Pe, Ir; 1979 v N; 1980 v Pe, A, Bel; 1981 v Is, Ni, W.

BURNS, T. (Celtic) (8): 1981 v Ni; 1982 v Holl, W; 1983 v Bel, Ni, Ca (2); 1988 v E.

BUSBY, M. W. (Manchester City) (1): 1934 v W.

CADDEN, C. (Motherwell) (2): 2018 v Mx.

CADDIS, P. (Birmingham) (1): 2016 v CZR.

CAIRNEY, T. (Fulham) (2): 2017 v Ca; 2018 v Cr.

CAIRNS, T. (Rangers) (8): 1920 v W; 1922 v E; 1923 v E, W; 1924 v Ni; 1925 v W, E, Ni.

CALDERHEAD, D. (Q.O.S. Wanderers) (1): 1889 v Ni.

CALDERWOOD, C. (Tottenham Hotspur, Aston Villa) (36): 1995 v Ru, Sm, J, Ec, Fi. 1996 v Gr, Fin, Se, Sm, US, U, Holl, E, Sw; 1997 v A (2), La, Se (2), Est (2); 1998 v Blr, La, Fr, D, Fin, Co, US, Br, N. 1999 v Lth, Est, Fi, CzR. 2000 v Bos (2).

CALDERWOOD, R. (Cartvale) (3): 1885 v Ni, E, W.

CALDOW, E. (Rangers) (40): 1957 Sp (2), Sw, WG, E; 1958 v Ni, W, Sw, Par, H, Pol, Y, Fr; 1959 v E, W, Ni, WG, Holl, Por; 1960 v E, W, Ni, A, H, T; 1961 v E, W, Ni, Ei (2), Cz; 1962 v Ni, W, E, Cz (2), U; 1963 v W, Ni, E.

CALDWELL, G. (Newcastle, Hibernian, Celtic, Wigan) (54): 2002 v Fr, Nig, Skor, SA, HK; 2004 v R, D, Est, Trin; 2005 v H, Sp, Slo, N, Mo, I, Blr; 2006 v Slo, US, Sw, Bul, J; 2007 v Lth, Fr, Uk, A; 2008 v SA, Cro, CzR; 2009 v Mac, Ice (2), N, Arg, Holl; 2010 v N, J, W, CzR; 2011 v CzR, Br, W; 2012 v D, CzR, Lth, Sp, Cy, Slo, US; 2013 v Aus, Mac, W (2), Bel, Ser (2).

CALDWELL, S. (Newcastle, Sunderland, Burnley, Wigan) (12): 2001 v Pol; 2003 v Ei; 2004 v W, Trin; 2005 v Mo; 2006 v A, Slo, US, Sw; 2010 v N; 2011 v Fi, Ni.

CALLAGHAN, P. (Hibernian) (1): 1900 v Ni.

CALLAGHAN, W. C. (Dunfermline Ath.) (2): 1970 v Ei, W.

CAMERON, C. (Hearts, Wolves) (28): 1999 v G, Fi; 2000 v Lth, Fr, Ei; 2001 v La, Sm, Cro, Aus, Sm, Pol; 2002 v Cro, Bel, La, Fr; 2003 v Ei, A, Lth, G; 2004 v N, Fi, G, Lth, W, R, D, 2005 v Sp, Mo.

CAMERON, J. (Rangers) (1): 1886 v NI.

CAMERON, J. (Queen's Park) (1): 1896 v Ni.

CAMERON, J. (St Mirren, Chelsea) (2): 1904 v Ni; 1909 v E.

CAMPBELL, C. (Queen's Park) (13): 1874 v E; 1876 v W; 1877 v E, W; 1878 v E; 1879 v E; 1880 v E; 1881 v E; 1882 v E; 1884 v E; 1885 v E; 1886 v E.

CAMPBELL, H. (Renton) (1): 1889 v W.

CAMPBELL, J. (Sheffield W.) (1): 1913 v W.

CAMPBELL, J. (South Western) (1): 1880 v W.

CAMPBELL, J. (Kilmarnock) (2): 1891 v Ni; 1892 v W.

CAMPBELL, J. (Celtic) (12): 1893 v E, Ni; 1898 v E, Ni; 1900 v E, Ni; 1901 v E, W, Ni; 1902 v W, Ni; 1903 v W.

CAMPBELL, J. (Rangers) (4): 1899 v E, W, Ni; 1901 v Ni.

CAMPBELL, K. (Liverpool, Partick Th.) (8): 1920 v E, W, Ni; 1921 v W, Ni; 1922 v W. Ni, E.

CAMPBELL, P. (Rangers) (2): 1878 v W; 1879 v W.

CAMPBELL, P. (Morton) (1): 1898 v W.

CAMPBELL, R. (Falkirk, Chelsea) (5): 1947 v Bel, L; 1950 v Sw, Por, Fr.

CAMPBELL, W. (Morton) (5): 1946 v Sw; 1947 v Ni; 1948 v E, Bel, Sw.

CANERO, P. (Leicester) (1): 2004 v D.

CARABINE, J. (Third Lanark) (3): 1938 v Holl; 1939 v E, Ni.

CARR, W. M. (Coventry City) (6): 1970 v Ni, W, E; 1971 v D; 1972 v Pe; 1973 v D.

CASSIDY, J. (Celtic) (4): 1921 v W, Ni; 1923 v Ni; 1924 v W.

CHALMERS, S. (Celtic) (5): 1965 v W, Fin; 1966 v Por, Br; 1967 v Ni.

CHALMERS, W. (Rangers) (1): 1885 v Ni.

CHALMERS, W. S. (Queen's Park) (1): 1929 v Ni.

CHAMBERS, T. (Hearts) (1): 1894 v W.

CHAPLIN, G. D. (Dundee) (1): 1908 v W.

CHEYNE, A. G. (Aberdeen) (5): 1929 v E, N, G, Holl; 1930 v Fr.

CHRISTIE, A. J. (Queen's Park) (3): 1898 v W; 1899 v E, Ni.

CHRISTIE, R. M. (Queen's Park) (1): 1884 v E.

CHRISTIE, R (Aberdeen) (3): 2018 v Holl, H, Mx.

CLARK, J. (Celtic) (4): 1966 v Br; 1967 v W, Ni, USSR.

CLARK, R. B. (Aberdeen) (17): 1968 v W, Holl; 1970 v Ni; 1971 v W, Ni, E, D, Por, USSR; 1972 v Bel, Ni, W, E, Cz, Br; 1973 v D, E.

CLARKE, S. (Chelsea) (6): 1988 v H, Bel, Bul, S.Ar, Ma; 1984 v Holl.

CLARKSON, D. (Motherwell) (2): 2008 v CzR; 2009 v Arg.

CLELAND, J. (Royal Albert) (1): 1891 v Ni.

CLEMENTS, R. (Leith Ath.) (1): 1891 v Ni.

CLUNAS, W. L. (Sunderland) (2): 1924 v E; 1926 v W.

COLLIER, W. (Raith R.) (1): 1922 v W.

COLLINS, J. (Hibs, Celtic, Monaco, Everton) (58): 1988 v S.Ar; 1990 v EG, Pol, Ma; 1991 v Sw, Bul, Ni, Fin; 1993 v Por (2), Ma, G, Est (2); 1994 v Sw, Holl (2), A; 1995 v Fin, Fi (2), Ru (2), Gr, Sm. 1996 v Gr, Fin, Se, Sm, Aus, D, US, U, Holl, E, Sw; 1997 v A (2), La, Se (2), Est, Ma; 1998 v Blr, La, Fr, Fin, Co, US, Br, M, N. 1999 v Lth. 2000 v Bos (2), Est, E (2).

COLLINS, R. Y. (Celtic, Everton, Leeds Utd) (31): 1951 v W, Ni, A; 1955 v Y, A, H; 1956 v Ni, W; 1957 v E, W, Sp (2), Sw, WG; 1958 v Ni, W, Sw, H, Pol, Y, Fr, Par; 1959 v E, W, Ni, WG, Holl, Por; 1965 v E, Pol, Sp.

COLLINS, T. (Hearts) (1): 1909 v W.

COLMAN, D. (Aberdeen) (4): 1911 v E, W, Ni; 1913 v Ni.

COLQUHOUN, E. P. (Sheffield Utd) (9): 1972 v Por, Holl, Pe, Y, Cz, Br; 1973 v D (2), E.

COLQUHOUN, J. (Hearts) (1): 1988 v S.Ar, Malta.

COMBE, J. R. (Hibernian) (3): 1948 v E, Bel, Sw.

COMMONS. K (Derby, Celtic) (12): 2009 v Ni, Mac, Ice, Arg; 2010 v N, Holl; 2011 v Fi, Ni, Br; 2013 v M, Bel, Est.

CONN, A. (Hearts) (1): 1956 v A.

CONN, A. (Tottenham H.) (2): 1975 v Ni, E.

CONNACHAN, E. D. (Dunfermline Ath.) (2): 1962 v Cz, U.

CONNELLY, G. (Celtic) (2): 1974 v Cz, WG.

CONNOLLY, J. (Everton) (1): 1973 v Sw.

CONNOR, J. (Airdrie) (1): 1886 v Ni.

CONNOR, J. (Sunderland) (4): 1930 v Fr; 1932 v Ni; 1934 v E; 1935 v Ni.

CONNOR, R. (Dundee, Aberdeen) (4): 1986 v Holl; 1988 v S.Ar; 1989 v E; 1991 v R.

CONWAY, C. (Dundee United, Cardiff) (7): 2010 v J; 2011 v Ni; 2012 v Cy; 2013 v Cro; 2014 v E, US, N.

COOK, W. L. (Bolton W.) (3): 1934 v E; 1935 v W, Ni.

COOKE, C. (Dundee, Chelsea) (16): 1966 v W, I, Por, Br; 1968 v E, Holl; 1969 v W, Ni, A, WG, Cy (2); 1970 v A; 1971 v Bel; 1975 v Sp, Por.

COOPER, D. (Rangers, Motherwell) (22): 1980 v Pe, A; 1984 v W, E; 1985 v Y, Ice, Sp (2), W; 1986 v EG, Aus (2), Holl, WG, U; 1987 v Bul, L, Ei, Br; 1990 v N, Eg.

CORMACK, P. B. (Hibernian, Nottingham F.) (9): 1966 v Br; 1969 v D; 1970 v Ei, WG; 1971 v D, W, Por, E; 1972 v Holl.

COWAN, J. (Aston Villa) (3): 1896 v E; 1897 v E; 1898 v E.

COWAN, J. (Morton) (25): 1948 v Bel, Sw, Fr; 1949 v E, W, Fr; 1950 v E, W, Ni, Sw, Por, Fr; 1951 v E, W, Ni, A (2), D, Fr, Bel; 1952 v Ni, W, USA, Se.

COWAN, W. D. (Newcastle Utd) (1): 1924 v E.

COWIE, D. (Dundee) (20): 1953 v E, Se; 1954 v Ni, W, Fin, N, A, U; 1955 v W, Ni, A, H; 1956 v W, A; 1957 v Ni, W; 1958 v H, Pol, Y, Par.

COWIE, D. (Watford, Cardiff) (9): 2010 v J, W; 2011 V Br; 2012 v D, CzR, Lth, Sp, Cy, US.

COX, S. (Rangers) (25): 1948 v Fr; 1949 v E, Fr; 1950 v E, Fr, W, Ni, Sw, Por; 1951 v E, D, Fr, Bel, A; 1952 v Ni, W, USA, D, Se; 1953 v W, Ni, E; 1954 v W, Ni, E.

CRAIG, A. (Motherwell) (3): 1929 v Ni, Holl; 1932 v E.

CRAIG, J. (Celtic) (1): 1977 v Se.

CRAIG, J. P. (Celtic) (1): 1968 v W.

CRAIG, T. (Rangers) (8): 1927 v Ni; 1928 v Ni; 1929 v N, G, Holl; 1930 v Ni, E, W.

CRAIG, T. B. (Newcastle Utd) (1): 1976 v Sw.

CRAINEY, S (Celtic, Southampton, Blackpool) (12): 2002 v Fr, Nig; 2003 v D, Fi; 2004 v R, D; 2011 v Fi, Br, W; 2012 v D, Lth, Cy.

CRAPNELL, J. (Airdrie) (9): 1929 v E, N, G; 1930 v Fr; 1931 v Ni, Sw; 1932 v E, Fr; 1933 v Ni.

CRAWFORD, D. (St Mirren, Rangers) (3): 1894 v W, Ni; 1900 v W.

CRAWFORD, J. (Queen's Park) (5): 1932 v Fr, Ni; 1933 v E, W, Ni.

CRAWFORD, S. (Raith Rovers, Dunfermline, Plymouth) (25): 1995 v Ec; 2001 v Pol; 2002 v Fr; 2003 v Fi, Ice (2), Can, Por, Ei, A, Lth, Nz, G; 2004 v N, Fi, Lth, Holl, R, Est, Trin; 2005 v H, Sp, Slo, Mo, Se.

CRERAND, P. T. (Celtic, Manchester Utd) (16): 1961 v Ei (2), Cz; 1962 v Ni, W, E, Cz (2), U; 1963 v W, Ni; 1964 v Ni; 1965 v E, Pol, Fin; 1966 v Pol.

CRINGAN, W. (Celtic) (5): 1920 v W; 1922 v E, Ni; 1923 v W, E.

CROSBIE, J. A. (Ayr Utd, Birmingham C.) (2): 1920 v W; 1922 v E.

CROAL, J. A. (Falkirk) (3): 1913 v Ni; 1914 v E, W.

**MORTON'S goalkeeper Jimmy Cowan, with 141
appearances during a nine-year spell**

**JACKIE HUSBAND, Willie Thornton, and
Adam McLean, of Partick Thistle in July 1962**

CROPLEY, A. J. (Hibernian) (2): 1972 v Por, Bel.

CROSS, J. H. (Third Lanark) (1): 1903 v Ni.

CRUICKSHANK, J. (Hearts) (6): 1964 v WG; 1970 v W, E; 1971 v D, Bel; 1976 v R.

CRUM, J. (Celtic) (2): 1936 v E; 1939 v Ni.

CULLEN, M. J. (Luton Town) (1): 1956 v A.

CUMMING, D. S. (Middlesbrough) (1): 1938 v E.

CUMMING, J. (Hearts) (9): 1955 v E, H, Por, Y; 1960 v E, Pol, A, H, T.

CUMMING, J. (Rangers) (2): 2018 v Holl, H.

CUMMINGS, G. (Partick Th., Aston Villa) (9): 1935 v E; 1936 v W, Ni, E; 1937 v G; 1938 v W, Ni, Cz; 1939 v E.

CUMMINGS, W. (Chelsea) (1): 2002 v HK.

CUNNINGHAM, A. N. (Rangers) (12): 1920 v Ni; 1921 v W, E; 1922 v Ni; 1923 v E, W; 1924 v E, Ni; 1926 v E, Ni; 1927 v E, W.

CUNNINGHAM, W. C. (Preston NE) (8): 1954 v N (2), U, Fin, A; 1955 v W, E, H.

CURRAN, H. P. (Wolves) (5): 1970 v A; 1971 v Ni, E, D, USSR.

DAILLY, C. (Derby, Blackburn, West Ham, Rangers) (67): 1997 v W, Ma, Blr; 1998 v Blr, La, Fr, D, Fin, Co, US, Br, N, M; 1999 v Lth; 2000 v Bos (2), Est, Lth, E (2), Fr, Holl, Ei; 2001 v La, Sm, Aus, Pol; 2002 v Cro, Bel, La, Fi, Nig, Skor, SA, HK; 2003 v D, Fi, Ice (2), Can, Por, Ei, A, Lth, Nz; 2004 v N, G, Lth, Holl, W, R, D; 2005 v Mo, Blr; 2006 v A, I, Blr, Slo, US, Sw; 2007 v Fi, Lth, Fr, A; 2008 v Uk, CzR.

DALGLISH, K. (Celtic, Liverpool) (102): 1972 v Bel, Holl; 1973 v D (2), E (2), W, Ni, Sw, Br; 1974 v Cz (2), WG (2), Ni, W, E, Bel, N, Z, Br, Y; 1975 v EG, Sp (2), Se, Por, W, Ni, E, R; 1976 v D (2), R, Sw, Ni, E; 1977 v Fin, Cz, W (2), Se, Ni, E, Ch, Arg, Br; 1978 v EG, Cz, W, Bul, Ni, W, E, Pe, Ir, Holl; 1979 v A, N, Por, W, Ni, E, Arg, N; 1980 v Pe, A, Bel (2), Por, Ni, W, E, Pol, H; 1981 v Se, Por, Is; 1982 v Se, Ni, Por, Sp, Holl, Ni, W, E, Nz, Br; 1983 v Bel, Sw; 1984 v U, Bel, EG; 1985 v Y, Ice, Sp, W; 1986 v EG, Aus, R; 1987 v Bul, L.

DAVIDSON, C. (Blackburn Rovers, Leicester, Preston NE) (19): 1999 v Lth, Est, Fi, CzR (2), G, Fi; 2000 v Est, Bos, Lth, E, Fr; 2001 v La, Pol; 2002, La; 2003 v Ice, Can; 2010 v N, Mac.

DAVIDSON, D. (Queen's Park) (5): 1878 v W; 1879 v W; 1880 v W; 1881 v E, W.

DAVIDSON, J. A. (Partick Th.) (8): 1954 v N (2), A, U; 1955 v W, Ni, E, H.

DAVIDSON, M. (St Johnstone) (1): 2013 v Lux.

DAVIDSON, S. (Middlesbrough) (1): 1921 v E.

DAWSON, A. (Rangers) (5): 1980 v Pol, H; 1983 v Ni, Ca (2).

DAWSON, J. (Rangers) (14): 1935 v Ni; 1936 v E; 1937 v G, E, W, Ni, A, Cz; 1938 v W, Holl, Ni; 1939 v E, Ni, H.

DEANS, J. (Celtic) (2): 1975 v EG, Sp.

DELANEY, J. (Celtic, Manchester Utd) (13): 1936 v W, Ni; 1937 v G, E, A, Cz; 1938 v Ni; 1939 v W, Ni; 1947 v E; 1948 v E, W, Ni.

DEVINE, A. (Falkirk) (1): 1910 v W.

DEVLIN, P. (Birmingham City) (10): 2003 v Can, Por, Ei, A, Ice, Lth, Nz, G; 2004 v N, Fi.

DEWAR, G. (Dumbarton) (2): 1888 v Ni; 1889 v E.

DEWAR, N. (Third Lanark) (3): 1932 v E, Fr; 1933 v W.

DICK, J. (West Ham Utd) (1): 1959 v E.

DICKIE, M. (Rangers) (3): 1897 v Ni; 1899 v Ni; 1900 v W.

DICKOV, P. (Manchester City, Leicester, Blackburn) (10): 2001 v Sm, Cro, Aus; 2003 v Fi; 2004 v Fi, Holl (2), W; 2005 v N, Slo.

DICKSON, W. A (Dundee Strathmore) (1): 1888 v Ni.

DICKSON, W. (Kilmarnock) (5): 1970 v Ni, W, E; 1971 v D, USSR.

DIVERS, J. (Celtic) (1): 1895 v W.

DIXON, P. (Dundee Utd) (3): 2013 v Mac, Lux, Ser.

DAVIDSON, S. (Middlesbrough) (1): 1921 v E.

DOBIE, S. (WBA) (6): 2002 v Skor, SA, HK; 2003 v D, Fi, Por.

DOCHERTY, T. H. (Preston NE, Arsenal) (25): 1952 v W; 1953 v E, Se; 1954 v N (2), A, U; 1955 v W, E, H (2), A; 1957 v E, Y, Sp (2), Sw, WG; 1958 v Ni, W, E, Sw; 1959 v W, E, Ni.

DODDS, D. (Dundee Utd) (2): 1984 v U, Ni.

DODDS, J. (Celtic) (3): 1914 v E, W, Ni.

DODDS, W. (Aberdeen, Dundee Utd, Rangers) (26): 1997 v La, W, Blr; 1998 v Blr. 1999 v Est, Fi, G, Fi, CzR. 2000 v Bos (2), Est, Lth, E (2), Fr, Holl, Ei; 2001 v La, Sm (2), Aus, Bel, Pol; 2002 v Cro, Bel.

DOIG, J. E. (Arbroath, Sunderland) (5): 1887 v Ni; 1889 v Ni; 1896 v E; 1899 v E; 1903 v E.

DONACHIE, W. (Manchester City) (35): 1972 v Pe, Ni, E, Y, Cz, Br; 1973 v D, E, W, Ni; 1974 v Ni; 1976 v R, Ni, W, E,; 1977 v Fin, Cz, W (2), Se, Ni, E, Ch, Arg, Br; 1978 v EG, W (2), Bul, E, Ir, Holl; 1979 v A, N, Por.

DONALDSON, A. (Bolton) (6): 1914 v E, Ni, W; 1920 v E, Ni; 1922 v Ni.

DONNACHIE, J. (Oldham Ath.) (3): 1913 v E; 1914 v E, Ni.

DONNELLY, S. (Celtic) (10): 1997 v W, Ma; 1998 La, Fr, D, Fin, Co, US. 1999 v Est. Fi.

DORRANS, G. (West Bromwich Albion) (12): 2010 v J, W, CzR; 2011 v CzR, Sp; 2012 v D, Lth, Slo; 2013 v W; 2014 v Cro; 2016 v Pol, Gib.

DOUGALL, C. (Birmingham City) (1): 1947 v W.

DOUGALL, J. (Preston NE) (1): 1939 v E.

DOUGAN, R. (Hearts) (1): 1950 v Sw.

DOUGLAS, A. (Chelsea) (1): 1911 v Ni.

DOUGLAS, B. (Wolves) (1): 2018 v H.

DOUGLAS, J. (Renfrew) (1): 1880 v W.

DOUGLAS, R. (Celtic, Leicester) (18): 2002 v Nig, SA, HK; 2003 v D, Fi, Ice (2), Por, Nz, G; 2004 v Fi, H, G, Lth, Holl (2), W; 2005 v I; 2006 v A.

DOWDS, P. (Celtic) (1): 1892 v Ni.

DOWNIE, R. (Third Lanark) (1): 1892 v W.

DOYLE, D. (Celtic) (8): 1892 v E; 1893 v W; 1894 v E, Ni; 1897 v E; 1898 v E, Ni.

DOYLE, J. (Ayr Utd) (1): 1976 v R.

DRUMMOND, J. (Falkirk, Rangers) (14): 1892 v Ni; 1894 v Ni; 1895 v Ni, E; 1896 v E, Ni; 1897 v Ni; 1898 v E; 1900 v E; 1901 v E; 1902 v E, W, Ni; 1903 v Ni.

DUNBAR, M. (Cartvale) (1): 1886 v Ni.

DUNCAN, A. (Hibernian) (6): 1975 v Por, W, Ni, E, R; 1976 v D.

DUNCAN, D. (Derby Co.) (14): 1933 v E, W; 1934 v A, W; 1935 v E, W; 1936 v E, W, Ni; 1937 v G, E, W, Ni; 1938 v W.

DUNCAN, D. M. (East Fife) (1): 1948 v Bel, Sw, Fr.

DUNCAN, J. (Alexandra Ath.) (2): 1878 v W; 1882 v W.

DUNCAN, J. (Leicester City) (1): 1926 v W.

DUNCANSON, J. (Rangers) (1): 1947 v Ni.

DUNLOP, J. (St Mirren) (1): 1890 v W.

DUNLOP, W. (Liverpool) (1): 1906 v E.

DUNN, J. (Hibernian, Everton) (6): 1925 v W, Ni; 1927 v Ni; 1928 v Ni, E; 1929 v W.

DURIE, G. S. (Chelsea, Tottenham, Rangers) (43): 1988 v Bul; 1989 v I, Cy; 1990 v Y, EG, Eg, Se; 1991 v Sw, Bul (2), USSR, Sm (2), 1992 v Sw, R, Ni, Fin, Ca, N, Holl, G; 1993 v Sw, I, Holl (2). 1996 US, Holl, E, Sw; 1997 v A, Se, Ma, Blr; 1998 Blr, La, Fr, Fin, Co, Br, N, M.

DURRANT, I. (Rangers, Kilmarnock) (20): 1988 v H, Bel, Ma, Sp; 1989 v N; 1993 v Sw, Por (2), I; 1994 v I, Ma. 1999 v Est, Fi, G, Fi, CzR. 2000 v Bos; Est, Holl, Ei.

DYKES, J. (Hearts) (2): 1938 v Holl; 1939 v Ni.

EASSON, J. F. (Portsmouth) (3): 1931 v A, Sw; 1934 v W.

ELLIOTT, M. (Leicester City) (18): 1998 v Fr, D, Fin. 1999, v Lth, Fi, CzR, Fi, Holl, Ei; 2001 v La, Sm (2), Cro, Aus, Bel; 2002 v Cro, Bel, La.

ELLIS, J. (Mossend Swifts) (1): 1892 v Ni.

EVANS, A. (Aston Villa) (4): 1982 v Holl, Ni, E, Nz.

EVANS, R. (Celtic, Chelsea) (48): 1949 v E, W, Ni, Fr; 1950 v W, Ni, Sw, Por; 1951 v E, A; 1952 v Ni; 1953 v Se; 1954 v Ni, W, E, N, Fin; 1955 v Ni, Por, Y, A, H; 1956 v E, Ni, W, A; 1957 v WG, Sp; 1958 v Ni, W, E, Sw, H, Pol, Y, Par, Fr; 1959 v E, WG, Holl, Por; 1960 v E, Ni, W, Pol; 1960 v A, H, T.

EWART, J. (Bradford City) (1): 1921 v E.

EWING, T. (Partick Th.) (2): 1958 v W, E.

FARM, G. N. (Blackpool) (10): 1953 v W, Ni, E, Se; 1954 v Ni, W, E; 1959 v WG, Holl, Por.

FERGUSON, B. (Rangers, Blackburn, Rangers) (45): 1999 v Lth. 2000 v Bos, Est, E (2), Fr, Ei; 2001 v La, Aus, Bel; 2003 v D, Fi, Ice (2), Ei; 2004 v N, Fi, G, Lth, Holl (2); 2005 v H, Sp, Slo, N, Mo (2), I, Blr; 2006: v I, N, Blr, Sw; 2007 v Fr, Uk, Geo, I, A, Fi; 2008 v Fr, Uk, Geo, I; 2009 v Arg, Holl.

FERGUSON, D. (Rangers) (2): 1988 v Ma, Co.

FERGUSON, D. (Dundee United, Everton) (7): 1992 v US, Ca, Holl; 1993 v G; 1995 v Gr; 1997 v A, Est.

FERGUSON, I. (Rangers) (9): 1989 v I, Cy, Fr; 1993 v Ma, Est; 1994 v Ma, A, Holl; 1997 v Est.

FERGUSON, J. (Vale of Leven) (6): 1874 v E; 1876 v E, W; 1877 v E, W; 1878 v W.

FERGUSON, R. (Kilmarnock) (7): 1966 v W, E, Holl, Por, Br; 1967 v W, Ni.

FERNIE, W. (Celtic) (12): 1954 v Fin, A, U; 1955 v W, Ni; 1957 v E, Ni, W, Y; 1958 v W, Sw, Par.

FINDLAY, R. (Kilmarnock) (1): 1898 v W.
FITCHIE, T. T. (Woolwich Arsenal, Queen's Park) (4): 1905 v W: 1906 v W, Ni; 1907 v W.
FLAVEL, R. (Airdrie) (2): 1947 v Bel, L.
FLECK, R. (Norwich City) (4): 1990 v Arg, Se, Br; 1991 v USSR.
FLEMING, C. (East Fife) (1): 1954 v Ni.
FLEMING, J. W. (Rangers) (3): 1929 v G, Holl; 1930 v E.
FLEMING, R. (Morton): 1886 v Ni.
FLETCHER, D. (Manchester Utd, WBA), Stoke (80): 2004 v N, Lth, Holl (2), W, D, Est, Trin; 2005 v H, Sp, Slo, N, Mo (2), Blr; 2006 v I, N, Blr, Slo, US, Sw, Bul, J; 2007 v Fi (2), Lth, Fr, Uk, A; 2008 v SA, Lth, Fr, Geo, I, Cro, CzR. 2009 v Ni, Mac, Ice (2), N, Holl; 2010 v N, Mac, Holl, W, CzR; 2011 v Se, Lth, Li, CzR, Sp, Fi. 2012 v CzR, Lth, Sp, Cy; 2013 v W, Bel, Lux; 2014 v Pol; 2015 v Ger, Pol, Ei, Ni, Q; 2016 v Pol, Gib, CZR, I, Fr; 2017 v Ma, Lth, Slv, E, Ca; 2018 v Slv, Slo.
FLETCHER, S. (Hibs, Burnley, Wolves, Sunderland, Sheffield W) (31): 2008 v Cro; 2009 v N, Holl, Ice; 2010 v Mac, W, J; 2011 v Se; 2013 v W (2), Bel, Est; 2014 v US, Pol; 2015 v G, Geo, Pol, Ei, Ni, Gib, Ei; 2016 v Geo, G, Pol, Gib, D, I, Fr; 2017 v Ma, Slv; 2018 v Slo
FORBES, A. R. (Sheffield Utd, Arsenal) (14): 1947 v Bel, L, E; 1948 v W, Ni; 1950 v E, Por, Fr; 1951 v W, Ni, A; 1952 v W, D, Se.
FORBES, J. (Vale of Leven) (5): 1884 v E, W, Ni; 1887 v W, E.
FORD, D. (Hearts) (3): 1974 v Cz, WG, W.
FORREST, J. (Motherwell) (1): 1958 v E.
FORREST, J. (Rangers, Aberdeen) (5): 1966 v W, I; 1971 v Bel, D, USSR.
FORREST, J. (Celtic) (22): 2011 v Ei; 2012 v D, Li, Sp, Slo; 2013 v Mac, Ser; 2014 v E, Bel; 2015 v Q; 2016 v Geo, G, Pol; 2017 v Ma, Lth, E, Slo; 2018 v Lth, Ma, Slv, Holl, N.
FORSYTH, A. (Partick Th., Manchester Utd) (10): 1972 v Y, Cz, Br; 1973 v D, E; 1975 v Sp, Ni, R, EG; 1976 v D.
FORSYTH, C. (Kilmarnock) (4): 1964 v E; 1965 v W, Ni, Fin.
FORSYTH, C. (Derby County) (4): 2014 v Nig; 2015 v Ni, Q, Ei.
FORSYTH, T. (Motherwell, Rangers) (22): 1971 v D; 1974 v Cz; 1976 v Sw, Ni, W, E; 1977 v Fin, Se, W, Ni, E, Ch, Arg, Br; 1978 v Cz, W, Ni, W, E, Pe, Ir, Holl.
FOX, D. (Celtic, Southampton) (4): 2010 v W; 2013 v Aus, W, Bel.
FOYERS, R. (St Bernard's) (2): 1893 v W; 1894 v W.
FRASER, D. M. (WBA) (2): 1968 v Holl; 1969 v Cy.
FRASER, J. (Moffat) (1): 1891 v Ni.
FRASER, M. J. E. (Queen's Park) (5): 1880 v W; 1882 v W, E; 1883 v W, E.
FRASER, J. (Dundee) (1): 1907 v Ni.
FRASER, R. (Bournemouth) (3): 2017 v E; 2018 v Holl, H.
FRASER, W. (Sunderland) (2): 1955 v W, Ni.
FREEDMAN, D. (Crystal Palace) (2): 2002 v L1, Fr.
FULTON, W. (Abercorn) (1): 1884 v Ni.
FYFE, J. H. (Third Lanark) (1): 1895 v W.
GABRIEL, J. (Everton) (2): 1961 v W; 1964 v N.
GALLACHER, K. W. (Dundee Utd, Coventry, Blackburn Rov, Newcastle) (53): 1988 v Co, E; 1989 v N; I; 1991 v Sm (2); 1992 v R, Ni, N, Holl, G, CIS; 1993 v Sw, Por (2), Est (2); 1994 v I, Ma; 1996 v Aus, D, U, Holl; 1997 v Se (2), Est (2), A, W, Ma, Blr; 1998 v Blr, La, Fr, Fin, US, Br, N, M. 1999 v Lth, Est, Fi, CzR. 2000 v Bos (2), Lth, E, Fr, Ei; 2001 v Sm (2), Cro, Bel.
GALLACHER, P. (Sunderland) (1): 1935 v Ni.

GALLACHER, P. (Dundee United) (8): 2002 v HK; 2003 v Can, Ei, A, Lth, R, D, Est.

GALLAGHER, H. K. (Airdrie, Newcastle Utd, Chelsea, Derby C.) (20): 1924 v Ni; 1925 v E, W, Ni; 1926 v W, E, Ni; 1927 v E, W, Ni; 1928 v E, W; 1929 v E, W, Ni; 1930 v W, Ni, Fr; 1934 v E; 1935 v E.

GALLOWAY, M. (Celtic) (1): 1992 v R.

GALLAGHER, P. (Blackburn Rov) (1): 2004 v W.

GALT, J. H. (Rangers) (2): 1908 v W, Ni.

GARDINER, I. (Motherwell) (1): 1958 v W.

GARDNER, D. R. (Third Lanark) (1): 1897 v W.

GARDNER, R. (Queen's Park, Clydesdale) (5): 1872 v E; 1873 v E; 1874 v E; 1875 v E; 1878 v E.

GEMMELL, T. (St Mirren) (2): 1955 v Por, Y.

GEMMELL, T. (Celtic) (18): 1966 v E; 1967 v W, Ni, E, USSR; 1968 v Ni, E; 1969 v W, Ni, E, D, A, WG, Cy; 1970 v E, Ei, WG; 1971 v Bel.

GEMMILL, A. (Derby Co., Nottingham F., Birmingham City) (43): 1971 v Bel; 1972 v Por, Holl, Pe, Ni, W, E; 1976 v D, R, Ni, W, E; 1977 v Fin, Cz, W (2), Ni, E, Ch, Arg, Br; 1978 v EG, Bul, Ni, W, E, Pe, Ir, Holl; 1979 v A, N. Por, N; 1980 v A, Por, Ni, W, E, H; 1981 v Se, Por, Is, Ni.

GEMMILL, S. (Nottingham F, Everton) (25): 1995 v J, Ec, Fi; 1996 v Sm, D, US; 1997 v Est, Se, W, Ma, Blr; 1998 v D, Fin; 1999 v G, Fi; 2001 v Sm; 2002 v Cro, Fr, Nig, Skor, SA, HK; 2003 v Can, Ei, A.

GIBB, W. (Clydesdale) (1): 1873 v E.

GIBSON, D. W. (Leicester City) (7): 1963 v A, N, Ei, Sp; 1964 v Ni; 1965 v W, Fin.

GIBSON, J. D. (Partick Th., Aston Villa) (8): 1926 v E; 1927 v E, W, Ni; 1928 v E, W; 1930 v W, Ni.

GIBSON, N. (Rangers, Partick Th.) (14): 1895 v E, Ni; 1896 v E, Ni; 1897 v E, Ni; 1898 v E; 1899 v E, W, Ni; 1900 v E, Ni; 1901 v W; 1905 v Ni.

GILCHRIST, J. E. (Celtic) (1): 1922 v E.

GILHOOLEY, M. (Hull City) (1): 1922 v W.

GILKS, M. (Blackpool) (3): 2013 v Aus, Lux; 2014 v Mac.

GILLESPIE, G. (Rangers, Queen's Park) (7): 1880 v E, W; 1882 v E; 1886 v W; 1890 v W; 1891 v Ni.

GILLESPIE, G. T. (Liverpool) (13): 1988 v Bel, Bul, Sp; 1989 v N, Fr, Ch; 1990 v Y, EG, Eg, Pol, Ma, Br; 1991 v Bul.

GILLESPIE, Jas. (Third Lanark) (1): 1898 v W.

GILLESPIE, John (Queen's Park) (1): 1896 v W.

GILLESPIE, R. (Queen's Park) (4): 1927 v W; 1931 v W; 1932 v Fr; 1933 v E.

GILLICK, T. (Everton) (5): 1937 v A, Cz; 1939 v W, Ni, H.

GILMOUR, J. (Dundee) (1): 1931 v W.

GILZEAN, A. J. (Dundee, Tottenham H.) (22): 1964 v W, E, N, WG; 1965 v Ni, Sp; 1966 v Ni, W, Pol, I; 1968 v W; 1969 v W, E, WG, Cy (2), A; 1970 v Ni, E, WG, A; 1971 v Por.

GLAVIN, R. (Celtic) (1): 1977 v Se.
GLASS S. (Newcastle Utd) (1): 1999 v Fi.
GLEN, A. (Aberdeen) (2): 1956 v E, Ni.
GLEN, R. (Renton, Hibernian) (3): 1895 v W; 1896 v W; 1900 v Ni.
GOODWILLIE, D. (Dundee Utd, Blackburn) (3): 2011 v Fi; 2012 v Lth, Sp.
GORAM, A. L. (Oldham, Hibs, Rangers) (42): 1986 v EG, R, Holl; 1987 v Br; 1989 v Y, I; 1990 v EG, Pol, Ma; 1991 v R (2), Sw, Bul (2), USSR, Sm (2); 1992 v Sw, Fin, N, Holl, G, CIS; 1993 v Sw, Por (2), I, Ma; 1994 v Holl; 1995 v Fin, Fi, Ru, Gr; 1996 v Se, D, Holl, Sw, E, Col; 1997 A, La, Est; 1998 v D.
GORDON, C. (Hearts, Sunderland, Celtic) (52): 2004 v Trin; 2005 v Sp, Slo, N, Mo (2), I, Blr; 2006 v A, I, N, Blr, Slo, US, Sw; 2007 v Fi (2), Lth, Fr, Uk, Geo, I, A; 2008 v SA, Lth, Fr, Uk, Geo, I, Cro, CzR; 2009 v Ni, Mac, Ice (2), N; 2010 v Mac, J, CzR; 2011 v Fi; 2015 v E, Ni, Q; 2016 v D; 2017 v E, Slo, E; 2018 v Lth, Ma, Slv, Slo, Holl.
GORDON, J. E. (Rangers) (10): 1912 v E, Ni; 1913 v E, Ni, W; 1914 v E, Ni; 1920 v W, E, Ni, U.
GOSSLAND, J. (Rangers) (1): 1884 v Ni.
GOUDLE, J. (Abercorn) (1): 1884 v Ni.
GOUGH, C. R. (Dundee Utd, Tottenham H., Rangers) (61): 1983 v Sw, Ni, W, E, Ca (3); 1984 v U, Bel, EG, Ni, W, E, Fr; 1985 v Sp, E, Ice; 1986 v W, EG, Aus, Is, R, E, D, WG, U; 1987 v Bul, L, Ei (2), Bel, E, Br; 1988 v H, S.Ar, Sp, Co, E; 1989 v Y, I, Cy (2), Fr; 1990 v Fr, Arg, EG, Pol, Ma, Cr; 1991 v USSR, Bul; 1992 v Sm, Ni, Ca, N, Holl, G, CIS; 1993 v Sw, Por.
GOULD, J. (Celtic) (2): 2000 v Lth; 2001 v Aus.
GOURLAY, J. (Cambuslang) (1): 1886 v Ni; 1888 v W.
GOVAN, J. (Hibernian) (6): 1948 v E, W, Bel, Sw, Fr; 1949 v Ni.
GOW, D. R. (Rangers) (1): 1888 v E.
GOW, J. J. (Queen's Park) (1): 1885 v E.
GOW, J. R. (Rangers) (1): 1888 v Ni.
GRAHAM, A. (Leeds Utd) (11): 1978 v EG; 1979 v A, N, W, Ni, E, Arg, N; 1980 v A, Pe; 1981 v W.
GRAHAM, G. (Arsenal, Manchester Utd) (12): 1972 v Por, Holl, Ni, Y, Cz, Br; 1973 v D (2), E, W, Ni, Br.
GRAHAM, J. (Annbank) (1): 1884 v Ni.
GRAHAM, J. A. (Arsenal) (1): 1921 v Ni.
GRANT, J. (Hibernian) (2): 1959 v W, Ni.
GRANT, P. (Celtic) (2): 1989 v E, Ch.
GRAY, A, (Hibernian) (1): 1903 v Ni.
GRAY, A. (Bradford) (2): 2003 v Lth, Nz.
GRAY, A. M. (Aston Villa, Wolverhampton W., Everton) (20): 1976 v R, Sw; 1977 v Fin, Cz; 1979 v A, N; 1980 v Por, E; 1981 v Se, Por, Is, Ni; 1982 v Se, Ni; 1983 v Ni, W, E, Ca (2); 1985 v Ice.
GRAY, D. (Rangers) (10): 1929 v W, Ni, G, Holl; 1930 v W, E, Ni; 1931 v W; 1933 v W, Ni.
GRAY, E. (Leeds Utd) (12): 1969 v E, Cy; 1970 v WG, A; 1971 v W, Ni; 1972 v Bel, Holl; 1976 v W, E; 1977 v Fin, W.
GRAY, F. T. (Leeds Utd, Nottingham F.) (32): 1976 v Sw; 1979 v N, Por, W, Ni, E, Arg; 1980 v Bel; 1981 v Se, Por, Is (2), Ni, (2), W, E; 1982 v Se, Ni, Por, Sp, Holl, W, Nz, Br, USSR; 1983 v EG, Sw, (2), Bel, W, E, Ca.

GRAY, W. (Pollokshields Ath.) (1): 1886 v E.

GREEN, A. (Blackpool, Newcastle) (6): 1971 v Bel, Por, Ni, E; 1972 v W, E.

GREER, G. (Brighton, Blackburn) (11): 2014 V US, N, Pol, Nig; 2015 v Pol, Ni, Gib; 2015 v Q; 2016 v Gib, D, Fr.

GREIG, J. (Rangers) (44): 1964 v E, WG; 1965 v W, Ni, E, Fin (2), Sp, Pol; 1966 v Ni, W, E, Pol, I (2), Por, Holl, Br; 1967 v W, Ni, E; 1968 v Ni, W, E, Holl; 1969 v W, Ni, E, D, A, WG, Cy (2); 1970 v W, E, Ei, WG, A; 1971 v D, Bel, W, Ni, E; 1976 v D.

GRAY, W. (Pollokshields Ath.) (1): 1886 v E.

GRIFFITHS, L. (Wolves, Celtic) (17): 2013 v Lux, Cro; 2014 v E, Bel; 2015 v Q; 2016 v Geo, D; 2017 v Lth, Slv, E, Ca, Slo, E; 2018 v Lth, Ma, Slv, Slo.

GUILLILAND, W. (Queen's Park) (4): 1891 v W; 1892 v Ni; 1894 v E; 1895 v E.

GUNN, B. (Norwich City) (6): 1990 v Eg; 1993 v Est (2); 1994 v Sw, I, Holl.

HADDOCK, H. (Clyde) (6): 1955 v E, H (2), Por, Y; 1958 v E.

HADDOW, D. (Rangers) (1): 1894 v E.

HAFFEY, F. (Celtic) (2): 1960 v E; 1961 v E.

HAMILTON, A. (Queen's Park) (4): 1885 v E, W; 1886 v E; 1888 v E.

HAMILTON, A. W. (Dundee) (24): 1962 v Cz, U, W, E; 1963 v W, Ni, E, A, N, Ei; 1964 v Ni, W, E, N, WG; 1965 v Ni, W, E, Fin (2), Pol, Sp; 1966 v Pol, Ni.

HAMILTON, G. (Aberdeen) (5): 1947 v Ni; 1951 v Bel, A; 1954 v N (2).

HAMILTON, S. (Port Glasgow Ath.) (1): 1906 v Ni.

HAMILTON, J. (Queen's Park) (3): 1892 v W; 1893 v E, Ni.

HAMILTON, J. (St Mirren) (1): 1924 v Ni.

HAMILTON, R. C. (Rangers, Dundee) (11): 1899 v E, W, Ni; 1900 v W; 1901 v E, Ni; 1902 v W, Ni; 1903 v E; 1904 v Ni; 1911 v W.

HAMILTON, T. (Hurlford) (1): 1891 v Ni.

HAMILTON, T. (Rangers) (1): 1932 v E.

HAMILTON, W. M. (Hibernian) (1): 1965 v Fin.

HAMMELL, S. (Motherwell) (1): 2005 v Se.

HANLEY, G (Blackburn Rovs, Newcastle, Norwich) (29): 2011 v W, Ei; 2012 v D; 2013 v Lux, W, Cro (2), Ser; 2014 v E, Bel, Mac, Cro, US, Nig; 2015 v Q, Geo, Ei; 2015 v Geo, G, Pol, D; 2016 v I, Fr; 2017 v Ma, Lth, Slv, E; 2018 v Ma, Cr.

HANNAH, A. B., (Renton) (1): 1888 v W.

HANNAH, J. (Third Lanark) (1): 1889 v W.

HANSEN, A. D. (Liverpool) (26): 1979 v W, Arg; 1980 v Bel, Por; 1981 v Se, Por, Is; 1982 v Se, Ni (2), Por, Sp, W, E, Nz, Br, USSR; 1983 v EG, Sw (2), Bel; 1985 v W; 1986 v R; 1987 v Ei (2), L.

HANSEN, J. (Partick Th.) (2): 1972 v Bel, Y.

HARKNESS, J. D. (Queen's Park, Hearts) (12): 1927 v E, Ni; 1928 v E; 1929 v W, E, Ni; 1930 v E, W; 1932 v W, Fr; 1934 v Ni, W.

HARPER, J. M. (Aberdeen, Hibernian) (4): 1973 v D (2); 1976 v D; 1978 v Ir.

HARPER, W. (Hibernian, Arsenal) (11): 1923 v E, Ni, W; 1924 v E, Ni, W; 1925 v E, Ni, W; 1926 v E, Ni.

HARRIS, J. (Partick Th.) (2): 1921 v W, Ni.

HARRIS, N. (Newcastle Utd) (1): 1924 v E.

HARROWER, W. (Queen's Park) (3): 1882 v E; 1884 v Ni; 1886 v W.

HARTFORD, R. A. (WBA, Manchester City, Everton) (50): 1972 v Pe, W, E, Y, Cz, Br; 1976 v D, R, Ni; 1977 v Cz, W, (2), Se, Ni, E, Ch, Arg, (cont..)

Br; 1978 v EG, Cz, W (2), Bul, E, Pe, Ir, Holl; 1979 v A, N, Por, W, Ni, E, Arg, N; 1980 v Pe, Bel; 1981 v Ni (2), Is, W, E; 1982 v Se, Ni (2), Por, Sp, W, E, Br.

HARTLEY, P. (Hearts, Celtic, Bristol City) (25): 2005 v I, Mo; 2006 v I, N, Blr, Slo, US; 2007 v Fi (2), Lth, Fr, Uk, Geo, I, A; 2008 v Fr, I, Cro, CzR; 2009 v Mac, Ice, Arg; 2010 v Mac, Holl, CzR.

HARVEY, D. (Leeds Utd.) (16): 1973 v D; 1974 v Cz, WG, Ni, W, E, Bel, Z, Br, Y; 1975 v EG, Sp (2); 1976 v D (2); 1977 v Fin.

HASTINGS, A. C. (Sunderland) (2): 1936 v Ni; 1938 v Ni.

HAUGHNEY, M. (Celtic) (1): 1954 v E.

HAY, D. (Celtic) (27): 1970 v Ni, W, E; 1971 v D, Bel, W, Por, Ni; 1972 v Por, Bel, Holl; 1973 v W, Ni, E, Sw, Br; 1974 v Cz (2), WG, Ni, W, E, Bel, N, Z, Br.

HAY, J. (Celtic, Newcastle Utd) (11): 1905 v Ni; 1909 v Ni; 1910 v W, Ni, E; 1911 v Ni, E; 1912 v E, W; 1914 v E, Ni.

HEGARTY, P. (Dundee Utd.) (8): 1979 v W, Ni, E, Arg, N; 1980 v W, E; 1983 v Ni.

HEGGIE, C. (Rangers) (1): 1886 v Ni.

HENDERSON, G. H. (Rangers) (1): 1904 v Ni.

HENDERSON, J. G. (Portsmouth, Arsenal) (7): 1953 v Se; 1954 v Ni, E, N; 1956 v W; 1959 v W, Ni.

HENDERSON, W. (Rangers) (30): 1963 v W, Ni, E, A, N, Ei, Sp; 1964 v W, Ni, E, N, WG; 1965 v Fin, Pol, E, Sp; 1966 v Ni, W, Pol, I, Holl; 1967 v W, Ni; 1968 v Holl; 1969 v Ni, E, Cy; 1970 v Ei; 1971 v Por.

HENDRY C. (Blackburn R., Rangers, Bolton) (51): 1993 v Est (2); 1994 v Ma, Holl (2), A; 1995 v Fin, Fi, Gr, Ru, Sm; 1996 v Fin, Se, Sm, Aus, D, US, U, Holl, E, Sw; 1997 A (2), Se (2), Est (2); 1998 La, D, Fin, Co, US, Br, N, M. 1999 v Lth, Est, Fi, G. 2000 v Bos (2), Est, E (2), Fr; 2001 v La, Sm (2), Cro, Aus, Bel.

HENDRY J. (Celtic) (2): 2018 v H, Mx.

HEPBURN, J. (Alloa Ath.) (1) 1891 v W.

HEPBURN, R. (Ayr Utd) (1): 1932 v Ni.

HERD, A. C. (Hearts) (1): 1935 v Ni.

HERD, D. G. (Arsenal): (5): 1959 v E, W, Ni; 1961 v E, Cz.

HERD, G. (Clyde) (5): 1958 v E; 1960 v H, T; 1961 v W, Ni.

HERRIOT, J. (Birmingham City) (8): 1969 v Ni, E, D, Cy (2), W; 1970 v Ei, WG.

HEWIE, J. D. (Charlton Ath.) (19): 1956 v E, A; 1957 v E, Ni, W, Y, Sp (2), Sw, WG; 1958 v H, Pol, Y, Fr; 1959 v Holl, Por; 1960 v Ni, W, Pol.

HIGGINS, A. (Kilmarnock) (1): 1885 v Ni.

HIGGINS, A. (Newcastle Utd) (4): 1910 v E, Ni; 1911 v E, Ni.

HIGHET, T. C. (Queen's Park) (4): 1875 v E; 1876 v E, W; 1878 v E.

HILL, D. (Rangers) (3): 1881 v E, W; 1882 v W.

HILL, D. A. (Third Lanark) (1): 1906 v Ni.

HILL, F. R. (Aberdeen) (3): 1930 v Fr; 1931 v W, Ni.

HILL, J. (Hearts) (2): 1891 v E; 1892 v W.

HOGG, G. (Hearts) (2): 1896 v E, Ni.

HOGG, J. (Ayr Utd.) (1): 1922 v Ni.

HOGG, R. M. (Celtic) (1): 1937 v Cz.

HOLM, A. H. (Queen's Park) (3): 1882 v W; 1883 v E, W.

HOLT, D. D. (Hearts) (5): 1963 v A, N, Ei, Sp; 1964 v WG.

HOLT, G. (Kilmarnock, Norwich) (10): 2001 v La, Cro; 2002 v Fr; 2004 v W, Est, Trin; 2005 v H, Slo, N, Mo.

HOLTON, J. A. (Manchester Utd.) (15): 1973 v W, Ni, E, Sw, Br; 1974 v Cz, WG, Ni, W, E, N, Z, Br, Y; 1975 v EG.

HOPE, R. (WBA) (2): 1968 v Holl; 1969 v D.

HOPKIN, D. (Crystal Palace, Leeds) (7): 1997 v Ma, Blr; 1998 v Blr, La; 1999 v CzR. 2000 v Bos (2).

HOULISTON, W. (Queen of the South) (3): 1949 v E, Ni, Fr.

HOUSTON, S. M. (Manchester Utd.) (1): 1976 v D.

HOWDEN, W. (Partick Th.) (1): 1905 v Ni.

HOWE, R. (Hamilton Accies) (2): 1929 v N, Holl.

HOWIE, J. (Newcastle Utd.) (3): 1905 v E; 1906 v E; 1908 v E.

HOWIE, H. (Hibernian) (1): 1949 v W.

HOWIESON, J. (St Mirren) (1): 1927 v Ni.

HUGHES, J. (Celtic) (8): 1965 v Pol, Sp; 1966 v Ni, I (2); 1968 v E; 1969 v A; 1970 v Ei.

HUGHES, R. (Portsmouth, Grimsby) (5): 2004 v Est, Trin; 2005 v N, Se; 2006 v A.

HUGHES, S. (Norwich City) (1): 2010 v J.

HUGHES, W. (Sunderland) (1): 1975 v Se.

HUMPHRIES, W. (Motherwell) (1): 1952 v Se.

HUNTER, A. (Kilmarnock, Celtic) (4): 1972 v Pe, Y; 1973 v E; 1974 v Cz.

HUNTER, J. (Dundee) (1): 1909 v W.

HUNTER, J. (Third Lanark, Eastern) (4): 1874 v E, 1875 v E, 1876 v E, 1877 v W.

HUNTER, R. (St Mirren) (1): 1890 v Ni.

HUNTER, W. (Motherwell) (3): 1960 v H, T; 1961 v W.

HUSBAND, J. (Partick Th.) (1): 1947 v W.

HUTCHISON, D. (Everton, Sunderland, West Ham) (26): 1999 v CzR, G; 2000 v. Bos, Est, Lth, E (2); Fr, Holl, Ei; 2001 v La, Sm (2), Cro, Aus, Bel; 2002 v Cro, Bel, La; 2003 v Ei, A, Ice, Lth; 2004 v N, Lth, Holl.

HUTCHISON, T. (Coventry City) (17): 1974 v Cz (2), WG (2), Ni, W, Bel, N, Z, Y; 1975 v EG, Sp (2), Por, E, R; 1976 v D.

HUTTON, A. (Rangers, Tottenham, Aston Villa) (50): 2007 v A; 2008 v SA, Lth, Fr, Uk, I, Cro; 2009 v Arg, Holl, Ice; 2010 v N, Mac, Holl, W, CzR; 2011 v Lth, Li, CzR, Ni, Br; 2012 v CzR, Li, Sp; 2013 v Aus, Mac, W (2), Bel, Est, Ser (2), Cro; 2014 v E, Bel, Mac, Cro, US, N, Pol, Nig; 2015 v v G, Geo, Pol, Gib, Ei; 2016 v Geo, G, Pol, Gib, CZR.

HUTTON, J. (Aberdeen, Blackburn R.) (10): 1923 v E, W, Ni; 1924 v Ni; 1926 v W, E, Ni; 1927 v Ni; 1928 v W, Ni.

HUTTON, J. (St Bernard's) (1): 1887 v Ni.

HYSLOP, T. (Stoke City, Rangers) (2): 1896 v E; 1897 v E.

IMLACH, J. J. S. (Nottingham F.) (4): 1958 v H, Pol, Y. Fr.

IMRIE, W. N. (St Johnstone) (2): 1929 v N, G.

INGLIS, J. (Kilmarnock Ath.) (1): 1884 v Ni.

INGLIS, J. (Rangers) (2): 1883 v E, N.

IRONS, J. H. (Queen's Park) (1): 1900 v W.

IRVINE, B. (Aberdeen) (9): 1991 v R; 1993 v G, Est (2); 1994 v Sw, I, Ma, A, Holl.

IWELUMO, C. (Wolves) (4): 2009 v N, Arg; 2011 v Se, CzR.

JACK, R. (Rangers) (1): 2018 v Holl.

JACKSON, A. (Cambuslang) (2): 1886 v W, 1888 v Ni.

JACKSON, A. (Aberdeen, Huddersfield Town) (17): 1925 v E, W, Ni; 1926 v E, W, Ni; 1927 v W, Ni; 1928 v E, W; 1929 v E, W, Ni; 1930 v E, W, Ni, Fr.

JACKSON, C. (Rangers) (8): 1975 v Se, Por, W; 1976 v D, R, Ni, W, E.

JACKSON D. (Hibs, Celtic) (28): 1995 v Ru, Sm, J, Ec, Fi. 1996 v Gr, Fin, Se, Sm, Aus, D, US; 1997 v La, Se (2), Est, A, W, Ma, Blr; 1998 v D, Fin, Co, US, Br, N. 1999 v Lth, Est.

JACKSON, J. (Partick Th., Chelsea) (8): 1931 v A, I, Sw; 1933 v E; 1934 v E; 1935 v E; 1936 v W, Ni.

JACKSON, T. A. (St Mirren) (6): 1904 v W, E, Ni; 1905 v W; 1907 v W, Ni.

JAMES, A. (Preston NE, Arsenal) (8): 1926 v W; 1928 v E; 1929 v E, Ni; 1930 v E, W, Ni; 1933 v W.

JARDINE, A. (Rangers) (38): 1971 v D; 1972 v Por, Bel, Holl; 1973 v E, Sw, Br; 1974 v Cz (2), WG (2), Ni, W, E, Bel, N, Z, Br, Y; 1975 v EG, Sp (2), Se, Por, W, Ni, E; 1977 v Se, Ch, Br; 1978 v Cz, W, Ni, Ir; 1980 v Pe, A. Bel (2).

JARVIE, A. (Airdrie) (3): 1971 v Por, Ni, E.

JESS, E. (Aberdeen) (18): 1993 v I, Ma; 1994 v Sw, I, Holl (2), A; 1995 v Fin; 1996 v Se, Sm, US, U, E; 1998 v D; 1999 v CzR (2), G, Fi.

JENKINSON, T. (Hearts) (1): 1887 v Ni.

JOHNSTON, A. (Sunderland, Rangers, Middlesbrough) (18): 1999 v Est, Fi, CzR (2), G, Fi; 2000 v Est, Fr, Ei; 2001 v Sm (2), Cro; 2002 v Nig, Skor, SA, HK; 2003 v D, Fi.

JOHNSTON, L. H. (Clyde) (2): 1948 v Bel, Sw.

JOHNSTON, M. (Watford, Celtic, Nantes, Rangers) (38): 1984 v W, E, Fr; 1985 v Y, Ice, Sp (2), W; 1986 v EG; 1987 v Bul, Ei (2), L; 1988 v H, Bel, L. S.Ar, Sp, Co, E; 1989 v N, Y, I, Cy (2), Fr, E, Ch; 1990 v Fr, N, EG, Pol, Ma, Cr, Se, Br; 1992 v Sw, Sm.

JOHNSTON, R. (Sunderland) (1): 1938 v Cz.

JOHNSTON, W. (Rangers, WBA) (22): 1966 v W, E, Pol, Holl; 1968 v W, E; 1969 v Ni; 1970 v Ni; 1971 v D; 1977 v Se, W, Ni, E, Ch, Arg, Br; 1978 v EG, Cz, W (2), E, Pe.

JOHNSTONE, D. (Rangers) (14): 1973 v W, Ni, E, Sw, Br; 1975 v EG, Se; 1976 v Sw, Ni, E; 1978 v Bul, Ni, W; 1980 v Bel.

JOHNSTONE, J. (Abercorn) (1): 1888 v W.

JOHNSTONE, J. (Celtic) (23): 1965 v W, Fin; 1966 v E; 1967 v W, USSR; 1968 v W; 1969 v A, WG; 1970 v E, WG; 1971 v D, E; 1972 v Por, Bel, Holl, Ni, E; 1974 v W, E, Bel, N; 1975 v EG, Sp.

JOHNSTONE, JAS. (Kilmarnock) (1): 1894 v W.

JOHNSTONE, J. A. (Hearts) (3): 1930 v W; 1933 v W, Ni.

JOHNSTONE, R. (Hibernian, Manchester City) (17): 1951 v E, D, Fr; 1952 v Ni, E; 1953 v E, Se; 1954 v W, E, N, Fin; 1955 v Ni, H, E; 1956 v E, Ni, W.

JOHNSTONE, W. (Third Lanark) (3): 1887 v Ni; 1889 v W; 1890 v E.

JORDAN, J. (Leeds Utd, Manchester Utd, AC Milan) (52): 1973 v E, Sw, Br; 1974 v Cz (2), WG, Ni, W, E, Bel, N, Z, Br, Y; 1975 v EG, Sp (2); 1976 v Ni, W, E; 1977 v Cz, W, Ni, E; 1978 v EG, Cz, W, Bul, Ni, E, Pe, Ir, Holl; 1979 v A, Por, W, Ni, E, N; 1980 v Bel, Ni, W, E, Pol; 1981 v Is, W, E; 1982 v Se, Holl, W, E, USSR.

KAY, J. L. (Queen's Park) (6): 1880 v E; 1882 v E, W; 1883 v E, W; 1884 v E.

KEILLOR, A. (Montrose, Dundee) (6): 1891 v W; 1892 v Ni; 1894 v Ni; 1895 v W; 1896 v W; 1897 v W.

KEIR, L. (Dumbarton) (5): 1885 v W: 1886 v Ni; 1887 v E, W; 1888 v E.

KELLY, H. T. (Blackpool) (1): 1952 v USA.

KELLY, J. (Renton, Celtic) (8): 1888 v E; 1889 v E; 1890 v E; 1892 v E; 1893 v E, Ni; 1894 v W; 1896 v Ni.

KELLY, J. C. (Barnsley) (2): 1949 v W, Ni.

KELLY, L (Kilmarnock) (1): 2013 v Lux.

KELSO, R. (Renton, Dundee) (8): 1885 v W, Ni; 1886 v W; 1887 v E, W; 1888 v E, Ni; 1898 v Ni.

KELSO, T. (Dundee) (1): 1914 v W.

KENNAWAY, J. (Celtic) (1): 1934 v A.

KENNEDY, A. (Eastern, Third Lanark) (6): 1875 v E; 1876 v E, W; 1878 v E; 1882 v W; 1884 v W.

KENNEDY, J. (Celtic) (6): 1964 v W, Fr, WG; 1965 v W, Ni, Fin.

KENNEDY, J. (Celtic) (2): 2004 v R.

KENNEDY, J. (Hibernian) (1): 1897 v W.

KENNEDY, S. (Aberdeen) (8): 1978 v Bul, W, E, Pe, Holl; 1979 v A, Por; 1982 v Por.

KENNEDY, S, (Partick Th.) (1): 1905 v W.

KENNEDY, S. (Rangers) (5): 1975 v Se, Por, W, Ni, E.

KENNETH, G. (Dundee United) (2): 2011 v Se, Fi.

KER, G. (Queen's Park) (5): 1880 v E; 1881 v E, W; 1882 v W, E.

KER, W. (Granville, Queen's Park) (2): 1872 v E; 1873 v E.

KERR, A. (Partick Th.) (2): 1955 v A, H.

KERR, B. (Newcastle Utd, Coventry) (3): 2003 v Nz; 2004 v Est; 2004: v Trin.

KERR, P. (Hibernian) (1): 1924 v Ni.

KEY, G. (Hearts) (1): 1902 v Ni.

KEY, W. (Queen's Park) (1): 1907 v Ni.

KING, A. (Hearts, Celtic) (6): 1896 v E, W; 1897 v Ni; 1898 v Ni; 1899 v Ni, W.

KING, J. (Hamilton Accies) (2): 1933 v Ni; 1934 v Ni.

KING, W. S. (Queen's Park) (1): 1929 v W.

KINGSLEY, S. (Swansea) (1): 2016 v Fr.

KINLOCH, J. D. (Partick Th.) (1): 1922 v Ni.

KINNAIRD, A. F. (Wanderers) (1): 1873 v E.

KINNEAR, D. (Rangers) (1): 1938 v Cz.

KYLE, K. (Sunderland, Kilmarnock) (10): 2002 v Skor, SA, HK; 2003 v D, Fi, Can, Por, Nz; 2004 v D; 2010 v W.

LAMBERT, P. (Motherwell, Borussia Dortmund, Celtic) (40): 1995 v J, Ec; 1997 v La, Se (2), A, Blr; 1998 v Blr, La, Fin, Co, US, Br, N, M; (cont)...

1999 v Lth, CzR (2), G, Fi; 2000 v Bos, Lth, Holl, Ei; 2001 v Bel, Sm; 2002 v Cro, Bel, Fr, Nig; 2003 v D, Fi, Ice (2), Por, Ei, Lth, G; 2004 v N, G.

LAMBIE, J. A. (Queen's Park) (3): 1886 v Ni; 1887 v Ni; 1888 v E.

LAMBIE, W. A. (Queen's Park) (9): 1892 v Ni; 1893 v W; 1894 v E; 1895 v E, Ni; 1896 v E, Ni; 1897 v E, Ni.

LAMONT, D. (Pilgrims): 1885 v Ni.

LANG, A. (Dumbarton) (1): 1880 v W.

LANG, J. J. (Clydesdale, Third Lanark) (2): 1876 v W; 1878 v W.

LATTA, A. (Dumbarton) (2): 1888 v W; 1889 v E.

LAW, D. (Huddersfield Town, Manchester Utd, Torino, Manchester City) (55): 1959 v W, Ni, Holl, Por; 1960 v Ni, W; 1960 v E, Pol, A; 1961 v E, Ni; 1962 v Cz (2), E; 1963 v W, Ni, E, A, N, Ei, Sp; 1964 v W, E, N, WG;1965 v W, Ni, E, Fin (2), Pol, Sp; 1966 v Ni, E, Pol; 1967 v W, E, USSR; 1968 v Ni; 1969 v Ni, A, WG; 1972 v Pe, Ni, W, E, Y, Cz, Br; 1974 v Cz (2), WG (2), Ni, Z.

LAW, G. (Rangers) (3): 1910 v E, Ni, W.

LAW, T. (Chelsea) (2): 1928 v E, 1930 v E.

LAWRENCE, J. (Newcastle Utd.) (1): 1911 v E.

LAWRENCE, T. (Liverpool) (3): 1963 v Ei; 1969 v W, WG.

LAWSON, D. (St Mirren) (1): 1923 v E.

LECKIE, R. (Queen's Park) (1): 1872 v E.

LEGGAT, G. (Aberdeen, Fulham) (18): 1956 v E; 1957 v W; 1958 v Ni, H, Pol, Y, Par; 1959 v E, W, Ni, WG, Holl; 1960 v E, Ni, W, Pol, A, H.

LEIGHTON, J. (Aberdeen, Manchester Utd, Hibernian, Aberdeen) (91): 1983 v EG, Sw (2), Bel, W, E, Ca (2); 1984 v U, Bel, Ni, W, E, Fr; 1985 v Y, Ice, Sp (2), W, E, Ice; 1986 v W, EG, Aus (2), Is, D, WG, U; 1987 v Bul, Ei (2), L, Bel, E; 1988 v H, Bel, Bul, L, S.Ar, Ma, Sp, Co, E; 1989 v N, Cy (2), Fr, E, Ch; 1990 v Y, Fr, N, Arg, Ma, Cr, Se, Br; 1994 v Ma, A, Holl; 1995 v Gr, Ru, Sm, J, Ec, Fi. 1996 v Gr, Fin, Se, Sm, Aus, D, US;1997 v Se (2), Est, A, W, Ma, Blr.1998 v Blr, La, D, Fin, US, Br, N, M. 1999 v Lth, Est.

LENNIE, W. (Aberdeen) (2): 1908 v W, Ni.

LENNOX, R. (Celtic) (10): 1967 v Ni, E, USSR; 1968 v W, L; 1969 v D, A. WG, Cy; 1970 v W.

LESLIE, L. G. (Airdrie) (5): 1961 v W, Ni, Ei (2), Cz.

LEVEIN, C. (Hearts) (16): 1990 v Arg, EG, Eg, Pol, Ma, Se; 1991 R, Sm; 1993 v Por (2), G; 1994 v Sw, Holl; 1995 v Fin, Fi, Ru.

LIDDELL, W. (Liverpool) (28): 1947 v W, Ni; 1948 v E, W, Ni; 1950 v E, W, Por, Fr; 1951 v W, Ni, E, A; 1952 v W, Ni, E, USA, D, Se; 1953 v W, Ni, E; 1954 v W; 1955 v Por, Y, A, H; 1956 v Ni.

LIDDLE, D. (East Fife) (3): 1931 v W, A, I, Sw.

LINDSAY, D. (St Mirren) (1): 1903 v Ni.

LINDSAY, J. (Dumbarton) (8): 1880 v W; 1881 v W, E; 1884 v W, E; 1885 v W, E; 1886 v E.

LINDSAY, J. (Renton) (3): 1888 v E; 1893 v E, Ni.

LINWOOD, A. B. (Clyde) (1): 1950 v W.
LITTLE, R. J. (Rangers) (1): 1953 v Se.
LIVINGSTONE, G. T. (Man City, Rangers) (2): 1906 v E; 1907 v W.
LOCHHEAD, A. (Third Lanark) (1): 1889 v W.
LOGAN, J. (Ayr Utd) (1): 1891 v W.
LOGAN, T. (Falkirk) (1): 1913 v Ni.
LOGIE, J. T. (Arsenal) (1): 1953 v Ni.
LONEY, W. (Celtic) (2): 1910 v W, Ni.
LONG, H. (Clyde) (1): 1947 v Ni.
LONGAIR, W. (Dundee) (1): 1894 v Ni.
LORIMER, P. (Leeds Utd) (21): 1970 v A; 1971 v W, Ni; 1972 v Ni, W, E; 1973 v D (2), E (2); 1974 v WG, E, Bel, N, Z, Br, Y; 1975 v Sp; 1976 v D (2), R.
LOVE, A. (Aberdeen) (3): 1931 v A, I, Sw.
LOW, A. (Falkirk) (1): 1934 v Ni.
LOW, T. P. (Rangers) (1): 1897 v Ni.
LOW, W. L. (Newcastle U) (5): 1911 v E, W; 1912 v Ni; 1920 v E, Ni.
LOWE, J. (Cambuslang) (1): 1891 v Ni.
LOWE, J. (St Bernard's) (1): 1887 v Ni.
LUNDIE, J. (Hibernian) (1): 1886 v W.
LYALL, J. (Sheffield W.) (1): 1905 v E.
McADAM, J. (Third Lanark) (1): 1880 v W.
McALLISTER, B. (Wimbledon) (3): 1997 v W, Ma, Blr.
McALLISTER, G. (Leicester City, Leeds Utd, Coventry) (57): 1990 v EG, Pol, Ma; 1991 v R, Sw (2), Bul, USSR, Sm, (2); 1992 v Ni, Fin, US, Ca, N, Holl, G, CIS; 1993 v Sw, Por, I, Ma; 1994 v Sw, I, Ma, Holl (2), A; 1995 v Fin, Ru (2), Gr, Sm. 1996 v Gr, Fin, Se, Sm, Aus, D, US, U, Holl, E, Sw; 1997 v A (2), La, Est (2), Se, W, Ma, Blr; 1998 v Blr, La, Fr; 1999 v CzR.
McALLISTER, J. (Livingston) (1): 2004 v Trin.
McARTHUR, D. (Celtic) (3): 1895 v E, Ni; 1899 v W.
McARTHUR, J. (Wigan, Crystal Palace) (32): 2011 v Fi, Ni, Br, W; 2012 v Cy, Slo, US; 2013 v Bel, Est, W, Mac, Cro, Ser; 2014 v Cro, N; 2015 v G, Geo, Ni, Q, Ei; 2016 v Pol, I, Fr; 2017 v Lth, Slv, E, E; 2018 v Lth, Ma, Slv, Slo.
McATEE, A. (Celtic) (1): 1913 v W.
McAULAY, J. (Dumbarton, Arthurlie) (2): 1882 v W; 1884 v Ni.
McAULAY, J. (Dumbarton) (8): 1883 v E, W; 1884 v E; 1885 v E; 1886 v E; 1887 v E, W.
McAULEY, R. (Rangers) (2): 1932 v Ni, W.
McAVENNIE, F. (West Ham Utd., Celtic) (5): 1986 v Aus (2), D, WG; 1988 v S.Ar.
McBAIN, E. (St Mirren) (1): 1894 v W.
McBAIN, N. (Manchester Utd., Everton) (3): 1922 v E; 1923 v Ni; 1924 v W.
McBRIDE, J. (Celtic) (2): 1967 v W, Ni.
McBRIDE, P. (Preston NE) (6): 1904 v E; 1906 v E; 1907 v E, W; 1908 v E; 1909 v W.
McBURNIE, O. (Barnsley) (4): 2018 v Cr, H, Pe, Mx.
McCALL, J. (Renton) (5): 1886 v W; 1887 v E, W; 1888 v E; 1890 v E.

McCALL, S. M. (Everton, Rangers) (40) 1990 v Arg, EG, Eg, Pol, Ma, Cr, Se, Br; 1991 v Sw, USSR, Sm (2); 1992 v Sw, R, US, Ca, N, Holl, G, CIS; 1993 v Sw, Por (2); 1994 v I, Holl (2), A; 1995 v Fin, Ru, Gr; 1996 v Gr, D, US, U, Holl, E, Sw; 1997 v A, La; 1998 v D.

McCALLIOG, J. (Sheffield W., Wolverhampton W.) (5): 1967 v E, USSR; 1968 v Ni; 1969 v D; 1971 v Por.

McCALLUM, N. (Renton) (1): 1888 v Ni.

McCANN, N. (Hearts, Rangers, Southampton) (26): 1999 v Lth,   CzR. 2000 v Bos; Est, E, Fr, Holl, Ei; 2001 v La, Sm, Aus; 2002 v Cro, La, Fr, Nig; 2003 v Ei; 2004 v Fi, G, Holl (2), R, D; 2005 v I, 2006 v I, N, US.

McCANN, R. J. (Motherwell) (5): 1959 v WG; 1960 v E, Ni, W; 1961 v E.

McCARTNEY, W. (Hibernian) (1): 1902 v Ni.

McCLAIR, B. (Celtic, Manchester Utd) (30): 1987 v L, Ei, E, Br; 1988 v Bul, Ma, Sp; 1989 v N, Y, I, Cy, Fr; 1990 v N, Arg; 1991 v Bul (2), Sm; 1992 v Sw, R, Ni, US, Ca, N, Holl, G, CIS; 1993 v Sw, Por, Est (2).

McCLORY, A. (Motherwell) (3): 1927 v W; 1928 v Ni; 1935 v W.

McCLOY, J. (Ayr Utd) (2): 1924 v E; 1925 v E.

McCLOY, P. (Rangers) (4): 1973 v W, Ni, Sw, Br.

McCOIST, A. (Rangers, Kilmarnock) (61): 1986 v Holl; 1987 v L, Ei, Bel, E, Br; 1988 v H, Bel, Ma, Sp, Co, E; 1989 v Y, Fr, Cy, E; 1990 v Y, Fr, N, EG, Eg, Pol, Ma, Cr, Se, Br; 1991 v R, Sw, Bul (2), USSR; 1992 v Sw, Sm, Ni, Fin, US, Ca, N, Holl, G, CIS; 1993 v Sw, Por (2), I, Ma. 1996 v Gr, Fin, Sm, Aus, D, U, E, Sw; 1997 v A (2), Se, Est; 1998 v Blr. 1999 v Lth, Est.

McCOLL, A. (Renton) (1): 1888 v Ni.

McCOLL, I. M. (Rangers) (14): 1950 v E, Fr; 1951 v W, Ni, Bel; 1957 v E, Ni, W, Y, Sp, Sw, WG; 1958 v Ni, E.

McCOLL, R. S. (Queen's Park, Newcastle Utd.) (13): 1896 v W, Ni; 1897 v Ni; 1898 v Ni; 1899 v Ni; E, W; 1900 v E, W; 1901 v E, W; 1902 v E; 1908 v Ni.

McCOLL, W. (Renton) (1): 1895 v W.

McCOMBIE, A. (Sunderland, Newcastle) (4): 1903 v E, W; 1905 v E, W.

McCORKINDALE, J. (Partick Th.) (1): 1891 v W.

McCORMACK, R. (Motherwell, Cardiff, Leeds, Fulham) (13): 2008 v CzR; 2009 v Holl, Ice; 2010 v N, W; 2011 v W, Ei; 2013 v Aus; 2014 v Bel, US, Pol; 2016 v CZR, I.

McCORMICK, R. (Abercorn) (1): 1886 v W.

McCRAE, D. (St Mirren) (2): 1929 v N, G.

McCREADIE, A. (Rangers) (2): 1893 v W; 1894 v E.

McCREADIE, E. G. (Chelsea) (23): 1965 v E, Sp, Fin, Pol; 1966 v Por, Ni, W, Pol, I; 1967 v E, USSR; 1968 v Ni, W, E, Holl; 1969 v W, Ni, E, D, A, WG, Cy (2).

McCULLOCH, D. (Hearts, Brentford, Derby Co.) (7): 1935 v W; 1936 v E; 1937 v W, Ni; 1938 v Cz; 1939 v H, W.

McCULLOCH, L. (Wigan, Rangers) (18): 2005 v Mo (2), I, Blr; 2006 v Blr, Bul, J; 2007 v Fr, Geo, I, A; 2008 v Lth, Fr, Uk; I; 2011 v Lth, Li, Sp.

MacDONALD, A. (Rangers) (1): 1976 v Sw.

McDONALD, J. (Edinburgh University) (1): 1886 v E.

McDONALD, J. (Sunderland) (2): 1956 v W, Ni.

McDONALD, K. (Fulham) (1): 2018 v Cr.

MacDOUGALL, E. J. (Norwich City) (7): 1975 v Se, Por, W, Ni, E; 1976 v D, R.
McDOUGALL, J. (Liverpool) (2): 1931 v I, A.
McDOUGALL, J. (Airdrie) (1): 1926 v Ni.
McDOUGALL, J. (Vale of Leven) (5): 1877 v E, W; 1878 v E; 1879 v E, W.
McEVELEY, J. (Derby County) (3): 2008 v SA, Lth, Cro.
McFADDEN, J. (Motherwell, Everton, Birmingham) (48): 2002 v SA; 2003 v Can, A, Nz; 2004 v Fi, G, Lth, Holl (2), W, R, D, Est, Trin; 2005 v H, Sp, Slo, N, Se, Mo, Blr; 2006 v N, Slo, US, Sw, Bul, U; 2007 v Fi, Lth, Fr, Uk; 2008 v SA, Lth, Fr, Uk, Geo, I; 2009 v Ni, Mac, Ice, N, Arg; 2010 v N, Mac, W; 2011 v Se, Lth, Li.
McFADYEN, W. (Motherwell) (2): 1934 v A, W.
MACFARLANE, A. (Dundee) (5): 1904 v W; 1906 v W; 1908 v W; 1909 v Ni; 1911 v W.
MACFARLANE, W. (Hearts) (1): 1947 v L.
McFARLANE, R. (Morton) (1): 1896 v W.
McGARR, E. (Aberdeen) (2): 1970 v Ei, A.
McGARVEY, F. (Liverpool, Celtic) (7): 1979 v Ni, Arg; 1984 v U, Bel, EG, Ni, W.
McGEOCH, A. (Dumbreck) (4): 1876 v E, W; 1877 v E, W.
McGEOUCH, D. (Hibernian) (2): 2018 v Pe, Mx.
McGHEE, J. (Hibernian) (1): 1886 v W.
McGHEE, M. (Aberdeen) (4): 1983 v Ca (2); 1984 v Ni, E.
McGINLAY, J. (Bolton W.) (13): 1994 v A, Holl; 1995 v Fi (2), Ru (2), Gr, Sm; 1996 v Se; 1997 v Se, Est (2), A.
McGINN, J. (Hibernian) (9): 2016 v D; 2017 v Slv, Ca; 2018 v Lth, Holl, Cr, H, Pe, Mx.
McGONAGLE, W. (Celtic) (6): 1933 v E; 1934 v A, E, Ni; 1935 v Ni, W.
McGOWAN, J. (Partick Thistle) (1): 1946 v Bel.
McGRAIN, D. (Celtic) (62): 1973 v W, Ni, E, Sw, Br; 1974 v Cz (2), WG, W, E, Bel, N, Z, Br, Y; 1975 v Se, Por, W, Ni, E, R; 1976 v D (2), Sw, Ni, W, E; 1977 v Fin, Cz, W (2), Se, Ni, E, Ch, Arg, Br; 1978 v EG, Cz; 1980 v Bel, Por, Ni, W, E, Pol, H; 1981 v Se, Por, Is, (2), Ni (2), W, E; 1982 v Se, Sp, Holl, Ni, E, Nz, USSR.
McGREGOR, A. (Rangers, Besiktas, Hull, Cardiff City) (38): 2007 v A; 2009 v Ni, Arg, Holl; 2011 v Se, Lth, Li, CzR, Sp, Ni, Br, W, Ei; 2012 v D, CzR, Lth, Li, Sp, Cy, Slo, US; 2013 v Aus, Mac, W (2), Est, Ser, Cro; 2014 v E, Cro. Nig; 2015 v Ni; 2016 v Gib, CZR; 2017 v Ca; 2018 v Cr, H.
McGREGOR, C. (Celtic) (3): 2018 v Holl, Cr, H.
McGREGOR, J. C. (Vale of Leven) (4): 1877 v E, W; 1878 v E; 1880 v E.
McGRORY, J. E. (Kilmarnock) (3): 1965 v Ni, Fin; 1966 v Por.
McGRORY, J. (Celtic) (7): 1928 v Ni; 1931 v E; 1932 v Ni, W; 1933 v E, Ni; 1934 v Ni.
McGUIRE, W. (Beith) (2): 1881 v E, W.
McGURK, F. (Birmingham City) (1): 1934 v W.
McHARDY, H. (Rangers) (1): 1885 v Ni.
McINALLY, A. (Aston Villa, Bayern Munich) (8): 1989 v Cy, Ch; 1990 v Y, Fr, Arg, Pol, Ma, Cr.
McINALLY, J. (Dundee Utd) (10): 1987 v Bel, Br; 1988 v Ma; 1991 v Bul (2); 1992 v US, N, CIS; 1993 v G, Por.
McINALLY, T. B. (Celtic) (2): 1926 v Ni; 1927 v W.
McINNES, D. (WBA) (2): 2003 v D, Por.
McINNES, T. (Cowlairs) (1): 1889 v Ni.
McINTOSH, W. (Third Lanark) (1): 1905 v Ni.

ST MIRREN fans at a window display in Paisley before the 1959 Scottish Cup Final 3-1 win against Aberdeen

McINTYRE, A. (Vale of Leven) (2): 1878 v E; 1882 v E.

McINTYRE, H. (Rangers) (1): 1880 v W.

McINTYRE, J. (Rangers) (1): 1884 v W.

McKAY, B. (Rangers) (1): 2016 v Fr.

McKAY, D. (Celtic) (14): 1959 v E, WG, Holl, Por; 1960 v E, Pol, A, H, T; 1961 v W, Ni; 1962 v Ni, Cz, U.

McKAY, J. (Blackburn R.) (1): 1924 v W.

McKAY, R. (Newcastle Utd.) (1): 1928 v W.

McKEAN, R. (Rangers) (1): 1976 v Sw.

McKENNA, S. (Aberdeen) (4): 2018 v Cr, H, Pe, Mx.

McKENZIE, D. (Brentford) (1): 1938 v Ni.

MACKENZIE, J. A. (Partick Th.) (9): 1954 v W, E, N, Fin, A, U; 1955 v E, H; 1956 v A.

McKEOWN, M. (Celtic) (2): 1889 v Ni; 1890 v E.

McKIE, J. (East Stirling) (1): 1898 v W.

McKILLOP, T. R. (Rangers) (1): 1938 v Holl.

McKIMMIE, S. (Aberdeen) (40): 1989 v E, Ch; 1990 v Arg, Eg, Cr, Br; 1991 v R (2), Sw, Bul, Sm; 1992 v Sw, Ni, Fin, US, Ca, N, Holl, G, CIS. 1993 v Por, Est; 1994 v Sw, I, Holl (2), A; 1995 v Fin, Fi (2), Ru (2), Gr. 1996 v Gr, Fin, Se, D, U, Holl, E.

McKINLAY, D. (Liverpool) (2): 1922 v W, Ni.

McKINLAY, T. (Celtic) (22): 1996 v Gr, Fin, D, U, E, Sw; 1997 v A (2), La, Se (2), Est (2), W, Ma, Blr; 1998 v Blr, La, Fr, US, Br, M.

McKINLAY, W. (Dundee Utd, Blackburn R.) (29): 1994 v Ma, Holl (2), A; 1995 v Fi (2), Ru (2), Gr, Sm, J, Ec; 1996 v Fin, Se, Sm, Aus, D, Holl; 1997 v Se, Est; 1998 v La, Fr, D, Fin, Co, US, Br. 1999 v Est, Fi.

McKINNON, A. (Queen's Park) (1): 1874 v E.

McKINNON, R. (Rangers) (28): 1966 v W, E, I (2), Holl, Br; 1967 v W, Ni, E; 1968 v Ni, W, E, Holl; 1969 v D, A, WG, Cy; 1970 v Ni, W, E, Ei, WG, A; 1971 v D, Bel, Por, USSR, D.

McKINNON, R. (Motherwell) (3): 1994 v Ma; 1995 v J, Fi.

MACKINNON, J. (Dumbarton) (4): 1883 v E, W; 1884 v E, W.

McKINNON, W. W. (Queen's Park) (9): 1872 v E; 1873 v E; 1874 v E; 1875 v E; 1876 v E, W; 1877 v E; 1878 v E; 1879 v E.

McLAREN, A. (St Johnstone) (5): 1929 v N, G, Holl; 1933 v W, Ni.

McLAREN, A. (Preston NE) (4): 1947 v E, Bel, L; 1948 v W.

McLAREN, A. (Hearts, Rangers) (24): 1992 v US, Ca, N; 1993 v I, Ma, G, Est (2); 1994 v I, Ma, Holl, A; 1995 v Fin, Fi (2), Ru (2), Gr, Sm, J, Ec; 1996 v Fin, Se, Sm.

McLAREN, A. (Kilmarnock) (1): 2001 v Pol.

McLAREN, J. (Hibernian, Celtic) (3): 1888 v W; 1889 v E; 1890 v E.

McLAUGHLIN, J. (Hearts) (1): 2018 v Mx.

McLEAN, A. (Celtic) (4): 1926 v W, Ni; 1927 v W, E.

McLEAN, D. (St Bernard's) (2): 1896 v W; 1897 v Ni.

McLEAN, D. (Sheffield W.) (1): 1912 v E.

McLEAN, G. (Dundee) (1): 1968 v Holl.

McLEAN, K. (Aberdeen) (5): 2016 v CZR; 2018 v Holl, H, Pe, Mx.

McLEAN, T. (Kilmarnock) (6): 1969 v D, Cy, W; 1970 v Ni, W; 1971 v D.

McLEISH, A. (Aberdeen) (77): 1980 v Por, Ni, W, E, Pol, H; 1981 v Se, (cont...)

SCOTLAND v England May 1985 back (l-r): Richard Gough, Alex McLeish, Roy Aitken, Jim Leighton, Maurice Malpas, David Speedie, Steve Archibald, Willie Miller, Mo Johnston and Paul McStay; front: Jim Bett, Graeme Souness, Murdo MacLeod, Gordon Strachan

Is (2), Ni (2), E; 1982 v Se, Sp, Ni, Br; 1983 v Bel, Sw, W, E, Ca (3); 1984 v U, Bel, EG, Ni, W, E, Fr; 1985 v Y, Ice, (2), Sp (2), W, E; 1986 v W, EG, Aus (2), E, Holl, D; 1987 v Bel, E, Br; 1988 v Bel, Bul, L, S.Ar, Ma, Sp, Co, E; 1989 v N, Y, I, Cy (2), Fr, E, Ch; 1990 v Y, Fr, N, Arg, EG, Eg, Cr, Se, Br; 1991 v R, Sw, USSR, Bul; 1993 v Ma.

McLEOD, D. (Celtic) (4): 1905 v Ni; 1906 v E, W, Ni.

McLEOD, J. (Dumbarton) (5): 1888 v Ni; 1889 v W; 1890 v Ni; 1892 v E; 1893 v W.

MacLEOD, J. M. (Hibernian) (4): 1961 v E, Ei (2), Cz.

MacLEOD, M. (Celtic, Borussia Dort., Hibernian) (20): 1985 v E; 1987 v Ei, L, E, Br; 1988 v Co, E; 1989 v I, Ch; 1990 v Y, Fr, N, Arg, EG, Pol, Se, Br; 1991 v R, Sw, USSR.

McLEOD, W. (Cowlairs) (1): 1886 v Ni.

McLINTOCK, A. (Vale of Leven) (3): 1875 v E; 1876 v E; 1880 v E.

McLINTOCK, F. (Leicester City, Arsenal) (9): 1963 v N, Ei, Sp; 1965 v Ni; 1967 v USSR; 1970 v Ni; 1971 v W, Ni, E.

McLUCKIE, J. S. (Manchester City) (1): 1934 v W.

McMAHON, A. (Celtic) (6): 1892 v E; 1893 v E, Ni; 1894 v E; 1901 v Ni. 1902 v W.

McMANUS S. (Celtic) (26): 2007 v Uk, Geo, I, Fi, A; 2008 v SA, Lth, Fr, Uk, Geo, I, Cro, CzR; 2009 v Ni, Mac, Ice (2), Arg; 2010 v Mac, Holl, J, W; 2011 v Lth, Li, CzR, Sp.

McMENEMY, J. (Celtic) (12): 1905 v Ni; 1909 v Ni; 1910 v E, W; 1911 v Ni, W, E; 1912 v W; 1914 v W, Ni, E; 1920 v Ni.

McMENEMY, J. (Motherwell) (1): 1934 v W.

McMILLAN, J. (St Bernard's) (1): 1897 v W.

McMILLAN, I. L. (Airdrie, Rangers) (6): 1952 v E, USA, D; 1955 v E; 1956 v E; 1961 v Cz.

McMILLAN, T. (Dumbarton) (1): 1887 v Ni.

McMULLAN, J. (Partick Th., Manchester City) (16): 1920 v W; 1921 v W, Ni, E; 1924 v E, Ni; 1925 v E; 1926 v W, E; 1927 v E, W; 1928 v E, W; 1929 v W, E, Ni.

McNAB, A. (Morton) (2): 1921 v E, Ni.

McNAB, A. (Sunderland, WBA) (2): 1937 v A; 1939 v E.

McNAB, C. D. (Dundee) (6): 1931 v E, W, A, I, Sw; 1932 v E.

McNAB, J. S. (Liverpool) (1): 1923 v W.

McNAIR, A. (Celtic) (15): 1906 v W; 1907 v Ni; 1908 v E, W; 1909 v E; 1910 v W; 1912 v E, W, Ni; 1913 v E; 1914 v E, Ni; 1920 v E, W, Ni.

McNAMARA J. (Celtic, Wolves) (33): 1997 v La, Se, Est, W; 1998 v D, Co, US, N, M; 2000 v Holl; 2001 v Sm; 2002 v Bel, Fr; 2003 v Ice (2), Lth, Nz, G; 2004 v Fi, G, Lth, Holl (2), W, Trin; 2005 v Sp, Slo, Se, I, Mo; 2006 v A, I, N.

McNAMEE, D. (Livingston) (4): 2004 v Est, Trin; 2006 v Bul, J.

J. McNAUGHT, W. (Raith R.) (5): 1951 v A, W, Ni; 1952 v E; 1955 v Ni.

McNAUGHTON, K. (Aberdeen, Cardiff City) (4): 2002 v Nig; 2003 v D; 2005 v Se; 2008 v CzR.

McNEIL, H. (Queen's Park) (10): 1874 v E; 1875 v E; 1876 v E, W; 1877 v W; 1878 v E; 1879 v E, W; 1881 v E, W.

McNEIL, M. (Rangers) (2): 1876 v W; 1880 v E.

McNEILL, W. (Celtic) (29): 1961 v E, Ei (2), Cz; 1962 v Ni, E, Cz, U; 1963 v Ei, Sp; 1964 v W, E, WG; 1965 v E, Fin, Pol, Sp; 1966 v Ni, Pol; 1967 v USSR; 1968 v E; 1969 v Cy (2), W, E; 1970 v WG; 1972 v Ni, WG, E.

McPHAIL, J. (Celtic) (5): 1950 v W; 1951 v W, Ni, A; 1954 v Ni.

McPHAIL, R. (Airdrie, Rangers) (17): 1927 v E; 1929 v W; 1931 v E, Ni; 1932 v W, Ni, Fr; 1933 v E, Ni; 1934 v A, Ni; 1935 v E; 1937 v G, E, Cz; 1938 v W, Ni.

McPHERSON, D. (Kilmarnock) (1): 1892 v Ni.

McPHERSON, D. (Hearts, Rangers) (27): 1989 v Cy; E; 1990 v N, Ma, Cr, Se, Br; 1991 v Sw, Bul (2), USSR, Sm (2); 1992 v Sw, R, Ni, Fin, US, Ca, N, Holl, G, CIS; 1993 v Sw, I, Ma, Por.

McPHERSON, J. (Clydesdale) (1): 1875 v E.

McPHERSON, J. (Vale of Leven) (8): 1879 v E, W; 1880 v E; 1881 v W; 1883 v E, W; 1884 v E; 1885 v Ni.

McPHERSON, J. (Kilmarnock, Cowlairs, Rangers) (9): 1888 v W; 1889 v E; 1890 v Ni, E; 1892 v W; 1894 v E; 1895 v E, Ni; 1897 Ni.

McPHERSON, J. (Hearts) (1): 1891 v E.

McPHERSON, R. (Arthurlie) (1): 1882 v E.

McQUEEN, G. (Leeds Utd, Manchester Utd) (30): 1974 v Bel; 1975 v Sp (2), Por, W, Ni, E, R; 1976 v D; 1977 v Cz, W (2), Ni, E; 1978 v EG, Cz, W, Bul, Ni, W; 1979 v A, N, Por, Ni, E, N; 1980 v Pe, A, Bel; 1981 v W.

McQUEEN, M. (Leith Ath.) (2): 1890 v W; 1891 v W.

McRORIE, D. M. (Morton) (1): 1931 v W.

McSPADYEN, A. (Partick Th.) (2): 1939 v E, H.

McSTAY, P. (Celtic) (76): 1984 v U, Bel, Ni, W, E; 1985 v Ice, Sp (2), W; 1986 v EG, Aus, Is, U, Y; 1987 v Bul, Ei (2), L, Bel, E, Br; 1988 v H, Bel, Bul, L, S.Ar, Sp, Co, E; 1989 v N, Y, I, Cy (2), Fr, E, Ch; 1990 v Y, Fr, N, Arg, EG, Eg, Pol, Ma, Cr, Se, Br; 1991 v R, USSR, Bul; 1992 v Sm, Fin, US, Ca, N, Holl, G, CIS; 1993 v Sw, Por (2), I, Ma, Est (2); 1994 v I, Holl; 1995 v Fin, Fi, Ru; 1996 v Aus, 1997 v Est (2), A.

McSTAY, W. (Celtic) (13): 1921 v W, Ni; 1925 v E, Ni, W; 1926 v E, Ni, W; 1927 v E, Ni, W; 1928 v W, Ni.

McSWEGAN, G. (Hearts) (2): 2000 v Bos, Lth.

McTAVISH, J. (Falkirk) (1): 1910 v Ni.

McTOMINAY, S. (Manchester Utd) (2): 2018 v Cr, Pe.

McWHATTIE, G. C. (Queen's Park) (2): 1901 v W, Ni.

McWILLIAM, P. (Newcastle Utd) (8): 1905 v E; 1906 v E; 1907 v E, W; 1909 v E, W; 1910 v E; 1911 v W.

MACARI, L. (Celtic, Manchester Utd) (24): 1972 v W, E, Y, Cz, Br; 1973 v D, E (2), W; 1975 v Se, Por, W, E, R; 1977 v Ni, E, Ch, Arg; 1978 v EG, W, Bul, Pe, Ir.

MACAULEY, A. R. (Brentford, Arsenal) (7): 1947 v E; 1948 v E, W, Ni, Bel, Sw, Fr.

MACKAIL-SMITH, C. (Peterborough, Brighton) (6): 2011 v Br; 2012 v D, Sp, Cy, Slo, US.

MACKAY, D. C. (Hearts, Tottenham H) (22): 1957 v Sp; 1958 v Fr; 1959 v W, Ni, WG, E; 1960 v W, Ni, A, Pol, H, T; 1961 v W, Ni, E; 1963 v E, A, N; 1964 v Ni, W, N; 1966 v Ni.

MACKAY, G. (Hearts) (4): 1988 v Bul, L, S.Ar, Ma.

MACKAY, M. (Norwich) (5): 2004 v D, Est, Trin; 2005 v Sp, Slo.

MACKAY-STEVEN, G (Dundee Utd) (1): 2014 v US.

MACKIE, J. (QPR) (9): 2011 v CzR, Sp, Fi; 2012 v Cy, Slo; 2013 v Mac, W, Bel, Ser.

MADDEN, J. (Celtic) (2): 1893 v W; 1895 v W.

MAGUIRE, C. (Aberdeen) (2): 2011 v Ni; Ei.

MAIN, F. R. (Rangers) (1): 1938 v W.

MAIN, J. (Hibernian) (1): 1909 v Ni.

MALEY, W. (Celtic) (2): 1893 v Ni.

MALONEY, S. (Celtic, Aston Villa, Celtic, Wigan, Chicago Fire, Hull) (47): 2006 v Blr, US; 2007 v Geo, I, Fi, A; 2008 v Lth, Uk, Geo, Cro, CzR; 2009 v Mac, Ice, N, Arg; 2010 v Mac, Holl; 2011 v Sp, Fi; 2012 v US; 2013 v Aus, Mac, W (2), Bel, Est, Ser, Cro; 2014 v E, Bel, Mac, Nig; 2015 v Geo, Pol, Ei, E, Ni, Gib, Q, Ei; 2016 v Geo, G, Pol, Gib, D, Fr.

MALPAS, M. (Dundee Utd) (55): 1984 v Fr; 1985 v E, Ice; 1986 v W, Aus (2), Is, R, E, Holl, D, WG; 1987 v Bul, Ei, Bel; 1988 v Bel, Bul, L, S.Ar, Ma; 1989 v N, Y, I, Cy (2), Fr, E, Ch; 1990 v Y, Fr, N, Eg, Pol, Ma, Cr, Se, Br; 1991 v R (2), Bul (2), USSR, Sm (2); 1992 v Sw, Ni, Fin, US, Ca, Holl, G; 1993 v Sw, Por, I.

MARSHALL, D. (Celtic, Cardiff, Hull) (27): 2005 v H, Se; 2010 v N, Holl; 2014 v Bel, Mac, Cro, US, N, Pol; 2015 v G, Geo, Pol, Ei, E, E, Gib, Q, Ei; 2016 v Geo, G, Pol, I, Fr; 2017 v Ma, Lth, Slv.

MARSHALL, H. (Celtic) (2): 1899 v W; 1900 v Ni.

MARSHALL, G. (Celtic) (1): 1992 v US.

MARSHALL, J. (Middlesbrough, Llanelli) (7): 1921 v E, W, Ni; 1922 v E, W, Ni; 1924 v W.

MARSHALL, J. (Third Lanark) (4): 1885 v Ni; 1886 v W; 1887 v E, W.

MARSHALL, J. (Rangers) (3): 1932 v E; 1933 v E; 1934 v E.

MARSHALL, R. W. (Rangers) (2): 1892 v Ni; 1894 v Ni.

MARTIN, B. (Motherwell) (2): 1995 v J, Ec.

MARTIN, C. (Derby County, Fulham) (17): 2014 v Nig; 2015 v Geo, Pol, Ei, E; 2016 v Q, Gib, D; 2017 v Ma, Lth, Ca, Slo, E; 2018 v Lth, Ma, Slv, Slo.

MARTIN, F. (Aberdeen) (6): 1954 v N (2), A, U; 1955 v E, H.

MARTIN, N. (Hibernian, Sunderland) (3): 1965 v Fin, Pol; 1966 v I.

MARTIN, R. (Norwich) (29): 2011 v W; 2012 v Slo, US; 2013 v Aus, Cro; 2014 v E, Bel, Mac, Cro, N, Pol; 2015 v Q, Geo, Pol, Ei, E, Ni, Gib, Ei; 2016 v Geo, G, Pol, CZR, I, Fr; 2017 v Ma, Lth, Slv, Slo.

MARTIS, J. (Motherwell) (1): 1961 v W.

MASON, J. (Third Lanark) (7): 1949 v E, W, Ni; 1950 v Ni; 1951 v Ni, Bel, A.

MASSIE, A. (Hearts, Aston Villa) (18): 1932 v Ni, W, Fr; 1933 v Ni; 1934 v E, Ni; 1935 v E, Ni, W; 1936 v W, Ni, E; 1937 v G, E, W, Ni, A; 1938 v W.

MASSON, D. S. (QPR, Derby Co) (17): 1976 v Ni, W, E; 1977 v Fin, Cz, W, Ni, E, Ch, Arg, Br; 1978 v EG, Cz, W, Ni, E, Pe.

MATHERS, D. (Partick Th.) (1): 1954 v Fin.

MATTEO, D. (Leeds Utd) (6): 2001 v Aus, Sm, Bel; 2002 v Cro, Bel, Fr.

MAXWELL, W. S. (Stoke City) (1): 1898 v E.

MAY, J. (Rangers) (5): 1906 v W, Ni; 1908 v E, Ni; 1909 v W.

MAY, S. (Sheffield Wednesday) (1): 2015 v England.

MEECHAN, P. (Celtic) (1): 1896 v Ni.

MEIKLEJOHN, D. D. (Rangers) (15): 1922 v W; 1924 v W; 1925 v W, Ni, E; 1928 v W, Ni; 1929 v E, Ni; 1930 v E, Ni; 1931 v E; 1932 v W, Ni; 1934 v A.

MENZIES, A. (Hearts) (1): 1906 v E.

MERCER, R. (Hearts) (1): 1912 v W; 1913 v Ni.

MIDDLETON, R. (Cowdenbeath) (1): 1930 v Ni.

MILLAR, A. (Hearts) (1): 1939 v W.

MILLAR, J. (Rangers) (3): 1897 v E; 1898 v E, Ni.

MILLAR, J. (Rangers) (1): 1963 v A, Ei.

MILLER, C. (Dundee Utd) (1): 2001 v Pol.

MILLER, K. (Rangers, Wolves, Celtic, Derby, Rangers, Bursaspor, Cardiff, Vancouver) (69): 2001 v Pol; 2003 v A, Ice, Lth, G; 2004 v Lth, Holl (2), W, R, (cont...)

Est, Trin; 2005 v H, Sp, N, Mo (2), Se, I, Blr; 2006 v A, I, N, Blr, Slo, Sw; 2007 v Fi, Lth, Uk, Geo, I; 2008 v SA, Uk, Geo, I, Cro, CzR; 2009 v Ni, Mac, Ice (2), Holl; 2010 v N, Mac, Holl, W, CzR; 2011 v Lth, Li, CzR, Sp, Ni, Br, W, Ei; 2012 v D, CzR, Cy, Slo, US; 2013 v Mac, W (2), Bel, Lux, Est, Ser; 2014 v E.

MILLER, J. (St Mirren) (5): 1931 v E, I, Sw; 1932 v Fr; 1934 v E.

MILLER, L. (Dundee Utd, Aberdeen) (3): 2006 v J; 2009 v Arg; 2010 v J.

MILLER, P. (Dumbarton) (2): 1882 v E; 1883 v E, N.

MILLER, T. (Liverpool, Manchester Utd) (3): 1920 v E; 1921 v E, Ni.

MILLER, W. (Third Lanark) (1): 1876 v E.

MILLER, W. (Celtic) (6): 1947 v E, W, Bel, L; 1948 v W, Ni.

MILLER, W. (Aberdeen) (65): 1975 v R; 1978 v Bul; 1980 v Bel, W, E, Pol, H; 1981 v Se, Por, Is, Ni, CzR (2), W, E; 1982 v Ni, Por, Holl, Br, USSR; 1983 v EG, Sw (2), W, E, Ca (3); 1984 v U, Bel, EG, W, E, Fr; 1985 v Y, Ice, Sp (2), W, E, Ice; 1986 v W, EG, Aus (2), Is, R, E, Holl, D, WG, U; 1987 v Bul, E, Br; 1988 v H, L, S.Ar, Ma, Sp, Co, E; 1989 v N, Y; 1990 v Y, N.

MILLS, W. (Aberdeen) (3): 1936 v W, Ni; 1937 v W.

MILNE, J. V. (Middlesbrough) (2): 1938 v E; 1939 v E.

MITCHELL, D. (Rangers) (5): 1890 v Ni; 1892 v E; 1893 v E, Ni; 1894 v E.

MITCHELL, J. (Kilmarnock) (3): 1908 v Ni; 1910 v Ni, W.

MITCHELL, R. C. (Newcastle Utd.) (2): 1951 v D, Fr.

MOCHAN, N. (Celtic) (3): 1954 v N, A, U.

MOIR, W. (Bolton) (1): 1950 v E.

MONCUR, R. (Newcastle Utd.) (16): 1968 v Holl; 1970 v Ni, W, E, Ei; 1971 v D, Bel, W, Por, Ni, E, D; 1972 v Pe, Ni, W, E.

MORGAN, H. (St Mirren, Liverpool) (2): 1898 v W; 1899 v E.

MORGAN, L. (Celtic) (1): 2018 v Pe, Mx.

MORGAN, W. (Burnley, Manchester Utd) (21): 1968 v Ni; 1972 v Pe, W, Cz, Br; 1973 v D (2), E (2), W, Ni, Sw, Br; 1974 v Cz (2), WG (2), Ni, Bel, Br, Y.

MORRIS, D. (Raith R.) (6): 1923 v Ni; 1924 v E, Ni; 1925 v E, W, Ni.

MORRIS, H. (East Fife) (1): 1950 v Ni.

MORRISON, J. (West Brom) (46): 2008 v CzR; 2009 v Ni, N, Holl, Ice; 2011 v Se, Lth, Li, CzR, Sp, Ni, Br; 2012 v D, CzR, Lth, Sp, Cy, Slo; 2013 v Aus, Mac, W, Bel, Est, Ser, Cro (2); 2014 v E, Cro, Pol, Nig; 2015 v G, Geo, Pol, E, Ni, Gib, Q, Ei; 2016 v Geo, G; 2017 v E, Slo, E; 2018 v Ma, Slv.

MORRISON, T. (St Mirren) (1): 1927 v E.

MORTON, A. L. (Queen's Park, Rangers) (31): 1920 v W, Ni; 1921 v E; 1922 v E, W; 1923 v E, W, Ni; 1924 v E, W, Ni; 1925 v E, W, Ni; 1927 v E, Ni; 1928 v E, W, Ni; 1929 v E, W, Ni; 1930 v E, W, Ni; 1931 v E, W, Ni; 1932 v E, W, Fr.

MORTON, H. A. (Kilmarnock) (2): 1929 v G, Holl.

MUDIE, J. K. (Blackpool) (17): 1957 v W, Ni, E, Y, Sw, Sp (2), WG; 1958 v Ni, E, W, Sw, H, Pol, Y, Par, Fr.

MUIR, W. (Dundee) (1): 1907 v Ni.

MUIRHEAD, T. A. (Rangers) (8): 1922 v Ni; 1923 v E; 1924 v W; 1927 v Ni; 1928 v Ni; 1929 v W, Ni; 1930 v W.

MULGREW. C (Celtic, Blackburn) (36): 2012 v Slo, US; 2013 v Aus, Lux, Est, W; 2014 v E, Bel, Mac, Cro, US, Pol, Nig; 2015 v G, Ei, E, Q, Ei; 2016 v Geo, G, CZR, D, I, Fr; 2017 v Ca, Slo, E; 2018 v Lth, Ma, Slv, Slo, Holl, Cr, H, Pe, Mx.

MULHALL, G. (Aberdeen, Sunderland) (3): 1960 v Ni; 1963 v Ni; 1964 v Ni.

MUNRO, A. D. (Hearts, Blackpool) (3): 1937 v W, Ni; 1938 v Holl.

MUNRO, F. M. (Wolverhampton W.) (9): 1971 v Ni, E, D, USSR; 1975 v Se, W, Ni, E, R.

MUNRO, I. (St Mirren) (7): 1979 v Arg, N; 1980 v Pe, A, Bel, W, E.

MUNRO, N. (Abercorn) (2): 1888 v W; 1889 v E.

MURDOCH, J. (Motherwell) (1): 1931 v Ni.

MURDOCH, R. (Celtic) (12): 1966 v W, E, I (2); 1967 v Ni; 1968 v Ni; 1969 v W, Ni, E, WG, Cy; 1970 v A.

MURPHY, F. (Celtic) (1): 1938 v Holl.

MURPHY, J. (Rangers) (2): 2018 v Cr, Pe.

MURRAY, I. (Hibernian, Rangers) (6): 2003 v Can; 2005 v Se, Mo, Blr, Bul; 2006 v J.

MURRAY, J. (Renton) (1): 1895 v W.

MURRAY, J. (Hearts) (5): 1958 v E, H, Pol, Y, Fr.

MURRAY, J. W. (Vale of Leven) (1): 1890 v W.

MURRAY, P. (Hibernian) (2): 1896 v Ni; 1897 v W.

MURRAY, S. (Aberdeen) (1): 1972 v Bel.

MURTY, G. (Reading) (4): 2004 v W; 2006 v Bul, J; 2008 v Geo.

MUTCH, G. (Preston NE) (1): 1938 v E.

NAISMITH, S. (Kilmarnock, Rangers, Everton, Norwich) (45): 2007 v Fi; 2010 v Holl, W; 2011 v Lth, Li, CzR, Sp, Ni, W, Ei; 2012 v D, CzR, Li, Lth, Sp; 2013 v Aus, Mac, Lux, Est, Ser (2), Cro; 2014 v E, Mac, Cro, US, N, Pol, Nig; 2015 v Ger, Geo, Pol, Ei, Gib, Q, Ei; 2016 v Geo, Pol, Gib, I, Fr; 2017 v Ca, Slo.

NAPIER, C. E. (Celtic, Derby County) (5): 1932 v E; 1935 v E, W; 1937 v Ni, A.

NAREY, D. (Dundee Utd.) (35): 1977 v Se; 1979 v Psor, Ni, Arg; 1980 v Por, Ni, Pol, H; 1981 v W, E; 1982 v Holl, W, E, Nz, Br, USSR; 1983 v EG, Sw, Bel, Ni, W, E, Ca (3); 1986 v Is, R, Holl, WG, U; 1987 v Bul, E, Bel; 1989 v I, Cy.

NAYSMITH, G. (Hearts, Everton, Sheffield United) (46): 2000 v Ei; 2001 v La, Sm, Cro; 2002 v Cro, Bel; 2003 v D, Ice (2), Por, Ei, A, Lth, Nz, G; 2004 v N, Fi, G, Lth, Holl (2), W; 2005 v H, Sp, Slo, N, Mo, I; 2006 v Bul, J; 2007 v Fi (2), Lth, Geo, I, A; 2008 v Uk, I, Cro, CzR; 2009 v Ni, Mac, Ice (2), N, Holl.

NEIL, R. G. (Hibernian, Rangers) (2): 1896 v W; 1900 v W.

NEILL, R. W. (Queen's Park) (5): 1876 v W; 1877 v E, W; 1878 v W; 1880 v E.

NEILSON, R. (Hearts) (1); 2007 v Uk.

NELLIES, P. (Hearts) (2): 1914 v W, Ni.

NELSON, J. (Cardiff C.) (4): 1925 v W, Ni; 1928 v E; 1930 v Fr.

NEVIN, P. (Chelsea, Everton, Tranmere) (28): 1986 v R, E; 1987 v L, Ei, Bel; 1988 v L; 1989 v Cy, E; 1991 v R, Bul, Sm; 1992 v US, G, CIS; 1993 v Ma, Por, Est; 1994 v Sw, Ma, Holl (2), A. 1995 v Fi, Ru, Sm; 1996 v Se, Sm, Aus.

NIBLO, T. (Aston Villa) (1): 1904 v E.

NIBLOE, J. (Kilmarnock) (11): 1929 v E, N, Holl; 1930 v W; 1931 v E, Ni, A, I, Sw; 1932 v E, Fr.

NICHOLAS, C. (Celtic, Arsenal, Aberdeen) (20): 1983 v Sw, Ni, E, Ca (3); 1984 v Bel, Fr; 1985 v Y, Ice, Sp, W; 1986 v Is, R, E, D, U; 1987 v Bul, E; 1989 v Cy.

NICOL, S. (Liverpool) (27): 1985 v Y, Ice, Sp, W; 1986 v W, EG, Aus, E, D, WG, U; 1988 v H, Bul, S.Ar, Sp, Co, E; 1989 v N, Y, Cy, Fr; 1990 v Y, Fr; 1991 v Sw, USSR, Sm; 1992 Sw.

NICHOLSON, B. (Dunfermline) (3): 2001 v Pol; 2002 v La; 2005 v Se.

NISBET, J. (Ayr Utd.) (3): 1929 v N, G, Holl.

NIVEN, J. B. (Moffat) (1): 1885 v Ni.

O'CONNOR, G. (Hibernian, Lokomotiv Moscow, Birmingham City) (16): 2002 v Nig, Skor, HK; 2005 v I; 2006 v A, Slo, US; 2007 v Fi (2), Fr, A; 2008 v SA, Lth, Fr, Uk; 2010 v Holl.
O'DONNELL, F. (Preston NE, Blackpool) (6): 1937 v E, A, Cz; 1938 v E, W, Holl.
O'DONNELL, P. (Motherwell) (1): 1994 v Sw.
O'DONNELL, S. (Kilmarnock) (2): 2018 v Pe, Mx.
OGILVIE, D. H. (Motherwell) (1): 1934 v A.
O'HARE, J. (Derby County) (13): 1970 v W, Ni, E; 1971 v D, Bel, W, Ni; 1972 v Por, Bel, Holl, Pe, Ni, W.
O'NEIL, J. (Hibs) (1): 2001 v Pol.
O'NEIL, B. (Celtic, Wolfsburg, Derby, Preston) (7): 1996 v Aus; 1999 v G; 2000 v Lth, Holl, Ei; 2001 v Aus; 2006 v A.
ORMOND, W. E. (Hibernian) (6): 1954 v E, N, Fin, A, U; 1959 v E.
O'ROURKE, F. (Airdrie) (1): 1907 v Ni.
ORR, J. (Kilmarnock) (1): 1892 v W.
ORR, R. (Newcastle Utd.) (2): 1902 v E; 1904 v E.
ORR, T. (Morton) (2): 1952 v Ni, W.
ORR, W. (Celtic) (3): 1900 v Ni; 1903 v Ni; 1904 v W.
ORROCK, R. (Falkirk) (1): 1913 v W.
OSWALD, J. (Third Lanark, St Bernard's, Rangers) (3): 1889 v E; 1895 v E; 1897 v W.

PARKER, A. H. (Falkirk, Everton) (15): 1955 v Por, Y, A; 1956 v E, Ni, W, A; 1957 v Ni, W, Y; 1958 v Ni, W, E, Sw, Par.
PARLANE, D. (Rangers) (12): 1973 v E, Sw, Br; 1975 v Sp, Se, Por, W, Ni, E, R; 1976 v D; 1977 v W.
PARLANE, R. (Vale of Leven) (3): 1878 v W; 1879 v E, W.
PATERSON, C. (Hearts, Cardiff) (9): 2016 v I; 2017 v Ma, Lth, Slv, E; 2018 v Cr, H, Pe, Mx.
PATERSON, G. D. (Celtic) (1): 1939 v Ni.
PATERSON, J. (Leicester City) (1): 1920 v E.
PATERSON, J. (Cowdenbeath) (3): 1931 v A, I, Sw.
PATON, A. (Motherwell) (2): 1952 v D, Se.
PATON, D. (St Bernard's) (1): 1896 v W.
PATON, M. (Dumbarton) (5): 1883 E; 1884 v W; 1885 v W, E; 1886 v E.
PATON, R. (Vale of Leven) (2): 1879 v E, W.
PATRICK, J. (St Mirren) (2): 1897 E, W.
PAUL, J. McD. (Queen's Park) (3): 1909 v E, W, Ni.
PAUL, W. (Partick Th.) (3): 1888 v W; 1889 v W; 1890 v W.
PAUL, W. (Dykebar) (1): 1891 v Ni.
PEARSON, S. (Motherwell, Celtic, Derby County) (10): 2004: v Holl, W; 2005 v H, Sp, N, Se; 2008 v SA, Fr, Uke, Geo.
PEARSON, T. (Newcastle Utd.) (2): 1947 v E, Bel.
PENMAN, A. (Dundee) (1): 1966 v Holl.
PETTIGREW, W. (Motherwell) (5): 1976 v Sw, Ni, W; 1977 v W, Se.
PHILLIPS, J. (Queen's Park) (3): 1877 v E, W; 1878 v W.
PHILLIPS, M (Blackpool, QPR, West Brom) (12): 2012 v US; 2013 v Bel; 2016 v CZR, I; 2018 v Lth, Ma, Slv, Slo, Holl, Cr, H, Pe.
PLENDERLEITH, J. B. (Manchester City) (1): 1961 v Ni.
PORTEOUS, W. (Hearts) (1): 1903 v Ni.
PRESSLEY, S. (Hearts) (32): 2000 v Fr, Ei; 2003 v Ice (2), Can, (cont...)

Por, A, Lth, Nz, G; 2004 v N, G, Lth, Holl (2), R, D, Est, Trin; 2005 v H, I, Mo, Blr; 2006 v A, N, Blr, Slo, US; 2007 v Fi, Lth, Fr, Uk.

PRINGLE, C. (St Mirren) (1): 1921 v W.

PROVAN, D. (Rangers) (5): 1964 v Ni, N; 1966 v I (2), Holl.

PROVAN, D. (Celtic) (10): 1980 v Bel (2), Por, Ni; 1981 v Is, W, E; 1982 v Se, Por, Ni.

PURSELL, P. (Queen's Park) (1): 1914 v W.

QUASHIE, N. (Portsmouth, Southampton, WBA) (14): 2004 v Est, Trin; 2005 v H, Sp, Slo, Se, I; 2006 v A, I, Slo, US, Sw; 2007 v Fi, Lth.

QUINN, J. (Celtic) (11): 1905 v Ni; 1906 v Ni, W; 1908 v Ni, E; 1909 v E; 1910 v E, Ni, W; 1912 v E, W.

QUINN, P. (Motherwell) (4): 1961 v E, Ei (2); 1962 v U.

RAE, G. (Dundee, Rangers, Cardiff) (14): 2001 v Pol; 2002 v La, G; 2004 v N, Fi, G, Lth, Holl, R; 2006 v Bul, J; 2008 v Cro, CzR; 2009 v Ice.

RAE, J. (Third Lanark) (2): 1889 v W; 1890 v Ni.

RAESIDE, J. S. (Third Lanark) (1): 1906 v W.

RAISBECK, A. G. (Liverpool) (8): 1900 v E; 1901 v E; 1902 v E; 1903 v E, W; 1904 v E; 1906 v E; 1907 v E.

RANKIN, G. (Vale of Leven) (2): 1890 v Ni; 1891 v E.

RANKIN, R. (St Mirren) (3): 1929 v N, G, Holl.

REDPATH, W. (Motherwell) (9): 1949 v W, Ni; 1951 v E, D, Fr, Bel, A; 1952 v Ni, E.

REID, J, G. (Airdrie) (3): 1914 v W; 1920 v W; 1924 v Ni.

REID, R. (Brentford) (2): 1938 v E, Ni.

REID, W. (Rangers) (9): 1911 v E, W, Ni; 1912 v Ni; 1913 v E, W, Ni; 1914 v E, Ni.

REILLY, L. (Hibernian) (38): 1949 v E, W, Fr; 1950 v W, Ni, Sw, Fr; 1951 v W, E, D, Fr, Bel, A; 1952 v Ni, W, E, USA, D, Se; 1953 v Ni, W, E, Se; 1954 v W; 1955 v H (2), Por, Y, A, E; 1956 v E, W, Ni, A; 1957 v E, Ni, W, Y.

RENNIE, H. G. (Hearts, Hibs) (13): 1900 v E, Ni; 1901 v E; 1902 v E, Ni, W; 1903 v Ni, W; 1904 v Ni; 1905 v W; 1906 v Ni; 1908 v Ni, W.

RENNY-TAILYOUR, H. W. (Royal Engineers) (1): 1873 v E.

RHODES, J. (Huddersfield, Blackburn, Middlesbrough, Sheffield W) (14): 2012 v Cy; 2013 v Aus, Mac, Lux, Est, Wal, Ser (2), Cro; 2014 v E, Bel; 2015 V Ni, Gib; 2017 v Ca.

RHIND, A. (Queen's Park) (1): 1872 v E.

RICHMOND, A. (Queen's Park) (1): 1906 v W.

RICHMOND, J. T. (Clydesdale, Queen's Park) (3): 1877 v E; 1878 v E; 1882 v W.

RING, T. (Clyde) (12): 1953 v Se; 1955 v W, Ni, E, H; 1957 v E, Sp (2), Sw, WG; 1958 v Ni, Sw.

RIOCH, B. D. (Derby County, Everton) (24): 1975 v Por, W, Ni, E, R; 1976 v D (2), R, Ni, W, E; 1977 v Fin, Cz, W (2), Ni, E, Ch, Br; 1978 v Cz, Ni, E, Pe, Holl.

RIORDAN, D. (Hibernian) (3): 2006 v A; 2010 v J, W.

RITCHIE, A. (East Stirling) (1): 1891 v W.

RITCHIE, H. (Hibernian) (2): 1923 v W; 1928 v Ni.

RITCHIE, J. (Queen's Park) (1): 1897 v W.

RITCHIE, M. (Bournemouth, Newcastle) (16): 2015 v Ni, Gib, Q, Ei; 2016 v G, Pol, Gib, D, I, Fr; 2017 v Ma, Lth, Slv, E; 2018 v Lth, Cr.

RITCHIE, P. (Hearts, Bolton, Walsall) (7): 1999 v G, Czr, E; 2000 v Lth, Fr, Holl; 2004 v W.

RITCHIE, W. (Rangers) (1): 1962 v U.
ROBB, D. T. (Aberdeen) (5): 1971 v W, E, Por, D, USSR.
ROBB, W. (Rangers, Hibernian) (2): 1926 v W; 1928 v W.
ROBERTSON, A. (Clyde) (5): 1955 v Por, A, H; 1958 v Sw, Par.
ROBERTSON, A. (Dundee Utd, Hull City, Liverpool) (22): 2014 v Pol, Nig; 2015 v Geo, Ei, E, Gib; 2016 v Geo, Gib, CZR, Fr; 2017 v Ma, Lth, Ca, Slo, E; 2018 v Lth, Ma, Slv, Slo, Holl, Cr, H..
ROBERTSON, D. (Rangers) (3): 1991 v Ni; 1994 v Sw, Holl.
ROBERTSON, G. (Motherwell, Sheffield W.) (4): 1910 v W; 1912 v W; 1913 v E, Ni.
ROBERTSON, G. (Kilmarnock) (1): 1938 v Cz.
ROBERTSON, H. (Dundee) (1): 1962 v Cz.
ROBERTSON, J. (Dundee) (2): 1931 v A, I.
ROBERTSON, J. (Hearts) (16): 1991 v R, Sw, Bul, Sm (2); 1992 v Ni, Fin; 1993 v I, Ma, G, Est; 1995 v J, Ec, Fi. 1996 v Gr, Se.
ROBERTSON, J. N. (Nottingham F., Derby County) (28): 1978 v Ni, W, Ir; 1979 v Por, N; 1980 v Pe, A, Bel (2), Por; 1981 v Se, Por, Is, Ni (2), E; 1982 v Se, Ni (2), E, Nz, Br, USSR; 1983 v EG, Sw; 1984 v U, Bel.
ROBERTSON, J. G. (Tottenham H.) (1): 1965 v W.
ROBERTSON, J. T. (Everton, Southampton, Rangers) (16): 1898 v E; 1899 v E; 1900 v E, W; 1901 v W, Ni, E; 1902 v W, Ni, E; 1903 v E, W; 1904 v E, W, Ni; 1905 v W.
ROBERTSON, P. (Dundee) (1): 1903 v Ni.
ROBERTSON, S. (Dundee United) (2): 2009 v Arg; 2011 v Se.
ROBERTSON, T. (Queen's Park) (4): 1889 v Ni; 1890 v E; 1891 v W; 1892 v Ni.
ROBERTSON, T. (Hearts) (1): 1898 v Ni.
ROBERTSON, W. (Dumbarton) (2): 1887 v E, W.
ROBINSON, R. (Dundee) (4): 1974 v WG; 1975 v Se, Ni, R.
ROBSON, B. (Dundee United, Celtic, Middlesbrough) (16): 2008 v SA, CzR; 2009 v Ni, Mac, Ice, N; 2010 v W, CzR; 2011 v Se, Li, CzR, W, Ei; 2012 v CzR, Cy, Slo.
ROSS, M. (Rangers) (13): 2002 v Skor, SA, HK; 2003 v D, Fi, Ice, Can, Por, Nz, G; 2004 v N, G, Holl.
ROUGH, A. (Partick Th., Hibernian) (53): 1976 v Sw, Ni, W, E; 1977 v Fin, Cz, W (2), Se, Ni, E, Ch, Arg, Br; 1978 v Cz, W, Ni, E, Pe, Ir, Holl; 1979 v A, Por, W, Arg, N; 1980 v Pe, A, Bel (2), Por, W, E, Pol, H; 1981 v Se, Por, Is (2), Ni, W, E; 1982 v Se, Ni, Sp, Holl, W, E, Nz, Br, USSR; 1986 v W, E.
ROUGVIE, D. (Aberdeen) (1): 1984 v Ni.
ROWAN, A. (Caledonian, Queen's Park) (2): 1880 v E; 1882 v W.
RUSSELL, D. (Hearts, Celtic) (6): 1895 v E, Ni; 1897 v W; 1898 v Ni; 1901 v W, Ni.
RUSSELL, J. (Cambuslang) (1): 1890 v Ni.
RUSSELL, J. (Derby County, Sporting Kansas City) (5): 2015 v E, Ni, Q; 2016 v Gib; 2018 v Mx.
RUSSELL W. F. (Airdrie) (2): 1924 v W; 1925 v E.
RUTHERFORD, E. (Rangers) (1): 1948 v F.
ST JOHN, I. (Motherwell, Liverpool) (21): 1959 v WG; 1960 v E, Ni, W, Pol, A; 1961 v E; 1962 v Ni, W, E, Cz (2), U; 1963 v W, Ni, (cont).. E, N, Ei, Sp; 1964 v Ni; 1965 v E.
SAUNDERS, S. (Motherwell) (1): 2011 v Fi.
SAWERS, W. (Dundee) (1): 1895 v W.
SCARFF, P. (Celtic) (1): 1931 v Ni.

SCHAEDLER, E. (Hibernian) (1): 1974 v WG.

SCOTT, A. S. (Rangers, Everton) (16): 1957 v Ni, Y, WG; 1958 v W, Sw; 1959 v Por; 1962 v Ni, W, E, Cz, U; 1964 v W, N; 1965 v Fin; 1966 v Por, Br.

SCOTT, J. (Hibernian) (1): 1966 v Holl.

SCOTT, J. (Dundee) (2): 1971 v D, USSR.

SCOTT, M. (Airdrie) (1): 1898 v W.

SCOTT, R. (Airdrie) (1): 1894 v Ni.

SCOULAR, J. (Portsmouth) (9): 1951 v D, Fr, A; 1952 v E, USA, D, Se; 1953 v W, Ni.

SELLAR, W. (Battlefield, Queen's Park) (9): 1885 v E; 1886 v E; 1887 v E, W; 1888 v E; 1891 v E; 1892 v E; 1893 v E, Ni.

SEMPLE, W. (Cambuslang) (1): 1886 v W.

SEVERIN, S. (Hearts, Aberdeen) (15): 2002 v La, Skor, SA, HK; 2003 v D, Ice, Can, Por; 2005 v H, Se; 2006 v A, Bul, J; 2007 v Fi, Lth.

SHANKLY, W. (Preston NE) (5): 1938 v E; 1939 v E, W, Ni, H.

SHARP, G. M. (Everton) (12): 1985 v Ice; 1986 v W, Aus (2), Is, R, U; 1987 v Ei; 1988 v Bel, Bul, L, Ma.

SHARP, J. (Dundee, Woolwich Arsenal, Fulham) (5): 1904 v W; 1907 v W, E; 1908 v E; 1909 v W.

SHAW, D. (Hibernian) (8): 1947 v W, Ni; 1948 v E, Bel, Sw, Fr; 1949 v W, Ni.

SHAW, F. W. (Pollokshields Ath.) (2): 1884 v E, W.

SHAW, J. (Rangers) (4): 1947 v E, Bel, L; 1948 v Ni.

SHEARER, D. (Aberdeen) (7) 1994 v A, Holl; 1995 v Fin, Ru, Sm, Fi. 1996 v Gr.

SHEARER, R. (Rangers) (4): 1961 v E, Ei (2), Cz.

SHINNIE, A. (Inverness CT) (1): 2013 v Lux.

SHINNIE, G. (Aberdeen) (2): 2018 v Pe, Mx.

SILLARS, D. C. (Queen's Park) (5): 1891 v Ni; 1892 v E; 1893 v W; 1894 v E; 1895 v W.

SIMPSON, J. (Third Lanark) (3): 1895 v E, W, Ni.

SIMPSON, J. (Rangers) (14): 1935 v E, W, Ni; 1936 v E, W, Ni; 1937 v G, E, W, Ni, A, Cz; 1938 v W, Ni.

SIMPSON, N. (Aberdeen) (4): 1983 v Ni; 1984 v Fr; 1987 v E; 1988 v E.

SIMPSON, R. C. (Celtic) (5): 1967 v E, USSR; 1968 v Ni, E; 1969 v A.

SINCLAIR, G. L. (Hearts) (3): 1910 v Ni; 1912 v W, Ni.

SINCLAIR, J. W. E. (Leicester City) (1): 1966 v Por.

SKENE, L. H. (Queen's Park) (1): 1904 v W.

SLOAN, T. (Third Lanark) (1): 1904 v W.

SMELLIE, R. (Queen's Park) (6): 1887 v Ni; 1888 v W; 1889 v E; 1891 v E; 1893 v E, Ni.

SMITH, A. (Rangers) (20): 1898 v E; 1900 v E, Ni, W; 1901 v E, Ni, W; 1902 v E, Ni, W; 1903 v E, Ni, W; 1904 v Ni; 1905 v W; 1906 v E, Ni; 1907 v W; 1911 v E, Ni.

SMITH, D. (Aberdeen, Rangers) (2): 1966 v Holl; 1968 v Holl.

SMITH, G. (Hibernian) (18): 1947 v E, Ni; 1948 v W, Bel, Sw, Fr; 1952 v E, USA, D; 1955 v Por, Y, A, H; 1956 v E, Ni, W; 1957 v Sp (2), Sw.

SMITH, H. G. (Hearts) (3): 1988 v S.Ar; 1991 Ni; 1992 v Ca.

SMITH, J. (Rangers) (2): 1935 v Ni; 1938 v Ni.

SMITH, J. (Ayr United) (1): 1924 v E.

SMITH, J. (Aberdeen, Newcastle Utd.) (4): 1968 v Holl; 1974 v WG, Ni, W.

SMITH, J. (Celtic) (2): 2003 v Ei, A.

SMITH, J. E. (Celtic) (2); 1959 v H, Por.

SMITH, Jas (Queen's Park) (1): 1872 v E.

SMITH, J. (Mauchline, Edinburgh University, Queen's Park) (10): 1877 v E, W; 1879 v E, W; 1880 v E; 1881 v W, E; 1883 v E, W; 1884 v E.

SMITH, N. (Rangers) (12): 1897 v E; 1898 v W; 1899 v E, W, Ni; 1900 v E, W, Ni; 1901 v Ni, W; 1902 v E, Ni.

SMITH, R. (Queen's Park) (2): 1872 v E; 1873 v E.

SNODGRASS, R. (Leeds Utd, Norwich, West Ham, Aston Villa) (25): 2011 v Ni, Br; 2012 v D, Lth, Slo; 2013 v Aus, Est, W, Ser, Cro; 2014 v E, Bel, Cro, US, N; 2016 v CZR, Fr; 2017 v Ma, Lth, Slv, E, Ca, Slo, E; 2018 v Slo.

SMITH, T. M. (Kilmarnock, Preston NE) (2): 1934 v E; 1938 v E.

SOMERS, P. (Celtic) (4): 1905 v E, Ni; 1907 v Ni; 1909 v W.

SOMERS, W. S. (Third Lanark, Queen's Park) (3): 1879 v E, W; 1880 v W.

SOMERVILLE, G. (Queen's Park) (1): 1886 v E.

SOUNESS, G. J. (Middlesbrough, Liverpool, Sampdoria, Rangers) (54): 1975 v EG, Sp, Se; 1978 v Bul, W, E, Holl; 1979 v A. N, W, Ni, E; 1980 v Pe, A, Bel, Por, Ni; 1981 v Por, Is (2); 1982 v Ni, Por, Sp, W, E, Nz, Br, USSR; 1983 v EG, Sw (2), Bel, W, E, Ca (3); 1984 v U, Ni, W; 1985 v Y, Ice (3), Sp (2), W, E; 1986 v EG, Aus (2), R, E, D, WG.

SPEEDIE, D. R. (Chelsea, Coventry City) (10): 1985 v E; 1986 v W, EG, Aus, E; 1989 v Y, I, Cy (2), Ch.

SPEEDIE, F. (Rangers) (3): 1903 v E, W, Ni.

SPENCER, J. (Chelsea, QPR) (14): 1995 v Ru, Gr, Sm, J; 1996 v Fin, Aus, D, US, U, Holl, E, Sw; 1997 v La, W.

SPEIRS, J. H. (Rangers) (1): 1908 v W.

STANTON, P. (Hibernian) (16): 1966 v Holl; 1969 v Ni; 1970 v Ei, A; 1971 v D, Bel, Por, USSR, D; 1972 v Por, Bel, Holl, W; 1973 v W, Ni; 1974 v WG.

STARK. J. (Rangers) (2): 1909 v E, Ni.

STEEL, W. (Morton, Derby County, Dundee) (30): 1947 v E, Bel, L; 1948 v Fr, E, W, Ni; 1949 v E, W, Ni, Fr; 1950 v E, W, Ni, Sw, Por, Fr; 1951 v W, Ni, E, A (2), D, Fr, Bel; 1952 v W; 1953 v W, E, Ni, Se.

STEELE, D. M. (Huddersfield) (3): 1923 v E, W, Ni.

STEIN, C. (Rangers, Coventry City) (21): 1969 v W, Ni, D, E, Cy (2); 1970 v A, Ni, W, E, Ei, WG; 1971 v D. USSR, Bel, D; 1972 v Cz; 1973 v E (2), W, Ni.

STEPHEN, J. F. (Bradford) (2): 1947 v W; 1948 v W.

STEVENSON, G. (Motherwell) (12): 1928 v W, Ni; 1930 v Ni, E, Fr; 1931 v E, W; 1932 v W, Ni; 1933 v Ni; 1934 v E; 1935 v Ni.

STEVENSON, L. (Hibernian) (1): 2018 v Pe.

STEWART, A. (Queen's Park) (2): 1888 v Ni; 1889 v W.

STEWART, A. (Third Lanark) (1): 1894 v W.

STEWART, D. (Dumbarton) (1): 1888 v Ni.

STEWART, D. (Queen's Park) (3): 1893 v W; 1894 v Ni; 1897 v Ni.

STEWART, D. S. (Leeds Utd.) (1): 1978 v EG.

STEWART, G. (Hibernian, Man City) (4): 1906 v W, E; 1907 v E, W.

STEWART, J. (Kilmarnock, Middlesbrough) (2): 1977 v Ch; 1979 v N.

STEWART, M. (Manchester Utd, Hearts) (4): 2002 v Nig, Skor, SA; 2009 v Ni.

STEWART, R. (West Ham Utd.) (10): 1981 v W, Ni, E; 1982 v Ni, Por, W; 1984 v Fr; 1987 v Ei (2), L.

STEWART, W. E. (Queen's Park) (2): 1898 v Ni; 1900 v Ni.

STOCKDALE, R. (Middlesbrough) (5): 2002 v Nig, Skor, SA, HK; 2003 v D.

STORRIER, D. (Celtic) (3): 1899 v E, W, Ni.

STRACHAN, G. (Aberdeen, Manchester Utd., Leeds Utd.) (50): 1980 v Ni, W, E, Pol, H; 1981 v Se, Por; 1982 v Ni, Por, Sp, Holl, Nz, Br, USSR; 1983 v EG, Sw (2), Bel, Ni, W, E, Ca (3); 1984 v EG, Ni, E, Fr; 1985 v Sp, E, Ice; 1986 v W, Aus, R, D, WG, U; 1987 v Bul, Ei (2); 1988 v H; 1989 v Fr; 1990 v Fr; 1991 v USSR, Bul, Sm; 1992 v Sw, R, Ni, Fin.

STURROCK, P. (Dundee Utd.) (20): 1981 v W, Ni, E; 1982 v Por, Ni, W, E; 1983 v EG, Sw, Bel, Ca (3); 1984 v W; 1985 v Y; 1986 v Is, Holl, D, U; 1987 v Bel.

SULLIVAN, N. (Wimbledon, Spurs) (28): 1997 v W; 1998 Fr, Co. 1999 v Fi (2), CzR (2), G. 2000 v Bos (2), Est, E (2) Fr, Holl, Ei; 2001 v La, Sm (2), Cro, Bel, Pol; 2002 v Cro, Bel, La, Fr, Skor; 2003 v Ei.

SUMMERS, W. (St Mirren) (1): 1926 v E.

SYMON, J. S. (Rangers) (1): 1939 v H.

TAIT, T. S. (Sunderland) (1): 1911 v W.

TAYLOR, J. (Queen's Park) (6): 1872 v E; 1873 v E; 1874 v E; 1875 v E; 1876 v E, W.

TAYLOR, J. D. (Dumbarton, St Mirren) (4): 1892 v W; 1893 v W; 1894 v Ni; 1895 v Ni.

TAYLOR, W. (Hearts) (1): 1892 v E.

TEALE, G. (Wigan, Derby) (13): 2006 v Sw, Bul, J; 2007 v Fi (2), Fr, Geo, I; 2008 v SA, Lth, Cro; 2009 v Holl, Ice.

TELFER, P. (Coventry) (1): 2000 v Fr.

TELFER, W. (Motherwell) (2): 1933 v Ni; 1934 v Ni.

TELFER, W. D. (St Mirren) (1): 1954 v W.

TEMPLETON, R. (Aston Villa, Newcastle Utd., Woolwich Arsenal, Kilmarnock) (11): 1902 v E; 1903 v E, W; 1904 v E; 1905 v W; 1908 v Ni; 1910 v E, Ni; 1912 v E, Ni; 1913 v W.

THOMPSON, S. (Dundee United, Rangers) (16): 2002 v Fr, Nig, HK; 2003 v D, Fi, Ice, Can, Ei, A, G; 2004 v Fi, G, R; 2005 v H, N, Mo.

THOMSON, A. (Arthurlie) (1): 1886 v Ni.

THOMSON, A. (Third Lanark) (1): 1889 v W.

THOMSON, A. (Airdrie) (1): 1909 v Ni.

THOMSON, A. (Celtic) (3): 1926 v E; 1932 v Fr; 1933 v W.

THOMSON, C. (Hearts, Sunderland) (21): 1904 v Ni; 1905 v E, (cont...)

UNISON
Scotland

SHOW RACISM THE <u>RED</u> CARD ⚔

Enjoy the season.
Support your
team. **And let's
<u>kick racism</u> and
<u>homophobia</u> out of
football.**

Three simple ways to join UNISON today
and get essential cover wherever you work

Join online at
joinunison.org

Call us on
0800 171 2193

Ask your UNISON rep
for an application form

Your public services trade union

Ni, W; 1906 v W, Ni; 1907 v E, W, Ni; 1908 v E, W, Ni; 1909 v W; 1910 v E; 1911 v Ni; 1912 v E, W; 1913 v E, W; 1914 v E, Ni.
THOMSON, C. (Sunderland) (1): 1937 v Cz.
THOMSON, D. (Dundee) (1): 1920 v W.
THOMSON, J. (Celtic) (4): 1930 v Fr; 1931 v E, W, Ni.
THOMSON, J. J. (Queen's Park) (3): 1872 v E; 1873 v E; 1874 v E.
THOMSON, J. R. (Everton) (1): 1933 v W.
THOMSON, K. (Rangers) (3): 2009 v Ni; 2010 v CzR; 2011 v Se.
THOMSON, R. (Celtic) (1): 1932 v W.
THOMSON, R. W. (Falkirk) (1): 1927 v E.
THOMSON, S. (Rangers) (2): 1884 v W, Ni.
THOMSON, W. (Dumbarton) (4): 1892 v W; 1893 v W; 1898 v Ni, W.
THOMSON, W. (Dundee) (1): 1896 v W.
THOMSON, W. (St Mirren) (7): 1980 v Ni; 1981 v Ni (2); 1982 v Por; 1983 v Ni, Ca; 1984 v EG.
THORNTON, W. (Rangers) (7): 1947 v W, Ni; 1948 v E, Ni; 1949 v Fr; 1952 v D, Se.
TIERNEY, K. (Celtic) (9): 2016 v D; 2017 v Slv, Slo, E; 2018 v Lth, Ma, Slv, Slo, Holl.
TONER, W. (Kilmarnock) (2): 1959 v W, Ni.
TOWNSLEY, T. (Falkirk) (1926 v W.
TROUP, A. (Dundee, Everton) (5): 1920 v E; 1921 v W, Ni; 1922 v Ni; 1926 v E.
TURNBULL, E. F. (Hibernian) (9): 1948 v Bel, Sw, Fr; 1951 v A; 1958 v H, Pol, Y, Par, Fr.
TURNER, T. (Arthurlie) (1): 1884 v W.
TURNER, W. (Pollokshields Ath.) (2): 1885 v Ni; 1886 v Ni.

URE, J. F. (Dundee, Arsenal) (11): 1962 v W, Cz; 1963 v W, Ni, E, A, N, Sp; 1964 v Ni, N; 1968 v Ni.
URQUHART, D. (Hibernian) (1): 1934 v W.

VALLANCE, T. (Rangers) (7): 1877 v E, W; 1878 v E; 1879 v E, W; 1881 v E, W.
VENTERS, A. (Cowdenbeath, Rangers) (3): 1934 v Ni; 1936 v E; 1939 v E.

WADDELL, T. S. (Queen's Park) (6): 1891 v Ni; 1892 v E; 1893 v E, Ni; 1895 v E, Ni.
WADDELL, W. (Rangers) (17): 1947 v W; 1949 v E, W, Ni, Fr; 1950 v E, Ni; 1951 v E, D, Fr, Bel, A; 1952 v Ni, W; 1954 v Ni; 1955 v W, Ni.
WALES, H. M. (Motherwell) (1): 1933 v W.
WALKER, A. (Celtic) (3): 1988 v Co; 1995 v Fin, Fi.
WALKER, F. (Third Lanark) (1): 1922 v W.
WALKER, G. (St Mirren) (4): 1930 v Fr; 1931 v Ni, A, Sw.
WALKER, J. (Hearts, Rangers) (5): 1895 v Ni; 1897 v W; 1898 v Ni; 1904 v W, Ni.
WALKER, J. (Swindon T.) (9): 1911 v E, W, Ni; 1912 v E, W, Ni; 1913 v E, W, Ni.
WALKER, N. (Hearts, Partick Thistle) (2): 1993 v G, 1996 US.
WALKER, R. (Hearts) (29): 1900 v E, Ni; 1901 v E, W; 1902 v E, W, Ni; 1903 v E, W, Ni; 1904 v E, W, Ni; 1905 v E, W, Ni; 1906 v Ni; 1907 (cont...)

RANGERS player Willie Waddell in action for Scotland in 1951, he played 17 times for his country

v E, Ni; 1908 v E, W, Ni; 1909 v E, W; 1912 v E, W, Ni; 1913 v E, W.
WALKER, T. (Hearts) (20): 1935 v E, W; 1936 v E, W, Ni; 1937 v G, E, W, Ni, A, Cz; 1938 v E, W, Ni, Cz, Holl; 1939 v E, W, Ni, H.
WALKER, W. (Clyde) (2): 1909 v Ni; 1910 v Ni.
WALLACE, I. A. (Coventry City) (3): 1978 v Bul; 1979 v Por, W.
WALLACE, L. (Hearts, Rangers) (10): 2010 v J, W, CzR; 2011 v Se, Li; 2012 v US; 2014 v Mac, US; 2017 v E, Ca.
WALLACE, R. (Preston NE) (1): 2010 v J.
WALLACE, W. S. B. (Hearts, Celtic) (7): 1965 v Ni; 1966 v E, Holl; 1967 v E, USSR; 1968 v Ni; 1969 v E.
WARDHAUGH, J. (Hearts) (2): 1955 v H; 1957 v Ni.
WARK, J. (Ipswich Town, Liverpool) (29): 1979 v W, Ni, E, Arg, N; 1980 v Pe, A, Bel (2); 1981 v Is; 1982 v Se, Sp, Holl, Ni, Nz, Br, USSR; 1983 v EG, Sw (2), Ni, E; 1984 v U, Bel, EG, E, Fr; 1985 v Y.
WATSON, A. (Queen's Park) (3): 1881 v E, W; 1882 v E.
WATSON, J. (Sunderland, Middlesbrough) (6): 1903 v E, W; 1904 v E; 1905 v E; 1909 v E, Ni.
WATSON, J. (Motherwell, Huddersfield) (2): 1948 v Ni; 1954 v Ni.
WATSON, J. A. K. (Rangers) (1): 1878 v W.
WATSON, P. R. (Blackpool) (1): 1934 v A.
WATSON, R. (Motherwell) (1): 1971 v USSR.
WATSON, W. (Falkirk) (1): 1898 v W.
WATT, A. (Charlton) (1): 2016 v CZR.
WATT, F. (Kilbirnie) (4): 1889 v W, Ni; 1890 v W; 1891 v E.
WATT, W. W. (Queen's Park) (1): 1887 v Ni.
WAUGH, H. (Hearts) (1): 1938 v Cz.
WEBSTER, A. (Hearts, Rangers) (28): 2003 v A, Nz, G; 2004 v N, Fi, W, Est, Trin; 2005 v H, Sp, Slo, N, Mo (2), Se, Blr; 2006 v A, I, N, Slo, US, Sw; 2010 v CzR; 2012 v US; 2013 v Aus, Mac, Est, Ser.
WEIR, A. (Motherwell) (6): 1959 v WG; 1960 v E, Por, A, H, T.
WEIR, D. (Hearts, Everton, Rangers) (69): 1997 v W, Ma; 1998 v Fr, D, Fin, N, M; 1999 v Est, Fi, CzR (2), G, Fi; 2000 v Bos (2), Est, Lth, E (2), Holl; 2001 v La, Sm (2), Cro, Aus, Bel, Pol; 2002 v Cro, Bel, La, Fr, Nig, Skor, SA, HK; 2003 v D, Fi; 2005 v I, Mo, Blr; 2006 v I, N, Blr, Slo, US, Sw, Bul, J; 2007 v Fi (2), Lth, Fr, Uk, Geo, I, A; 2008 v Lth, Fr, Uk, Geo, I; 2009 v Ni, N; 2010 v Mac, Holl; 2011 v Lth, Li, CzR, Sp.
WEIR, J. (Third Lanark) (1): 1887 v Ni.
WEIR, J. B. (Queen's Park) (4): 1872 v E; 1874 v E; 1875 v E; 1878 v W.
WEIR, P. (St Mirren, Aberdeen) (6): 1980 v N, W, Pol, H; 1983 v Sw; 1984 v Ni.
WHITE, J. (Albion Rovers, Hearts) (2): 1922 v W; 1923 v Ni.
WHITE, J. A. (Falkirk, Tottenham H.) (22): 1959 v WG, Holl, Por; 1960 v Ni, W, Pol, A, T; 1961 v W; 1962 v Ni, W, E, Cz (2); 1963 v W, Ni, E; 1964 v Ni, W, E, N, WG.
WHITE, W. (Bolton W.) (2): 1907 v E; 1908 v E.
WHITELAW, A. (Vale of Leven) (2): 1887 v Ni; 1890 v W.
WHITTAKER, S. (Rangers, Norwich) (31): 2010 v N, Mac, Holl, J, CzR; 2011 v Se, Lth, CzR, Sp, Br, W, Ei; 2012 v Lth, Cy, US; 2013 v Lux, Cro, Ser; 2014 v E, Bel, Mac, US, N, Nig; 2015 v G, Pol, Ei, E, Ni; 2016 v Pol, D.
WHYTE, D. (Celtic, Middlesbrough, Aberdeen) (12): 1988 v Bel, L; 1989 v Ch; 1992 v US; 1993 v Por, I; 1995 v J, Ec, US; 1997 v La; 1998 v Fin; 1999 v G.
WILKIE, L. (Dundee) (11): 2002 v SA, HK; 2003 v Ice (2), Can, Por, A, Lth; 2004 v Fi, Holl (2).

WILLIAMS, G. (Nottingham Forest) (5): 2002 v Nig, Skor, SA, HK, Por.
WILSON, A. (Sheffield W.) (6): 1907 v E; 1908 v E; 1912 v I; 1913 v E, W; 1914 v Ni.
WILSON, A. (Portsmouth) (1): 1954 v Fin.
WILSON, A. N. (Dunfermline, Middlesbrough) (12): 1920 v E, W, Ni; 1921 v E, W, Ni; 1922 v E, W, Ni; 1923 v E, W, Ni.
WILSON, D. (Queen's Park) (1): 1900 v W.
WILSON, D. (Oldham) (1): 1913 v E.
WILSON, D. (Rangers) (22): 1961 v E, W, Ni, Ei (2), Cz; 1962 v Ni, W, E, Cz, U; 1963 v W, E, A, N, Ei, Sp; 1964 v E, WG; 1965 v Ni, E, Fin.
WILSON, D. (Liverpool) (5): 2011 v Fi, Ni, Br; 2012 v D, CzR.
WILSON, G. W. (Hearts, Everton, Newcastle Utd.) (6): 1904 v W; 1905 v E, Ni; 1906 v W; 1907 v E; 1909 v E.
WILSON, H. (Newmilns, Sunderland, Third Lanark) (4): 1890 v W; 1897 v E; 1902 v W; 1904 v Ni.
WILSON, I. A. (Leicester, Everton) (5): 1987 v E, Br; 1988 v Bel, Bul, L.
WILSON, J. (Vale of Leven) (4): 1888 v W; 1889 v E; 1890 v E; 1891 v E.
WILSON, M. (Celtic) (1): 2011 v Ni.
WILSON, P. (Celtic) (4): 1926 v Ni; 1930 v Fr; 1931 v Ni; 1933 v E.
WILSON, P. (Celtic) (1): 1975 v Sp.
WILSON, R. P. (Arsenal) (2): 1972 v Por, Holl.
WINTERS, R. (Aberdeen) (1): 1999 v G.
WISEMAN, W. (Queen's Park) (2): 1927 v W; 1930 v Ni.
WOOD, G. (Everton, Arsenal) (4): 1979 v Ni, E, Arg; 1982 v Ni.
WOODBURN, W. A. (Rangers) (24): 1947 v E, Bel, L; 1948 v W, Ni; 1949 v E, Fr; 1950 v E, W, Ni, Por, Fr; 1951 v E, W, Ni, A (2), D, Fr, Bel; 1952 v E, W, Ni, USA.
WOTHERSPOON, D. N. (Queen's Park) (2): 1872 v E; 1873 v E.
WRIGHT, K. (Hibs) (1): 1992 v Ni.
WRIGHT, S. (Aberdeen) (2): 1993 v G, Est.
WRIGHT, T. (Sunderland) (3): 1953 v W, Ni, E.
WYLIE, T. G. (Rangers) (1): 1890 v Ni.

YEATS, R. (Liverpool) (2): 1965 v W; 1966 v I.
YORSTON, B. C. (Aberdeen) (1): 1931 v Ni.
YORSTON, H. (Aberdeen) (1): 1955 v W.
YOUNG, A. (Hearts, Everton) (8): 1960 v E, A, H, T; 1961 v W, Ni, Ei; 1966 v Por.
YOUNG, A. (Everton) (2): 1905 v E; 1907 v W.
YOUNG, G. A. (Rangers) (53): 1947 v E, Ni, Bel, L; 1948 v E, Ni, Bel, Sw, Fr; 1949 v E, W, Ni, Fr; 1950 v E, W, Ni, Sw, Por, Fr; 1951 v E, W, Ni, A (2), D, Fr, Bel; 1952 v E, W, Ni, USA, D, Se; 1953 v W, E, Ni, Se; 1954 v Ni, W; 1955 v W, Ni, Por, Y; 1956 v Ni, W, E, A; 1957 v E, Ni, W, Y, Sp, Sw.
YOUNG, J. (Celtic) (1): 1906 v Ni.
YOUNGER, T. (Hibernian, Liverpool) (24): 1955 v Por, Y, A, H; 1956 v E, Ni, W, A; 1957 v E, Ni, W, Y, Sp (2), Sw, WG; 1958 v Ni, W, E, Sw, H, Pol, Y, Par.

WORLD CUP WINNERS

Year	Winners		Runners-up		Venue
1930	URUGUAY	4	Argentina	2	Uruguay
1934	ITALY	2	Czechoslovakia	1	Italy
			(after extra time)		
1938	ITALY	4	Hungary	2	France
1950	URUGUAY	2	Brazil	1	Brazil
1954	W GERMANY	3	Hungary	2	Switzerland
1958	BRAZIL	5	Sweden	2	Sweden
1962	BRAZIL	3	Czechosl'kia	1	Chile
1966	ENGLAND	4	W Germany	2	England
			(after extra time)		
1970	BRAZIL	4	Italy	1	Mexico
1974	W GERMANY	2	Holland	1	W Germany
1978	ARGENTINA	3	Holland	1	Argentina
			(after extra time)		
1982	ITALY	3	W Germany	1	Spain
1986	ARGENTINA	3	W Germany	2	Mexico
1990	W GERMANY	1	Argentina	0	Italy
1994	BRAZIL	0	Italy	0	America
			(after extra time, Brazil won 3-2 on penalties)		
1998	FRANCE	3	Brazil	0	France
2002	BRAZIL	2	Germany	0	Japan
2006	ITALY	1	France	1	Germany
			(after extra time, Italy won 5-3 on penalties)		
2010	SPAIN	1	Holland	0	South Africa
			(after extra time)		
2014	GERMANY	1	Argentina	0	Brazil

EUROPEAN CHAMPIONSHIP WINNERS

Year	Winners		Runners-up		Venue
1960	RUSSIA	2	Yugoslavia	1	France
1964	SPAIN	2	Russia	1	Spain
1968	ITALY	2	Yugoslavia	0	Italy
			(aet in replay after 1-1 draw)		
1972	W GERMANY	3	Russia	0	Belgium
1976	CZECHOSLOVAKIA	2	W Germany	2	Yugoslavia
			(Czechoslovakia won 5-3 on penalties)		
1980	W GERMANY	2	Belgium	1	Italy
1984	FRANCE	2	Spain	0	France
1988	HOLLAND	2	Russia	0	West Germany
1992	DENMARK	2	Germany	0	Sweden
1996	GERMANY	2	Czech Rep	1	England
			(1-1 full time. Germany scored Golden Goal in extra time)		
2000	FRANCE	2	Italy	1	Holland
			(1-1 full time. France scored Golden Goal in extra time)		
2004	GREECE	1	Portugal	0	Portugal
2008	SPAIN	1	Germany	0	Austria
2012	SPAIN	4	Italy	0	Ukraine
2016	PORTUGAL	1	France	0	France
			(after extra time)		

EUROPEAN SUPER CUP

1972	AJAX	3	Rangers	2
	Rangers	1	AJAX	3
1973	AC Milan	0	AJAX	1
	AJAX	6	AC Milan	0
		1974 – Not contested		
1975	Bayern Munich	0	DYNAMO KIEV	1
	DYNAMO KIEV	2	Bayern Munich	0

1976	Bayern Munich	2	ANDERLECHT	1
	ANDERLECHT	4	Bayern Munich	1
1977	Hamburg	1	LIVERPOOL	1
	LIVERPOOL	6	Hamburg	0
1978	ANDERLECHT	3	Liverpool	1
	Liverpool	2	ANDERLECHT	1
1979	NOTTS FOREST	1	Barcelona	1
	Barcelona	1	NOTTS FOREST	1
1980	Nottingham Forest	2	VALENCIA	1
	VALENCIA	1	Nottingham Forest	0
1981 – Not contested				
1982	Barcelona	1	ASTON VILLA	0
	ASTON VILLA	3	Barcelona	0
1983	Hamburg	1	ABERDEEN	0
	ABERDEEN	2	Hamburg	0
1984	JUVENTUS	2	Liverpool	0
1985	Juventus v Everton not played due to Uefa ban on English clubs			
1986	ST BUCHREST	1	Dynamo Kiev	0
1987	Ajax	1	FC PORTO	0
	FCPORTO	1	Ajax	0
1988	MECHELEN	3	PSV Eindhoven	0
	PSV Eindhoven	1	MECHELEN	0
1989	Barcelona	1	AC MILAN	1
	AC MILAN	1	Barcelona	0
1990	Sampdoria	1	AC MILAN	1
	AC MILAN	2	Sampdoria	0
1991	MANCHESTER UTD	1	Red Star Belgrade	0
1992	Werder Bremen	1	BARCELONA	1
	BARCELONA	2	Werder Bremen	1
1993	PARMA	0	AC Milan	1
	AC Milan	0	PARMA	2
(aet, 90mins 0-1, agg.1-2 for Parma)				
1994	Arsenal	0	AC MILAN	0
	AC MILAN	2	Arsenal	0
1995	Real Zaragoza	1	AJAX	1
	AJAX	4	Real Zaragoza	0
1996	Paris St Germain	0	JUVENTUS	1
	JUVENTUS	6	Paris St Germain	1
1997	BARCELONA	1	Borussia Dortmund	0
	Borussia Dortmund	1	BARCELONA	0
1998	Real Madrid	0	CHELSEA	1
1999	LAZIO	2	Manchester United	1
2000	GALATASARAY	2	Real Madrid	1
(1-1 full time. Galatasaray scored golden goal in extra time)				
2001	LIVERPOOL	3	Bayern Munich	2
2002	REAL MADRID	3	Feyenoord	1
2003	AC MILAN	1	FC Porto	0
2004	Porto	2	VALENCIA	1
2005	LIVERPOOL	3	CSKA Moscow	1
(aet, 90mins 1-1)				
2006	SEVILLA	3	Barcelona	0
2007	AC MILAN	3	Sevilla	1
2008	Manchester Utd	2	ZENIT	2
2009	BARCELONA	1	Shakhtar Donetsk	0
(after extra time)				
2010	Inter Milan	0	ATLÉTICO MADRID	2
2011	BARCELONA	2	Porto	0
2012	ATLETICO MADRID	4	Chelsea	1
2013	BAYERN MUNICH	2	Chelsea	2
(Bayern win 5-4 on penalties)				
2014	REAL MADRID	2	Sevilla	0
2015	BARCELONA	5	Sevilla	4
(after extra time)				
2016	REAL MADRID	3	Sevilla	2
(after extra time)				
2017	REAL MADRID	2	Manchester Utd	1

EUROPEAN CUP FINALS

Year	Winners	Runners-up
1956	REAL MADRID 4	Rheims 3
	(Paris, 38,000)	
1957	REAL MADRID 2	Fiorentina 0
	(Madrid, 124,000)	
1958	REAL MADRID 3	AC Milan 2
	After extra time (Brussels, 67,000)	
1959	REAL MADRID 2	Rheims 0
	(Stuttgart, 80,000)	
1960	REAL MADRID 7	Eintracht 3
	(Glasgow, 127,261)	
1961	BENFICA 3	Barcelona 2
	(Berne, 28,000)	
1962	BENFICA 5	Real Madrid 3
	(Amsterdam, 65,000)	
1963	AC MILAN 2	Benfica 1
	(Wembley, 45,000)	
1964	INTER MILAN 3	Real Madrid 1
	(Vienna, 74,000)	
1965	INTER MILAN 1	Benfica 0
	(Milan, 80,000)	
1966	REAL MADRID 2	Partisan Belgrade 1
	(Brussels, 55,000)	
1967	CELTIC 2	Inter Milan 1
	(Lisbon, 56,000)	
1968	MAN UNITED 4	Benfica 1
	(Wembley, 100,000)	
1969	AC MILAN 4	Ajax 1
	(Madrid, 50,000)	
1970	FEYENOORD 2	Celtic 1
	(Milan, 50,000)	
1971	AJAX 2	Panathinaikos 0
	(Wembey, 90,000)	
1972	AJAX 2	Inter Milan 0
	(Rotterdam, 67,000)	
1973	AJAX 1	Juventus 0
	(Belgrade, 93,500)	
1974	BAYERN MUNICH 4	Atletico Madrid 0
	(Brussels, 65,000) (after 1-1 draw)	
1975	BAYERN MUNICH 2	Leeds 0
	(Paris, 50,000)	
1976	BAYERN MUNICH 1	St Etienne 0
	(Glasgow, 54,864)	

1977	LIVERPOOL 3	Borussia MG.................. 1

(Rome, 57,000)

1978	LIVERPOOL 1	Bruges 0

(Wembley, 92,000)

1979	NOTTS FOREST 1	Malmo 0

(Munich, 57,500)

1980	NOTTS FOREST 1	Hamburg...................... 0

(Madrid, 50,000)

1981	LIVERPOOL 1	Real Madrid 0

(Paris, 48,360)

1982	ASTON VILLA 1	Bayern Munich 0

(Rotterdam, 46,000)

1983	HAMBURG................. 1	Juventus 0

(Athens, 75,000)

1984	LIVERPOOL 1	Roma............................ 1

(Rome, 69,693)

Liverpool won 4-2 on penalties

1985	JUVENTUS................ 1	Liverpool...................... 0

(Brussels, 58,000)

1986	S BUCHAREST 0	Barcelona 0

Steaua Bucharest won 2-0 on penalties (Seville, 70,000)

1987	PORTO...................... 2	Bayern Munich 1

(Vienna, 59,000)

1988	PSV........................... 0	Benfica 0

(Stuttgart, 70,000)

PSV Eindhoven won 6-5 on penalties

1989	AC MILAN 4	Steau Bucharest 0

(Barcelona, 97,000)

1990	AC MILAN 1	Benfica 0

(Vienna, 57,500)

1991	R.S. BELGRADE 0	Marseille 0

(Bari, 56,000)

Red Star won 5-3 on penalties

1992	BARCELONA 1	Sampdoria.................... 0

After extra time

(Wembley, 70,000)

1993	MARSEILLE 1	AC Milan 0

(Munich, 65,000)

1994	AC MILAN 4	Barcelona.................... 0

(Athens, 75,000)

1995	AJAX......................... 1	AC Milan 0

(Vienna, 49,000)

1996	JUVENTUS................ 1	Ajax............................. 1

(Rome, 67,000)

(1-1 full time. Juventus won 4-2 on penalties)

1997	B DORTMUND 3	Juventus 1

(Munich, 55,500)

1998   REAL MADRID 1   Juventus 0
(Amsterdam, 45,000)
1999   MANCHESTER UTD. 2   Bayern Munich 1
(Barcelona, 90,000)

2000   REAL MADRID 3   Valencia 0
(Paris, 73,000)
2001   BAYERN MUNICH 1   Valencia 1
(1-1 full-time, Bayern won 5-4 on penalties)
(Milan, 80,000)
2002   REAL MADRID 2   Bayer Leverkusen 1
(Glasgow, 52,000)
2003   AC MILAN 0   Juventus 0
(0-0 after extra time. AC Milan won 3-2 on penalties)
(Manchester, 63,000)
2004   PORTO...................... 3   Monaco 0
(Gelsenkirchen, 52,000)
2005   LIVERPOOL 3   AC Milan 3
(3-3 after extra time, Liverpool won 3-2 on penalties)
(Istanbul, 65,000)
2006   BARCELONA 2   Arsenal 1
(Paris, 79,500)
2007   AC MILAN 2   Liverpool 1
(Athens, 74,000)
2008   MANCHESTER UTD..... 1   Chelsea 1
(1-1 full-time, Manchester Utd won 6-5 on penalties)
(Moscow, 69,552)
2009   BARCELONA 2   Manchester Utd 0
(Rome, 72,700)
2010   INTER MILAN 2   Bayern Munich 0
(Madrid, 80,100)
2011   BARCELONA 3   Manchester Utd 1
(Wembley, 87,695)
2012   CHELSEA 1   Bayern Munich 1
(1-1 full-time, Chelsea won 4-3 on penalties)
(Munich, 69,901)
2013   BAYERN MUNICH 2   B Dortmund 1
(Wembley, 86,298)
2014   REAL MADRID 4   Atletico Madrid 1
(after extra time, 1-1 after 90 minutes)
(Lisbon, 60,976)
2015   BARCELONA 3   Juventus 1
(Berlin, 70,442)
2016   REAL MADRID 1   Atletico Madrid 1
(1-1 full-time, Real Madrid won 5-3 on penalties)
(Milan, 71,942)
2017   REAL MADRID 4   Juventus 1
(Cardiff, 65,842)
2017   REAL MADRID 4   Juventus 1
(Cardiff, 65,842)
2018   REAL MADRID 3   Liverpool 1
(Kiev, 61,561)

EUROPEAN CUP-WINNERS' CUP FINALS

1961   Rangers..................0   FIORENTINA 2
                        (Ibrox, 80,000)
        FIORENTINA..................2   Rangers....................1
                        (Florence, 50,000)
                        Aggregate 4-1
1962   ATLETICO MADRID 1   Fiorentina................................1
                        (Glasgow, 27,389)
        ATLETICO MADRID 3   Fiorentina................................0
                        (Stuttgart, 45,000)
1963   SPURS..........................5   Atletico Madrid....................1
                        (Rotterdam, 25,000)
1964   SPORTING LISBON ...1   MTK Budapest..................0
                        (Antwerp, 18,000)
                   After 3-3 draw in Brussels
1965   WEST HAM..................2   Munich 1860...................1
                        (Wembley, 100,000)
1966   BOR. DORTMUND.......2   Liverpool 1
                        (Hampden, 41,657)
1967   BAYERN MUNICH.......1   Rangers................................0
                        (Nuremberg, 69,480 aet)
1968   AC MILAN.....................2   S.V. Hamburg 0
                        (Rotterdam, 60,000)
1969   S BRATISLAVIA...........3   Barcelona 2
                        (Basle, 40,000)
1970   MANCHESTER CITY ...2   Gornik..................................1
                        (Vienna, 10,000)
1971   CHELSEA.....................2   Real Madrid 1
                   (Athens, 24,000, after 1-1 draw)
1972   RANGERS.....................3   Moscow Dynamo..................2
                        (Barcelona, 35,000)
1973   AC MILAN 1   Leeds United....................0
                        (Salonika, 45,000)
1974   AC MAGDEBURG........2   AC Milan.............................0
                        (Rotterdam, 5,000)
1975   DYNAMO KIEV.............3   Ferencvaros........................0
                        (Basle, 13,000)
1976   ANDERLECHT..............4   West Ham 2
                        (Brussels, 58,000)
1977   SV HAMBURG..............2   Anderlecht 0
                        (Amsterdam, 65,000)
1978   ANDERLECHT..............4   Austria Wein 0
                        (Paris, 48,679)

1979	BARCELONA..............4	Fortuna Dusseldorf..............3

(Basel, 58,000)

1980	VALENCIA..................0	Arsenal 0

(Brussels, 40,000, Valencia won 5-4 on penalties)

1981	DYNAMO TBILISI 2	Carl Zeiss Jena 1

(Dusseldorf, 9,000)

1982	BARCELONA..............2	Standard Liege..................1

(Barcelona, 100,000)

1983	ABERDEEN..................2	Real Madrid..........................1

(Gothenburg, 17,804)

1984	JUVENTUS...................2	FC Porto............................1

(Basle, 60,000)

1985	EVERTON......................3	Rapid Vienna........................1

(Rotterdam, 30,000)

1986	DYNAMO KIEV.............3	Atletico Madrid ....0.

(Lyon, 39,300)

1987	AJAX 1	Lokomotiv Leipzig 0

(Athens, 35,000)

1988	KV MECHELEN............1	Ajax 0

(Strasbourg, 39,446)

1989	BARCELONA................2	Sampdoria 0

(Berne, 45,000)

1990	SAMPDORIA.................2	Anderlecht 0

(Gothenburg, 20,103)

1991	MANCHESTER UTD.....2	Barcelona 1

(Rotterdam, 50,000)

1992	WERDER BREMEN 2	Monaco 0

(Lisbon, 50,000)

1993	Antwerp 0	PARMA 3

(Wembley, 50,000)

1994	Parma...........................0	ARSENAL...............................1

(Copenhagen, 33,765)

1995	Arsenal 1	REAL ZARAGOZA.................2

(aet, 90 minutes 1-1) (Paris, 42,000)

1996	PARIS ST GERMAIN....1	Rapid Vienna........................0

(Brussels, 50,000)

1997	BARCELONA................1	Paris St Germain..................0

(Rotterdam, 40,000)

1998	CHELSEA......................1	VfB Stuttgart............................0

(Stockholm, 30, 216)

1999	LAZIO............................2	Real Mallorca...........................1

(Villa Park, 30,000)

EUROPA LEAGUE FINALS
(FORMERLY FAIRS CITIES CUP, UEFA CUP)

1958	London	2	BARCELONA	2
	BARCELONA	6	London	0
			(agg: 8-2)	
1960	Birmingham	0	BARCELONA	0
	BARCELONA	4	Birmingham	1
			(agg: 4-1)	
1961	Birmingham	2	ROMA	2
	ROMA	2	Birmingham	0
			(agg: 4-2)	
1962	VALENCIA	6	Barcelona	2
	Barcelona	1	VALENCIA	1
			(agg 7-3)	
1963	Dynamo Zagreb	1	VALENCIA	2
	VALENCIA	2	Dynamo Zagreb	0
			(agg: 4-1)	
1964	REAL ZARAGOZA	2	Valencia	1
			(Barcelona)	
1965	FERENCVAROS	1	Juventus	0
			(Turin)	
1966	BARCELONA	0	Real Zaragoza	1
	Real Zaragoza	2	BARCELONA	4
			(agg: 4-3)	
1967	DINAMO ZAGREB	2	Leeds United	0
	Leeds United	0	DINAMO ZAGREB	0
			(agg: 2-0)	
1968	LEEDS UNITED	1	Ferencvaros	0
	Ferencvaros	0	LEEDS UNITED	0
			(agg: 1-0)	
1969	NEWCASTLE UTD	3	Ujpest Dozsa	0
	Ujpest Dozsa	2	NEWCASTLE UTD	3
			(agg: 6-2)	
1970	Anderlecht	3	ARSENAL	1
	ARSENAL	3	Anderlecht	0
			(agg: 4-3)	
1971	Juventus	2	LEEDS UNITED	2
	LEEDS UNITED	1	Juventus	1
			(agg: 3-3)	
			Leeds won on away goals	
1972	Wolves	1	TOTTENHAM	2
	TOTTENHAM	1	Wolves	1
			(agg: 3-2)	
1973	LIVERPOOL	3	Borussia M	0
	Borussia M	2	LIVERPOOL	0
			(agg: 3-2)	
1974	Tottenham Hostpur	2	FEYENOORD	2
	FEYENOORD	2	Tottenham Hotspur	0
			(agg: 4-2)	
1975	BORUSSIA M	0	Twente	0
	Twente	1	BORUSSIA M	5
			(agg: 5-1)	

1976	LIVERPOOL	3	FC Bruges	2
	Bruges	1	LIVERPOOL	1

(agg 4-3)

1977	JUVENTUS	1	Athletic Bilbao	0
	Athletic Bilbao	2	JUVENTUS	1

(agg: 2-2. Juventus won on away goals)

1978	Bastia	0	PSV EINDHOVEN	0
	PSV EINDHOVEN	3	Bastia	0

(agg: 3-0)

1979	Red Star Belgrade	1	BORUSSIA M	1
	BORUSSIA M	1	Red Star Belgrade	0

(agg: 2-1)

1980	Borussia M	3	EINTRACHT	2
	EINTRACHT	1	Borussia M	0

(agg: 3-3. Eintracht won on away goals)

1981	IPSWICH	3	AZ 67	0
	AZ 67	4	IPSWICH	2

(agg: 5-4)

1982	GOTHENBURG	1	Hamburg	0
	Hamburg	0	GOTHENBURG	3

(agg: 4-0)

1983	ANDERLECHT	1	Benfica	0
	Benfica	1	ANDERLECHT	1

(agg: 2-1)

1984	Anderlecht	1	TOTTENHAM	1
	TOTTENHAM	1	Anderlecht	1

(agg: 2-2. Tottenham won 4-3 on penalties)

1985	Videoton	0	REAL MADRID	3
	REAL MADRID	0	Videoton	1

(agg: 3-1)

1986	REAL MADRID	5	Cologne	1
	Cologne	2	REAL MADRID	0

(agg: 5-3)

1987	GOTHENBURG	1	Dundee United	0
	Dundee United	1	GOTHENBURG	1

(agg: 2-1)

1988	Espanyol	3	BAYER LEVERKUSEN	0
	BAYER LEVERKUSEN	3	Espanyol	0

(agg: 3-3. Leverkusen won 3-2 on penalties)

1989	NAPOLI	2	Stuttgart	1
	Stuttgart	3	NAPOLI	3

(agg: 5-4)

1990	JUVENTUS	3	Fiorentina	1
	Fiorentina	0	JUVENTUS	0

(agg: 3-1)

1991	INTER MILAN	2	Roma	0
	Roma	1	INTER MILAN	0

(agg: 2-1)

1992	Torino	2	AJAX	2
	AJAX	0	Torino	0

(agg: 2-2. Ajax win on away goals rule)

1993	Borussia Dortmund	1	JUVENTUS	3
	JUVENTUS	3	Borussia Dortmund	0
		(agg: 6-1)		
1994	Salzburg	0	INTER MILAN	1
	INTER MILAN	1	Salzburg	0
		(agg: 2-0)		
1995	PARMA	1	Juventus	0
	Juventus	1	PARMA	1
		(agg: 2-1)		
1996	BAYERN MUNICH	2	Bordeaux	0
	Bordeaux	1	BAYERN MUNICH	3
		(agg: 5-1)		
1997	Schalke	1	INTER MILAN	0
	INTER MILAN	1	Schalke	0
	(agg: 1-1. Schalke win 4-1 on penalties)			
1998	INTER MILAN	3	Lazio	0
		(Paris)		
1999	PARMA	3	Marseille	0
		(Moscow)		
2000	GALATASARAY	0	Arsenal	0
	(Galatasaray won 4-1 on penalties)			
		(Copenhagen)		
2001	LIVERPOOL	5	Alaves	4
	(4-4 full-time. Liverpool win with golden goal)			
		(Dortmund)		
2002	Borussia Dortmund	2	FEYENOORD	3
		(Rotterdam)		
2003	Celtic	2	PORTO	3
	(2-2 after 90 mins.)			
		(Seville)		
2004	VALENCIA	2	Marseille	0
		(Gothenburg)		
2005	Sporting Lisbon	1	CSKA MOSCOW	3
		(Lisbon)		
2006	Middlesbrough	0	SEVILLA	4
		(Eindhoven)		
2007	SEVILLA	1	Espanyol	1
	(aet 2-2, Sevilla win 3-1 on pens)			
		(Glasgow)		
2008	ZENIT	2	Rangers	0
		(Manchester)		
2009	SHAKHTAR	2	Werder Bremen	1
	(1-1 after 90 mins.)			
		(Istanbul)		
2010	ATLETICO MADRID	2	Fulham	1
	(1-1 after 90 mins.)			
		(Hamburg)		
2011	PORTO	1	Braga	0
		(Dublin)		
2012	ATLETICO MADRID	3	Athletic Bilbao	0
		(Bucharest)		
2013	Benfica	1	CHELSEA	2
		(Amsterdam)		
2014	SEVILLA	0	Benfica	0
	(Sevilla won 4-2 on penalties)			
		(Turin)		
2015	Dnipro Dnipropetrovsk	2	SEVILLA	3
		(Warsaw)		
2016	Liverpool	1	SEVILLA	3
		(Basel)		
2017	Ajax	0	MANCHESTER UTD	2
		(Stockholm)		
2018	Marseille	0	ATHLETICO MADRID	3
		(Lyon)		

GAMES TO REMEMBER

1967   England..................2   SCOTLAND 3
(Home Internationals, Wembley, April 15. Att: 100,000)
SCOTLAND: Simpson, Gemmell, McCreadie, Greig, McKinnon, Baxter, Wallace, Bremner, McCalliog, Law, Lennox. Scorers: Law, Lennox, McCalliog.
ENGLAND: Banks, Cohen, Wilson, Stiles, J Charlton, Moore, Ball, Greaves, R Charlton, Hurst, Peters. Scorers: J. Charlton, Hurst.

1967   CELTIC 2   Inter Milan...................... 1
(European Cup Final, Lisbon, May 25. Attendance 56,000)
CELTIC: Simpson, Craig, Gemmell, Murdoch, McNeill, Clark, Johnstone, Wallace, Chalmers, Auld, Lennox. Scorers: Gemmell (63), Chalmers (85).
INTER MILAN: Sarti, Burgnich, Facchetti, Bedin, Guarneri, Picchi, Domenghini, Cappellini, Mazzola, Bicicli, Corso. Scorer: Mazzola (7 pen).

1972   RANGERS 3   Moscow Dynamo 2
(Cup-Winners' Cup Final, Barcelona, May 24. Att: 35,000)
RANGERS: McCloy, Jardine, Mathieson, Greig, D Johnstone, Smith, McLean, Conn, Stein, MacDonald, W Johnston. Scorers: Stein (24), Johnston (40, 49).
MOSCOW DYNAMO: Pilgui, Basalev, Dolmatov, Zykov, Dobbonosov, (Gerschkovitch), Zhukov, Baidatchini, Jakubik (Eschtrekov), Sabo, Makovikov, Evryuzhikbin. Scorers: Eschtrekov (55) Makovikov (87).

1978   Holland 2   SCOTLAND 3
(World Cup finals, Mendoza, June 11. Att: 35,130)
HOLLAND: Jongbloed, Suurbier, Krol, Rijsbergen (Wildschut), Poortvleit, W van de Kerkhof, Neeskens (Boskamp, Jansen, R va n de Kerkhof, Rep, Resenbrink. Scorers: Resenbrink (34pen), Rep (71).
SCOTLAND: Rough, Donachie, Buchan, Rioch, Dalglish, Jordan Hartford, Kennedy, Forsyth, Gemmill, Souness. Scorers: Dalglish (43), Gemmill (47pen, 68).

2007   France 0   SCOTLAND 1
(EURO 2008 Qualifier, Paris, September 12. Att: 42,000)
FRANCE: Landreau, Lassana Diarra, Thuram, Escude, Abidal (Benz ema), Ribery, Viera (Nasri), Makelele, Malouda, Trezeguet, Anelka.
SCOTLAND: Gordon, Hutton, McManus, Weir, Alexander, McCulloch, Ferguson, Fletcher (Pearson), Brown, Hartley, McFadden (O'Connor). Scorer: McFadden (64).

2017   Barcelona...............6   Paris Saint Germain.......1
(Champions League last 16, Barcelona, March 8. Att: 96,290)
BARCELONA: Stegen, Umtiti, Piqué, Mascherano; Rakiti (84 Gomez) Busquets, Iniesta (65 Turin) Rafinha (76 Roberto), Suárez, Messi, Neymar. Scorers: Suárez (3), Kurzawa (40) (own goal), Messi (50), Neymar (88,90+1pen), Roberto (90+5)
PARIS SAINT GERMAIN: Trapp, Meunier, Marquinhos (90 Krychowiak), Kurzawa, Thiago Silva, Matuidi, Draxler (75 Aurier), Lucas (55 di Maria), Verratti, Rabiot, Cavani. Scorer: Cavani (62).

SCOTTISH CLUBS IN EUROPE
A COMPLETE HISTORY
Abbreviations EC (European Champions Cup), ECWC (European Cup-Winners' Cup), FC (Fairs Cities Cup) UEFA (Uefa Cup) w (won) l (lost) p (preliminary) q (qualifying round)

ABERDEEN

Opponents	Venue	Res	Scorers	Rnd
		1967-68 ECWC		
KR Reykjavic (Iceland)	H	W10-1	Munro 3, Storrie 2 Smith 2, McMillan, Petersen,Taylor	1
	A	W4-1	Storrie 2 Buchan, Munro	
Standard Liege (Belgium)	A	L0-3		2
	H	W2-0	Munro, Melrose	
		1968-69 FC		
Slavia Sofia (Bulgaria)	A	D0-0		1
	H	W2-0	Robb, Taylor	
Real Zaragossa (Spain)	H	W2-1	Forrest, Smith	2
	A	L0-3		
		1970-71 ECWC		
Honved (Hungary)	H	W3-1	Graham, Harper, S Murray	1
	A	L1-3	S Murray	
		1971-72 UEFA		
Celta Vigo (Spain)	A	W2-0	Harper, o.g.	1
	H	W1-0	Harper	
Juventus (Italy)	A	L0-2		2
	H	D1-1	Harper	
		1972-73 UEFA		
Borussia Moench. (West Germany)	H	L2-3	Harper, Jarvie	1
	A	L3-6	Harper 2, Jarvie	
		1973-74 UEFA		
Finn Harps (Rep of Ireland)	H	W4-1	R Miller, Jarvie 2, Graham	1
	A	W3-1	Robb, Graham, R Miller	
Tottenham H (England)	H	D1-1	Hermiston pen	2
	A	L1-4	Jarvie	
		1977-78 UEFA		
RWD Molenbeek (Belgium)	A	D0-0		1
	H	L1-2	Jarvie	
		1978-79 ECWC		
Marek Stanke (Bulgaria)	A	L2-3	Jarvie, Harper	1
	H	W3-0	Strachan, Jarvie, Harper	
Fortuna Dusseldorf (West Germany)	A	L0-3		2
	H	W2-0	McLelland, Jarvie	
		1979-80 UEFA		
Eintracht Frankfurt (West Germany)	H	D1-1	Harper	1
	A	L0-1		
		1980-81 EC		
Austria Vienna (Austria)	H	W1-0	McGhee	1
	A	D0-0		
Liverpool (England)	H	L0-1		2
	A	L0-4		

Opponents	Venue	Res	Scorers	Rnd
		1981-82 UEFA		
Ipswich Town (England)	A	D1-1	Hewitt	1
Arges Pitesti (Romania)	H	W3-1	Strachan, pen, Weir 2	2
	A	D2-2	Strachan, pen,Hewitt	
SV Hamburg (West Germany)	H	W3-2	Black, Watson, Hewitt	3
	A	L1-3	McGhee	
		1982-83 ECWC		
Sion (Switzerland)	H	W7-0	Black 2, Strachan, Hewitt, Simpson, McGhee, Kennedy	P
	A	W4-1	Hewitt, Miller, McGhee 2	
Dinamo Tirana (Albania)	H	W1-0	Hewitt	1
	A	D0-0		
Lech Poznan (Poland)	H	W2-0	McGhee, Weir	2
	A	W1-0	Bell	
Bayern Munich (West Germany)	A	D0-0		QF
	H	W3-2	Simpson, McLeish, Hewitt	
Waterschei (Belgium)	H	W5-1	Black, Simpson McGhee 2, Weir	SF
	A	L0-1		
Real Madrid (Spain)	N	W2-1	Black, Hewitt	F
		1983-84 (European Super Cup)		
Hamburg (West Germany)	A	D0-0		
	H	W2-0	Simpson, McGhee	
		1983-84 ECWC		
Akranes (Iceland)	A	W2-1	McGhee 2	1
	H	D1-1	Strachan, pen	
Beveren (Belgium)	A	D0-0		2
	H	W4-1	Strachan 2, 1 pen, Simpson, Weir	
Ujpest Dozsa (Hungary)	A	L0-2		QF
	H	W3-0	McGhee 3	
Porto (Portugal)	A	L0-1		SF
	H	L0-1		
		1984-85 EC		
Dynamo Berlin (East Germany)	H	W2-1	Black 2	1
	A	L1-2	Angus	
		1985-86 EC		
Akranes (Iceland)	A	W3-1	Black, Hewitt, Stark	1
	H	W4-1	Simpson, Hewitt Gray, Falconer	
Servette (Switzerland)	A	D0-0		2
	H	W1-0	McDougall	
IFK Gothenburg (Sweden)	H	D2-2	J Miller, Hewitt	QF
	A	D0-0		
		1986-87 ECWC		
Sion (Switzerland)	H	W2-1	Bett (pen), Wright	1
	A	L0-3		
		1987-88 UEFA		
Bohemians (Rep of Ireland)	A	D0-0		1
	H	W1-0	Bett pen	
Feyenoord (Holland)	H	W2-1	Falconer, J Miller	2
	A	L0-1		

Opponents	Venue	Res	Scorers	Rnd
1988-89 UEFA				
Dynamo Dresden	H	D0-0		1
(East Germany)	A	L0-2		
1989-90 UEFA				
Rapid Vienna	H	W2-1	C Robertson, Grant	1
(Austria)	A	L0-1		
1990-91 ECWC				
Salamis	A	W2-0	Mason, Gillhaus	1
(Cyprus)	H	W3-0	C Robertson, Gillhaus, Jess	
Legia Warsaw	H	D0-0		2
(Poland)	A	L0-1		
1991-92 UEFA				
BK Copenhagen	H	L0-1		1
(Denmark)	A	L0-2		
1993-94 ECWC				
Valur	A	W3-0	Shearer, Jess 2	1
(Iceland)	H	W4-0	Jess 2, Miller, Irvine	
Torino	A	L2-3	Paatelainen, Jess	
(Italy)	H	L1-3	Richardson	
1994-95 UEFA				
Skonto Riga	A	D0-0		P
(Latvia)	H	D1-1	Kane	
1996-97 UEFA				
Vilnius	A	W4-1	Dodds 2, Glass, Shearer	Q
(Lithuania)	H	L1-3	Irvine	
Barry Town	H	W3-1	Windass, Glass, Young	1
(Wales)	A	D3-3	Dodds 2, Rowson	
Brondby	H	L0-2		2
(Denmark)	A	D0-0		
2000-01 UEFA				
Bohemians	H	L1-2	Winters	Q
(Rep of Ireland)	A	W1-0	Morrison og	
2002-2003 UEFA				
Nistru Otaci	H	W1-0	Mackie	Q
(Moldova)	A	D0-0		
Hertha Berlin	H	D0-0		1
(Germany)	A	L0-1		
2007-08 UEFA CUP				
Dnipro	H	D0-0		1
(Ukraine)	A	D1-1	Mackie	
GROUP STAGE				
Pana'ikos (Greece)	A	L0-3		
L Moscow (Russia)	H	D1-1	Diamond	
A Madrid (Spain)	A	L0-2		
FC Cop'hagen (Den)	H	W4-0	Smith, Smith, o.g, Foster	
LAST 32				
Bayern Munich	H	D2-2	Walker, Aluko	
(Germany)	A	L1-5	Lovell	
2009-10 UEFA EUROPA LEAGUE				
Sigma Olomouc	H	L1-5	Mulgrew	Play-off
(Czech Rep)	A	L0-3		
2014-15 UEFA EUROPA LEAGUE				
Daugava Riga	H	W5-0	Logan, McGinn, Rooney 2	Q1
			Hayes	
(Latvia)	A	W3-0	Rooney 3	
Groningen	H	D0-0		Q2
(Holland)	A	W2-1	Rooney, McGinn	
Real Sociedad	A	L0-2		Q3
(Spain)	H	L2-3	Pawlett, Reynolds	

Opponents	Venue	Res	Scorers	Rn
		2015-16 UEFA EUROPA LEAGUE		
Shkendija	A	D1-1	McGinn	Q1
(Macedonia)	H	D0-0		
Rijeka	A	W3-0	Considine, Pawlett, McLean	Q2
(Croatia)	H	D2-2	McGinn, Hayes	
Kairat	A	L1-2	McLean	Q3
(Kazakhstan)	H	D1-1	McLean	
		2016-17 UEFA EUROPA LEAGUE		
C S Fola Esch	H	W3-1	Logan, McGinn, Rooney	Q1
(Luxembourg)	A	L0-1		
Ventspils	H	W3-0	Stockley, Rooney, Burns	Q2
(Latvia)	A	L0-1		
Maribor	H	D1-1	Hayes	Q3
(Slovenia)	A	L0-1		
		2017-18 UEFA EUROPA LEAGUE		
Siroki Brijeg	H	D1-1	Christie	Q1
(Bosnia)	A	W2-0	Stewart, Mackay-Steven	
Apollon Limassol	H	W2-1	Christie, Shinnie	Q2
(Cyprus)	A	L0-2		

AIRDRIE

Opponents	Venue	Res	Scorers	Rnd
		1992-93 ECWC		
Sparta Prague	H	L0-1		1
(Czechoslovakia)	A	L1-2	Black	

CELTIC

Opponents	Venue	Res	Scorers	Rnd
		1962-63 FC		
Valencia	A	L2-4	Carrol 2	1
(Spain)	H	D2-2	Crerand, o.g.	
		1963-64 ECWC		
Basle	A	W5-1	Divers, Hughes 3, Lennox	1
(Switzerland)	H	W5-0	Johnstone, Divers 2, Murdoch, Chalmers	
Dynamo Zagreb	H	W3-0	Chalmers 2, Hughes	2
(Yugoslavia)	A	L1-2	Murdoch	
Slovan Bratislava	H	W1-0	Murdoch pen	QF
(Czechoslovakia)	A	W1-0	Hughes	
MTK Budapest	H	W3-0	Johnstone, Chalmers 2	SF
(Hungary)	A	L0-4		
		1964-65 FC		
Leixoes	A	D1-1	Murdoch	1
(Portugal)	H	W3-0	Murdoch, pen, Chalmers	
Barcelona	A	L1-3	Hughes	2
(Spain)	H	D0-0		
		1965-66 ECWC		
Go Ahead	A	W6-0	Gallacher 2, Hughes, Johnstone 2 Lennox	1
(Holland)	H	W1-0	McBride	

Opponents	Venue	Res	Scorers	Rn
Aarhus (Denmark)	A	W1-0	McBride	2
	H	W2-0	McNeill, Johnstone	
Dynamo Kiev (USSR)	H	W3-0	Gemmell, Murdoch 2	QF
	A	D1-1	Gemmell	
Liverpool (England)	H	W1-0	Lennox	SF
	A	L0-2		
1966-67 EC				
Zurich (Switzerland)	H	W2-0	Gemmell, McBride	1
	A	W3-0	Gemmell 2, 1 pen, McBride	
Nantes (France)	A	W3-1	McBride, Lennox, Chalmers	2
	H	W3-1	Johnstone, Lennox, Chalmers	
Vojvodina (Yugoslavia)	A	L0-1		QF
	H	W2-0	Chalmers, McNeill	
Dukla Prague (Czechoslovakia)	H	W3-1	Johnstone, Wallace, 2	SF
	A	D0-0		
Inter Milan (Italy)	N	W2-1	Gemmell, Chalmers	F
1967-68 EC				
Dymano Kiev (USSR)	H	L1-2	Lennox	1
	A	D1-1	Lennox	
1968-69 EC				
St Etienne (France)	A	L0-2		1
	H	W4-0	Gemmell pen, Craig Chalmers, McBride	
Red Star Belgrade (Yugoslavia)	H	W5-1	Murdoch, Johnstone 2, Lennox, Wallace	2
	A	D1-1	Wallace	
AC Milan (Italy)	A	D0-0		QF
	H	L0-1		
1969-70 EC				
Basle (Switzerland)	A	D0-0		1
	H	W2-0	Hood, Gemmell	
Benfica (Portugal)	H	W3-0	Gemmell, Wallace, Hood	2
	A	L0-3		
Fiorentina (Italy)	H	W3-0	Auld, Wallace, o.g.	QF
	A	L0-1		
Leeds United (England)	A	W1-0	Connelly	SF
	H	W2-1	Hughes, Murdoch	
Feyenoord (Holland)	N	L1-2	Gemmell	F
1970-71 EC				
KPV Kokkola (Finland)	H	W9-0	Hood 3, Wilson 2, Hughes McNeill, Johnstone, Davidson	1
	A	W5-0	Wallace 2, Callaghan Davidson, Lennox	
Waterford (Rep of Ireland)	A	W7-0	Wallace 3, Murdoch 2 Macari 2	2
	H	W3-2	Hughes, Johnstone 2	
Ajax (Holland)	A	L0-3		QF
	H	W1-0	Johnstone	
1971-72 EC				
BK 1903 Copenhagen (Denmark)	A	L1-2	Macari	1
	H	W3-0	Wallace 2, Callaghan	

Opponents	Venue	Res	Scorers	Rn
Sliema W (Malta)	H	W5-0	Gemmell, Macari 2 Hood, Brogan	2
	A	W2-1	Hood, Lennox	
Ujpest Dozsa (Hungary)	A	W2-1	Macari, o.g.	QF
	H	D1-1	Macari	
Inter Milan (Italy)	A	D0-0		SF
	H	D0-0	lost on penalties	

1972-73 EC

Rosenborg (Norway)	H	W2-1	Macari, Deans	1
	A	W3-1	Macari, Hood, Dalglish	
Ujpest Dozsa (Hungary)	H	W2-1	Dalglish 2	2
	A	L0-3		

1973-74 EC

Turku (Finland)	A	W6-1	Callaghan 2, Hood, Johnstone, Deans, Connelly, pen	1
	H	W3-0	Deans, Johnstone 2	
Vejle (Denmark)	H	D0-0		2
	A	W1-0	Lennox	
Basle (Switzerland)	A	L2-3	Wilson, Dalglish	QF
	H	W4-2	Dalglish, Deans, Callaghan, Murray	
Atletico Madrid (Spain)	H	D0-0		SF
	A	L0-2		

1974-75 EC

Olympiakos (Greece)	H	D1-1	Wilson	1
	A	L0-2		

1975-76 ECWC

Valur (Iceland)	A	W2-0	Wilson McDonald	1
	H	W7-0	Edvaldsson, Dalglish McCluskey, pen, Deans Hood 2, Callaghan	
Boavista (Portugal)	A	D0-0		2
	H	W3-1	Dalglish, Edvaldsson, Deans	
Zwickau (East Germany)	H	D1-1	Dalglish	QF
	A	L0-1		

1976-77 UEFA

Wisla Krakow (Poland)	H	D2-2	McDonald, Dalglish	1
	A	L0-2		

1977-78 EC

Jeunesse D'Esch (Luxembourg)	H	W5-0	McDonald, Wilson, Craig 2, McLaughlin	1
	A	W6-1	Lennox 2, Glavin, Edvaldsson 2, Craig	
SW Innsbruck (Austria)	H	W2-1	Craig, Burns	2
	A	L0-3		

1979-80 EC

Partizan Tirana (Albania)	A	L0-1		1
	H	W4-1	McDonald, Aitken 2 Davidson	
Dundalk (Rep of Ireland)	H	W3-2	McDonald, Burns McCluskey	2
	A	D0-0		

Opponents	Venue	Res	Scorers	Rn
Real Madrid	H	W2-0	McCluskey, Doyle	QF
(Spain)	A	L0-3		
1980-81 ECWC				
Diosgyor	H	W6-0	McGarvey 2, Sullivan	P
(Hungary)			McCluskey 2, o.g.	
	A	L1-2	Nicholas	
Timisorara	H	W2-1	Nicholas 2	1
(Romania)	A	L0-1	lost on away goals	
1981-82 EC				
Juventus	H	W1-0	MacLeod	1
(Italy)	A	L0-2		
1982-83 EC				
Ajax	H	D2-2	Nicholas, McGarvey	1
(Holland)	A	W2-1	Nicholas, McCluskey	
Real Sociedad	A	L0-2		2
(Spain)	H	W2-1	MacLeod 2	
1983-84 UEFA				
Aarhus	H	1-0	Aitken	1
(Denmark)	A	W4-1	MacLeod, McGarvey,	
			Aitken, Provan	
Sporting Lisbon	A	L0-2		2
(Portugal)	H	W5-0	Burns, McAdam, McClair	
			MacLeod, McGarvey	
Notts Forest	A	D0-0		3
(England)	H	L1-2	MacLeod	
1984-85 ECWC				
Gent	A	L0-1		1
(Belgium)	H	W3-0	McGarvey 2, McStay	
Rapid Vienna	A	L1-3	McClair	2
(Austria)	H	W3-0	McClair, MacLeod, Burns	
(Uefa ordered match to be replayed)				
	N	L0-1		
1985-86 ECWC				
Atletico Madrid	A	D1-1	Johnston	1
(Spain)	H	L1-2	Aitken	
1986-87 EC				
Shamrock Rov	A	W1-0	MacLeod	1
(Rep of Ireland)	H	W2-0	Johnston 2	
Dymano Kiev	H	D1-1	Johnston	2
(USSR)	A	L1-3	McGhee	
1987-88 UEFA				
Bor Dortmund	H	W2-1	Walker, Whyte	1
(West Germany)	A	L0-2		

Opponents	Venue	Res	Scorers	Rn
			1988-89 EC	
Honved	A	L0-1		1
(Hungary)	H	W4-0	Stark, Walker, McAvennie, McGhee	
Werder Bremen	H	L0-2		2
(West Germany)	A	D0-0		
			1989-90 ECWC	
Part Belgrade	A	L1-2	Galloway	1
(Yugoslavia)	H	W5-4	Dziekanowski 4 Walker	
			1991-92 UEFA	
Ekeren	H	W2-0	Nicholas 2, 1 pen	1
(Belgium)	A	D1-1	Galloway	
Neuchatel Xamax	A	L1-5	O'Neill	2
(Switzerland)	H	W1-0	Miller	
			1992-93 UEFA	
Cologne	A	L0-2		1
(Germany)	H	W3-0	McStay, Creaney, Collins	
Bor Dortmund	A	L0-1		2
(Germany)	H	L1-2	Creaney	
			1993-94 UEFA	
Young Boys	A	D0-0		1
(Switzerland)	H	W1-0	og	
Sporting Lisbon	H	W1-0	Creaney	2
(Portugal)	A	L0-2		
			1995-96 ECWC	
Dinamo Batumi	A	W3-2	Thom 2, Donnelly	1
(Georgia)	H	W4-0	Thom 2, Donnelly, Walker	
Paris St Germain	A	L0-1		2
(France)	H	L0-3		
			1996-97 UEFA	
Kosice	A	D0-0		Q
(Poland)	H	W1-0	Cadete	
Hamburg	H	L0-2		1
(Germany)	A	L0-2		
			1997-98 UEFA	
Inter Cable-Tel	A	W3-0	Thom pen, Johnson pen, Wieghorst	Q
(Wales)	H	W5-0	Thom pen, Jackson, Johnson, Hannah, Hay	
Tirol Innsbruck	A	L1-2	Stubbs	Q
(Austria)	H	W6-3	Donnelly 2, 1 pen, Thom Burley 2, Wieghorst	
Liverpool	H	D2-2	McNamara, Donnelly	1
(England)	A	D0-0		
			1998-99 EC	
St Patrick's	H	D0-0		P
(Rep of Ireland)	A	W2-0	Brattbakk, Larsson	
Croatia Zagreb	H	W1-0	Jackson	P
(Croatia)	A	L0-3		

Opponents	Venue	Res	Scorers	Rnd
		UEFA		
Vitoria Guimareas (Portugal)	A	W2-1	Larsson, Donnelly	1
	H	W2-1	Stubbs, Larsson	
FC Zurich (Switzerland)	H	D1-1	Brattbakk	2
	A	L2-4	O'Donnell, Larsson	
		1999-2000 UEFA		
Cwmbran Town (Wales)	A	W6-0	Berkovic, Larsson 2, Tebily, Viduka, Brattbakk	Q
	H	W4-0	Brattbakk, Smith, Mjallby, Johnson	
Hapoel Tel Aviv (Israel)	H	W2-0	Larsson 2	1
	A	W1-0	Larsson	
Lyon (France)	A	L0-1		2
	H	L0-1		
		2000-2001 UEFA		
Jeunesse Esch (Luxembourg)	A	W4-0	Moravcik 2, Larsson, Petta	Q
	H	W7-0	Burchill 3, Berkovic 2, Riseth, Petrov	
HJK Helsinki (Finland)	H	W2-0	Larsson 2	1
	A	L1-2	Sutton	
Bordeaux (France)	A	D1-1	Larsson pen	2
	H	L1-2 (aet)	Moravcik	
		2001-2002 EC		
Ajax (Holland)	A	W3-1	Petta, Agathe, Sutton	Q3
	H	L0-1		
		FIRST GROUP STAGE		
Juventus (Italy)	A	L2-3	Petrov, Larsson	
Porto (Portugal)	H	W1-0	Larsson	
Rosenborg (Norway)	H	W1-0	Thompson	
Porto	A	L0-3		
Rosenborg	A	L0-2		
Juventus	H	W4-3	Valgaeren, Sutton 2, Larsson	
		UEFA		
Valencia (Spain)	A	L0-1		3
	H	W1-0	Larsson	
		(aet, Valencia won 5-4 on penalties)		
		2002-2003 EC		
FC Basel (Switzerland)	H	W3-1	Larsson pen, Sutton, Sylla	Q3
	A	L0-2		
		UEFA		
FK Suduva (Lithuania)	H	W8-1	Larsson 3, Petrov, Sutton, Lambert, Hartson, Valgaeren	1
	A	W2-0	Fernandez, Thompson	
Blackburn (England)	H	W1-0	Larsson	2
	A	W2-0	Larsson, Sutton	
Celta Vigo (Spain)	H	W1-0	Larsson	3
	A	L1-2	Hartson	

Opponents	Venue	Res	Scorers	Rnd
VfB Stuttgart	H	W3-1	Lambert, Maloney, Petrov	4
(Germany)	A	L2-3	Thompson, Sutton	
Liverpool	H	D1-1	Larsson	QF
(England)	A	W2-0	Thompson, Hartson	
Boavista	H	D1-1	Larsson	SF
(Portugal)	A	W1-0	Larsson	
Porto	N	L 2-3 (aet)	Larsson 2	F

2003-2004 EC

FBK Kaunas	A	W4-0	Larsson, Sutton, Maloney, Miller	Q2
(Lithuania)	H	W1-0	Gvildys (og)	
MTK Hungaria	A	W4-0	Larsson, Agathe, Petrov, Sutton	Q3
(Hungary)	H	W1-0	Sutton	

GROUP STAGE

Bayern Munich	A	L1-2	Thompson	
(Germany)	H	D0-0		
Lyon	H	W2-0	Miller, Sutton	
(France)	A	L2-3	Hartson, Sutton	
Anderlecht	A	L0-1		
(Belgium)	H	W3-1	Larsson, Miller, Sutton	

UEFA

Teplice	H	W3-0	Larsson 2, Sutton	3
(Czech Republic)	A	L0-1		
Barcelona	H	W1-0	Thompson	4
(Spain)	H	D0-0		
Villarreal	H	D1-1	Larsson	QF
(Spain)	A	L0-2		

2004-05 EC
GROUP STAGE

Barcelona	H	L1-3	Sutton	
(Spain)	A	D1-1	Hartson	
AC Milan	A	L1-3	Varga	
(Italy)	H	D0-0		
Shakhtar Dontesk	A	L0-3		
(Ukraine)	H	W1-0	Thompson	

2005-2006 EC

Artmedia Bratislava	A	L0-5		Q2
(Slovakia)	H	W4-0	Thompson pen, Hartson, McManus, Beattie	

2006-2007 EC
GROUP STAGE

Manchester Utd	H	W1-0	Nakamura	
(England)	A	L2-3	Vennegoor, Nakamura	
FC Copenhagen	H	W1-0	Miller	
(Denmark)	A	L1-3	Jarosik	
Benfica	H	W3-0	Miller 2, Pearson	
(Portugal)	A	L0-3		

Opponents	Venue	Res	Scorers	Rnd
		LAST 16		
AC Milan	H	D0-0		
(Italy)	A	D0-0		
		(AC Milan win 1-0 after extra-time)		
		2007-08 EC		
Spartak Moscow	A	D1-1	Hartley	Q2
(Russia)	H	D1-1	McDonald	
		GROUP STAGE		
Shakhtar Donetsk	A	L0-2		
(Ukraine)	H	W2-1	Jarosik, Donati	
AC Milan	H	W2-1	McManus, McDonald	
(Italy)	A	L0-1		
Benfica	A	L0-1		
(Portugal)	H	W1-0	McGeady	
		LAST 16		
Barcelona	H	L2-3	Vennegoor, Robson	
(Spain)	A	L0-1		
		2008-09 EC		
		GROUP STAGE		
Aalborg BK	H	D0-0		
(Denmark)	A	L1-2	Robson	
Villarreal	A	L0-1		
(Spain)	H	W2-0	Maloney, McGeady	
Manchester United	A	L0-3		
(England)	H	D1-1	McDonald	
		2009-10 EC		
Dinamo Moscow	H	L0-1		Q3
(Russia)	A	W2-0	McDonald, Samaras	
Arsenal	H	L0-2		Play-off
(England)	A	L1-3	Donati	
		UEFA Europa League		
		GROUP STAGE		
Hapoel Tel-Aviv	A	L1-2	Samaras	
(Israel)	H	W2-0	McDonald, Robson	
Rapid Vienna	H	D1-1	McDonald	
(Austria)	A	D3-3	Fortune 2, McGowan	
Hamburg	H	L0-1		
(Germany)	A	D0-0		
		2010-11 EC		
Braga	A	L0-3		Q3
(Portugal)	H	W2-1	Hooper, Juarez	
		UEFA Europa League		
		Play-off Round		
Utrecht	H	W2-0	Juarez, Samaras	
(Holland)	A	L0-4		

2011-12 UEFA Europa League
Play-off Round

FC Sion	H	D0-0	
(Switzerland)	A	DL1-3	Mulgrew

(Celtic were awarded 3-0 wins in both legs after Sion were found guilty by UEFA of fielding five ineligible players over the two games)

GROUP STAGE

Atletico Madrid	A	L0-2		
(Spain)	H	L0-1		
Udinese	H	D1-1	Ki	
(Italy)	A	D1-1	Hooper	
Rennes	A	D1-1	Ledley	
(France)	H	W3-1	Hooper, Stokes 2	

2012-13 EC

HJK Helsinki	H	W2-1	Hooper, Mulgrew	Q3
(Finland)	A	W2-0	Ledley, Samaras	

Play-off Round

Helsingborg	A	W2-0	Commons, Samaras
(Sweden)	H	W2-0	Hooper, Wanyama

Group Stage

Benfica	H	D0-0	
(Portugal)	A	L1-2	Samaras
Spartak Moscow	A	W3-2	Hooper, Kombarov (og), Samaras
(Russia)	H	W2-1	Hooper, Commons
Barcelona	A	L1-2	Samaras
(Spain)	H	W2-1	Wanyama, Watt

Round of 16

Juventus	H	L0-3	
(Italy)	A	L0-2	

2013-14 EC

Cliftonville	A	W3-0	Lustig, Samaras, Forrest	Q2
(Northern Ireland)	H	W2-0	Ambrose, Samaras	
Elfsborg	H	W1-0	Commons	Q3
(Sweden)	A	D0-0		

Play-off Round

Shakhter Karagandy	A	L0-2	
(Kazakhstan)	H	W3-0	Commons, Samaras, Forrest

Group Stage

Milan	A	L0-2	
(Italy)	H	L0-3	
Barcelona	H	L0-1	
(Spain)	A	L1-6	Samaras
Ajax	H	W2-1	Forrest, Kayal
(Holland)	A	L0-1	

2014-15 EC

KR Reykjavik	A	W1-0	McGregor	Q2
(Iceland)	H	W4-0	van Dijk 2, Pukki 2	
Legia Warsaw	A	L1-4	McGregor	Q3
(Poland)	H	L0-2		

(Celtic given 3-0 win after 2nd leg result annulled by Uefa as Legia fielded a player who should have been serving a suspension. The decision meant Celtic won the tie on the away goals rule.)

Opponents	Venue	Res	Scorers	Rnd
			Play-off Round	
Maribor	A	D1-1	McGregor	
(Slovenia)	H	L0-1		
			UEFA Europa League	
			GROUP STAGE	
Red Bull Salzburg	A	D2-2	Wakaso, Brown	
(Austria)	H	L1-3	Johansen	
Dinamo Zagreb	H	W1-0	Commons	
(Croatia)	A	L3-4	Commons, Scepovic, Pivari, og	
Astra Giugiu	H	W2-1	Scepovic, Johansen	
(Romania)	A	D1-1	Johansen	
			Round of 32	
Inter Milan	H	D3-3	Armstrong, Campagnaro, og, Guidetti	
(Italy)	A	L0-1		
			2015-16 EC	
Stjarnan	H	W2-0	Boyata, Johansen	Q2
(Iceland)	A	W4-1	Biton, Mulgrew, Griffiths, Johansen	
Qarabag	H	W1-0	Boyata	Q3
(Azerbaijan)	A	D0-0		
			Play-off Round	
Malmo	H	W3-2	Griffiths 2, Biton	
(Sweden)	A	L0-2		
			UEFA Europa League	
			GROUP STAGE	
Ajax	A	D2-2	Bitton, Lustig	
(Holland)	H	L1-2	McGregor	
Fenerbahce	H	D2-2	Griffiths, Commons	
(Turkey)	A	D1-1	Commons	
Molde	A	L1-3	Commons	
(Norway)	H	L1-2	Commons	
			2016-17 EC	
Lincoln Red Imps	A	L0-1		Q2
(Gibraltar)	H	W3-0	Lustig, Griffiths, Roberts	
Astana	A	D1-1	Griffiths	Q3
(Kazakhstan)	H	W2-1	Griffiths, Dembele	
Hapoel Be'er Sheva	H	W5-2	Rogic Griffiths 2, Dembele, Brown	PO
(Israel)	A	L0-2		
			GROUP STAGE	
Barcelona	H	L0-7		
(Spain)	A	L0-2		
Manchester City	H	D3-3	Dembele 2, Sterling og	
(England)	A	D1-1	Roberts	
Borussia M'gladbach	H	L0-2		
(Germany)	A	D1-1	Dembele	

Opponents	Venue	Res	Scorers	Rnd
		2017-18 EC		
Linfield	A	W2-0	Haughey OG, Rogic	Q2
(Northern Ireland)	H	W4-0	Sinclair 2, Rogic, Armstrong	
Rosenborg	H	D0-0		Q3
(Norway)	A	W1-0	Forrest	
Astana	H	W5-0	Postnikov OG, Sinclair 2	PO
			Forrest, Shitov OG	
(Kazakhstan)	A	L3-4	Sinclair, Ntcham, Griffiths	
		GROUP STAGE		
PSG	H	L0-5		
(France)	A	L1-7	Dembele	
Bayern Munich	A	L0-3		
(Germany)	A	L1-2	McGregor	
Anderlecht	A	W3-0	Griffiths, Roberts, Sinclair	
(Belgium)	H	L0-1		
		UEFA Europa League		
		Last 32		
Zenit	H	W1-0	McGregor	
(Russia)	A	L0-3		

DUNDEE

Opponents	Venue	Res	Scorers	Rnd
		1962-63 EC		
FC Cologne	H	W8-1	Gilzean 3, Wishart, Smith	P
(West Germany)			Robertson, Penman, og	
	A	L0-4		
Sporting Lisbon	A	L0-1		1
(Portugal)	H	W4-1	Gilzean 3, Cousin	
Anderlecht	A	W4-1	Gilzean 2, Cousin, Smith	QF
(Belgium)	H	W2-1	Cousin, Smith	
AC Milan	A	L1-5	Cousin	SF
(Italy)	H	W1-0	Gilzean	
		1964-65 ECWC		
Bye				1
Real Zaragossa	H	D2-2	Murray, Houston	2
(Spain)	A	L1-2	Robertson	
		1967-68 FC		
DWS Amsterdam	A	L1-2	McLean	1
(Holland)	H	W3-0	Wilson, McLean 2, 1 pen	
FC Liege	H	W3-1	Stuart 2, Wilson	2
(Belgium)	A	W4-1	McLean 4	
		Bye in Round 3		
Zurich	H	W1-0	Easton	QF
(Switzerland)	A	W1-0	Wilson	
Leeds United	H	D1-1	Wilson	SF
(England)	A	L0-2		

Opponents	Venue	Res	Scorers	Rnd
		1971-72 UEFA		
Akademisk	H	W4-2	Bryce 2, Wallace, Lambie	1
(Denmark)	A	W1-0	Duncan	
Cologne	A	L1-2	Kinninmonth	2
(West Germany)	H	W4-2	Duncan 3, Wilson	
AC Milan	A	L0-3		3
(Italy)	H	W2-0	Wallace, Duncan	
		1973-74 UEFA		
Twente Ensch.	H	L1-3	Stewart	1
(Holland)	A	L2-4	Johnston, Scott	
		1974-75 UEFA		
RWD Molenbeek	A	L0-1		1
(Belgium)	H	L2-4	Duncan, Scott	
		2003-04 UEFA		
Vllaznia Shkoder	A	W2-0	Lovell, Novo	Q
(Albania)	H	W4-0	Novo 2, Sara, Rae	
Perugia	H	L1-2	Novo	1
(Italy)	A	L0-1		

DUNDEE UNITED

Opponents	Venue	Res	Scorers	Rnd
		1966-67 FC		
Bye				1
Barcelona	A	W2-1	Hainey, Seeman	2
(Spain)	H	W2-0	Mitchell, Hainey	
Juventus	A	L0-3		3
(Italy)	H	W1-0	Dossing	
		1969-70 FC		
Newcastle Utd	H	L1-2	Scott	1
(England)	A	L0-1		
		1970-71 FC		
Grasshoppers	H	W3-2	Reid I, Markland, Reid A	1
(Switzerland)	A	D0-0		
Sparta Prague	A	L1-3	Traynor	2
(Czechoslovakia)	H	W1-0	Gordon	
		1974-75 ECWC		
Jiul Petrosani	H	W3-0	Narey, Copland, Gardner	1
(Romania)	A	L0-2		
Bursaspor	H	D0-0		2
(Turkey)	A	L0-1		
		1975-76 UEFA		
Keflavik	A	W2-0	Narey 2	1
(Iceland)	H	W4-0	Hall 2, Hegarty, pen, Sturrock	
Porto	H	L1-2	Rennie	2
(Portugal)	A	D1-1	Hegarty	

Opponents	Venue	Res	Scorers	Rnd
		1977-78 UEFA		
KB Copenhagen	H	W1-0	Sturrock	1
(Denmark)	A	L0-3		
		1978-79 UEFA		
Standard Liege	A	L0-1		1
(Belgium)	H	D0-0		
		1979-80 UEFA		
Anderlecht	H	D0-0		1
(Belgium)	A	D1-1	Kopel	
Diosgyor	H	L0-1		2
(Hungary)	A	L1-3	Kopel	
		1980-81 UEFA		
Slask Wroclaw	A	D0-0		1
(Poland)	H	W7-2	Dodds 2, Pettigrew 3, Stark, Payne pen	
Lokeren	H	D1-1	Pettigrew	
(Belgium)	A	D0-0		
		1981-82 UEFA		
Monaco	A	W5-2	Bannon 2, 1 pen, Dodds 2, Kirkwood	1
(France)	H	L1-2	Milne	
Borussia M.	A	L0-2		2
(West Germany)	H	W5-0	Milne, Kirkwood, Hegarty, Sturrock, Bannon	
Winterslag	A	D0-0		3
(Belgium)	H	W5-0	Bannon, Narey, Hegarty Milne 2	
Radnicki Nis	H	W2-0	Narey, Dodds	QF
(Yugoslavia)	A	L0-3		
		1982-83 UEFA		
PSV Eindhoven	H	D1-1	Dodds	1
(Holland)	A	W2-0	Kirkwood, Hegarty	
Viking Stavanger	A	W3-1	Milne 2, Sturrock	2
(Norway)	H	D0-0		
Werder Bremen	H	W2-1	Milne, Narey	3
(West Germany)	A	D1-1	Hegarty	
Bohemians	A	L0-1		QF
(Czechoslovakia)	H	D0-0		
		1983-84 EC		
Hamrun Spartans	A	W3-0	Reilly, Bannon, Stark	1
(Malta)	H	W3-0	Milne, Kirkwood 2	
Standard Liege	A	D0-0		2
(Belgium)	H	W4-0	Milne 2, Hegarty, Dodds	
Rapid Vienna	A	L1-2	Stark	QF
(Austria)	H	W1-0	Dodds	
AS Roma	H	W2-0	Dodds, Stark	SF
(Italy)	A	L0-3		
		1984-85 UEFA		
AIK Stockholm	A	L0-1		1
(Sweden)	H	W3-0	Sturrock, Milne 2	

Opponents	Venue	Res	Scorers	Rnd
ASK Linz	A	W2-1	Kirkwood, Bannon pen	2
(Austria)	H	W5-1	Hegarty, Coyne 2,	
			Gough Beaumont	
Manchester Utd	A	D2-2	Hegarty, Sturrock	3
(England)	H	L2-3	Dodds, Hegarty	
1985-86 UEFA				
Bohemians	A	W5-2	Sturrock 3, Bannon 2	1
(Rep of Ireland)	H	D2-2	Milne, Redford	
Vardar Skopje	H	W2-0	Redford, Gough	2
(Yugoslavia)	A	D1-1	Hegarty	
Neuchatel Xamax	H	W2-1	Dodds, Redford	3
(Switzerland)	A	L1-3	Redford	
1986-87 UEFA				
Lens	A	L0-1		1
(France)	H	W2-0	Milne, Coyne	
Uni. Craiova	H	W3-0	Redford 2, Clark	2
(Romania)	A	L0-1		
Hadjuk Split	H	W2-0	McInally, Clark	3
(Yugoslavia)	A	D0-0		
Barcelona	H	W1-0	Gallacher	QF
(Spain)	A	W2-1	Clark, Ferguson	
Borussia Moench.	H	D0-0		SF
(West Germany)	A	W2-0	Ferguson, Redford	
IFK Gothenburg	A	L0-1		F
(Sweden)	H	D1-1	Clark	
1987-88 UEFA				
Coleraine	A	W1-0	Sturrock	1
(Northern Ireland)	H	W3-1	Gallacher, Sturrock, Clark	
Vitkovice	H	L1-2	Ferguson	2
(Czechoslovakia)	A	D1-1	og	
1988-89 ECWC				
Floriana	A	D0-0		1
(Malta)	H	W1-0	Meade	
Din. Bucharest	H	L0-1		2
(Romania)	A	D1-1	Beaumont	
1989-90 UEFA				
Glentoran	A	W3-1	Cleland, McInally, Hinds	1
(Northern Ireland)	H	W2-0	Clark, Gallacher	
Antwerp	A	L0-4		2
(Belgium)	H	W3-2	Paatelainen, O'Neill, Clark	
1990-91 UEFA				
FH Hafnafjordur	A	W3-1	Jackson, Cleland, og	1
(Iceland)	H	D2-2	Connolly, og	
Arnhem	A	L0-1		2
(Holland)	H	L0-4		
1993-94 UEFA				
Brondby	A	L0-2		1
(Denmark)	H	W3-1	McKinlay, Crabbe, Clark	

Opponents	Venue	Res	Scorers	Rnd
		1994-95 ECWC		
Tatran Presov	H	W3-2	Petric, Nixon, Hannah	1
(Slovakia)	A	L1-3	Nixon	
		1997-98 UEFA		
C E Principat	A	W8-0	Zetterlund, Winters 4,	Q
(Andorra)			McSwegan 3	
	H	W9-0	Olofsson, Zetterlund,	
			Winters 2, McLaren,	
			McSwegan 3, Thompson	
Trabzonspor	A	L0-1		Q
(Turkey)	H	D1-1	McLaren	
		2005-06 UEFA		
MyPa 47	A	D0-0		Q2
(Finland)	H	D2-2	Kerr, Samuel	
		2010-11 UEFA Europa League		
		Play-off Round		
AEK Athens	H	L0-1		
(Greece)	N	D1-1	Daly	
(Matched moved to Panionios due to pitch problems)				
		2011-12 UEFA Europa League		
Slask Wroclaw	A	L0-1		Q2
(Poland)	H	W3-2	Watson, Goodwillie, Daly	
(Slask Wroclaw through on away goals)				
		2012-13 UEFA Europa League		
Dynamo Moscow	H	D2-2	Flood, Watson	Q3
(Russia)	A	L0-5		

DUNFERMLINE

Opponents	Venue	Res	Scorers	Rnd
		1961-62 ECWC		
St Patrick's Ath	H	W4-1	Melrose, Peebles,	1
(Rep of Ireland)			Dickson, Macdonald	
	A	W4-0	Peebles 2, Dickson 2	
Vardar Skopje	H	W5-0	Smith, Dickson 2,	2
(Yugoslavia)			Melrose, Peebles	
	A	L0-2		
Ujpest Dozsa	A	L3-4	Smith, Macdonald 2	QF
(Hungary)	H	L0-1		
		1962-63 FC		
Everton	A	L0-1		1
(England)	H	W2-0	Miller, Melrose	
Valencia	A	L0-4		2
(Spain)	H	W6-2	Melrose, Sinclair 2	
			McLean, Peebles, Smith	
	N	L0-1		
		1964-65 FC		
Oergryte	H	W4-2	McLaughlin 2, Sinclair 2	1
(Sweden)	A	D0-0		
Stuttgart	H	W1-0	Callaghan	2
(West Germany)	A	D0-0		

Opponents	Venue	Res	Scorers	Rnd
Athletico Bilbao	A	L0-1		3
(Spain)	H	W1-0	Smith	
	A	L1-2	Smith	

1965-66 FC

Bye				1
KB Copenhagen	H	W5-0	Fleming, Paton 2,	2
(Denmark)			Robertson, Callaghan	
	A	W4-2	Edwards, Paton, Fleming,	
			Ferguson	
Spartak Brno	H	W2-0	Paton, Ferguson, pen	3
(Czechoslovakia)	A	D0-0		
Real Zaragossa	H	W1-0	Paton	QF
(Spain)	A	L2-4	Ferguson 2	

1966-67 FC

Frigg Oslo	A	W3-1	Fleming 2, Callaghan	1
(Norway)	H	W3-1	Delaney 2 Callaghan	
Dynamo Zagreb	H	W4-2	Delaney, Edwards,	2
(Yugoslavia)			Ferguson 2	
	A	L0-2		

1968-69 ECWC

Apoel	H	W10-1	Robertson 2, Renton 2,	1
(Cyprus)			Barry, Callaghan W 2, Gardner	
			Edwards, Callaghan T	
	A	W2-0	Gardner, Callaghan W	
Olymp. Piraeus	H	W4-0	Edwards 2, Fraser,	2
(Greece)			Mitchell	
	A	L0-3		
West Bromwich	H	D0-0		QF
(England)	A	W1-0	Gardner	
Slovan Bratislava	H	D1-1	Fraser	SF
(Czechoslovakia)	A	L0-1		

1969-70 FC

Bordeaux	H	W4-0	Paton 2, Mitchell, Gardner	1
(France)	A	L0-2		
Gwardia Warsaw	H	W2-1	McLean, Gardner	2
(Poland)	A	W1-0	Renton	
Anderlecht	A	L0-1		3
(Belgium)	H	W3-2	McLean 2, Mitchell	
FH Hafnarfjordur	A	D2-2	Brewster, Skerla	Q2
(Iceland)	H	L1-2	Dempsey	

2004-05 UEFA

2007-08 UEFA

BK Hacken	H	D1-1	Hamilton	Q2
BK Hacken	A	L0-1		

FALKIRK

Opponents	Venue	Res	Scorers	Rnd

2009-10 UEFA Europa League

Vaduz	H	W1-0	Flynn	Q2
(Liechtenstein)	A	L0-2		

GRETNA

Opponents	Venue	Res	Scorers	Rnd
		2006-07 UEFA		
Derry City	H	L1-5	McGuffie	Q
(Ireland)	A	D2-2	Graham, Baldacchino	

HEARTS

Opponents	Venue	Res	Scorers	Rnd
		1958-59 EC		
Standard Liege	A	L1-5	Crawford	P
(Belgium)	H	W2-1	Bauld	
		1960-61 EC		
Benfica	H	L1-2	Young	P
(Portugal)	A	L0-3		
		1961-62 FC		
Union St Gilloise	A	W3-1	Blackwood, Davidson 2	1
(Belgium)	H	W2-0	Wallace, Stenhouse	
Inter Milan	H	L0-1		2
(Italy)	A	L0-4		
		1963-64 FC		
Lausanne	A	D2-2	Traynor, Ferguson	1
(Switzerland)	H	D2-2	Cumming, Hamilton J	
	A	L2-3	Wallace, Ferguson	
		1965-66 FC		
Bye				1
Valerengen	H	W1-0	Wallace	2
(Norway)	A	W3-1	Kerrigan 2, Traynor	
Real Zaragossa	H	D3-3	Anderson, Wallace, Kerrigan	3
(Spain)	A	D2-2	Anderson, Wallace	
	A	L0-1		
		1976-77 ECWC		
Lokomotiv Leipzig	A	L0-2		1
(East Germany)	H	W5-1	Kay, Gibson 2, Brown, Busby	
SV Hamburg	A	L2-4	Park, Busby	2
(West Germany)	H	L1-4	Gibson	
		1984-85 UEFA		
Paris St Germain	A	L0-4		1
(France)	H	D2-2	Robertson 2	
		1986-87 UEFA		
Dukla Prague	H	W3-2	Foster, Clark, Robertson	1
(Czechoslovakia)	A	L0-1		
		1988-89 UEFA		
St Patrick's Ath	A	W2-0	Foster pen, Galloway	1
(Rep of Ireland)	H	W2-0	Black, Galloway	
FK Austria	H	D0-0		2
(Austria)	A	W1-0	Galloway	

Opponents	Venue	Res	Scorers	Rnd
Velez Mostar (Yugoslavia)	H	W3-0	Bannon, Galloway, Colquhoun	3
	A	L1-2	Galloway	
Bayern Munich (West Germany)	H	W1-0	Ferguson	QF
	A	L0-2		
1990-91 UEFA				
Dnepr (USSR)	A	D1-1	Robertson	1
	H	W3-1	McPherson, Robertson 2	
Bologna (Italy)	H	W3-1	Foster 2, Ferguson	2
	A	L0-3		
1992-93 UEFA				
Slavia Prague (Czech Rep)	A	L0-1		1
	H	W4-2	Mackay, Baird, Levein, Snodin	
Standard Liege (Belgium)	H	L0-1		2
	A	L0-1		
1993-94 UEFA				
Atletico Madrid (Spain)	H	W2-1	Robertson, Colquhoun	1
	A	L0-3		
1996-97 ECWC				
Red Star Belgrade (Yugoslavia)	A	D0-0		1
	H	D1-1	McPherson	
1998-99 ECWC				
Lantana (Estonia)	A	W1-0	Makel	Q
	H	W5-0	Hamilton, Fulton, McCann, Flogel, Holmes	
Real Mallorca (Spain)	H	L0-1		1
	A	D1-1	Hamilton	
2000-2001 UEFA				
IBV (Iceland)	A	W2-0	Severin, Jackson	Q
	H	W3-0	McSwegan, Tomaschek, O'Neil	
Stuttgart (Germany)	A	L0-1		1
	H	W3-2	Pressley, Petric, Cameron pen	
2003-2004 UEFA				
Zeljeznicar (Bosnia)	H	W2-0	de Vries, Webster	1
	A	D0-0		
Bordeaux (France)	A	W1-0	de Vries	2
	H	L0-2		
2004-05 UEFA				
Sporting Braga (Portugal)	H	W3-1	Webster, Hartley, Kisnorbo	1
	A	D2-2	de Vries 2	

Opponents	Venue	Res	Scorers	Rnd
		GROUP STAGE		
Feyenoord (Hol)	A	L0-3		
Shalke (Ger)	H	L0-1		
FC Basel (Swi)	A	W2-1	Wyness, Neilson	
Ferencvaros (Hun)	A	L0-1		
		2006-07 EC		
NK Siroki Brijeg	H	W3-0	o.g, Tall, Bednar	Q
(Bosnia)	A	D0-0		
AEK Athens	H	L1-2	Mikoliunas	Q
(Greece)	A	L0-3		
		UEFA		
Sparta Prague	H	L0-2		1
(Czech Rep)	A	D0-0		
		2009-10 UEFA Europa League		
Dinamo Zagreb	A	L0-4		Play-off
(Croatia)	H	W2-0	Stewart, Zaliukas	
		2011-12 UEFA Europa League		
Paksi	A	D1-1	Hamill	Q3
(Hungary)	H	W4-1	Stevenson 2, Driver, Skacel	
		Play-off Round		
Tottenham	H	L0-5		
(England)	A	D0-0		
		2012-13 UEFA Europa League		
Liverpool	H	L0-1		Play-off
(England)	A	D1-1	Templeton	
		2016-17 UEFA Europa League		
FC Infonet	H	W2-1	Bauben, Kalimullin OG	Q1
(Estonia)	A	W4-2	Paterson, Rossi Branco 2 Ozturk	
Birkirkara	A	D0-0		Q2
(Malta)	H	L1-2	Sammon	

HIBERNIAN

Opponents	Venue	Res	Scorers	Rnd
		1955-56 EC		
Rot-Weiss Essen	A	W4-0	Turnbull 2, Reilly, Ormond	1
(West Germany)	H	D1-1	Buchanan J	
Djurgaarden	H	W3-1	Combe, Mulkerrin, og	QF
(Sweden)	A	W1-0	Turnbull pen	
Reims	A	L0-2		SF
(France)	H	L0-1		
		1960-61 FC		
Barcelona	A	D4-4	McLeod, Preston Baker 2	QF
(Spain)	H	W3-2	Baker, Preston, Kinloch	
AS Roma	H	D2-2	Baker, McLeod	SF
(Italy)	A	D3-3	Baker 2, Kinloch	
	A	L0-6		
		1961-62 FC		
Belenenses	H	D3-3	Fraser 2, Baird pen	1
(Portugal)	A	W3-1	Baxter 2, Stevenson	
Red Star Belgrade	A	L0-4		2
(Yugoslavia)	H	L0-1		
		1962-63 FC		
Stavenet	H	W4-0	Byrne 2, Baker, og	1
(Denmark)	A	W3-2	Stevenson 2, Byrne	

Opponents	Venue	Res	Scorers	Rnd
DOS Utrecht	A	W1-0	Falconer	2
(Holland)	H	W2-1	Baker, Stevenson	
Valencia	A	L0-5		QF
(Spain)	H	W2-1	Preston, Baker	
1965-66 FC				
Valencia	H	W2-0	Scott, McNamee	1
(Spain)	A	L0-2		
	A	L0-3		
1967-68 FC				
Porto	H	W3-0	Cormack 2, Stevenson	1
(Portugal)	A	L1-3	Stanton pen	
Napoli	A	L1-4	Stein	2
(Italy)	H	W5-0	Duncan, Quinn, Cormack	
			Stanton, Stein	
Leeds United	A	L0-1		3
(England)	H	D1-1	Stein	
1968-69 FC				
Ljubljana	A	W3-0	Stevenson, Stein, Marinello	1
(Yugoslavia)	H	W2-1	Davis 2	
Lokomotiv Leipzig	H	W3-1	McBride 3	2
(East Germany)	A	W1-0	Grant	
SV Hamburg	A	L0-1		3
(West Germany)	H	W2-1	McBride 2	
1970-71 FC				
Malmo FF	H	W6-0	McBride 3 Duncan 2, Blair	1
(Sweden)	A	W3-2	Duncan, McEwan, Stanton	
Vitoria Giumaraes	H	W2-0	Duncan, Stanton	2
(Portugal)	A	L1-2	Graham	
Liverpool	H	L0-1		3
(England)	A	L0-2		
1972-73 ECWC				
Sporting Lisbon	A	L1-2	Duncan	1
(Portugal)	H	W6-1	Gordon 2, O'Rourke 3, og	
Besa	H	W7-1	Cropley, O'Rourke 3,	2
(Albania)			Duncan 2, Brownlie	
	A	D1-1	Gordon	
Hadjuk Split	H	W4-2	Gordon 3, Duncan	QF
(Yugoslavia)	A	L0-3		
1973-74 UEFA				
Keflavik	H	W2-0	Black, Higgins	1
(Iceland)	A	D1-1	Stanton	
Leeds United	A	D0-0		2
(England)	H	D0-0		
1974-75 UEFA				
Rosenborg	A	W3-2	Stanton, Gordon, Cropley	1
(Norway)	H	W9-1	Harper 2, Munro 2, Stanton 2,	
			Cropley 2 pens, Gordon	
Juventus	H	L2-4	Stanton, Cropley	2
(Italy)	A	L0-4		

Opponents	Venue	Res	Scorers	Rnd
		1975-76 UEFA		
Liverpool	H	W1-0	Harper	1
(England)	A	L1-3	Edwards	
		1976-77 UEFA		
Sochaux	H	W1-0	Brownlie	1
(France)	A	D0-0		
Osters Vaxjo	H	W2-0	Blackley, Brownlie pen	2
(Sweden)	A	L1-4	Smith	
		1978-79 UEFA		
Norrkoping	H	W3-2	Higgins 2, Temperley	1
(Sweden)	A	D0-0		
Strasbourg	A	L0-2		2
(France)	H	W1-0	McLeod pen	
		1989-90 UEFA		
Videoton	H	W1-0	Mitchell	1
(Hungary)	A	W3-0	Houchen, Evans, Collins	
FC Liege	H	D0-0		
(Belgium)	A	L0-1		
		1992-93 UEFA		
Anderlecht	H	D2-2	Beaumont, McGinlay	1
(Belgium)	A	D1-1	Jackson	
		2001-02 UEFA		
AEK Athens	A	L0-2		1
(Greece)	H	W3-2 (aet)	Luna 2, Zitelli	
		2005-06 UEFA		
Dnipro	H	D0-0		1
(Ukraine)	A	L1-5	Riordan	
		2010-11 UEFA Europa League		
Maribor	A	L0-3		3
(Slovenia)	H	L2-3	De Graaf 2	
		2013-14 UEFA Europa League		
Malmo	A	L0-2		Q2
(Sweden)	H	L0-7		
		2016-17 UEFA Europa League		
Brondby IF	H	L0-1		Q2
(Denmark)	A	W1-0	Gray (Lost 5-3 on pens after aet)	

INVERNESS CT

Opponents	Venue	Res	Scorers	Rnd
		2015-16 UEFA Europa League		
Astra Giurgiu	H	L0-1		Q1
(Romania)	A	D0-0		

KILMARNOCK

Opponents	Venue	Res	Scorers	Rnd
		1964-65 FC		
Eintracht Frankfurt	A	L0-3		1
(West Germany)	H	W5-1	Hamilton, McIlroy, Sneddon McFadzean, McInally	
Everton	H	L0-2		2
(England)	A	L1-4	McIlroy	
		1965-66 EC		
Nendori Tirana	A	D0-0		P
(Albania)	H	W1-0	Black	
Real Madrid	H	D2-2	McLean pen, McInally	1
(Spain)	A	L1-5	McIlroy	

Opponents	Venue	Res	Scorers	Rnd
		1966-67 FC		
Bye				1
Antwerp	A	W1-0	McInally	2
(Belgium)	H	W7-2	McInally 2, Queen 2	
			McLean 2, Watson	
La Gantoise	H	W1-0	Murray	3
(Belgium)	A	W2-1	McInally, McLean	
Lokomotiv Leipzig	A	L0-1		QF
(East Gemany)	H	W2-0	McFadzean, McIlroy	
Leeds United	A	L2-4	McIlroy 2	SF
(England)	H	D0-0		
		1969-70 FC		
Zurich	A	L2-3	McLean J, Mathie	1
(Switzerland)	H	W3-1	McGrory, Morrison, McLean T	
Slavia Sofia	H	W4-1	Mathie 2, Cook, Gilmour	2
(Bulgaria)	A	L0-2		
Dynamo Bacau	H	D1-1	Mathie	3
(Romania)	A	L0-2		
		1970-71 FC		
Coleraine	A	D1-1	Mathie	1
(Northern Ireland)	H	L2-3	McLean T, Morrison	
		1997-98 ECWC		
Shelbourne	H	W2-1	Wright 2	Q
(Rep of Ireland)	A	D1-1	McIntyre	
Nice	A	L1-3	Wright	1
(France)	H	D1-1	Reilly	
		1998-99 UEFA		
Zeljeznicar	A	D1-1	McGowne	P
(Bosnia)	H	W1-0	Mahood	
Sigma Olomouc	A	L0-2		P
(Czech Rep)	H	L0-2		
		1999-2000 UEFA		
KR Reyjkavic	A	L0-1		Q
(Iceland)	H	W2-0	Wright, Bagan	
Kaislerlautern	A	L0-3		1
(Germany)	H	L0-2		
		2001-2002 UEFA		
Glenavon	A	W1-0	Innes	Q
(Northern Ireland)	H	W1-0	Mitchell	
Viking Stavanger	H	D1-1	Dargo	1
(Norway)	A	L0-2		

LIVINGSTON

Opponents	Venue	Res	Scorers	Rnd
		2002-2003 UEFA		
Vaduz	A	D1-1	Rubio	Q
(Liechtenstein)	H	D0-0		
Sturm Graz	A	L2-5	Zarate, Lovell	1
(Austria)	H	W4-3	Wilson 2 (1 pen), Xausa,	
			Andrews	

MORTON

Opponents	Venue	Res	Scorers	Rnd
		1968-69 FC		
Chelsea	A	L0-5		1
(England)	H	L3-4	Thorop, Mason, Taylor	

MOTHERWELL

Opponents	Venue	Res	Scorers	Rnd
		1991-92 FC		
Katowice	A	L0-2		1
(Poland)	H	W3-1	Kirk 2, Cusack	
		1994-95 UEFA		
Hanvar	H	W3-0	Coyne, McGrillen, Kirk	P
(Faroe Islands)	A	W4-1	Kirk 2, Davies, Burns	
Bor Dortmund	A	L0-1		1
(Germany)	H	L0-2		
		1995-96 UEFA		
My-Pa 47	H	L1-3	McSkimming	P
(Finland)	A	W2-0	Burns, Arnott	
		2008-09 UEFA		
AS Nancy	A	L0-1		1
(France)	H	L0-2		
		2009-10 UEFA Europa League		
Llanelli	H	L0-1		Q1
(Wales)	A	W3-0	Sutton 2, Murphy	
Flamurtari Vlorë	A	L0-1		Q2
(Albania)	H	W8-1	Murphy 3, Slane, Forbes 2, Hutchinson, McHugh	
Steaua Bucharest	A	L0-3		Q3
(Romania)	H	L1-3	Forbes	
		2010-11 UEFA Europa League		
Breidablik	H	W1-0	Forbes	2
(Iceland)	A	W1-0	Murphy	
Aalesunds	A	D1-1	Murphy	3
(Norway)	H	W3-0	Murphy, Sutton, Page	
Odense	A	L1-2	Hateley	Play-off
(Denmark)	H	L0-1		
		2012-13 EC		
Panathinaikos	H	L0-2		3
(Greece)	A	L0-3		
		2012-13 UEFA Europa League		
Levante	H	L0-2		Play-off
(Spain)	A	L0-1		
		2013-14 UEFA Europa League		
Kuban Krasnodar	H	L0-2		Q3
(Russia)	A	L0-1		
		2014-15 UEFA Europa League		
Stjarnan	H	D2-2	Law 2	Q1
(Iceland)	A	L2-3	Hammell, Ainsworth	

PARTICK THISTLE

Opponents	Venue	Res	Scorers	Rnd
		1963-64 FC		
Glentoran	A	W4-1	Hainey, Yard 2, Wright	1
(Northern Ireland)	H	W3-0	Smith 2, Harvey, pen.	
Spartak Brno	H	W3-2	Yard, Harvey, pen,	2
(Czechoslovakia)			Ferguson	
	A	L0-4		
		1972-73 UEFA CUP		
Honved	A	L0-1		1
(Hungary)	H	L0-3		

QUEEN OF THE SOUTH

Opponents	Venue	Res	Scorers	Rnd
		2008-09 UEFA		
FC Nordsjaelland	H	L1-2	O'Connor	Q
(Denmark)	A	L1-2	Harris	

RAITH ROVERS

Opponents	Venue	Res	Scorers	Rnd
		1995-96 UEFA		
Gotu	H	W4-0	Dair, Rougier, Cameron	P
(Faroe Islands)			McAnespie	
	A	D2-2	Lennon, Crawford	
Akranes	H	W3-1	Lennon 2, Wilson	1
(Iceland)	A	L0-1		
Bayern Munich)	H	L0-2		2
(Germany)	A	L1-2	Lennon	

RANGERS

Opponents	Venue	Res	Scorers	Rnd
Bye				P
		1956-57 EC		
Nice	H	W2-1	Murray, Simpson	1
(France)	A	L1-2	Hubbard pen	
	N	L1-3	og	
		1957-58 EC		
St Etienne	H	W3-1	Kichenbrand, Scott,	P
(France)			Simpson	
	A	L1-2	Wilson	
AC Milan	H	L1-4	Murray	1
(Italy)	A	L0-2		
		1959-60 EC		
Anderlecht	H	W5-2	Millar, Scott, Matthew,	P
(Belgium)			Baird 2	
	A	W2-0	Matthew, McMillan	

Opponents	Venue	Res	Scorers	Rnd
Red Star	H	W4-3	McMillan, Scott, Wilson	1
Bratislava			Millar	
(Czechoslovakia)	A	D1-1	Scott	
Sparta Rotterdam	A	W3-2	Wilson, Baird, Murray	QF
(Holland)	H	L0-1		
	N	W3-2	Baird 2, og	
Eintracht Frankfurt	A	L1-6	Caldow pen	SF
(West Germany)	H	L3-6	McMillan 2, Wilson	
		1960-61 ECWC		
Ferencvaros	H	W4-2	Davis, Millar 2, Brand	P
(Hungary)	A	L1-2	Wilson	
Borussia Moench	A	W3-0	Millar, Scott, McMillan	QF
(West Germany)	H	W8-0	Baxter, Brand 3, Millar 2	
			Davis, og	
Wolves	H	W2-0	Scott, Brand	SF
(England)	A	D1-1	Scott	
Fiorentina	H	L0-2		F
(Italy)	A	L1-2	Scott	
		1961-62 EC		
Monaco	A	W3-2	Baxter, Scott 2	P
(France)	H	W3-2	Christie 2, Scott	
Vorwaerts	A	W2-1	Caldow pen, Brand	1
(East Germany)	H	W4-1	McMillan 2 Henderson, og	
Standard Liege	A	L1-4	Wilson	
(Belgium)	H	W2-0	Brand, Caldow	
		1962-63 ECWC		
Seville	H	W4-0	Millar 3, Brand	1
(Spain)	A	L0-2		
Tottenham	A	L2-5	Brand, Millar	2
(England)	H	L2-3	Brand, Wilson	
		1963-64 EC		
Real Madrid	H	L0-1		P
(Spain)	A	L0-6		
		1964-65 EC		
Red Star Belgrade	H	W3-1	Brand 2, Forrest	P
(Yugoslavia)	A	L2-4	Greig, McKinnon	
	N	W3-1	Forrest 2, Brand	
Rapid Vienna	H	W1-0	Wilson	1
(Austria)	A	W2-0	Forrest, Wilson	
Inter Milan	A	L1-3	Forrest	QF
(Italy)	H	W1-0	Forrest	
		1966-67 ECWC		
Glentoran	A	D1-1	McLean	1
(Northern Ireland)	H	W4-0	Johnston, Smith D,	
			Setterington, McLean	

Opponents	Venue	Res	Scorers	Rnd
Bor Dortmund	H	W2-1	Johansen, Smith A	2
(West Germany)	A	D0-0		
Real Zaragoza	H	W2-0	Smith, Willoughby	QF
(Spain)	A	L0-2		
Slavia Sofia	A	W1-0	Wilson	SF
(Bulgaria)	H	W1-0	Henderson	
Bayern Munich	N	L0-1		F
(West Germany)				

1967-68 FC

Opponents	Venue	Res	Scorers	Rnd
Dynamo Dresden	A	D1-1	Ferguson	1
(East Germany)	H	W2-1	Penman, Greig	
FC Cologne	H	W3-0	Ferguson 2, Henderson	2
(West Germany)	A	L1-3	Henderson	
Bye				3
Leeds United	H	D0-0		QF
(England)	A	L0-2		

1968-69 FC

Opponents	Venue	Res	Scorers	Rnd
Vojvodina	H	W2-0	Greig pen, Jardine	1
(Yugoslavia)	A	L0-1		
Dundalk	H	W6-1	Henderson 2, Greig	2
(Rep of Ireland)			Ferguson 2, og	
	A	W3-0	Mathieson, Stein 2	
DWS Amsterdam	A	W2-0	Johnstone, Henderson	3
(Holland)	H	W2-1	Smith, Stein	
Athletic Bilbao	H	W4-1	Ferguson, Penman,	QF
(Spain)			Persson, Stein	
Newcastle Utd	H	D0-0		SF
(England)	A	L0-2		

1969-70 ECWC

Opponents	Venue	Res	Scorers	Rnd
Steaua Bucharest	H	W2-0	Johnston 2	1
(Romania)	A	D0-0		
Gornik Zabrze	A	L1-3	Persson	2
(Poland)	H	L1-3	Baxter	

1970-71 FC

Opponents	Venue	Res	Scorers	Rnd
Bayern Munich	A	L0-1		1
(West Germany)	H	D1-1	Stein	

1971-72 ECWC

Opponents	Venue	Res	Scorers	Rnd
Rennes	A	D1-1	Johnston	1
(France)	H	W1-0	MacDonald	
Sporting Lisbon	H	W3-2	Stein 2, Henderson	2
(Portugal)	A	L3-4	Stein 2, Henderson	
Torino	A	D1-1	Johnston	QF
(Italy)	H	W1-0	MacDonald	
Bayern Munich	A	D1-1	og	SF
(West Germany)	H	W2-0	Jardine, Parlane	
Dynamo Moscow	N	W3-2	Johnston 2, Stein	F
(USSR)				

Opponents	Venue	Res	Scorers	Rnd
		1972-73 European Super Cup		
Ajax	H	L1-3	MacDonald	
(Holland)	A	L2-3	MacDonald, Young	
		1973-74 ECWC		
Ankaragucu	A	W2-0	Conn, McLean	1
(Turkey)	H	W4-0	Greig 2, O'Hara, Johnstone	
Borussia Moench.	A	L0-3		2
(West Germany)	H	W3-2	Conn, Jackson, MacDonald	
		1975-76 EC		
Bohemians	H	W4-1	Fyfe, Johnstone, O'Hara	1
(Rep of Ireland)			og	
	A	D1-1	Johnstone	
St Etienne	A	L0-2		2
(France)	H	L1-2	MacDonald	
		1976-77 EC		
Zurich	H	D1-1	Parlane	1
(Switzerland)	A	L0-1		
		1977-78 ECWC		
Young Boys	H	W1-0	Greig	P
(Switzerland)	A	D2-2	Johnstone, Smith	
Twente Enschede	H	D0-0		1
(Holland)	A	L0-3		
		1978-79 EC		
Juventus	A	L0-1		1
(Italy)	H	W2-0	MacDonald, Smith	
PSV Eindhoven	H	D0-0		2
(Holland)	A	W3-2	MacDonald, Johnstone	
			Russell	
FC Cologne	A	L0-1		QF
(West Germany)	H	D1-1	McLean	
		1979-80 ECWC		
Lillestrom	H	W1-0	Smith	P
(Norway)	A	W2-0	MacDonald A, Johnstone	
Fortuna Dusseldorf	H	W2-1	MacDonald A, McLean	1
(West Germany)	A	D0-0		
Valencia	A	D1-1	McLean	2
(Spain)	H	L1-3	Johnstone	
		1981-82 ECWC		
Dukla Prague	A	L0-3		1
(Czechoslovakia)	H	W2-1	Bett, MacDonald J	
		1982-83 UEFA		
Borussia Dortmund	A	D0-0		1
(West Germany)	H	W2-0	Cooper, Johnstone	
FC Cologne	H	W2-1	Johnstone, McClelland	2
(West Germany)	A	L0-5		

Opponents	Venue	Res	Scorers	Rnd
		1983-84 ECWC		
Valetta (Malta)	A	W8-0	Paterson, McPherson 4 MacDonald, Prytz 2	1
	H	W10-0	Mitchell 2, MacDonald 3 Dawson, MacKay, Davis 2, Redford	
Porto (Portugal)	H	W2-1	Clark, Mitchell	2
	A	L0-1		
		1984-85 UEFA		
Bohemians (Rep of Ireland)	A	L2-3	McCoist, McPherson	1
	H	W2-0	Paterson, Redford	
Inter Milan (Italy)	A	L0-3		2
	H	W3-1	Mitchell, Ferguson 2	
		1985-86 UEFA		
Osasuna (Spain)	H	W1-0	Paterson	1
	A	L0-2		
		1986-87 UEFA		
Ilves (Finland)	H	W4-0	Fleck 3, McCoist	1
	A	L0-2		
Boavista (Portugal)	H	W2-1	McPherson, McCoist	2
	A	W1-0	Ferguson	
Borussia Moench. (West Germany)	H	D1-1	Durrant	3
	A	D0-0		
		1987-88 EC		
Dynamo Kiev (USSR)	A	L0-1		1
	H	W2-0	Falco, McCoist	
Gornik Zabrze (Poland)	H	W3-1	McCoist, Durrant, Falco	2
	A	D1-1	McCoist pen	
Steaua Bucharest (Romania)	A	L0-2		QF
	H	W2-1	Gough, McCoist pen	
		1988-89 UEFA		
Katowice (Poland)	H	W1-0	Walters	1
	A	W4-2	Butcher 2, Durrant Ferguson	
FC Cologne (West Germany)	A	L0-2		2
	H	D1-1	Drinkell	
		1989-90 EC		
Bayern Munich (West Germany)	H	L1-3	Walters, pen	1
	A	D0-0		
		1990-91 EC		
Valetta (Malta)	A	W4-0	McCoist, Hateley, Johnston 2	1
	H	W6-0	Dodds, Spencer, Johnston 3, McCoist	
Red Star Belgrade (Yugoslavia)	A	L0-3		2
	H	D1-1	McCoist	

Opponents	Venue	Res	Scorers	Rnd
		1991-92 EC		
Sparta Prague	A	L0-1		1
(Czechoslovakia)	H	W2-1	McCall 2	
		1992-93 EC		
Lyngby	H	W2-0	Hateley, Huistra	1
(Denmark)	A	W1-0	Durrant	
Leeds United	H	W2-1	og, McCoist	2
(England)	A	W2-1	Hateley, McCoist	
		GROUP STAGE		
Marseille	H	D2-2	McSwegan, Hateley	
(France)				
CSKA Moscow	A	W1-0	Ferguson	
(Russia)				
FC Bruges	A	D1-1	Huistra	
(Belgium)				
FC Bruges	H	W2-1	Durrant, Nisbet	
Marseille	H	D1-1	Durrant	
CSKA Moscow	H	D0-0		
		1993-94 EC		
Levski Sofia	H	W3-2	McPherson, Hateley 2	1
(Bulgaria)	A	L1-2	Durrant	
		1994-95 EC		
AEK Athens	A	L0-2		1
(Greece)	H	L0-1		
Anorthosis	H	W1-0	Durie	P
(Cyprus)	A	D0-0		
		1995-96 EC		
		GROUP STAGE		
Steaua Bucharest	A	L0-1		
(Romania)				
Borussia Dort	H	D2-2	Gough, Ferguson	
(Germany)				
Juventus	A	L1-4	Gough	
(Italy)				
Juventus	H	L0-4		
Steaua Bucharest	H	D1-1	Gascoigne	
Borussia Dort	A	D2-2	Laudrup, Durie	
		1996-97 EC		
Vladikavkaz	H	W3-1	McInnes, McCoist, Petric	Q
(Russia)	A	W7-2	McCoist 3, van Vossen	
			Laudrup 2, Miller	
		GROUP STAGE		
Grasshoppers	A	L0-3		
(Switzerland)				

Opponents	Venue	Res	Scorers	Rnd
Auxerre	H	L1-2	Gascoigne	
(France)				
Ajax	A	L1-4	Durrant	
(Holland)				
Ajax	H	L0-1		
Grasshoppers	H	W2-1	McCoist 2, 1 pen	
Auxerre	A	L1-2	Gough	
1997-98 EC				
Gotu	A	W5-0	Negri, Durie 2, McCoist 2	Q
(Faroe Islands)	H	W6-0	Durie, Negri 2, McCoist	
			Albertz, Ferguson	Q
Gothenburg	A	L0-3		Q
(Sweden)	H	D1-1	Miller	
UEFA				
Strasbourg	A	L1-2	Albertz	1
(France)	H	L1-2	Gattuso	
1998-99 UEFA				
Shelbourne	A	W5-3	Albertz 2, 1 pen,	Q
(Rep of Ireland)			Amato 2, van Bronckhorst	
	H	W2-0	Johansson 2	
PAOK Salonika	H	W2-0	Kanchelskis, Wallace	Q
(Greece)	A	D0-0		
Beitar	A	D1-1	Albertz	1
(Israel)	H	W4-2	Gattuso, Porrini,	
			Johansson, Wallace	
Bayer Leverkusen	A	W2-1	van Bronckhorst,	2
(Germany)			Johansson	
	H	D1-1	Johansson	
Parma	H	D1-1	Wallace	3
(Italy)	A	L1-3	Albertz	
1999-2000 EC				
FC Haka	A	W4-1	Amoruso, Mols 2	Q
(Finland)			Johansson	
	H	W3-0	Wallace, Mols, Johansson	
Parma	H	W2-0	Vidmar, Reyna	Q
(Italy)	A	L0-1		
GROUP STAGE				
Valencia	A	L0-2		
(Spain)	H	L1-2	Moore	
Bayern Munich	H	D1-1	Albertz	
(Germany)	A	L0-1		
PSV Eindhoven	A	W1-0	Albertz	
(Holland)	H	W4-1	Amoruso Mols 2, McCann	

Opponents	Venue	Res	Scorers	Rnd
			UEFA	
Bor Dortmund	H	W2-0	Kohler og, Wallace	
(Germany)	A	L0-2		
			(Dortmund won 3-1 on penalties)	
			2000-2001 EC	
Zalgiris Kaunas	H	W4-1	Johnston, Albertz, Dodds 2	Q2
(Lithuania)	A	D0-0		
Herfolge BK	A	W3-0	Albertz, Dodds, Amoruso	Q3
(Denmark)	H	W3-0	Wallace, Johnston, Kanchelskis	
			GROUP STAGE	
Sturm Graz	H	W5-0	Mols, de Boer, Albertz,	
(Austria)			van Bronckhorst, Dodds	
	A	L0-2		
Monaco	A	W1-0	van Bronckhorst	
(France)	H	D2-2	Miller, Mols	
Galatasaray	A	L2-3	Kanchelskis, van Bronckhorst	
(Turkey)	H	D0-0		
			UEFA	
Kaiserslautern	H	W1-0	Albertz	3
(Germany)	A	L0-3		
			2001-2002 EC	
NK Maribor	A	W3-0	Flo 2, Nerlinger	Q2
(Slovenia)	H	W3-1	Caniggia 2, Flo	
Fenerbahce	H	D0-0		Q3
(Turkey)	A	L1-2	Ricksen	
			UEFA	
Anzhi	N	W1-0	Konterman	1
(Russia)				
Moscow Dynamo	H	W3-1	Amoruso, Ball, de Boer	2
(Russia)	A	W4-1	de Boer, Ferguson, Flo	
			Lovenkrands	
PSG	H	D0-0		3
(France)	A	D0-0		
			(aet, Rangers won 4-3 on penalties)	
Feyenoord	H	D1-1	Ferguson pen	4
(Holland)	A	L2-3	McCann, Ferguson pen	
			2002-2003 UEFA	
Viktoria Zizkov	A	L0-2		1
(Czech Republic)	H	W3-1	de Boer 2, McCann	
			(aet, 2-0 after 90 mins. Zizkov won on away goals)	
			2003-2004 EC	
FC Copenhagen	H	D1-1	Lovenkrands	Q3
(Denmark)	A	W2-0	Arteta, Arveladze	
			GROUP STAGE	
VfB Stuttgart	H	W2-1	Nerlinger, Lovenkrands	
(Germany)	A	L0-1		
Panathinaikos	H	D1-1	Emerson	
(Greece)	H	L1-3	Mols	
Manchester Utd	H	L0-1		
(England)	A	L0-3		

Opponents	Venue	Res	Scorers	Rnd
			2004-05 EC	
CSKA Moscow	A	L1-2	Novo	Q3
(Russia)	H	D1-1	Thompson	
			UEFA	
Maritimo	A	L0-1		1
(Portugal)	H	W1-0	Prso	
			(aet, Rangers win 4-2 on penalties)	
			GROUP STAGE	
Amica Wronki (Pol)	A	W5-0	Lovenkrands, Novo, Ricksen, Arveladze, Thompson	
Graz AK (Aut)	H	W3-0	Novo, Arveladze, Namouchi	
AZ Alkmaar (Hol)	A	L0-1		
Auxerre (Fra)	H	L0-2		
			2005-06 EC	
A Famagusta	A	W2-1	Novo, Ricksen	Q3
(Cyprus)	H	W2-0	Buffel, Prso	
			GROUP STAGE	
Porto	H	W3-2	Lovenkrands, Prso, Kyrgiakos	
(Portugal)	A	D1-1	McCormack	
Inter Milan	A	L0-1		
(Italy)	H	D1-1	Lovenkrands	
Artmedia Bratislava	H	D0-0		
(Slovakia)	A	D2-2	Prso, Thompson	
			LAST 16	
Villarreal	H	D2-2	Lovenkrands, Pena og	
(Spain)	A	D1-1	Lovenkrands	
			2006-07 UEFA	
Molde	H	W2-0	Buffel, Ferguson	1
(Denmark)	A	D0-0		
			GROUP STAGE	
Livorno (Italy)	A	W3-2	Adam, Boyd, Novo,	
Maccabi Haifa (Is)	H	W2-0	Novo, Adam	
Auxerre (Fra)	A	D2-2	Novo, Boyd	
P. Belgrade (Cro)	H	W1-0	Hutton	
			LAST 32	
Hapoel Tel Aviv	H	W4-0	Ferguson 2, Boyd, Adam	
(Israel)	A	L1-2	Novo	
			LAST 16	
Osasuna	H	D1-1	Hemdani	
(Spain)	A	L0-1		
			2007-08 EC	
Zeta	H	W2-0	Weir, McCulloch	
(Montenegro)	A	W1-0	Beasley	
Red Star	H	W1-0	Novo	
(Serbia)	A	D0-0		
			GROUP STAGE	
VfB Stuttgart	H	W2-1	Adam, Darcheville	
(Germany)	A	L2-3	Adam, Ferguson	
Lyon	H	W3-0	McCulloch, Cousin, Beasley	
(France)	H	L0-3		
Barcelona	H	D0-0		
(Spain)	A	L0-2		

UEFA
LAST 32

Panathinaikos	H	D0-0	
(Greece)	A	D1-1	Novo

LAST 16

Werder Bremen	H	W2-0	Cousin, Davis
(Germany)	A	L0-1	

QUARTER-FINAL

Sporting Lisbon	H	D0-0	
(Portugal)	A	W2-0	Darcheville, Whittaker

SEMI-FINAL

Fiorentina	H	D0-0	
Fiorentina	A	D0-0	(aet, Rangers win 4-2 on penalties)

FINAL

Zenit St Petersburg	N	L0-2	

2008-09 EC

FBK Kaunas	H	D0-0		Q
(Lithuania)	A	L1-2	Thomson	

2009-10 EC
GROUP STAGE

Stuttgart	A	D1-1	Bougherra
(Germany)	H	L0-2	
Sevilla	H	L1-4	Novo
(Spain)	A	L0-1	
Unirea Urziceni	H	L1-4	Gomes og
(Romania)	A	D1-1	McCulloch

2010-11 EC
GROUP STAGE

Manchester Utd	A	D0-0	
(England)	H	L0-1	
Bursaspor	H	W1-0	Naismith
(Turkey)	A	D1-1	Miller
Valencia	H	D1-1	Edu
(Spain)	A	L0-3	

UEFA EUROPA LEAGUE
LAST 32

Sporting Lisbon	H	D1-1	Whittaker
(Portugal)	A	D2-2	Diouf, Edu
(Rangers through on away goals)			

LAST 16

PSV Eindhoven	A	D0-0	
(Holland)	H	L0-1	

2011-12 EC

Malmo	H	L0-1		Q
(Sweden)	A	D1-1	Jelavic	

UEFA EUROPA LEAGUE
Play-off Round

NK Maribor	A	L1-2	Ortiz
(Slovenia)	H	D1-1	Bocanegra

2017-18 UEFA EUROPA LEAGUE

Progres Niederkorn	H	W1-0	Miller	Q1
(Luxembourg)	A	L0-2		

ST JOHNSTONE

Opponents	Venue	Res	Scorers	Rnd
		1971-72 UEFA		
SV Hamburg	A	L1-2	Pearson	1
(West Germany)	H	W3-0	Hall, Pearson, Whitelaw	
Vasas Budapest	H	W2-0	Connolly pen, Pearson	2
(Hungary)	A	L0-1		
Zeljeznicar	H	W1-0	Connolly	3
(Yugoslavia)	A	L1-5	Rooney	
		1999-2000 UEFA		
VPS Vaasa	A	D1-1	Lowndes	Q
(Finland)	H	W2-0	Simao 2	
Monaco	A	L0-3		1
(France)	H	D3-3	Leonard og, Dasovic, O'Neil	
		2012-13 UEFA Europa League		
Eski ehirspor	A	L0-2		Q2
(Turkey)	H	D1-1	Tade	
		2013-14 UEFA Europa League		
Rosenborg	A	W1-0	Wright	Q2
(Norway)	H	D1-1	May	
Minsk	A	W1-0	MacLean	Q3
(Belarus)	H	L0-1		
		(aet, Minsk win 3-2 on penalties)		
		2014-15 UEFA Europa League		
Lucern	A	D1-1	MacLean	Q2
(Switzerland)	H	D1-1	May	
		(aet, St Johnstone win 5-4 on penalties)		
Spartak Trnava	H	L1-2	Mackay	Q3
(Switzerland)	A	D1-1	May	
		2015-16 UEFA Europa League		
Alashkert	A	L0-1		Q1
(Armenia)	H	W2-1	O'Halloran, McKay	
		2017-18 UEFA Europa League		
FK Trakai	H	L0-2	Shaughnessy	Q1
(Armenia)	A	L0-1		

ST MIRREN

Opponents	Venue	Res	Scorers	Rnd
		1980-81 UEFA		
Elfsborg	A	W2-1	Somner, Abercromby	1
(Sweden)	H	D0-0		
St Etienne	H	D0-0		2
(France)	A	L0-2		
		1983-84 UEFA		
Feyenoord	H	L0-1		1
(Holland)	A	L0-2		
		1985-86 UEFA		
Slavia Prague	A	L0-1		1
(Czechoslovakia)	H	W3-0	Gallagher, McGarvey 2	
Hammarby	D	D3-3	Gallagher 3	2
(Sweden)	H	L1-2	McGarvey	
		1987-88 ECWC		
Tromso	H	W1-0	McDowall	1
(Norway)	A	D0-0		
Mechelen	A	D0-0		2
(Belgium)	H	L0-2		

SCOTTISH JUNIOR CUP

1886-87	Fairfield (Govan)......... 3	Edinburgh Woodburn 1
	(after protest)	
1887-88	Wishaw Thistle............ 3	Maryhill.............................1
1888-89	Burnbank Swifts........ 4	W Benhar Violet................1
1889-90	Burnbank Swifts........ 3	Benburb 1 ....
	(after protest)	
1890-91	Vale of Clyde 2	Chryston Ath......................0
	(after a draw)	
1891-92	Minerva...................... 5	W Benhar Violet................2
1892-93	Vale of Clyde 3	Dumbarton Fern................2
	(after a draw)	
1893-94	Ashfield...................... 3	Renfrew V...........................0
1894-95	Ashfield...................... 2	West Calder Wan..............1
	(after a draw)	
1895-96	Cambuslang Hibs 3	Parkhead...........................1
1896-97	Strathclyde................. 2	Dunfermline Juniors..........0
	(after protest)	
1897-98	Dalziel Rovers............ 2	Parkhead 1
1898-99	Parkhead 4	Westmarch XI 1
1899-00	Maryhill 3	Rugby XI.............................2
1900-01	Burnbank Ath............. 2	Maryhill..............................0
1901-02	Glencairn 1	Maryhill..............................0
	(after a draw)	
1902-03	Parkhead 3	Larkhall Th 0
1903-04	Vale of Clyde 3	Parkhead............................0
1904-05	Ashfield...................... 2	Renfrew Vic. 1
1905-06	Dunipace Juniors 1	Rob Roy.............................0
	(after a draw)	
1906-07	Strathclyde................. 1	Maryhill XI 0
	(after two draws)	
1907-08	Larkhall Th 1	QP Hampden XI 0
1908-09	Kilwinning R 1	Strathclyde........................0
	(after a draw)	
1909-10	Ashfield...................... 3	Kilwinning R.......................0
	after protest	
1910-11	Burnbank Ath.............. 1	Petershill...........................0
	(after a draw)	
1911-12	Petershill.................... 5	Denny Hibs 0
1912-13	Inverkeithing Utd........ 1	Dunipace Juniors 0
1913-14	Larkhall Th 1	Ashfield..............................0
	(after two draws)	
1914-15	Parkhead 2	Port Glasgow Ath 0
1915-16	Petershill.................... 2	Parkhead............................0
1916-17	St Mirren Juniors........ 1	Renfrew Juniors.................0
	(after a draw)	
1917-18	Petershill awarded cup, no final tie	

1918-19	Glencairn	1	St Anthony's	0
	(after a draw)			
1919-20	Parkhead	2	Cambuslang R	0
1920-21	Rob Roy	1	Ashfield	0
1921-22	St Roch's	2	Kilwinning R	1
	(after protest)			
1922-23	Musselb'gh Bruntonian	2	Arniston R	0
1923-24	Parkhead	3	Baillieston Juniors	1
	(after a draw)			
1924-25	Saltcoats Vics	2	St Anthony's	1
	(after two draws)			
1925-26	Strathclyde	2	Bridgeton Wav	0
	(after a draw)			
1926-27	Glencairn	2	Cambuslang R	1
1927-28	Maryhill Hibs	6	Burnbank Ath	2
1928-29	Dundee Violet	4	Denny Hibs	0
1929-30	Newtongrange Star	3	Hall Russell's	0
1930-31	Denny Hibs	1	Burnbank Ath	0
	(replay ordered, Denny failed to appear)			
1931-32	Perthshire	2	Rob Roy	1
1932-33	Yoker Ath	4	Tranent Juniors	2
	(after a draw)			
1933-34	Benburb	3	Bridgeton Wav	1
1934-35	Tranent	6	Petershill	1
1935-36	Benburb	1	Yoker Ath	0
	(after a draw)			
1936-37	Arthurlie	5	Rob Roy	1
1937-38	Cambuslang R	3	Benburb	2
1938-39	Glencairn	2	Shawfield	1
1939-40	Maryhill	1	Morton Juniors	0
1940-41	Perthshire	3	Armadale Th	1
	(after two draws)			
1941-42	Clydebank	4	Vale of Clyde	2
1942-43	Rob Roy	3	Benburb	1
	(after two draws)			
1943-44	Perthshire	1	Blantyre Vics	0
1944-45	Burnbank Ath	3	Cambuslang R	1
	(after protest)			
1945-46	Fauldhouse Utd	2	Arthurlie	0
1946-47	Shawfield	2	Bo'ness Utd	1
	(after a draw)			
1947-48	Bo'ness Utd	2	Irvine Meadow	1
1948-49	Auchinleck Talbot	3	Petershill	2
1949-50	Blantyre Vics	3	Cumnock	0
1950-51	Petershill	1	Irvine Meadow	0
1951-52	Kilbirnie Ladeside	1	Camelon	0
1952-53	Vale of Leven	1	Annbank Utd	0
1953-54	Sunnybank	2	Lochee Harp	1

1954-55	Kilsyth R	4	Duntocher Hibs	1
	(after a draw)			
1955-56	Petershill	4	Lugar Boswell Th	1
1956-57	A'deen Bnks o' Dee	1	Kilsyth R	0
1957-58	Shotts Bon Accord	2	Pumpherston	0
1958-59	Irvine Meadow	2	Shettleston	1
1959-60	St Andrew's	3	Greenock	1
1960-61	Dunbar United	2	Cambuslang R	0
	(after a draw)			
1961-62	Rob Roy	1	Renfrew	0
	(after a draw)			
1962-63	Irvine Meadow	2	Glenafton Ath	1
1963-64	Johnstone Burgh	3	Cambuslang R	0
	(after a draw)			
1964-65	Linlithgow Rose	4	Baillieston	1
1965-66	Bonnyrigg Rose	6	Whitburn	1
	(after a draw)			
1966-67	Kilsyth R	3	Glencairn	1
	(after a draw)			
1967-68	Johnstone Burgh	4	Glenrothes	3
	(after a draw)			
1968-69	Cambuslang R	1	Rob Roy	0
1969-70	Blantyre Vics	1	Penicuick Ath	0
	(ater a draw)			
1970-71	Cambuslang R	2	Newtongrange Star	1
1971-72	Cambuslang R	3	Bonnyrigg Rose	2
	(after 1-1 draw)			
1972-73	Irvine Meadow	1	Cambuslang R	0
	(after two draws)			
1973-74	Cambuslang R	3	Linlithgow Rose	1
1974-75	Glenrothes	3	Glencairn	0
1975-76	Bo'ness Utd	3	Darvel	0
1976-77	Kilbirnie Ladeside	3	Rob Roy	1
1977-78	Bonnyrigg Rose	1	Stonehouse Violet	0
1978-79	Cumnock	1	Bo'ness Utd	0
1979-80	Baillieston	2	Benburb	0
	(after a draw)			
1980-81	Pollok	1	Arthurlie	0
1981-82	Baillieston	0	Blantyre Vics	1
1982-83	East Kilbride Th	2	Bo'ness Utd	0
1983-84	Baillieston	0	Bo'ness Utd	2
1984-85	Pollok	3	Petershill	1
	(after 1-1 draw)			
1985-86	Auchinleck Talbot	3	Pollok	2
1986-87	Auchinleck Talbot	1	Kilbirnie Ladeside	0
	(after 1-1 draw)			
1987-88	Auchinleck Talbot	1	Petershill	0
1988-89	Cumnock	1	Ormiston Primrose	0
1989-90	Hill o' Beath	1	Lesmahagow	0

1990-91	Auchinleck Talbot 1	Newtongrange Star 0
1991-92	Auchinleck Talbot 4	Glenafton............................0
1992-93	Glenafton..................... 1	Tayport................................0
1993-94	Largs Thistle................ 1	Glenafton............................0
1994-95	Camelon...................... 2	Whitburn.............................0
1995-96	Camelon...................... 0	Whitburn.............................2

(after extra time)

1996-97	Pollok 3	Tayport................................1
1997-98	Arthurlie 4	Pollok 0
1998-99	Kilwinning Rangers.... 1	Kelty Hearts.......................0
1999-2000	Johnstone Burgh 2	Whitburn.............................2

(aet, 2-2 full time. Whitburn won 4-3 on penalties)

2000-01	Renfrew 0	Carnoustie Panmure 0

(aet, Renfrew won 6-5 on penalties)

2001-02	Linlithgow Rose.......... 1	Auchinleck Talbot..............0
2002-03	Tayport........................ 1	Linlithgow Rose 0

(after extra time)

2003-04	Carnoustie Panmure....0	Tayport................................0

(aet, Carnoustie won 4-1 on penalties)

2004-05	Lochee United..............0	Tayport................................2
2005-06	Auchinleck Talbot........2	Bathgate Thistle.................1
2006-07	Kelty Hearts.................1	Linlithgow Rose..................2

(after extra time)

2007-08	Bathgate Thistle...........2	Cumnock 1
2008-09	Auchinleck Talbot........2	Clydebank 1
2009-10	Largs Thistle................0	Linlithgow Rose..................1
2010-11	Auchinleck Talbot........2	Musselburgh.......................1

(after extra time)

2011-12	Auchinleck Talbot........1	Shotts Bon Accord 2
2012-13	Auchinleck Talbot 1	Linlithgow Rose..................0
2013-14	Glenafton Athletic.........0	Hurlford United...................3
2014-15	Auchinleck Talbot........2	Musselburgh.......................1
2015-16	Beith.............................1	Pollok 1

(aet, Beith won 4-3 on penalties)

2016-17	Auchinleck Talbot........1	Glenafton 2
2017-18	Auchinleck Talbot........3	Hurlford Utd.......................2

AUCHINLECK TALBOT players are overjoyed after winning the 2018 Scottish Junior Cup

Pic: SNS

JUNIOR CONTACTS

ANNBANK UTD...S Taylor, 07870 649413

ARDEER THISTLE...P McBlain, 07767 898818

ARDROSSAN WINTON ROVERS........B Macnamara, 07969 241895

ARTHURLIE..T Stevenson, 07886 324644

ASHFIELD...T Robertson, 07801 394259

AUCHINLECK TALBOT..............................H Dumigan, 07929 525494

BEITH..R McCarter, 07501 897050

BELLSHILL...E Lynas, 07749 826357

BENBURB..A Wiseman, 07969 954415

BLANTYRE VICS..D Sinclair, 07831 327483

CAMBUSLANG RANGERS............................ S Wilson, 07951 595710

CARLUKE ROVERS....................................... M Black, 07454 249194

CLYDEBANK... M Bamford, 07817 619286

CRAIGMARK BURNTONIANS.................. D Conway, 07748 550589

CUMBERNAULD UTD.................................A Robertson, 07533 194432

CUMNOCK..G Morton, 07966 767405

DALRY..H Aitken, 07968 862364

DARVEL...J MacLachlan, 07748 828380

DUNIPACE... I Duncan, 01324 813463

EAST KILBRIDE THISTLE........................P Kelsall, 07954 309949

FORTH WANDERERS .... S Barrett, 07990 578773

GIRVAN .... A Sinclair, 07759 753425

GLASGOW PERTHSHIRE .... Ms C Cunningham, 07854 183775

GLENAFTON ATHLETIC ....J Stewart, 07831 232638

GREENOCK..N Martin, 07958 450467

HURLFORD...G Jaconelli, 07858 667131

IRVINE MEADOW........................... Mrs L McFarlane, 07854 767062

IRVINE VICTORIA .... D Loach, 07969 486913

JOHNSTONE BURGH ....R Cantwell, 07719 323744

KELLO ROVERS .... Ms G Keggans, 07800 864158

KILBIRNIE LADESIDE ....G Ronney, 07889 403298

KILSYTH RANGERS ....W Dunbar, 07776 066696

KILWINNING RANGERS ....A Poole, 07767 258306

KIRKINTILLOCH ROB ROY .... C O'Brien, 07955 095707

LANARK UNITED ....T Anderson, 07721 047708

LARGS THISTLE ....D Scott, 07852 2314975

LARKHALL THISTLE......................................H Kerr, 07746 875347

LESMAHAGOW ....A Irving, 07963 770172

LUGAR BOSWELL THISTLE .... K Young, 07812 046194

MARYHILL...G Anderson, 07693 804869

MAYBOLE.. A Meek, 01655 883419
MUIRKIRK.. B Tait, 07596 089828
NEILSTON...M Kirkland, 07900 202569
NEWMAINS UTD COMMUNITY FC ....J Devine, 07833 187781
PETERSHILL...D Crozier, 07711 867748
POLLOK.. F McNeill, 07518 768422
PORT GLASGOW..P Loughlin, 07946 814951
ROSSVALE...A Sandilands, 07908 713302
RENFREW..G Johnston, 07724 807774
ROYAL ALBERT ATHLETIC...................... P Higgins, 01698 888498
RUTHERGLEN GLENCAIRN.................... A Forbes, 07787 737654
SALTCOATS VICTORIA............................... G Hunter, 07505 488430
ST ANTHONY'S..F McKenna, 07790 169666
ST ROCH'S...A Cameron, 07513 231176
SHETTLESTON ....L Turnbull, 07415 628354
SHOTTS BON ACCORD ....A Hendry, 07760 571381
THORNIEWOOD UTD ....I McLaughlin, 07758 249811
TROON ....Ms S Hamilton, 07932 214639
VALE OF CLYDE...J Wilson, 07772 973091
VALE OF LEVEN...A Wallace, 07950 075210
WHITLETTS VICTORIA..................................J Shields, 07918 030175
WISHAW .... R Watson, 07764 223057
YOKER ATHLETIC ....J Cuthbertson, 07769 586845

Annbank Utd (New Pebble Pk), **Ardeer Thistle** (Ardeer Stdm),
Ardrossan Winton Rovers (Winton Pk), **Arthurlie** (Dunterlie Pk),
Ashfield (Saracen Pk), **Auchinleck Talbot** (Beechwood Pk), **Beith Juniors**
(Bellsdale Pk), **Bellshill Ath** (Rockburn Pk), **Benburb** (New Tinto Pk), **Blantyre V**
(Castle Pk), **Cambuslang Rangers** (Somervell Pk),
Carluke Rov (Jock Cumming Stdm), **Clydebank** (sharing Holm Pk),
Craigmark Burtonians (Station Pk), **Cumbernauld Utd** (Guy's Meadow),
Cumnock (Townhead Pk), **Dalry Th** (Merksworth Pk), **Darvel** (Recreation Pk),
Dunipace (Westfield Pk), **East Kilbride Th** (Show Park), **Forth W** (Kingshill Pk),**Gir
van** (Hamilton Park), **Glasgow Perthshire** (Keppoch Pk),
Glenafton Athletic (Loch Pk), **Greenock** (Ravenscraig Stadium),
Hurlford Utd (Blair Pk), **Irvine Meadow** (Meadow Pk), **Irvine Vics** (Victoria Pk), **Jo
hnstone Burgh** (Keanie Pk), **Kello Rovers** (Nithside Pk),
Kilbirnie Ladeside (Valefield Pk), **Kilsyth Rangers** (Duncansfield Pk),
Kilwinning Rangers (Abbey Pk), **Kirkintilloch Rob Roy**
(sharing Guy's Meadow), **Lanark Utd** (Moor Pk), **Largs Th** (Barrfields Stdm),
Larkhall Th (Gasworks Pk), **Lesmahagow** (Craighead Pk), **Lugar Boswell Th**
(Rosebank Pk), **Maryhill** (Lochburn Pk), **Maybole** (Ladywell Stadium),
Muirkirk (Burnside Pk), **Neilston** (Brig o'Lea Stadium), **Newmains United
Community FC** (Victoria Pk), **Petershill** (New Petershill Pk),
Pollok (Newlandsfield Pk), **Port Glasgow** (Port Glasgow Community
Stadium), **Renfrew** (Tileworks Pk), **Rossvale FC** (Sharing Petershill Park),
Royal Albert (Tileworks Pk), **Rutherglen Glencairn** (Clyde Gateway Stadium), **Salt
coats Vics** (Campbell Pk), **St Anthony's** (McKenna Pk), **St Roch's** (James McGrory
Stadium), **Shettleston** (Greenfield Pk), **Shotts Bon Accord** (Hannah Pk), **Thorniew
ood Utd** (Robertson Pk), **Troon** (Portland Pk), **Vale of Clyde** (Fullarton Pk),
Vale of Leven (Millburn Pk), **Whitletts Vics** (Dam Park Stadium),
Wishaw (The Beltane), **Yoker Athletic** (Holm Pk).

FA CUP WINNERS

1872 Wanderers 1 Royal
Engineers 0
1873 Wanderers 2 Oxford Uni 0
1874 Oxford Uni 2 Royal
Engineers 0
1875 Royal Enginers 2 Old
Etonians 0 (after 1-1 draw)
1876 Wanderers 3 Old
Etonians 0 (after 1-1 draw)
1877 Wanderers 2 Oxford Uni
1 (aet)
1878 Wanderers 3 Royal
Enginers 1
1879 Old Etonians 1 Clapham
Rovers 0
1880 Clapham Rovers 1 Oxford
Uni 0
1881 Old Carthusians 3 Old
Etonians 0
1882 Old Etonians 1
Blackburn R 0
1883 Blackburn Oly 2 Old
Etonians 1 (aet)
1884 Blackburn R 2 Queen's
Park 1
1885 Blackburn R 2 Queen's
Park 0
1886 Blackburn R 2 WBA 0 (after
a 0-0 draw)
1887 Aston V 2 WBA 0
1888 WBA 2 Preston 1
1889 Preston 3 Wolves 0
1890 Blackburn R 6 Sheff Wed 1
1891 Blackburn R 3 Notts Co 1
1892 WBA 3 Aston V 0
1893 Wolves 1 Everton 0
1894 Notts Co 4 Bolton 1
1895 Aston V 1 WBA 0
1896 Sheff Wed 2 Wolves 1
1897 Aston V 3 Everton 2
1898 Notts Forest 3 Derby 1
1899 Sheff Utd 4 Derby 1

1900 Bury 4 Southampton 0
1901 Tottenham H 3 Sheff U 1
(after 2-2 draw)
1902 Sheff U 2 Southampton 1
(after 1-1 draw)
1903 Bury 6 Derby 0
1904 Man City 1 Bolton 0
1905 Aston V 2 Newcastle 0
1906 Everton 1 Newcastle 0
1907 Sheff W 2 Everton 1
1908 Wolves 3 Newcastle 1
1909 Man U 1 Bristol C 0
1910 Newcastle 2 Barnsley 0
(after 1-1 draw)
1911 Bradford C 1 Newcastle 0
(after 0-0 draw)
1912 Barnsley 1 West Brom 0
(aet, after 0-0 draw)
1913 Aston Villa 1 Sunderland 0
1914 Burnley 1 Liverpool 0
1915 Sheff U 3 Chelsea 0
1920 Aston V 1 Huddersfield
0 (aet)
1921 Tottenham 1 Wolves 0
1922 Huddersfield 1 Preston 0
1923 Bolton 2 West Ham 0
1924 Newcastle 2 Aston Villa 0
1925 Sheff U 1 Cardiff 0
1926 Bolton 1 Man City 0
1927 Cardiff 1 Arsenal 0
1928 Blackburn 3 Huddersfield 1
1929 Bolton 2 Portsmouth 0
1930 Arsenal 2 Huddersfield 0
1931 West Brom 2 Birmingham 1
1932 Newcastle 2 Arsenal 1
1933 Everton 3 Man City 0
1934 Man City 2 Portsmouth 1
1935 Sheffield W 4 West Brom 2
1936 Arsenal 1 Sheffield U 0
1937 Sunderland 3 Preston 1
1938 Preston 1 Huddersfield 0
(after extra time)

1939 Portsmouth 4 Wolves 1
1946 Derby 4 Charlton 1 (aet)
1947 Charlton 1 Burnley 0 (aet)
1948 Man Utd 4 Blackpool 2
1949 Wolves 3 Leicester 1
1950 Arsenal 2 Liverpool 0
1951 Newcastle 2 Blackpool 0
1952 Newcastle 1 Arsenal 0
1953 Blackpool 4 Bolton 3
1954 WBA 3 Preston 2
1955 Newcastle 3 Man City 1
1956 Man City 3 Birmingham 1
1957 Aston Villa 2 Man Utd 1
1958 Bolton 2 Man Utd 0
1959 Notts Forest 2 Luton 1
1960 Wolves 3 Blackburn 0
1961 Tottenham 2 Leicester 0
1962 Tottenham 3 Burnley 1
1963 Man Utd 3 Leicester 1
1964 West Ham 3 Preston 2
1965 Liverpool 2 Leeds 1 (aet)
1966 Everton 3 Sheff Wed 2
1967 Tottenham 2 Chelsea 1
1968 West Brom 1 Everton 0 (aet)
1969 Man City 1 Leicester 0
1970 Chelsea 2 Leeds 1 (aet,
     first game a 2-2 draw)
1971 Arsenal 2 Liverpool 1 (aet)
1972 Leeds 1 Arsenal 0
1973 Sunderland 1 Leeds 0
1974 Liverpool 3 Newcastle 0
1975 West Ham 2 Fulham 0
1976 Southampton 1 Man U 0
1977 Man Utd 2 Liverpool 1
1978 Ipswich 1 Arsenal 0
1979 Arsenal 3 Man Utd 2
1980 West Ham 1 Arsenal 0
1981 Tottenham 3 Man City 2
     (after 1-1 draw)
1982 Tottenham 1 QPR 0
     (after 1-1 draw)
1983 Man Utd 4 Brighton 0
     (after 2-2 draw)
1984 Everton 2 Watford 0
1985 Man Utd 1 Everton 0 (aet)
1986 Liverpool 3 Everton 1
1987 Coventry 3 Tottenham 2
     (aet)
1988 Wimbledon 1 Liverpool 0

1989 Liverpool 3 Everton 2 (aet)
1990 Man Utd 1 Crystal P 0
     (after 3-3 draw)
1991 Tottenham 2 Notts Forest 1
     (aet)
1992 Liverpool 2 Sunderland 0
1993 Arsenal 2 Sheff Wed 1
     (aet, first game 1-1)
1994 Man Utd 4 Chelsea 0
1995 Everton 1 Man Utd 0
1996 Man Utd 1 Liverpool 0
1997 Chelsea 2 Middlesboro 0
1998 Arsenal 2 Newcastle 0
1999 Man Utd 2 Newcastle 0
2000 Chelsea 1 Aston V 0
2001 Liverpool 2 Arsenal 1
2002 Arsenal 2 Chelsea 0
2003 Arsenal 1 Southampton 0
2004 Man Utd 3 Millwall 0
2005 Arsenal 0 Man Utd 0
     (aet, Arsenal won 5-4
     on penalties)
2006 Liverpool 3 West Ham 3
     (aet, Liverpool won 3-1 on
     penalties)
2007 Chelsea 1 Man Utd 0
     (aet)
2008 Portsmouth 1 Cardiff 0
2009 Chelsea 2 Everton 1
2010 Chelsea 1 Portsmouth 0
2011 Manchester City 1 Stoke 0
2012 Chelsea 2 Liverpool 1
2013 Manchester City 0 Wigan 1
2014 Arsenal 3 Hull City 2 (aet)
2015 Arsenal 4 Aston Villa 0
2016 Manchester Utd 2
     Crystal Palace 1 (aet)
2017 Arsenal 2 Chelsea 1
2018 Chelsea 1 Manchester Utd 0

Pic: Getty

CHELSEA with the FA Cup

ENGLISH LEAGUE CHAMPIONS

1888-89	Preston NE
1889-90	Preston NE
1890-91	Everton
1891-92	Sunderland
1892-93	Sunderland
1893-94	Aston Villa
1894-95	Sunderland
1895-96	Aston Villa
1896-97	Aston Villa
1897-98	Sheffield United
1898-99	Aston Villa
1899-1900	Aston Villa
1900-01	Liverpool
1901-02	Sunderland
1902-03	The Wednesday
1903-04	The Wednesday
1904-05	Newcastle United
1905-06	Liverpool
1906-07	Newcastle United
1907-08	Manchester United
1908-09	Newcastle United
1909-10	Aston Villa
1910-11	Manchester United
1911-12	Blackburn Rovers
1912-13	Sunderland
1913-14	Blackburn Rovers
1914-15	Everton
1919-20	West Bromwich Albion
1920-21	Burnley
1921-22	Liverpool
1922-23	Liverpool
1923-24	Huddersfield Town
1924-25	Huddersfield Town
1925-26	Huddersfield Town
1926-27	Newcastle United
1927-28	Everton
1928-29	Sheffield Wednesday
1929-30	Sheffield Wednesday
1930-31	Arsenal
1931-32	Everton
1932-33	Arsenal
1933-34	Arsenal
1934-35	Arsenal
1935-36	Sunderland
1936-37	Manchester City
1937-38	Arsenal
1938-39	Everton
1946-47	Liverpool
1947-48	Arsenal
1948-49	Portsmouth
1949-50	Portsmouth
1950-51	Tottenham Hotspur
1951-52	Manchester United
1952-53	Arsenal
1953-54	Wolves
1954-55	Chelsea
1955-56	Manchester United
1956-57	Manchester United
1957-58	Wolves
1958-59	Wolves
1959-60	Burnley
1960-61	Tottenham Hotspur
1961-62	Ipswich Town
1962-63	Everton
1963-64	Liverpool
1964-65	Manchester United
1965-66	Liverpool
1966-67	Manchester United
1967-68	Manchester City
1968-69	Leeds United
1969-70	Everton
1970-71	Arsenal
1971-72	Derby County
1972-73	Liverpool
1973-74	Leeds United
1974-75	Derby County
1975-76	Liverpool
1976-77	Liverpool
1977-78	Nottingham Forest
1978-79	Liverpool
1979-80	Aston Villa
1980-81	Aston Villa
1981-82	Liverpool
1982-83	Liverpool
1983-84	Liverpool
1984-85	Everton
1985-86	Liverpool
1986-87	Everton
1987-88	Liverpool

1988-89	Arsenal	2004-05	Chelsea
1989-90	Liverpool	2005-06	Chelsea
1990-91	Arsenal	2006-07	Manchester United
1991-92	Leeds United	2007-08	Manchester United
PREMIER LEAGUE		2008-09	Manchester United
1992-93	Manchester United	2009-10	Chelsea
1993-94	Manchester United	2010-11	Manchester United
1994-95	Blackburn Rovers	2011-12	Manchester City
1995-96	Manchester United	2012-13	Manchester United
1996-97	Manchester United	2013-14	Manchester City
1997-98	Arsenal	2014-15	Chelsea
1998-99	Manchester United	2015-16	Leicester City
1999-00	Manchester United	2016-17	Chelsea
2000-01	Manchester United	2017-18	Manchester City
2001-02	Arsenal		
2002-03	Manchester United		
2003-04	Arsenal		

ENGLISH LEAGUE CUP WINNERS

1961	Aston Villa	1994	Aston Villa
1962	Norwich City	1995	Liverpool
1963	Birmingham City	1996	Aston Villa
1964	Leicester City	1997	Leicester City
1965	Chelsea	1998	Chelsea
1966	WBA	1999	Tottenham Hotspur
1967	Queen's Park Rangers	2000	Leicester City
1968	Leeds United	2001	Liverpool
1969	Swindon Town	2002	Blackburn Rovers
1970	Manchester City	2003	Liverpool
1971	Tottenham Hotspur	2004	Middlesbrough
1972	Stoke City	2005	Chelsea
1973	Tottenham Hotspur	2006	Manchester United
1974	Wolves	2007	Chelsea
1975	Aston Villa	2008	Tottenham Hotspur
1976	Manchester City	2009	Manchester United
1977	Aston Villa	2010	Manchester United
1978	Nottingham Forest	2011	Birmingham City
1979	Nottingham Forest	2012	Liverpool
1980	Wolves	2013	Swansea City
1981	Liverpool	2014	Manchester City
1982	Liverpool	2015	Chelsea
1983	Liverpool	2016	Manchester City
1984	Liverpool	2017	Manchester United
1985	Norwich City	2018	Manchester City
1986	Oxford United		
1987	Arsenal		
1988	Luton Town		
1989	Nottingham Forest		
1990	Nottingham Forest		
1991	Sheffield Wed.		
1992	Manchester United		
1993	Arsenal		

Pic: PA

MANCHESTER City celebrate beating Arsenal 3-0 in the final

**JOHN LAMBIE, former Partick Thistle manager
passed away on April 10, 2018**

**FORMER Celtic midfielder Liam Miller died aged 36 on
February 9, 2018 after a short illness**

FORMER Rangers midfielder Ray Wilkins passed away in April 2018 following a heart attack, aged 61

FORMER Aberdeen and Rangers midfielder Neale Cooper died suddenly in May 2018, aged just 54 Pic: SNS

NOTES